SECRET
ARMIES

SECRET ARMIES

Inside the American, Soviet and
European Special Forces

James Adams

THE ATLANTIC MONTHLY PRESS
NEW YORK

For Richard

First published in Great Britain in 1988 by Hutchinson
First published in the United States of America in 1988

Printed in the United States of America

FIRST EDITION

Library of Congress Cataloging-in-Publication Data

Adams, James, 1951–
  Secret armies.

  Bibliography: p.
  Includes index.
  1. Special forces (Military science)   2. Military
history, Modern—20th century.   I. Title.
U240.A3   1988   356'.167   88-3400
ISBN 0-87113-223-0

The Atlantic Monthly Press
19 Union Square West
New York, NY 10003

FIRST PRINTING

Contents

Author's Note

To some extent the title of this book is a misnomer. The existence of some of the forces mentioned has been openly acknowledged by government and, on occasion, by the groups themselves. Sometimes, therefore, they are not necessarily secret. However, in every case many of the operations they conduct, the training and equipment they use and their role in the execution of policy are highly classified. I feel that the title *Secret Armies* accurately reflects the role of these special forces in the world today.

Acknowledgements

I would like to thank René Riley who did some stunning research for me in the United States. She dealt patiently and expertly with my endless queries and found answers where none seemed possible. She has now joined *US News and World Report* where I am sure she has a great future. Harry Spry-Leverton also carried out some research in Britain.

Elizabeth Bode was also very helpful in supplying information and advice. My mother-in-law, Florence Frischer, put up with me for two months while I wrote some of this book. She tolerated the tension and drama with great good humour and patience.

A large number of people not only supplied information for this book but read the draft manuscript and offered valuable advice and criticism. I am grateful to them all for taking so much trouble to go through the manuscript, correct my mistakes and make suggestions for improvements. Many were or are connected with some branch of government service in different countries, for perfectly understandable reasons none of them wishes to be named.

Finally, and most importantly, I must thank my wife Patricia. Her encouragement and intelligent advice form the backdrop on which this book is written.

PART 1: INTRODUCTION

1

Another Type of War

Small wars play a very significant role in contemporary international geo-politics. It has been estimated that in 1986 there were forty armed conflicts taking place, involving forty-five of the world's 165 nations.[1]

This figure, startling as it is, still does not adequately reflect the true situation: neither the isolated activities of terrorist groups nor the many brief but bloody attempts at revolution in Third World countries are included in it, since these are generally defined as being at a lower level of conflict than formal warfare. Nevertheless, even with this limited definition, around five million people have been killed in current armed conflicts, some of which date back to the 1940s. Obviously, therefore, if all other acts of war were included, the statistics would be correspondingly more horrific.

All around the world, in countries both developed and less advanced, armed groups from every imaginable political background are fighting to change the systems that control their lives. This is clearly not a new phenomenon – but what is new is the scale of the instability and the involvement of outside countries in attempting to influence the outcome of such conflicts.

To understand how this has come about it is necessary to look at the evolution of military thinking in both west and east since World War II.

With the explosion of the first atomic device over Hiroshima in 1945 the traditional structures of the world's major armed forces were altered forever. Just as the introduction of the tank saw the elimination of the cavalry as an effective weapon of war, so nuclear weapons changed, and limited, the options available to military and political strategists. No longer could it be assumed that to achieve military or political advantage two protagonists had only to meet on the field of battle and engage in an extended period of hostilities, with probable high loss of life, until a victor emerged, after which the territory and economic assets of the vanquished would be there for the taking. Instead the deterrence doctrine known as Mutually Assured Destruction or MAD has grown up, by which both sides know that a war between them will surely result in the total destruction of themselves and their allies.

Since the atom bomb, therefore, although conventional wars are still possible among those nations who do not possess nuclear weapons (Iran and Iraq for example), those who do have nuclear arsenals, particularly the United States and the Soviet Union, have been obliged to deal with their differences by other means.

There is no doubt that the nuclear deterrent has imposed clear operational limits on both superpowers. They have had to confine their activities around the world to areas that will not lead to direct confrontations. There is no reason to suppose that the nuclear deterrent will not continue working for the foreseeable future. Certainly, there is no serious military strategist in west or east who believes that a conventional confrontation leading to nuclear war between the United States and the Soviet Union is likely.

Both sides still see the other as the main threat to international peace. But if history since World War II is any guide, they will go a long way to avoid a head-on conflict. In every post-war crisis that could have developed into a confrontation between the superpowers, both sides have taken positive steps to reduce tension. Even in Korea, Cuba, Vietnam, the various Israeli conflicts, and, more recently, the Iran-Iraq war, they have ultimately – even if in some cases belatedly – exercised restraint.

Thus, although the US and the USSR both appear to accept that the war their forces are specifically designed to fight is in fact the least probable, they also accept at the same time that those forces are necessary.

Two experts on military affairs, Maurice Tugwell and David Charters, have pointed out that, 'Although Soviet capabilities to project power improved markedly in the 1970s, direct confrontation between the United States and the Soviet Union is probably the least likely contingency, especially in the all-important Central Front of Western Europe. Outside Western Europe it is possible to visualise situations where the United States and Soviet Union might clash, for example, protecting respective clients or allies in the context of a major war in the Middle East. But it is difficult to estimate how likely or realistic such scenarios might be . . .

'The most likely threats to US interests may arise from local and regional conflicts and internal instability of US allies or clients.'[2]

In theory such a stand-off between the superpowers should bring about an unprecedented era of stability. In practice, however, both sides have continued to pursue territorial, economic or political advantage around the world, but always using means that will achieve the policy goals without bringing about a direct confrontation between them.

In fact, the interfering hand of either west or east (or both) can be found in every small war that is going on in the world today.

At the same time, economic influences have come to bear that have reduced the likelihood of conventional warfare, even between those non-nuclear nations who otherwise might normally have confronted each other eagerly on the battlefield. Weapons have become almost prohibitively expensive. The days when troops could be mustered under the flag of the local warlord, equipped with a few rudimentary armaments and sent off to war are gone. Today's high technology wars can only be waged by the very rich. One fighter aircraft costs what an entire squadron did in World War II and even equipping a basic platoon of infantry with the necessary logistics and fire support will be beyond many countries.[3]

At the same time, however, the more basic combat weapons are mass-produced in such quantities that they are readily accessible to even the most isolated terrorist or impoverished Third World dictator. So, while it may be impossibly expensive to fight a conventional war, it is relatively cheap to wage war by bomb or grenade or automatic rifle.

Both state-sponsored terrorism and international terrorism are relatively new phenomena. They emerged in the late 1960s, when Che Guevara posters appeared on the walls of thousands of student apartments around the world. It was a time when change through revolution seemed possible to many young people and when demonstrations against Vietnam, colonialism or any other manifestations of supposed establishment oppression were the accepted method of showing political commitment. To many, when existing governments in all their various forms appeared immovable in the face of justified demands for change, violence became an acceptable means of advancing political ends.

Simultaneously, as if in sympathy, terrorist groups emerged in the Middle East, Europe, the Far East and the Americas. There was no common hand guiding these groups – although many of them did identify with the left – but all were agreed that they wished to change the existing order in the societies in which they operated. The tacticians in the groups looked to the Brazilian revolutionary Carlos Marighella, and his *Mini-Manual of the Urban Guerrilla* became required reading.

'The urban guerrilla,' he wrote, 'is a man who fights the military dictatorship with arms, using unconventional methods. A political revolutionary and an ardent patriot, he is a fighter for his country's liberation, a friend of the people and of freedom. The urban guerrilla follows a political goal and only attacks government, the big capitalists and the foreign imperialists. The urban guerrilla is an implacable enemy of the government and systematically inflicts damage on the authorities and on the men who dominate the country and exercise power. The principal task of the urban guerrilla is to distract, to wear out, to demoralise the militarists, the military dictatorship and its repressive forces. The urban guerrilla is not afraid of dismantling and destroying the present . . . economic, political and social system for his aim is to help the rural guerrilla and to collaborate in the creation of a totally new and revolutionary social and political structure with the armed people in power.'

This call to arms was answered all over the world, and to many it was a terrifying time, a period when the peaceful societies we had all learned to take for granted seemed to be coming to an end. But such alarmist views have been proved premature. Although terrorism has been immensely successful in generating publicity for a cause (no one took the Palestinians seriously until they began hijacking aircraft in the late 1960s) it has been less successful in achieving political ends. No terrorist group in recent years has achieved its aims. On the other hand, it must be admitted that a long list of countries – including Israel, Angola, Algeria, Cuba, Nicaragua, Ethiopia and the Sudan – owe their existence to guerrilla warfare, which often uses terrorism as an effective tactic.

And anyway, political reality has not discouraged terrorist groups from forming, or failed to sustain those, such as the IRA or the PLO, with a longer life. Although many of the heroes of the revolutionary 1960s – Baader Meinhof, Japanese Red Army, the Angry Brigade – have disappeared, out of the ashes of that first wave of modern terrorism has emerged a new breed of killer who is better trained and better armed than his predecessor.

Furthermore, the dismantling of colonial empires at the end of the nineteenth century and the beginning of the twentieth, seems to have acted as a spur to many other groups who seek autonomy. Separatists like the Tamils in Sri Lanka, or the Basques in Spain, or the Kurds in Iraq, now believe that they can achieve their aims through violent means.

There is some confusion between official assessments of the

terrorist problem. One source suggests that 126 groups carried out 2,679 terrorist acts in 1984, while in the following year 147 groups carried out 2,818 operations. But in 1985 a total of 5,486 people were killed and 6,228 injured, an increase of 43% and 63% respectively over the previous year. Therefore, since the number of incidents increased by only 5%, this suggests that there is a trend towards using greater violence.[4]

On the other hand, the Rand Corporation, the respected California research organisation, says that there were 480 attacks in 1985 and 415 the following year, and the numbers killed and injured have remained the same.[5]

A further confusion, resulting from differing definitions of the subversive, the terrorist and the guerrilla, whether sponsored by outside countries or independent, has given rise in the US to a new blanket term: low intensity conflict.

The US Army defines low intensity conflict as 'a limited politico-military struggle to achieve political, social, economic, or psychological objectives. It is often protracted and ranges from diplomatic, economic and psycho-social pressures through terrorism and insurgency. Low intensity conflict is generally confined to a geographic area and is often characterised by constraints on the weaponry, tactics, and the level of violence. Low intensity conflict involves the actual or contemplated use of military capabilities up to, but not including, sustained combat between regular forces.'[6]

Such broad definitions accept that the problem embraces everything from the printing of subversive leaflets to a bomb planted by IRA terrorists in Harrods in London to the extended war being fought by the mujahedeen in Afghanistan. But there is agreement in both east and west – unadmitted, of course – that low intensity conflict has been and will continue to be their preferred means of warfare. This is what US Secretary of the Army, John Marsh, calls 'the twilight battlefield.'[7]

In January 1986 a two-day conference on low intensity conflict actually took place at Fort McNair, Washington DC, sponsored by the US Defense Secretary, Caspar Weinberger.

The conference was the first of its type and was attended by leading US defence and intelligence experts on counter terrorism and guerrilla warfare. The Secretary of State, George Shultz, spelt out the need for a new US defence initiative in an address that for the first time publicly advanced America's new thinking on low intensity conflict. 'The problem of low intensity warfare requires us to confront a host of political, military, intellectual, legal and moral questions. It is a complicated set of new and unconventional challenges to our policy.'

He went on: 'The ironic fact is, these new and elusive challenges have proliferated, in part, because of our success in deterring nuclear and conventional war. Our adversaries know they cannot prevail against us in either type of war. So they have done the logical thing: they have turned to other methods. Low intensity warfare is their answer to our conventional and nuclear strength – a flanking manoeuvre in military terms. Our policy . . . must be unambiguous. It must be clearly and unequivocally the policy of the United States to fight back – to resist challenges, to defend our interests, and to support those who put their own lives on the line in a common cause.

'Just as we turned to our men and women in uniform when new conventional and nuclear threats emerged, we are turning to you now for the new weapons, new doctrines, and new tactics that this new method of warfare requires.'[8]

Shultz was in fact simply making public a policy that had been laid down by President Ronald Reagan in 1982 (although the build-up had actually been authorised earlier) when he notified the military in a secret memorandum that action should be taken to improve America's ability to fight these types of wars. 'We must revitalise and enhance special operations forces to project United States power where the use of conventional forces would be premature, inappropriate or unfeasible,' said the President.

It has been one of the basic tenets of US foreign policy under President Reagan that what is seen as Soviet expansionism around the world should be restrained or repelled wherever and whenever possible. (This has come to be called the Reagan Doctrine.) In the aftermath of the Vietnam war, there had been little appetite among the American public to commit US troops to fight wars in foreign countries. And although sponsorship of groups such as UNITA in Angola or the mujahedeen in Afghanistan could, in part, overcome this problem there was still a feeling in government circles that not enough was being done to confront the Soviets.

Wherever Reagan and his advisers looked it seemed to them that America was retreating before the Russian bear. One senior administration official put it well when, over dinner in a Washington restaurant, he pulled out his pen and on the linen tablecloth drew a map that took in Cam Ran Bay in Vietnam, the Red Sea, Mozambique and the Caribbean. 'That shows you how the Soviets have been expanding in recent years,' he said. 'Everywhere you look they are gaining influence in countries that are strategically vital or that straddle key choke points on sea routes that are essential to the free world.'

As Noel Koch, who until his resignation in 1986 was Principal Deputy Assistant Secretary of Defense for International Security Affairs, puts it: 'Like the shark which must move constantly in order to survive, Soviet ideology is expansionist. Consistent with the keystone principle of that ideology, which is that man is solely and simply a creature of appetite, the Soviet Union is a predator state, which must eat others to live.'

To counter what it sees as these aggressive policies, such as the invasion of Afghanistan, Soviet support for the government of Nicaragua and the fostering of other liberation movements, the Reagan administration first devised a strategy of containment, of trying to prevent the Soviets from gaining influence in new areas of the world. This quickly evolved into the more aggressive policy of rollback, which aims to actively align under the western banner countries that are currently seen to be under communist influence. It is not clear exactly how this policy is intended to work: whether rollback means persuading countries to join the US camp or simply forcing them to leave the Soviet camp, it will presumably require a judicious combination of mailed fist and velvet glove. And, inevitably, the point men for rollback are, along with other covert intelligence agents, the special operations forces in the US and the allies' armed forces.

According to the initial lecture given to US students at the special warfare school at Fort Bragg, North Carolina, 'Special operations are operations conducted by specially trained, equipped and organised forces against strategic and tactical targets in pursuit of national political, military and economic and psychological objectives. These operations are conducted during periods of peace and hostilities.'

Those special operations are carried out by highly trained troops that, unlike their more conventional counterparts, act as guerrilla forces. Operating covertly on behalf of government, they are trained to fight in any climate or terrain and develop special skills in sabotage, assassination, reconnaissance and in the training of other guerrilla forces.

All the major military powers of both east and west have their own such forces, and these play an increasingly important role in the furthering of foreign policy goals. Together with genuine, if state-sponsored, subversives, terrorists and guerrillas, they are the secret armies that are fighting today's wars. They form the backbone of the armed foreign policy in the communist world and the bite that follows the diplomatic bark in the free world.

Conventional wars may well be a thing of the past. While all nations must be prepared to fight them, none of the major powers actually believes battle will ever be joined. Instead, a new, secret, battlefield has appeared where special operations forces act out their deadly games in a clandestine environment that is only rarely visible to the public. But it is here that the future of modern warfare lies and the skills and failings of the secret armies that wage war in the name of their governments hold the key to our security.

To understand how these secret armies have evolved to become such a vital tool of government policy, it is necessary to look back briefly at their evolution which began shortly after the Russian Revolution.

PART 2: EUROPE ABLAZE

2

Revolutionary Exports

It was the Russians who first really understood and exploited special forces. Faced with Napoleon's invasion in 1812, and using the example of Napoleon's own light troops, they extended the tactic to develop guerrilla forces which, trained and led by military officers, operated almost entirely behind enemy lines, harassing the communications and supply system of the army. Clausewitz noted that 'the Napoleonic army was surrounded by an armed populace.'[1]

Similar tactics were used against the Germans in 1917. Then in the aftermath of the World War I and the Civil War that immediately followed it, the new Soviet leaders developed the lessons learned in combat. They institutionalised a structure that combined a comprehensive unconventional warfare capability with both a strong military force to fight external wars and an effective intelligence apparatus to control internal dissent and assess the threat from external enemies.

In using the army to impose the collectivisation programme on the Soviet republics, Moscow also employed special forces that operated generally as a branch of the intelligence service, which was successively called Cheka, GPU, OGPU and the NKVD. This set an early precedent for special forces to be used either in combination with the regular army or completely independently, a technique that has continued basically unchanged.

At the heart of Soviet political thinking at this time was

the intention of spreading the Bolshevik revolution to the rest of the world. Lenin and senior army figures such as Marshal Mikhail Tukhachevsky believed that the Red Army could be in the vanguard of a worldwide revolution, and to aid directly countries whose workers were in revolt, the Red Army formed the world's first airborne forces. Even in those early days, their role was to have included not only supporting and arming the revolutionary workers but also assassinating the political leadership of the foreign country.[2]

Although the purges of the late 1930s effectively destroyed these special forces before they saw action, the Spanish Civil War of 1936–9 gave the Russians an excellent opportunity to test their theories for the export of revolution.

According to John Dziak, the US Defense Intelligence Agency's leading analyst on Soviet special forces, Stalin sent Jan Berzin, the head of Military Intelligence, to Madrid to mastermind Soviet support for the Republicans.[3] Berzin had three main tasks: to help defend Madrid with Soviet tanks, aircraft and advisers; to advise on operational planning; and, most importantly, to keep a small group of special purpose forces in a secret location ready to seize control of key points in the Spanish capital. Although the full details of this operation have never been revealed, it is clear that the Soviets intended to wrest control of Madrid from the Republicans so that they could control the nature of the communist state that they believed would emerge.

In addition, Berzin organised and ran a series of guerrilla operations behind the Nationalist lines, organised a series of assassinations of Nationalist leaders and Republican dissidents, and was instrumental in spiriting out of Spain the country's gold reserves. The gold reached Moscow and, despite repeated representations from the Spanish government, has never been returned.

The Spanish affair is important because it laid the foundations for a range of activities that have often been repeated and that still form a major part of Soviet use of special forces. The operation was run by the Glavnoye Razvedyvatelnoye

Upravleniye (GRU) or military intelligence; planning was in an advanced stage for the seizure of key points that would have given the Soviets a controlling influence on the government of the future; the GRU forces not only had a direct role in assassination and sabotage but also provided military assistance to indigenous guerrillas fighting behind enemy lines.

When World War II broke out in 1939, despite Stalin's purges the Soviets still had more experience of special forces work than any of the other protagonists. They had practised guerrilla and counter-insurgency tactics since the revolution, and this experience was put to good use when the Germans invaded in 1941.

The Central Committee of the Communist Party established a Central Staff for the Partisan Movement whose head reported directly to Stalin. They concentrated on infiltrating special forces behind the German lines who in turn raised local partisans to harass Hitler's advancing forces. Recruits were drawn primarily from the various intelligence agencies who already had the required training in assassination, explosives and espionage. There is no doubting the effectiveness of Soviet efforts in this area. A Soviet analysis of the campaign points out: 'During the war the partisans killed, wounded or took prisoner hundreds of thousands of German troops, collaborators, and officials of the occupying administration. They derailed more than 18,000 trains and destroyed or damaged thousands of locomotives and tens of thousands of railway cars and cisterns (tank cars). The partisan affected the morale of the German Army, keeping the German troops in a constant state of fear.'[4]

While the Russians may have had more experience in fighting a partisan war, faced with the overwhelming tactical superiority of the German forces the other allies had to adapt swiftly to meet the threat. Thus World War II laid the foundations for all special forces operations that followed. The techniques and equipment may have been improved but the basic lessons of strategic deception and guerrilla warfare remain well learned.

For the Soviets those lessons left them with a special forces organization that was totally integrated into their armed forces. Its tactics were designed to make maximum use of its unconventional warfare capability and they have continued to invest the men and material necessary to ensure its continued existence.

3

Churchill's Leopards

Hitler's blitzkreig tactics in the early days of World War II brought swift dividends. His well-armed, superbly trained and highly mobile army seemed unstoppable, and within four weeks of its move into Belgium and Holland on 10 May 1940 it was forcing the British to retreat via Dunkirk to prepare a final defence of their island.

Britain stood alone (the United States had not yet entered the war) and to the allied commanders in London a German invasion seemed inevitable; the tattered remnants of the British armed forces would not last long against it. However, rather than simply waiting for defeat, Britain's Prime Minister Winston Churchill was determined to take the attack to the Germans. In a memo dated 18 June 1940 he wrote to the Commander-in-Chief, Home Forces:

'We have always set our faces against this idea, but the Germans certainly gained in the last war by adopting it, and this time it has been a leading cause of their victory. There ought to be at least twenty thousand Storm Troops or "Leopards" drawn from existing units, ready to spring at the throat of any small landings or descents. These officers and men should be armed with the latest equipment, Tommy-guns, grenades etc., and should be given facilities in motor-cycles and armoured cars.'

Although preoccupation with a prospective invasion was understandable, even at this stage Churchill saw for these 'Leopards' a dual role, one that could take the battle to the enemy's heart. He therefore required the service chiefs additionally to provide:

'1. Proposals for organising the striking companies.
'2. Proposals for transporting and landing tanks on the [enemy] beaches.
'3. A proper system of espionage and intelligence along the whole coast.
'4. Deployment of parachute troops on a scale to equal five thousand.'[1]

Churchill's memorandum underlined the urgency that was to be given to creating a British special operations capability. In fact, some work had already been done, both in establishing a parachute school (which opened outside Manchester five days after Churchill wrote his note) and on recruiting men to form the 'Leopards' or Commandos as they became known.

On the same day that the parachute school opened, a small force of commandos landed on the French coast with the aim of taking prisoners for interrogation. That mission failed, as did another on Guernsey the following month. However, on the night of 18/19 July 1940 a small team destroyed a hydro-electric power station in Norway. From then on, the commandos went from strength to strength, attacking targets throughout Europe.

As the war progressed, so a wide range of innovative ideas were generated by those individuals of imagination and courage who always seem to come to the fore in time of war. Perhaps the most remarkable of these was David Stirling, then a subaltern in the Scots Guards. At 6ft 5in Stirling was a powerful figure, but his size was matched both by his qualities of leadership and by his vision. Service in North Africa had convinced him that the German lines of supply and communication, which now stretched across hundreds of miles of empty desert, would be particularly vulnerable to covert attack by small numbers of highly trained specialists. In particular, he felt that the enemy airfields, often lightly guarded since the threat in their rear was considered minimal by the Germans, might make profitable targets.

Stirling was convinced that small teams should be dropped by parachute behind enemy lines and that after their attack they would be able to work their way out on foot. To test this scheme he independently obtained the use of a Vickers Valentia aircraft. In an early jump, however, the inexperienced Stirling was badly injured and forced to spend two months in hospital. While there he prepared a detailed case explaining why he felt his idea should be approved, and submitted a memorandum written in pencil to the Commander-in-Chief, General Auchinleck.

Stirling's memorandum argued that the kind of force he had in mind should be small, should operate in groups of five (later changed to four), and should use surprise to overcome what would always be superior enemy forces. In addition, the members of his proposed group would all be volunteers, highly trained in all forms of warfare including escape and evasion, reconnaissance and sabotage, and capable of arriving at their target by sea, land or air. Above all, his force would carry out strategic tasks designed to influence the conduct of the war as a whole. This would distinguish Stirling's group from the commandos (from whom many of his recruits were to come) who carried out essentially tactical raids, designed to influence the course of a particular battle.

Authority was given for Stirling to form his group which was originally known as L Detachment, Special Air Service Brigade. There was no such Brigade but Britain at the time was involved in psychological warfare operations designed to convince the Germans that a full parachute and glider brigade was based in North Africa. Dummy drops had taken place and fake gliders had been built. Headquarters felt that to have some real soldiers actually operating under the bogus banner would give it additional credibility. Stirling agreed. Later the name of his group became simply the Special Air Service.

From the beginning Stirling established guidelines which,

together with his comments, are worth quoting at length here, since all other special operations forces in the western world have subsequently tried to emulate the SAS. As we shall see, however, very few have succeeded. The guidelines were:

'1.   The unrelenting pursuit of excellence.

'2.   Maintaining the highest standards of discipline in all aspects of the daily life of the SAS soldier, from the occasional precision drilling on the parade ground even to his personal turnout on leave. We always reckoned that a high standard of self-discipline in each soldier was the only effective foundation for Regimental discipline. Commitment to the SAS pursuit of excellence becomes a sham if any single one of the disciplinary standards is allowed to slip.

'3.   The SAS brooks no sense of class, and particularly not among the wives. This might sound a bit portentous but it epitomises the SAS philosophy. The traditional idea of a crack regiment was one officered by the aristocracy and, indeed, these regiments deservedly won great renown for their dependability and their gallantry in wartime and for their parade-ground panache in peacetime. In the SAS we share with the Brigade of Guards a deep respect for quality, but we have an entirely different outlook. We believe, as did the ancient Greeks who originated the word aristocracy, that every man with the right attitudes and talents, regardless of birth and riches, has a capacity in his own lifetime of reaching that status in its true sense; in fact in our SAS context an individual soldier might prefer to go on serving as an NCO rather than have to leave the Regiment in order to obtain an officer's commission. All ranks in the SAS are of "one company" in which a sense of class is both alien and ludicrous. A visit to the Sergeant's Mess at SAS HQ in Hereford vividly conveys what I mean.

'4.   Humility and humour: both these virtues are indispensable in the everyday life of officers and men – particularly so in the case of the SAS which is often regarded as an elite regiment. Without frequent recourse to humour and humility, out special status could cause resentment in other units of the British Army and an unbecoming conceit and big-headedness in our own soldiers.'2

The first raid launched by the SAS, on 17 November 1941, was a disaster. The team planned a simultaneous parachute assault on a number of German North African airfields. In the event, things went badly wrong. The night on which it took place was totally unsuitable for a parachute operation. There was no moon and the wind was so strong that no party was dropped within ten miles of the selected DZs. One of the five aircraft never dropped its stick of parachutists at all. Owing to the severity of the conditions two men were killed on landing, and of the rest only eighteen men and four officers even reached their rendezvous.

From then on Stirling preferred to make use of the Long Range Desert Group reconnaissance units to get his men to their targets, and the SAS went from strength to strength. In the North African campaign, their saboteurs destroyed more than 300 aircraft and numerous fuel dumps. Equally importantly, the Germans were forced to divert essential front-line troops to guard the rear area from their attacks.

If the commandos provided fertile recruiting ground for the SAS, they also sowed the seed for another élite unit that was to achieve on the sea what the SAS did on land – the Special Boat Service (later known as the Special Boat Squadron). Roger Courtney, a former big game hunter who had joined the commandos was convinced that small collapsible canoes used by the commandos in their training could be a useful tool for covert raiding on enemy installations on or near the sea. This initial idea was later expanded, and the SBS became adept at using midget submarines and converted fishing boats in addition to canoes. Unlike their counterparts in the SAS, SBS members often operated out of uniform, this justifying their motto: 'Not by strength, by guile'.

While the commandos, the SAS and the SBS formed the backbone of special operations forces in World War II, the allied approach to unconventional warfare was so unstructured that other groups, such as Popski's Private Army which successfully operated behind enemy lines in Italy and North Africa, also sprang up to fill a local tactical need or provide an outlet for creative fighting talent. All these groups were essentially simple adjuncts of the armed forces command structure. They would be given a particular task from senior officers, would do the job, and then would return for further instructions.

The British recognised, nevertheless, that if Churchill's encouragement to 'set Europe ablaze' was to be met, a great deal more would have to be done both to gather intelligence from the occupied territories and to foster resistance among the local people. Initially this work was performed by the agents of MI6, the Secret Intelligence Service, who in fact were geared for a largely peacetime role and proved fairly ineffective. In July 1940, therefore, the Special Operations Executive (SOE) was established with a brief to recruit and train agents to operate in enemy territory and to begin a psychological warfare operation against the Axis powers.

The group responsible for such propaganda, SO2, was highly imaginative, its actions ranging from radio broadcasts and fake newspapers, through the spreading of rumours about rail fare rises, to more risible items such as a report that Britain had released 1,000 Australian sharks into the sea off the coast of Tunis.[3]

More substantively, the SOE embarked on a major recruiting campaign, not just among British servicemen and women but also among the French, Norwegian and others who had fled the German occupation.

The British were essentially making up the rules as they went along, adapting or forming new groups to meet the fluid requirements of the war. It was not until the Americans joined the war that a more comprehensive strategy began to emerge.

4

The Men from Uncle

The United States entered the war in December 1941, after the Japanese attack on Pearl Harbour. It is hard to believe now, but at the beginning of World War II the United States had no external intelligence service and a standing armed force that was smaller than those of most European countries.

As the British had produced David Stirling and others, so the Americans found men like William (Wild Bill) Donovan to meet the need of the hour. Donovan was a much-decorated veteran of World War I, a lawyer of Irish descent yet an Anglophile, a teetotaller and a Catholic – and, perhaps most important, a good friend of President Roosevelt. In 1940 and early 1941 Donovan and others had tried to warn the President and Congress of the dangers of a possible Axis victory in Europe. Their message had met with some sympathy, particularly in the White House, and Donovan had been encouraged to travel frequently to Britain to sense the mood of the nation and provide personal reports to Roosevelt that would counterbalance the pessimistic assessments of the US Ambassador to London, Joseph Kennedy.[1]

Donovan was impressed by the work done by the SOE and other special forces and argued strongly that the United States should establish an organisation that could carry out sabotage, espionage, subversion and propaganda. The result was the creation of the Office of Co-ordinator of Information (COI) in July 1941 which in June 1942 became the Office of

Strategic Services (OSS) which in turn evolved into the
Central Intelligence Agency (CIA).

Under Donovan's inspired leadership, the OSS became
responsible for all black propaganda and psychological
warfare. These Donovan himself defined as, 'The co-ordination and use of all means, including moral and physical,
by which the end is attained – other than those of recognised
military operations, but including the psychological exploitation of the result of those recognised military actions –
which tend to destroy the will of the enemy to achieve victory
and to damage his political or economic capacity to do so;
which tend to deprive the enemy of the support, assistance
or sympathy of his allies or associates or of neutrals, or to
prevent his acquisition of such support, assistance, or
sympathy; or which tend to create, maintain, or increase the
will to victory of our own people and allies and to acquire,
maintain, or to increase the support, assistance and sympathy
of neutrals.'

This excellent definition still holds good and is seen by
many special forces as the rationale for all their work.

In addition to psychological warfare, Donovan thought
his new organisation should be responsible both for acts of
subversion and for intelligence gathering. This made it unique
and set a precedent in US unconventional warfare that was
to be followed for many years: this all-embracing authority
given to the OSS and later the CIA should be compared with
that given to other unconventional warfare organisations such
as the SAS, SBS or SOE, all of which had their compartment-
alised roles to perform without having total control of the
broad strategy. This assumption of power by Wild Bill
Donovan was eventually to make the CIA the most powerful
intelligence gathering and active organisation in the western
world.

One of the first things Donovan did was send large numbers
of OSS personnel to join with the SOE in infiltrating teams
into occupied Europe. Such groups consisted of three people
– generally an American, a Frenchman and a British member

of SOE – and were called Jedburgh teams after the town on the Scottish borders which had seen some early guerrilla warfare when a twelfth-century Scottish clan chief launched raids against the English invaders. The training was carried out in the grounds of an estate centred on the Elizabethan manor of Milton Hall, outside Peterborough. To many of the foreigners, particularly the Americans, the emphasis on discipline and fitness was perhaps as tiresome as the Scottish piper who woke them up at dawn every morning.

A graphic description of that time comes from Aaron Bank, an early American recruit to the OSS, who worked under-cover in France as part of a Jedburgh team and went on to play a key role in establishing Army special forces at Fort Bragg.

'Most of the training was conducted within the estate. Demolition charges were shaking the grounds and small-arms firing resounded from the area where fashionable ladies had played croquet. This is where Major Fairbairn, a British expert in the martial arts and the developer, with his partner Captain Sykes, of the famous Fairbairn-Sykes fighting knife, held sway with his instruction in instinctive firing. This was a method by which you aimed a handgun with your body rather than with your eyes on the sights – a specialty for night combat. Major Fairbairn was also highly visible in the sunken gardens where we practised silent killing with the use of the knife or the garrotte. Knife fighting was included. However, rather than the smell of blood, we'd inhale the fragrance of roses and the boxwood hedges. All day long the *da-de-da* of Morse code could be heard floating out of the library windows where we'd take turns tapping the sending keys.'[2]

SOE eventually recruited and trained as many as 10,000 people, and their efforts in building resistance among the occupied countries paid handsome dividends as the war went on. Resistance groups were trained, armed and, in many cases, led by members of the SOE and OSS whose activities spread beyond Europe to the Middle, Near and Far East.

A particularly significant demonstration of the potential of unconventional warfare occurred in Burma where the OSS trained local Kachin tribesmen in guerrilla action against the Japanese. The tribesmen, who were already adept jungle fighters, learned to gather intelligence, carry out sabotage missions, and help US pilots who had been shot down to escape back to allied lines. After three years of fighting, the OSS had 10,000 Kachins under their control and there is little doubt these men had a profound effect on the course of the war against the Japanese.

While the allies had been honing their skills in the unorthodox, their principal enemy the Germans had not been idle either. Their key player in this area was Otto Skorzeny, an Austrian who had joined the SS at the beginning of the war. He, like David Stirling, was a man of his time. Hitler personally selected him to form the Brandenbergers, an élite unit that was to carry out unconventional warfare against the allies. Its first major action occurred in 1943 when the Italian government arrested and imprisoned their leader, Benito Mussolini, and attempted to sue for peace with the allies. Hitler ordered Skorzeny to find Mussolini and bring him back to Germany. This was a seemingly impossible task as the Italian leader was being held in a ski hotel high in the Gran Sasso mountains, the only access to which was via a funicular railway. Not only was this well protected, but a frontal assault would inevitably alert the Italian troops, who might then execute Mussolini. Parachuting was impossible because of the high winds and rarefied air at that altitude, and so Skorzeny decided instead on a glider assault. This extremely dangerous manoeuvre took the Italian guards completely by surprise. After rescuing Mussolini, the Germans landed a tiny Storch aircraft on the plateau by the hotel and took the Italian leader to Germany.

A series of other daring operations consolidated Skorzeny's reputation as an innovative thinker. Then, during the Ardennes offensive in 1944, Hitler ordered him to form a brigade of American-uniformed Germans to infiltrate enemy

lines with two main objectives: to secure the vital Meuse
Bridges and to wage psychological warfare among the allied
troops. In fact, Skorzeny was unable to persuade the regular
army units to hand over enough captured American equipment for him fully to equip his troops and do the job properly.
But some did get through, and history has it that the ruse
was only discovered when one of the Germans asked an American to fill his jeep up with 'petrol' instead of asking for 'gas'.

More importantly, however, the news that Germans were
operating behind allied lines dressed as Americans caused
something close to panic, which was exacerbated when one
of the captured Germans 'confessed' that he and his
colleagues were on a mission to assassinate Eisenhower. This
disinformation had the effect of severely restricting the
Commander-in-Chief's movements for some days. All down
the American lines, US soldiers questioned other soldiers on
American historical or sporting trivia to try and sort the
genuine from the imposter. On one occasion, a bona fide US
general was arrested when he mistakenly insisted that the
Chicago White Sox, a baseball team, were in the National
League when every GI knew they were in the American
League.

After the war, David Stirling met with Otto Skorzeny who
told him that he had read every German intelligence report
on the activities of the commandos and the SAS to see what
he could learn. Many of the tactics he employed were the
direct result of lessons the British had learned with their own
special forces.

The Russians evidently learned a great deal from Skorzeny.
A key tactic of Soviet special forces in the event of an attack
today would be to infiltrate behind allied lines dressed in
Nato uniforms, to commit acts of sabotage and generally
cause chaos in the rear areas.

Indeed, as far as special operations were concerned, the
significance of World War II was that for the first time
different nations had an opportunity to build on the early
efforts of Napoleon, Wellington and others to extend the area

of battle away from the central front to the areas of greatest vulnerability in the enemy's rear. For the first time, guerrilla warfare and psychological warfare played a major part in the victory. Sabotage, the gathering of intelligence, and the raising of guerrilla armies in occupied territories had all proved their worth.

Nevertheless, the end of the war in 1945 demonstrated what has since become a repeating cliché: conventional military men see unconventional warfare as élitist, a drain on scarce resources in both men and equipment, and (although it may never be expressed in quite these terms) a subversive influence that thrives on operating outside traditional discipline and command structures.

Many of those who were to take up the cause of unconventional warfare in peacetime were veterans of World War II, men attempting to turn their experiences of that period to advantage during peacetime. Sadly, however, it is only war that cuts through the conventional thinking and brings to the fore exceptional men who are then allowed to think imaginatively. It was men like Stirling, Donovan, Popski and Skorzeny who made the SAS and other groups work. Peace brought the beginning of a new era, when special operations forces would fight for their existence against political and military prejudice.

5

End of Empire

In the post-World War II euphoria, there was a general assumption that, with the defeat of the Nazis, all threats to peace in the world had been removed. In fact, 1945 marked the beginning of the Cold War between west and east and the start of a series of campaigns that continue today and have as their aim the gaining of political influence through the use of covert military force.

With the exception of Winston Churchill, who had an obsessive dislike of the Soviets, and in particular of their leader, Joseph Stalin, allied leaders did not at this early stage see the spread of communism as a major issue. Agreements reached at Potsdam in July 1945 for the division of Europe between west and east as the spoils of war were already in place. One result of this sense of security, combined with the already mentioned antipathy of armed forces high commands for unconventional warfare, was the disbanding of all British special forces groups (with the exception of the Airborne). The SAS disappeared, but as a sop to its supporters 21 SAS (Territorials) was established. All the other allied special forces were subsumed into the regular forces which themselves were severely contracting as piecemeal demobilisation began.

However, relations with the Soviets swiftly deteriorated. Stalin had his problems. His economy was shattered by the war and Russian society could not afford to absorb the kind of massive demobilisation that was taking place in the allied armies. In consequence his armed forces were seen vastly to outnumber those of the allies, heightening the tension between the two sides. In this charged atmosphere, Churchill did his best to draw attention to what he saw as the Soviet menace. In a speech in the US in 1946 he received a standing ovation when he said:

'From Stettin in the Baltic to Trieste in the Adriatic, an Iron Curtain has descended across the Continent. Behind that line lie all the capitals of the ancient states of central and eastern Europe . . . all subject in one form or another, not only to Soviet influence but to a very high and in some cases increasing measure of control from Moscow.'[1]

Churchill was merely giving public voice to what would shortly become the cornerstone of allied foreign policy: the containment of the Soviet Union, the policies of which were seen as essentially expansionist. As one senior Truman adviser put it, the Soviet Union was a 'political force committed fanatically to the belief that with the US there can be no permanent *modus vivendi*, that it is desirable and necessary that the internal harmony of our society be disrupted, our traditional way of life be destroyed, the internal authority of our state be broken, if Soviet power is to be secure.'[2]

To counter the Soviets, therefore, the US first needed to establish an effective intelligence-gathering and special operations capability. A natural source for this was the OSS, by then renamed the CIA, which under Donovan had proved itself so capable during the war. At the end of 1947 President Truman signed National Security Directive NSC–10/2 which established the Office of Special Projects, swiftly renamed the Office of Policy Co-ordination, to act as the covert action arm of he CIA. The OPC was charged with carrying out 'any covert activities related to propaganda; preventive direct action, including sabotage, anti-sabotage, demolition and evacuation measures; subversion against hostile states, including assistance to underground resistance movements, guerrillas and refugee liberation groups; and support of indigenous anti-communist elements in threatened countries of the free world.'[3]

The first head of the OPC was Frank Wisner, a lawyer by training and a veteran of the OSS. As he spelled out in a memorandum to the Joint Chiefs of Staff in 1949, however, his perception of the role of the OPC was different in significant ways from that of the President and the NSC.

OPC's role, he stated, was 'to plan and to execute special (covert) operations or measures which are designed to reinforce or to accomplish United States foreign policy objectives; in peacetime, to formulate and execute plans to the necessary state of readiness in order that appropriate special (covert) operations may be executed in time of war as considered necessary by competent authority; in wartime, to plan and execute such special (covert) operations or measures as may be appropriate in the discharge of the OPC mission or as directed by competent authority.

'The techniques and means by which the OPC attains its objectives differ from those of the Department of State and the National Military Establishment inasmuch as OPC operations are conducted in a covert or clandestine manner to the end that official United States interest or responsibility is not permitted to appear and if such interest should inadvertently appear, it can plausibly be disclaimed by this government.'

Wisner listed seven objectives of the OPC:

'1. Political warfare including assistance to underground resistance movements and support of indigenous anti-communist elements in threatened countries of the free world.
'2. Psychological warfare including "black" and "grey" propaganda.
'3. Economic warfare.
'4. Evacuation, including the paramount responsibility for escape and evasion.
'5. Guerrilla and partisan-type warfare.
'6. Sabotage and counter-sabotage.
'7. Other covert operations (excluding espionage, counter-

espionage, and cover and deception for military
operations).'

In this manner, under the single OPC umbrella, the CIA
managed to embrace every aspect of covert warfare from
espionage to psychological operations and subversion. It was
an astonishing coup, the significance of which was little
appreciated at the time. It has to be remembered that the
US was new to the game of covert warfare and the politicians
who created first the OSS, and then the CIA with all its
offshoots, saw it simply as an effective tool of policy, one that
had been proven in combat and was now prepared to meet
the threats and problems of the new Cold War with the
Soviets.

The first targets of the OPC were the nationalist groups
now under communist control. Beginning in Lithuania and
spreading through the Balkans to the Baltic and back to the
Ukraine, from 1947 to the early 1950s the OPC with the
occasional help of British intelligence tried to foster revolution
against communist rule. In these early days, two key factors
emerged that are still evident today.

First, the western allies are politically inconsistent and
unreliable when fighting undercover wars. The will to fight
lasts as long as the war remains secret but dissipates as soon
as word of the operation leaks out. The US is particularly
vulnerable in this respect, so that time and again (in the
Ukraine, Albania, Tibet, Laos, Vietnam) revolutionaries
encouraged by US covert operators have been deserted, and
left to face almost certain death, as the American government
falls victim to political pragmatism brought on by a critical
electorate.

Secondly, allied nations place a high value on the life of an
individual intelligence operator. Even if a covert operation
costs only very few lives, it will be abandoned as too costly
by the west. By contrast, the Soviet Union has displayed a
consistent disregard for casualties. For example, in a ten year
campaign in Lithuania which ended in 1956 and was in part

supported by the OPC, although the Russians took 80,000
army casualties and had around 5,000 officials killed, there
was never any sign of weakening political resolve. In covert
warfare the Soviets have a major advantage in that they are
neither responsible to an electorate nor subject to the criticisms of a free press.

While the British and the Americans were doing their best
to undermine communism behind the Iron Curtain through
covert means, the rise in power and influence of the Soviet
Union and the teachings of Marx, Lenin and Mao Tse-tung
were acting as an inspiration to thousands of revolutionaries
around the world. The result was warfare on two levels: full
scale conflicts in Korea and Vietnam, and a rash of small
wars of national liberation sponsored by the Soviet Union
that threatened governments favourable to the west. Both
gave opportunities for special operations forces, but it was
the small wars that proved their usefulness.

The first of these began in Malaya when nearly 10,000
guerrillas took to the jungle in 1948 after a campaign of
urban terrorism had appeared to be having little effect. The
Malayan People's Anti-British Army were led by Chin Peng,
a communist with considerable experience of guerrilla warfare
fighting alongside the British against the Japanese. The intention of the rebels was so to terrorise the peasants that they
would gain a stranglehold on the countryside. With that
under control they would gradually be able to infiltrate the
urban areas once again. It was hoped that the Malayan
government would be powerless in the face of such a strategy,
backed up by extensive assassinations of local leaders, both
British and Malay.

As Malaya was still a British colony at this time, responsibility for the conduct of the war fell to the British government.
For the first two years of the war a moderately effective
campaign was fought by both the police and the army to
counter the guerrillas. But this effort was limited by the poor
training of the troops and tactics inadequate to fighting a
counter-insurgency war over large tracts of inhospitable

jungle where the indigenous population were either too terrified to supply information or else actively supported the communists.

In 1950, General Sir Harold Briggs was appointed Director of Operations and he consulted an SAS veteran, Mike Calvert, who had served in the SAS and fought against the Japanese in Burma. Calvert's assessment of the Malayan campaign had three key parts:

'1. A specially-trained force should be created that would be able to fight the communists on their own territory. This force would be able to live for long periods in the jungle and would not only gather valuable intelligence but would also deny the guerrillas any safe haven.

'2. Living and operating from their jungle hideouts, the guerrillas were almost entirely dependent for food, money and intelligence on the rural population. Calvert saw that if population areas could be denied them, then the guerrillas would be forced out into the open where they would be vulnerable. This involved not only discovering and patrolling the rural supply routes but also moving the population of some 410 villages to specially constructed fortified areas away from communist influence.

'3. If the guerrillas could force the local population to support them through terrorism, Calvert felt that the counter-force could win them over using a more humanitarian approach. If, he argued, the government forces could be shown to be on the side of the local people and if they could convince the villagers of their commitment to the war against the communists, then there was a good chance local support for the government forces would grow. This became known as the 'hearts-and-minds' campaign and has been imitated in countless campaigns ever since.'

Shortly after his report was submitted, Calvert was instructed to raise the force. His recruits came from the SAS Territorial unit, ex-SAS officers and men, a strong contingent from Rhodesia and others who simply volunteered for the job. They were called the Malayan Scouts (SAS) but were renamed 22 SAS Regiment in 1951.

What Calvert proposed seems with hindsight to be perfectly logical, and it seems extraordinary that such policies had not been adopted before. But this was a new kind of warfare, and the devising of new tactics and strategies took time. Malaya in many ways marked a number of firsts for special forces work. A broad strategy for counter-insurgency work was developed and effectively used; at a tactical level, for example, the insertion of special forces by parachute and their extraction by helicopter became an accepted method of operating. Above all, in the ten-year campaign, it was conclusively proved that small numbers of highly trained people, used properly, could influence the course of a war. It was a lesson that had already been learned in World War II, but it needed to be underlined by the Malaya Emergency before it was finally accepted by the army high command.

While the SAS were performing so effectively in Malaya, their fate was being decided back in London. As always with any special operations force, the SAS had their firm supporters (mainly those who had served with them and gone on to higher things) and their equally convinced detractors (usually conventional warfare men who had crossed the path of the SAS and come off worst). But on this occasion, fortunately, official discussions coincided with the preparation of a central staff study on the requirements and capabilities for fighting a war in Europe against the eastern bloc. And this study concluded that there was a requirement for two new types of operation behind enemy lines: long-term, deep penetration by forces that would target vulnerable individuals in the political or military structure of the enemy and commit acts of sabotage against targets that might be invulnerable to air attack; and short-term penetration for specific tactical reconnaissance or sabotage. It was suggested, therefore, that the former be carried out by the SAS and the latter by the Royal Marine commandos.

This recommendation was accepted, and in July 1957 it

was announced that the SAS would be given a permanent place in the order of battle as 22 SAS Regiment with two squadrons (later expanded to four).

For the next twenty years the SAS were repeatedly to prove their worth. Extensive campaigns were fought against communist guerrilla forces in Borneo, Brunei, Oman and Aden. In all of these, with the notable exception of Aden, the SAS were successful. The strategies and tactics that had proved their basic worth in Malaya proved equally effective in the jungles of Borneo or the high deserts of Oman. The two-tier approach, of taking the fight to the guerrillas and waging and winning a hearts-and-minds campaign among the locals, remained central to their success.

In Aden, the British were fighting a war against communist guerrillas who were ostensibly fighting for independence from the British colonialists. Substantial British regular forces were deployed in the country, augmented by the SAS. Both North and South Yemen had made a cottage industry out of tribal warfare, and as a result those seemingly backward people had a sensitive and sophisticated political nose. In Aden, the SAS waged a covert war in the mountains and in the bazaars, taking on the terrorists on their own turf. At the same time, they embarked on a hearts-and-minds campaign aimed at winning over the tribal leaders. Rural clinics were set up to bring modern medicine to tribesmen who still used herbal remedies centuries old; essential food supplies were brought to remote villages and even the occasional electricity generator was supplied to a village. But all of this had little effect as, from the beginning of the war in 1964, the British had made clear their intention of giving the country its independence in 1968, and the Adeni tribesmen therefore had no doubt who was going to win. The only question that remained to be settled was who would take power afterwards. The communists were seen by both sides to be the stronger contender and so the war in Aden was lost not because the tactics employed by the SAS and the regular forces were wrong but because there was a clear absence of political will to win.

This is a recurring theme throughout the history of low intensity conflict – as the CIA have found and, more recently, US Special Forces in supporting insurgencies. Without demonstrable evidence of political will, no indigenous people fighting for their own survival will believe for long in mere promises of support.

PART 3: COVERT ACTION

6

Guerrillas, Assassins and Subversives

If Malaya provided the impetus for Britain to establish a permanent SAS, the Korean War which began in June 1950 provided exactly the same motivation for the Americans. Until then, the US Army high command had accepted – even welcomed – CIA control of all special operations. But, once a real war (in the Army's view) came along, there was sharp resentment that the CIA had control of special operations, and a feeling that the Army should do more to control its own destiny.

The Korean War was in part a direct result of the dividing of the spoils that had occurred at the end of World War II. America and the Soviet Union had agreed to divide Korea at the 38th parallel. Although it was originally supposed to be a temporary arrangement, the division – like many in Europe – became permanent. Following its policy of containment the US was anxious to prevent any further expansion of Soviet influence in the area and gave clear support to the government of Syngman Rhee in the South while the Soviets equally strongly supported the communist regime of Kim Il Sung which they had created in the North. Both superpowers were determined to prevent reunification on the other's terms and so, when the North invaded the South in June 1950, a wider conflict was inevitable.

Although both Russian and Chinese troops were on hand

in North Korea, US intelligence assessments suggested that the Russians did not want a direct confrontation with the US. So President Truman, expecting a quick, clean war and determined to counter Soviet aggression, committed US forces to fight with South Korea. These men and materials were subsequently backed up by a United Nations force.

The American military quickly found itself without any clear ability either to counter communist propaganda and psychological operations or to wage a guerrilla war behind enemy lines. With the encouragement of the Army Secretary, Frank Pace, the army therefore created the Office of the Chief of Psychological Warfare in January 1951. The new division was to mastermind psychological warfare and other 'special operations', which included counter-insurgency work. Under General Robert McClure, the new team embarked on an ambitious programme of leafleting and radio broadcasts aimed at the Chinese and North Koreans.

At the same time, McClure set up a wider Special Operations Division, which basically consisted of two OSS veterans, Colonel Russ Volckmann and Aaron Bank, who had gained his experience with the Jedburgh teams in France. The two men spent some months examining the past performance of special operations forces in an attempt to devise a programme that would give them a peacetime role that could easily transfer to wartime.

The final study, according to Bank, isolated five main features:

'1. Europe, primarily the Soviet satellites, would be the main target area.

'2. Since the army had never conducted covert unconventional warfare operations in Europe, the OSS experience would be used as background for all theories of operations, training and organisation.

'3. Regardless of the formation of the unit, its mission must be strictly within the parameters of unconventional warfare.

'4. For administrative purposes, and to appease the

traditionalists and the orthodox in the service – those whose sole interest was in conventional forces (armour, infantry and artillery) – the unit would have to appear to be formed in companies and battalions, with command equivalents that would not threaten those of senior rank.

'5. It would form the core of a guerrilla force intended to conduct unconventional warfare under the direction and control of the army.'[1]

The role of this new force would include infiltration by air, sea or land deep into enemy-controlled territory. It would then remain in place to recruit, train, control and direct local guerrilla units in future special forces operations. These operations were defined as 'the organisation of resistance movements and operation of their component networks, conduct of guerrilla warfare, field intelligence gathering, espionage, sabotage, subversion and escape and evasion activities.'[2]

On 1 May 1952, the US Army agreed that a special forces capability was needed and the following month the 10th Special Forces Group (Airborne) was formed at Fort Bragg, North Carolina with Aaron Bank as its first commander. Bank was ordered to recruit three batches of 500 men each and he called for volunteers. These had to be Airborne trained, qualified in European languages and prepared to operate behind enemy lines. There was no shortage of volunteers from OSS veterans, Rangers and the Airborne.

The structure that Bank established remains largely in place today. The operational units were formed into A-teams of eight men commanded by a captain (this was later expanded to two officers and ten men); a B-team commanded by a major with three officers and nine men to co-ordinate the A-teams; and C-teams commanded by a lieutenant-colonel with two other officers and nine men, to liaise with host governments or groups, and to devise strategy. Ten A-teams made up a company commanded by the senior captain, three companies with one B-team would form a battalion and a group would have one C-team and three battalions.

Curiously, although the Korean War had acted as a spur for the US military to establish both a psychological warfare capability and a special forces unit, only the former was actually deployed in Korea.

Today, lecturers at Fort Bragg cite the Korean War to recruits as a classic example of how not to fight an unconventional war. From the beginning there was conflict between the CIA, which handled intelligence gathering and helped downed pilots in escape and evasion, the conventional military, which had their own reconnaissance and intelligence gathering apparatus, and various army groups which had responsibility for setting up and running individual unconventional warfare units. The units themselves were divided up into a myriad of groups that were nominally under the overall control of the 8th Army.

Official army records suggest for example that, although 20,000 North Korean defectors and South Korean troops were recruited to form the United Nations Partisan Forces in Korea, to undertake hit-and-run attacks against the enemy, its organisation was hopelessly unwieldy and in fact it contributed little.

From the outset of the conflict there was poor understanding of the potential for special operations forces, particularly in a strategic role. Intelligence was so poor that even the presence of an indigenous guerrilla force that had been operating in the North since 1949 was not known until some time after the war began. These guerrillas operated in the south-west of North Korea, an area that provided much of the food for the country, and properly exploited – which they never were – they could have performed a vital role in the war. The military high command also never used any special forces for deep penetration behind the enemy lines, either for intelligence gathering or sabotage. Although such operations had proved their worth only six years before, reconnaissance was confined to an area fifty miles north of the combat zone.

Korea was hardly a victory for the allies. To the blinkered conventional military mind, however, the war had shown that the massive use of conventional firepower could at least fight an enemy to a standstill – provided, of course, he obligingly fought the same kind of war. The United States armed forces thus had their prejudices reinforced. In both World War II and Korea, American military might had prevailed, and this fact was to colour official judgements on future fighting, especially in Vietnam.

The Soviets viewed the situation rather differently. They quickly recognised that an externally-sponsored conflict using large numbers of conventional forces would not succeed. For them to have any chance of winning, a new strategy was needed, one that would exploit the west's obsession with conventional warfare. Guerrilla warfare and terrorism was the answer.

If conventional military men in the west had not learned much from Korea, the Special Operations forces had. Today in his closing remarks about the Korean War to the recruits at Fort Bragg, the lecturer shows a slide which simply says:

There was no
Doctrine
Strategy
Command and Control
Training Base

These four fundamental requirements for unconventional warfare were to dog the US military for the next thirty years. At no time in any of the wars, big or small, that involved special forces, is there evidence that sufficient thought had been given to getting the basics of the business right. The US special forces themselves place the blame squarely with the men responsible for devising strategies, implementing policy and providing leadership who have never fully understood the nature of the complex weapon they have at their disposal.

In the autumn of 1953, the first opportunity arose to deploy the 10th Special Forces Group. Rioting in East Berlin against Soviet occupying forces led Washington to feel there was a

potential for using the special forces – the only force specifically trained to raise guerrilla armies in enemy territory –
in East Germany to take advantage of the obvious discontent.
Half of the 10th were therefore sent to a new base at Bad
Tolz in West Germany, the other half remaining behind in
the US as the 77th Special Forces Group. Not that the 10th
were in fact ever used to infiltrate behind the Iron Curtain,
but at least the riots provided an excuse for them to devise a
real warfighting strategy that then gained official approval.

At Bad Tolz, the special forces received training in languages and lock-picking (the local wine merchants suffered a
series of mysterious burglaries immediately afterwards). More
importantly, they gathered special equipment, such as secure
radios and explosives, either from their own armouries or
borrowed from the British, that turned them from a paper
unit into an organisation capable of actually operating behind
enemy lines for extended periods. While at Bad Tolz, the
men, who still wore the uniform and markings of the
Airborne, began experimenting with different caps and
badges to distinguish themselves from the common herd.
After various designs and colours had been tried, Aaron Bank
himself ordered a batch of green berets and designed the
Trojan Horse shoulder flash, both of which were to become
the hallmark of special forces in the US army.

Clearly there was now an understanding among some of
the military that the nature of warfare was changing. Not
only had the 10th been set up specifically to work behind
enemy lines raising resistance groups in time of a conventional
war in Europe, but – as Castro's coming to power brought
home – no longer was a massive conventional war in central
Europe or anywhere else even the most likely scenario.
Instead, strategists in the west appreciated that the kind of
revolutions that had brought Mao to power in China and
Castro in Cuba, and that had so ruthlessly repressed freedom
of expression in Hungary, required the development of a new
response.

This new response was first publicly articulated by President Kennedy in May 1961, in a message to the US Congress. In describing revolutionary warfare he said: 'They have fired no missiles; and their troops are seldom seen. They send arms, agitators, aid, technicians and propaganda to every troubled area. But where fighting is required, it is usually done by others – by guerrillas striking at night, by assassins striking alone . . . by subversives and saboteurs and insurrectionists, who in some cases control whole areas inside of independent nations. . . . We need a greater ability to deal with guerrilla forces, insurrection and subversion and we must help train local forces to be equally effective.'

He hammered home this message to a graduating class at West Point the following year. Over 400 of the 600 in the audience would later serve in Vietnam and twenty-one would be killed. Kennedy told the young soldiers: 'This is another type of war, new in its intensity, ancient in its origin – war by guerrillas, subversives, insurgents, assassins; war by ambush instead of by combat; by infiltration instead of aggression, seeking victory by eroding and exhausting the enemy instead of engaging him. . . . It requires in those situations where we must counter it – and these are the kind of challenges that will be before us in the next decade if freedom is to be saved – a whole new kind of strategy, a wholly different kind of force, and therefore, a new and wholly different kind of military training.'[3]

Kennedy's emphasis on the work of special forces was underlined later that same year when he paid a visit to their headquarters at Fort Bragg. He used the occasion to approve formally the wearing of the green beret but, more importantly, his trip served notice on the Army high command that the President required action in building up a special forces capability.

Among more conventional military men there had traditionally been a reluctance to commit valuable resources to special forces since a recognition of their role might imply a reduced role for the regular military and therefore a reduction in their own status in the bureaucracy. The intelligence community, on the other hand, saw the expansion of special forces as a threat to their own worldwide monopoly in covert wars. In fact it wasn't until the enforced cutbacks on CIA covert operations in the late 1970s that an alliance grew up between special forces and the Agency, where each could exploit the other's political influence to get a share of the covert action.

Meanwhile, however, each of the services tried to be the first to appear to fall in line with the President's wishes. the Navy formed SEALs (Sea Air Land teams, the US equivalent of the British SBS) while the Air Force developed the Air Commandos. The Army expanded their special forces to include the 1st Special Forces Group based in Okinawa with responsibility for the Far East, the 8th in Panama (Latin America), the 3rd and 6th at Fort Bragg (Africa and the Middle East), the 10th at Bad Tolz (Europe) and the 7th at Fort Bragg in reserve. Each had 1,500 men, a fourfold increase in the total strength. But in the rush to fill the places two of the cornerstones of special forces policy suffered: excellence and security.

From 1962 to 1964 the number of potential recruits rejected dropped from a high of 90 per cent to 30 per cent. Also, instead of taking only recruits who had already been trained by the Airborne, special forces began accepting untrained civilian volunteers. At the same time, anxious to demonstrate the special forces' capability to interested public officials, the army put on a show at Fort Bragg which included demonstrations of survival techniques such as catching, skinning and eating a snake. (Since then special forces have been known as 'the snake eaters'.)

The special forces themselves seemed to have a rather clearer understanding of their role, which was essentially to combat guerrilla forces operating in friendly countries. To that end, the writings of Mao Tse-tung, Che Guevara and the North Vietnamese leader Vo Nguyen Giap became required reading at Fort Bragg. But perhaps the most important lesson learned by recruits at the Special Warfare School were taught by Bernard Fall, a Frenchman who had written a brilliant and highly critical book on the French war in Algeria and Indo-China entitled *Street Without Joy*. Fall made the point that although the French had won the war in Algeria, in the process they had forfeited the support of the electorate at home. At the same time, they had so alienated large sections of the local population that their ability to govern was seriously hampered, and so they ultimately lost Algeria. This was a lesson taught to the American special services but never learned by the American government – as was to be so painfully demonstrated in Vietnam.

7

Vietnam: Futility and Frustration

The first US special forces had been sent to Vietnam in 1957 to train commandos of the Vietnamese army. There was nothing particularly significant in this as units were being deployed all over the world, from Ethiopia to Jordan.

Two years later, US special forces became involved in Laos where the pro-west government was under attack from communist Pathet Lao insurgents supported by as many as 10,000 North Vietnamese troops. Under the control of the CIA, the special forces teams were required first to train the local army in counter-insurgency tactics, and then to train selected local tribes to fight the Pathet Lao on their own terms. The campaign was only moderately successful. There was a great deal of political interference, and the special forces were never allowed the independence they needed to operate for long periods in the jungle. Instead, a great deal of time was spent at base camp on training programmes that had little relevance to what was going on in the countryside. Some progress was made, however, in training Meo and Kha tribesmen, who were to continue their fight against the communists for ten years after the US special forces left.

On 23 July 1962 a protocol was signed in Geneva calling on all foreign countries to withdraw their forces from Laos. All American servicemen left (although many CIA men stayed behind), while only forty North Vietnamese troops were counted going through the checkpoints out of the country.

Laos should have provided serious lessons for the US. After all, the withdrawal occurred at exactly the time when President Kennedy was considering increasing the US commitment to Vietnam. But in fact there was still disagreement within the US as to exactly how a counter-insurgency war should be fought.

Predictably, the military treated the problem as being concerned with the effective use of force. As they saw it, threats to a country invariably began outside that country and the solution was not only to attack the insurgents with all the force at your disposal but also to take the fight outside, to the sponsor of the insurgency. In the case of Vietnam, this was an argument both for dealing firmly with the Vietcong operating inside South Vietnam and for attacking the North with all the means at America's disposal, including bombing or even an amphibious invasion. In a war of attrition, it was argued, the stronger force must win.

This theory takes no account of the fact that insurgencies are essentially *political* wars, as Harry Summers points out in his excellent study of the Vietnam war, *On Strategy*. He recalls a conversation with a North Vietnamese colonel in Hanoi in April 1975. 'You know you never defeated us on the battlefield,' said the American colonel. The North Vietnamese thought about this for a moment. 'That may be so,' he replied, 'but it is also irrelevant.'[1]

The counter to the military argument was put by the White House and the State Department, who both felt that a more political approach would work. According to their theory, insurgency was only possible because of popular support for the insurgents inside a country's border. There might indeed be outside interference, but the war would be won by the people who gained the most popular support. Washington's strategy then would involve a broad hearts-and-minds campaign, backed up by limited counter-guerrilla action.

The most articulate advocate of the latter approach was a

British diplomat, Sir Robert Thompson, who had played a key role in Britain's campaign against the communists in Malaya and had moved to Saigon as Head of the British Advisory Mission there. Thompson argued in a paper delivered to the US government that if the Americans hoped to win the war, they should follow the example of the British in Malaya. In Thompson's view, the Vietcong's campaign was aimed at gaining control of the estimated 16,000 villages and hamlets in South Vietnam. They would never take on the opposing military in direct confrontation. Instead, they would concentrate their efforts on persuading or forcing villages to give them support. This would not only ensure them a ready supply of recruits but would also be a source of money, supplies and intelligence.

Thompson pointed out that when the French had been in Vietnam they had made the mistake of building a series of protected forts, behind which they sheltered their army. Although they won every direct battle with the Vietcong, they lost control of the villages, even those that lay far behind the forts. The Vietcong had no need to seek a direct conventional victory – instead they steadily whittled away support for the French behind their own lines.

The clear lesson was that America's fight would be won or lost in the villages. In Malaya the British had used what became known as the Oil Spot theory. A small force of specially-trained troops would move into an area, secure a village and train the local people to look after their own defence, with the outside forces providing rapid reinforcement, if necessary. Once one village was secured, the British unit would spread out, securing an ever wider area but always with the co-operation of the local people who would be armed, trained and responsible for their own welfare. Furthermore, the British had moved hundreds of villages, assembling what they called strategic hamlets which, after a period of training, looked after their own defences and protected each other from communist attack. The hamlets were supported by troops held in reserve and at no time were the communist guerrillas able to get back inside the ring of strategic hamlets to terrorise or gain supplies and intelligence.

Applying that same policy in Vietnam, Thompson argued, would have a double impact. First, the Vietcong would be forced to operate outside their most effective areas and in territory that was more suited to the US and Vietnamese forces. In their search for food and influence they would gradually be drawn into killing zones where the nature of the battle would be almost entirely determined by the allies. And secondly, those people involved in the strategic hamlet programme would benefit from such a firm demonstration of political will by the Saigon government. They would be convinced of its commitment to their security, and would see the positive improvements in land reform, crop production and health care that flowed from a comprehensive civil aid policy. These two tactical advantages would undermine the influence of the Vietcong, and the insurgency would wither for lack of popular support.

In principle, these ideas were well received by the White House. President Kennedy's support of unconventional warfare was well known and the Thompson plan perfectly articulated his thinking. Also, the figures seemed to support him. While the Vietcong were undeniably supported to a large degree by the government in Hanoi, intelligence analysis suggested that out of 35,000 Vietcong operating in the South in 1961, fully 34,600 had been recruited there.[2]

Before the conventional military became heavily involved in Vietnam, operations were controlled by the CIA. Thus it was they, not the army, that controlled the special forces in the early days. Because the CIA understood that the war was an internal problem and not a matter of cutting off the South from the North, they adopted Thompson's approach of the Oil Spot and used the British strategy to combat the Vietcong.

Ten A-teams were deployed in 1961 and 1962 around a village called Buon Enao in Darlac Province populated by the Rhade tribe. They rapidly established a network of fortified villages, armed the local militia in Civilian Irregular Defence

Groups (CIDG), set up local dispensaries, and involved the whole community in defending itself from the Vietcong. They established a mobile strike force composed entirely of local people and available to help any village in the area that came under attack. The programme was a remarkable success. After only two years, several hundred villages, some three hundred thousand civilians, and several hundred square miles of territory had been secured from the Vietcong and 38,000 local people had been armed and trained to defend themselves.[3]

Naturally, the CIA wanted to expand the programme and requested more special forces. But this coincided with an increase in the US military presence in Vietnam and gave the Army high command an opportunity to argue that the special forces should be under their control and not that of the CIA. The Army won that fight and from then on the special forces were never employed correctly and the strategic hamlet programme became hopelessly corrupted.

Over the course of the next nine years an average of 3,500 US special forces would serve each year in Vietnam and until the major expansion of US forces that took place in 1965 would do their best to carry out the President's instructions to fight a counter-insurgency war. The early field manuals prepared for the special forces, such as the 535-page FM 31–20 and the 114–page Handbook ST31-180, were almost entirely devoted to jungle warfare, presumably targeted at Vietnam. Designed in a handy size that fitted into the pocket for easy reference in the field, the handbooks covered anything from setting snares, to making a thermite bomb in a flower pot to raising and training a guerrilla army. And, if all else failed you could turn to the back cover of the Handbook and put your trust in the Lord with the Special Forces Prayer:

Almighty God, Who art the
Author of liberty and the
champion of the oppressed, hear
our prayer.

We, the men of Special Forces,
acknowledge our dependence upon
Thee in the preservation of human
freedom.
Go with us as we seek to defend
the defenceless and to free the
enslaved.

In 1965, the mission of special forces was defined as:

'a. To plan and conduct unconventional warfare operations in areas not under friendly control.
'b. To organise, equip, train, and direct indigenous forces in the conduct of guerrilla warfare.
'c. To train, advise and assist indigenous forces in the conduct of counter-insurgency and counter-guerrilla operations in support of US cold war objectives
'd. To perform such other special forces missions as may be directed or as may be inherent in or essential to the primary mission of guerrilla warfare.'[4]

By this time, clearly, the unconventional warfare role had been expanded from support of guerrilla fighting and escape and evasion, to include 'subversion against hostile states', a significant change that put special forces firmly on the offensive in the fight against the communist menace.

But, from the beginning, the US policy had been deeply flawed. The US forces were supposed to be merely 'advisers' and as such were subordinate to the Vietnamese military – which was corrupt, ineffective and divided about how to fight the war. In addition, US military commanders never fully accepted the White House/State Department argument that the war had to be won with the people, instead of by using maximum military force.

In 1970, just before the 5th Special Forces Group handed over control of their projects to the Vietnamese and headed back to Fort Bragg, they received a Civic Action Medal from the Chief of Staff of the Vietnamese Army which cited the setting up of 49,902 economic aid projects, 34,334 educational projects, 35,468 welfare projects, and 10,959 medical projects; supplying 14,934 transportation facilities; supporting nearly half a million refugees; digging 6,436 wells and repairing 1,949 kilometres of road; building 129 churches, 272 markets, 110 hospitals and 398 dispensaries; and building 1,003 classrooms and 670 bridges.[5]

On these apparently impressive figures it might be thought that the special forces alone should have won the war. However, the operations they conducted were not only too diverse to eliminate effectively Vietcong influence in any single area but were also constantly undermined by the Vietnamese and US military high commands.

The Vietnamese distrusted and disliked the tribes with whom the special forces operated. They were despised as backward and rebellious (the Montagnards helped support this prejudice by rebelling against their Vietnamese rulers in 1963 and 1964). And the US military, despite clear contrary instructions from Washington, insisted on a policy of search and destroy. For example, there was a standing order to American helicopters to fire on any village that contained a source of fire against them. This resulted in the levelling of many villages, the killing of thousands of civilians, and the total alienation of large sections of the population, who naturally came to believe the Vietcong propaganda that all Americans were butchering imperialists. In 1963, it was estimated that 30 per cent to 40 per cent of all those killed in the war were innocent bystanders.[6]

With the assassination of President Kennedy on 22 November 1963, control of the war passed to Lyndon Johnson, a man who knew nothing about warfare and in particular did not have Kennedy's understanding of how best to exploit special forces and their skills. The military shrewdly used the opportunity to press for a change of strategy in the war. They argued that they had been hampered in their planning by Washington's over-cautious approach and an obsession with the hearts-and-minds campaign in Vietnam.

They wanted swift solutions – but in a type of warfare that invariably requires years, rather than months, before policies bear fruit. It is this eagerness for action and answers, in fact, that has bedevilled America's approach to modern wars of terrorism or counter-insurgency.

Back in 1963 the military told President Johnson they wanted more troops and authorisation for the bombing not only of areas of South Vietnam occupied by the Vietcong but also of strategic targets in the North. The President agreed to both requests and thus committed the US to fighting an unconventional war by conventional means – a policy that has never proved successful in the history of warfare. According to official US estimates, in the year immediately following the bombing decisions recruitment of Vietcong guerrillas from among the villagers of South Vietnam increased almost four times – from 40,800 to between 105,900 and 135,900 – clear evidence that the hearts-and-minds campaign had been lost.[7]

The US military continued to pay lip service to the strategic hamlet concept and thousands were established. But responsibility for security rested firmly with the American and Vietnamese military and not with locally-trained militia. In fact, in the areas where the special forces had proved so successful in the early years, arms were actually taken away from the local people on the grounds that they could not be trusted, and this despite clear evidence to the contrary.

Although the special forces retained their training role, they were increasingly used for deep reconnaissance or search and destroy missions. These were essentially strike operations aimed at killing Vietcong and took no account of the steadily increasing support that the guerrillas were able to get inside South Vietnam.

The US commanders made exactly the same mistake in training the South Vietnamese army. The South Vietnamese were neither trained nor equipped to fight a counter-insurgency war simply because US generals continued to believe they were fighting a conventional war. Because they chose to think only in conventional terms, the Americans saw as the prime threat a massed invasion of the South by the North Vietnamese army. So they trained a huge army to fight a war that did not exist.

(Perhaps the best illustration of the American outlook comes from Guenther Lewy in his excellent book *America in Vietnam*. 'I'll be damned', one American officer is quoted as having said, 'if I permit the United States Army, its institutions, its doctrine and its traditions to be destroyed just to win this lousy war.')[8]

This basic error coloured all aspects of the war and was largely responsible for America's defeat. The Army continued to use all the methods of measuring success that had worked well in previous conventional wars. So, a victory in a set battle – almost invariably at a time and place of the Vietcong's choosing – repeatedly convinced them that overall victory was at hand. The simple expenditure of ammunition or the deployment of people often seemed to be sufficient. Throughout the campaign the military produced hopelessly over-optimistic reports on the course of the war claiming variously that it would be over within a year or within three years. Certainly, at the end of each year, the reports sent back to Washington from Saigon reported a steady march towards victory. Every year too, the Vietcong made more progress, controlling ever larger areas of territory and terrorising more and more people.

With the west's propaganda war being lost both at home and among the Vietnamese people, the North Vietnamese now felt confident enough to introduce large numbers of their own troops into the South. A war that had all the classic hallmarks of a counter-insurgency campaign now became both a guerrilla war and a more conventional conflict. As the French had discovered only ten years before, although the superior American firepower ensured victory in the set-piece battle, the Vietcong guerrillas held sway over ever greater parts of the countryside. And while losses among North Vietnam's conventional forces were far higher than among the Americans, General Giap, leader of the North's army, felt it was a price worth paying. As one American military analyst wrote: 'His is not an army that sends coffins north. It is by the traffic in homebound American coffins that Giap measures his success.'[9]

As late as 1968 when America was already looking for a way out of the war, Sir Robert Thompson was arguing that it was still not too late for the United States and the government of South Vietnam to change its policies and win the war. His article in *Foreign Affairs* is worth quoting at length as he clearly sets out a strategy and tactics for the war that apply equally to any similar conflict.

'The higher strategy of People's Revolutionary War,' he wrote, 'is conceived in the context of time, space and cost. Time (or perhaps patience) is the key to this strategy. Its value is greatly enhanced if there is a large measure of impatience on the other side. While the revolutionary forces are forged, the Government forces are infected with a growing sense of futility and frustration. Time also allows for the exploitation of opportunity, for advancing when possible or for taking "one step backward" when trends are unfavourable. It is part of the doctrine that victory is inevitable, even if it takes half a century.

'The answer in Vietnam is a complete switch of strategy to the indirect approach, with the emphasis on nation-building concurrent with limited pacification, and a mere containment of the military threat. It should be recognised that, even though an offensive action against the enemy's main force units may be tactically aggressive, it is strategically defensive, for the strategic offensive lies in the nation-building and the pacification. This strategic offensive requires an intensely practical approach in its initial stages to the rebuilding of the whole Vietnamese government machine: the selection and training of qualified administrators and technicians at all levels; the consolidation and clarification of the law; the promulgation of terms of service and simplified government procedures; the re-establishment of the civil courts, the revival of the ministries and of the administrative structure right down to the villages, so that requirements come up and action goes down; and the restoration of law and order which requires a professionally qualified police force (a task which alone will take ten years, not six months). Not until you get performance – and that is the key word – can you hope to have any semblance of democracy in Vietnam. Democracy is not elections and voting; it is the liberty of the individual and his protection by law, not just against the Vietcong but against all the local factional secret society cliques, so that he can make a free choice.

'Meanwhile, the major military task, apart from supporting pacification, is to prevent the enemy's main-force units from interfering with this strategic offensive. They do not have to be destroyed, though obviously "prevent" means that they must by kept stirred-up and occupied. Their eventual destruction will come in two ways. First, as their popular base within the country declines, so will their strength and capacity correspondingly decline, leading to a steady de-escalation of the conflict and, secondly, as the advance of pacification threatens their vital areas, so will they have to come out and fight for them on ground not of their own choosing.'[10]

But the advice came far too late. The only forces that could have carried out such a programme had begun a six-year handover to regular Vietnamese forces in 1964. The 5th Special Forces Group left Vietnam entirely on 31 December 1970, three years before the full scale withdrawal of American forces and five years before the embarrassing evacuation via the US embassy roof in Saigon of the last Americans in the country.

Even during the handover period, however, the special forces expanded their operations as they sought to take the fight to the guerrillas. *Mike Forces* were set up as quick reaction teams to protect the strategic hamlets attacked by the Vietcong, and units codenamed Projects *Omega*, *Delta*, *Sigma* and *Blackjack* were set up to carry out reconnaissance and sabotage missions deep into enemy-held territory. When at full strength, Project *Delta* numbered some 600 men and for two years was commanded by Charlie Beckwith who was later to set up and run Delta Force, a completely separate group established in 1977 for counter-terrorist work.

Unfortunately these missions served to tarnish the reputation of the special forces, not only in the eyes of the conventional military commanders but also in the eyes of the politicians and public back home. Although special forces played only a very minor role in the CIA-run Phoenix programme which resulted in more than 45,000 suspected Vietcong being assassinated and 30,000 jailed, there were widespread allegations of torture, assassination and simple brutality by special forces teams against those suspected of being Vietcong sympathisers or agents. While special forces personnel have always denied any such allegations, there seems little doubt that as the war dragged on the standard of their recruits fell, with a consequent reduction in discipline, and that overall frustration with the course of the war probably led to excesses.

One of the most spectacular, if unsuccessful, raids by special forces during the Vietnam War occurred on 21 November 1970, just one month before all special forces were withdrawn from the country. The raid was aimed at the Son Tay prison in North Vietnam twenty-four miles from Hanoi, which was believed to hold sixty-one American prisoners of war. The operation was to suffer from all the hallmarks of future assaults by US special operations forces in Iran and Grenada: poor command and control; an obsession with security; and an overly complex plan. On this occasion, the intelligence was excellent; it just didn't reach the people who needed it.[11]

Operation Ivory Coast was first proposed in May 1970, when intelligence analysts said that examination of aerial photographs taken by SR-71 Blackbird reconnaissance aircraft overflying North Vietnam combined with human intelligence and satellite photography suggested that American prisoners might be held at Son Tay. The idea was enthusiastically endorsed by General Donald Blackburn who at that time was Special Assistant for Counter-Insurgency and Special

Activities at the Pentagon. Blackburn had been involved in covert warfare in the Philippines, Laos and Vietnam and liked the idea of masterminding the first raid on a POW camp in North Vietnam.

A detailed assessment of the project followed and the chairman of the Joint Chiefs of Staff gave the go-ahead on 10 July. Blackburn chose as the force leader Colonel Arthur D. 'Bull' Simons who had served under him in Laos and had a distinguished record with the special forces in Vietnam. Simons in turn gathered fifty-eight volunteers from the special forces at Fort Bragg, including Captain Dick Meadows, who was to play such a vital part during the attempted assault on the US embassy in Teheran ten years later. The force was moved to Eglin Air Force Base in Florida for training.

The plan was extremely complex. An HH-53 Jolly Green Giant helicopter gunship would lead the assault. Its massive firepower would destroy the two main guard towers on the camp walls and clear the way for an HH-3 Sea King helicopter loaded with Dick Meadows and thirteen men which would crash-land inside the prison compound. After Meadows had rescued the prisoners, they would be taken outside the compound, loaded on board two other Jolly Green Giants and flown to safety under cover of A-1 Skyraider fighters with three C-130 Combat Talon transport aircraft co-ordinating the strike and creating diversions in the area.

Flying time to the target from a secret CIA base in Thailand was 3.4 hours and involved a complicated formula that took into account the different flying speeds and ranges of the aircraft. Also, using information gathered by the Defense Intelligence Agency, all aircraft were required to fly at very low levels along carefully-designed routes which were precisely timed to coincide with the movements of North Vietnamese radar dishes. If all went well, the US aircraft would always be flying through one spot while the radar was looking at another.

To practise the assault, Simons had constructed a complete mock-up of the prison compound at Eglin Air Force Base.

To avoid detection by overflying Soviet satellites, the whole construction was dismantled every time the DIA told them one was likely to be overhead. Altogether, the team made 368 practice flights spending 1,107 hours in the air.

After a full dress rehearsal on 7 October, the plan was first submitted to Henry Kissinger and then after some delay to President Nixon and a small group of officials at the White House on 18 November. Nixon gave his approval and the team, by then at their forward base in Thailand, headed into North Vietnam on the night of 21–22 November.

The operation was brilliantly executed. The assault force remained undetected on its way to Son Tay. The team backing up Meadows went slightly off course, came under heavy fire when they landed, and in the ensuing battle killed between one hundred and two hundred enemy soldiers. Meadows, meanwhile, had landed his team inside the compound without accident. Unfortunately, there were no prisoners there to be rescued.

SR-71 reconnaissance of the camp the previous month had shown that the prisoners had been evacuated and although additional reconnaissance before the assault had shown the camp was being used again, intelligence gathered by a DIA agent in Hanoi suggested that no Americans had been returned there. This information had been passed on to Blackburn who had refused to accept it and had not passed it on to his commanders. Instead, his commitment to the project appears to have overcome his good sense and the two teams were sent on a highly dangerous mission even though he knew it was likely to prove fruitless.

Both assault teams successfully returned to Thailand. But then a gaffe by President Nixon alerted the world to their failure. Hosting a Thanksgiving dinner in the White House for disabled Vietnam veterans, at which he had hoped to announce the triumph of the Son Tay rescue mission, the President, while signing souvenir matchbooks, began talking about the raid instead. The story appeared the next day in the *Washington Post*.

Between 1966 and 1973 some 119 missions were under-taken, ninety-eight of them raids attempting to rescue American prisoners. None was successful. One US soldier was rescued, only to die later from his wounds. But of all those missions, Son Tay was the most spectacular failure.

Such operations by US special operations forces, combined with an increasing focus on the covert activities of intelligence agencies in the west, generated a great deal of interest among politicians and the general public.

The Vietnam war had clearly shown how the skilful use of guerrilla forces can overwhelm an apparently more powerful adversary. The Vietcong employed classic guerrilla theory, first by operating in small bands inside the country and living off the local population, on whom they relied for food and intelligence. Then, once they felt powerful enough, they moved to a more conventional phase and met the enemy in larger numbers.

Neither the French nor the Americans understood this kind of war. US military commanders have often argued that the war was lost not because they fought badly but because the politicians refused to allow them to use all the force at their command and the media undermined the will of the people to support them. But even if the politicians had allowed the military to do everything they wanted – which would have included invading North Vietnam – there is absolutely no evidence to suggest that the war would have ended in the foreseeable future. On the contrary, the Vietcong would have redoubled their efforts and would surely have won substantial numbers of new recruits from a population that had seen confirmed the Vietcong's propaganda which depicted the United States as a warmonger. Vietcong guerrillas would have survived, however much direct force was used by the US military. It was not political will that was lacking in the Vietnam War, it was a basic understanding of the nature of modern unconventional warfare. As long as the US high command insisted on attacking the wrong targets with the wrong weapons at the wrong time, a Vietcong victory was inevitable.

Disillusionment with the Vietnam War came about not because the media undermined the US effort. During the Kennedy years there were few voices raised against America's involvement. On the contrary, there was a great deal of public support both for President Kennedy and the military effort. However, once it was seen that despite the massive investment of men and material there had been no significant gains, with the prospect of none in the future, it is hardly surprising that a certain cynicism began to develop. But the rot was started by the soldiers themselves, who began to tell a different story from that put out by military headquarters in Saigon. It was a story of increasing Vietcong influence, of huge search and destroy missions that found little and only destroyed local villages, of a population that increasingly saw the Americans and not the Vietcong as the aggressor.

With the politicians and the media conveniently available to shoulder the blame for the defeat, the US military saw little reason to do much about its own ability to fight future wars. The Vietnamese experience had very little impact on their strategic thinking. Little is taught at Fort Bragg about Vietnam, as the focus continues to be on a conventional war on the central front.

In the immediate aftermath of Vietnam it appeared easier for the military commanders to concentrate on something they knew well and for which detailed plans were already written – the US commitment to Nato – rather than worrying about unconventional warfare in or out of Nato. France was no longer a military member of Nato and so the US special forces wartime base west of Paris was not available. Also, current intelligence assessments tended to support the view that the traditional role for special forces – training guerrilla armies behind enemy lines – was anyway becoming irrelevant. Technological advances in both east and west made a quick conventional war in Europe the most probable threat. Allied assessments varied on the length of a conventional war between one week and thirty days (war stocks were supposed to last for a month but few senior officers believe a conventional assault by the Warsaw Pact can be defended longer than about ten days before nuclear weapons are used). In such circumstances, any war would be over long before the special forces could raise and train a guerrilla army.

Official US and Nato support for special forces was therefore difficult to find, and the result – at a time when other countries were developing their capability for unconventional warfare – was severe cutbacks. The 1st, 3rd, 6th, and 8th Special Forces Groups were disbanded. Units were withdrawn from Germany, Okinawa and Panama and numbers fell to a total of 3,600 in the remaining 5th, 7th and 10th Groups. This decline in numbers was matched by a fall in performance. With a lack of commitment from the service chiefs, few soldiers wanted to join special forces and so inevitably overall performance suffered. In this downward spiral, the future of special forces looked bleak indeed.

There was little interest, also, in what was happening in the communist bloc (in part because of a lack of information) even though in fact the changing nature of warfare was well understood by the Soviets.

8

Poisoning the Prague Spring

Obviously the Soviets understood just as well as the United States and other western countries that wars would never be the same again after the arrival of nuclear weapons. No longer would they be fought by massed armies. Instead any future territorial expansion would be brought about by policies which Soviet premier Nikita Khruschev articulated as 'support for wars of national liberation'. In 1974 this view was reinforced by the Soviet Defence Minister, Marshal Grechko, who wrote:

'At the present stage the historic function of the Soviet armed forces is not restricted to their function in defending our Motherland and the other socialist states. In its foreign policy activity the Soviet state purposefully opposes the export of counter-revolution and the policy of oppression, and the national imperialist's aggression in whatever distant region of our planet it may appear.'[1]

It is difficult to disentangle from the web of propaganda on both sides whether the US or the Soviet Union were first to begin developing their influence in Third World countries. Seen from Washington, Soviet influence and expansionist policies appeared to be everywhere from Cuba to Angola to Vietnam. Moscow, equally, saw America's hand in the Philippines, Iran and Central America. Confrontation in the covert battle for the hearts and minds of unaligned nations was inevitable and both sides established similar forces to deal with it, the US developing the CIA and special forces, and the Soviets the KGB and spetsnaz.

What is clear is that with the equalisation in the balance of power between the United States and the USSR, Moscow has been increasingly ready to use its military and economic muscle to intervene abroad. In Cuba, Angola, Nicaragua, Mozambique, Ethiopia and others, Moscow has frequently moved decisively to arm and train guerrillas or governments which support Moscow's brand of communism. With the notable exception of Afghanistan, this involvement overseas has stopped short of intervention with Soviet troops outside the communist bloc. However, extensive use has been made of surrogates like the Cubans and training teams to provide expertise on the ground.

While the KGB handled direct subversion, training, arming and funding of guerrilla movements, spetsnaz was available to project armed Soviet power beyond the country's borders. And the first real opportunity to test that capability came with the emergence of a liberal government in Czechoslovakia in 1968.

Under the moderate leadership of Alexander Dubcek, the Czech government attempted a series of reforms in the country's economy and political structure. Workers' councils, an early attempt at trade unionism, were authorised; the separation of the Party and the state was proposed, with a new federal structure of government, and the intelligence agencies to be monitored by committees of the National Assembly; political prisoners were released, and pro-Soviet Czechs were purged from influential positions in the security and party apparatus.[2]

Predictably enough, the Soviet Union saw in these reforms a potential blueprint for rebellion among other satellite states. For example in the Ukraine, where strong nationalist sentiment still existed despite a bloody post-war campaign to suppress dissidents, the KGB was already reporting renewed unrest as a result of the Czech experiment. If allowed to continue unchecked the Soviets feared it could signal the beginning of the end of the Union of Soviet Socialist Republics.

Over a period of eight months, the Soviets did everything they could to undermine by covert means the leadership of Dubcek and his reformist colleagues. The KGB was particularly active in trying to rally Czech hard-liners and oust Dubcek. Even so, support for the reforms was so widespread that it failed. The only course left open to the Kremlin was direct military intervention.

The Soviets alerted the Czech government that extensive manoeuvres would take place along its borders on 21 August. In fact, that exercise simply gave the Soviets the cover they needed to bring their troops forward, ready to cross the border at a moment's notice. On 16 August detailed briefings for infiltration and invasion were given to spetsnaz and other Warsaw Pact forces. The infiltration briefings included a film of Prague airport secretly taken by Soviet agents, and the detailed plans of all Czech airports which had been prepared for the Soviets by Colonel Miroslav Elias, a longtime KGB agent serving in the Ministry of Interior.

Just after 23.00 hours on the night of 20 August, the control tower at Prague airport received a distress signal from a Soviet cargo plane which asked permission to land. Permission was granted. Before the plane had come to a halt, spetsnaz units deployed from its cargo hold, and teamed up with others who had flown in earlier that day dressed in civilian clothes, pretending to be tourists. This apparently flimsy cover had worked simply because the head of passport control at the airport, Colonel Frantisek Stachovsky, was a KGB agent.

The spetsnaz, armed with Czech Skorpion sub-machine-guns, stormed the airport control tower, seizing it and other key points at the airport. Once the airport was secured the Soviet forces commandeered buses, cars and trucks to take them into the centre of Prague.

Meanwhile, the Soviet cargo plane, apparently unable to stop, had got stuck in the mud at the end of the runway. In fact, on board the plane was a homing beacon to guide other Soviet aircraft to the runway in case the control tower ceased to function. Immediately wave after wave of Soviet Antonov transports began flying into the airport to unload troops and vehicles. At the border, Warsaw Pact troops from Soviet, East German, Polish, Bulgarian and Hungarian divisions moved in as the advance guard of what was to be a 500,000-strong invasion force backed up by 5,000 tanks.

Other spetsnaz units had been infiltrated into Prague over the previous few days. These joined up with KGB units comprising agents from the Soviet embassy, sleepers already in place in the city, and agents inside the Czech government and security service. Their first targets were the radio and television stations which were immediately occupied by spetsnaz teams led by a traitorous Czech intelligence officer, Colonel Josef Rypl. KGB agents in the telephone exchanges and the media (the editor of *Rude Provo*, the main national newspaper, was a Soviet sympathiser, while the heads of both the official news agency and broadcasting were KGB agents) prevented any truthful information being broadcast to the nation. Although some back-up radio stations did operate some hours later, control of the main news outlets gave the Soviets vital breathing space in which to consolidate their hold on the country and prevent united opposition gaining any real momentum.

At the time of the invasion, the Party Praesidium was in session and just before midnight news of it reached the delegates by a secure telephone link. They immediately passed a resolution condemning the invasion as an act 'contrary to the fundamental principles of relations between Socialist states and a denial of the basic norms of international law.' The meeting then broke up and Dubcek and his cabinet retired to his office in the Central Committee building.

In emergency session, with the incessant noise of Soviet transport aircraft overhead to remind them of their vulnerability, the cabinet discussed the options available. In fact, the cabinet had nowhere to go and no options available.

Furthermore, Colonel Bohumil Molnar, the head of Regional Administration at the Ministry of the Interior and a long-time KGB agent, had supplied the invasion force with detailed plans of the Central Committee building and an escape route available to government officials through the city's sewer system. Shortly after 04.00 a black Volga saloon drew up outside the building. Inside were Molnar and two KGB agents. Backed up by units of spetsnaz dressed in their distinctive wine-coloured berets and striped sailor's jerseys under their paratrooper uniforms, the KGB headed towards Dubcek's office. A vivid description of the next few minutes comes from one of Dubcek's cabinet, Zdenek Mlynar, who subsequently defected to the west:

'Suddenly the door of Dubcek's office flew open and about eight soldiers and low-ranking officers with machine-guns rushed in, surrounded us from behind around a large table and aimed their weapons at the backs of our heads. Then two officers came into the room. One was a colonel, who was shorter than the other, almost dwarfish in stature, but to compensate he wore a whole row of medals, perhaps including the golden star signifying a Hero of the Soviet Union. He also had the arrogant authoritarian bearing of a sergeant major. He announced that he was "taking us into custody" and began to issue various commands. Then someone – perhaps it was Dubcek – said something and the colonel roared out: "No talking. Sit quietly. No talking Czech." If he hadn't added that last condescending phrase I might have tried to ignore him. But it suddenly and quite spontaneously provoked in me such feelings of anger, humiliation, fear and that strange sensation of immunity that comes to ex-rulers that I lost my temper and shouted imperiously to him in Russian: "Behave as you were told. Where do you think you are anyway? You are in the office of the First Secretary of the Communist Party. Do you have orders to silence us? Of course you don't. So obey your orders." '

Such defiance was largely wasted. The cabinet were kept under guard for the next five hours. At one stage the tension dissolved into laughter as the Chairman of the National Front, Frantisek Kriegel, lay down on the floor, rested his head on his briefcase and, worn out by the drama, promptly went to sleep. The sound of his stentorian snores almost provoked the guards into firing out of anger when they thought he was making a fool of them, but in fact he was genuinely asleep.

Later that day, those key members of Dubcek's cabinet who were considered part of the reformist movement were taken by car to the airport and flown by military transport to Moscow. A list of reformists who were considered a major security threat to the invasion forces had also been drawn up and over the next few weeks large numbers of them were liquidated by the KGB.

Without their leaders and with the military under the firm control of the KGB, the Czech people had little to do but passively protest against the invasion. They did so in their thousands but the demonstrations were essentially peaceful. Slogans sprang up across the country that were a bitter parody of those that were favoured by other protesters in the western world: 'Yankee Go Home' became 'Ivan Go Home', and signs saying 'USA in Vietnam, USSR in Czechoslovakia' appeared.

Over the next three days negotiations took place between the Czech cabinet and the Soviet Politburo, led by Leonid Brezhnev himself, to decide on what terms government by the Czechs would be allowed to resume. The Soviets made it clear that a return to any form of reformist communist government was unacceptable. Brezhnev told the Czechs that changes made to European frontiers after World War II were inviolate. He added that he had spoken personally to President Lyndon Johnson two days before the invasion and the US President had assured the Soviets that any action they took regarding Czechoslovakia or Hungary would not be opposed by the United States.

The situation was clearly hopeless and on 26 August Dubcek and his cabinet signed an agreement that accepted the presence of Soviet troops. Once that had been conceded, there was little else left to fight for, and subsequent agreements cancelled all the reforms that had been granted by Dubcek and his colleagues. Czechoslovakia was once again under the firm control of Moscow.

The invasion provided an excellent example of Soviet covert operations. Working in apparently perfect harmony, the KGB with its agents in place and the GRU with spetsnaz shock troops supported by overwhelming follow-on firepower, proved a devastating combination. Careful planning ensured that the invading forces quickly secured the airport, thus allowing the follow-on forces unopposed access to the country. Agents were already in place to take control of all communication centres. In addition, the isolation of the Czech leadership was correctly identified as being crucial to the whole enterprise. Once Dubcek and his immediate supporters had been taken under Soviet control, any real prospect of the invasion being opposed by the military vanished.

The tactics employed by the Soviets were to be put to good use again ten years later, during the invasion of Afghanistan. Indeed, unlike many of their counterparts in the west, Soviet military commanders seem to have learned much from their experiences with unconventional warfare, and have placed increasing emphasis on the capability of their spetsnaz forces in recent years.

But then, in 1970, a new form of revolutionary warfare emerged on the world scene to give special forces a new role and a new importance.

PART 4: BLOODY REVOLUTION

9

'There are no Innocents'

On 6 September 1970 – a day that became known in terrorist folklore as Skyjack Sunday – TWA flight 741 with 155 passengers and crew on board was hijacked in West Germany. The terrorists on board, all members of the Popular Front for the Liberation of Palestine, ordered the aircraft to fly to Jordan where it landed at a disused RAF base called Dawson's Field outside the country's capital, Amman.

Within a matter of hours it had been joined by a Swissair DC-8 also hijacked by PFLP terrorists. The aircraft were loaded with explosives and surrounded by well-armed PFLP supporters who threatened to blow up aircraft, passengers and crew unless terrorists held in jails in West Germany, Switzerland and Britain were released.

An El Al Boeing en route from Tel Aviv to New York was the target of four more PFLP hijackers. Two of them who tried to board the plane during a stopover in Amsterdam were bumped from the flight which was overbooked. (Showing considerable initiative they immediately switched targets, hijacked a PanAm 747 going to New York, forced it to fly to Cairo where they blew it up on the tarmac.) The other two, however, Leila Khaled, an attractive Palestinian in her early twenties and Patrick Arguello, a Nicaraguan leftist, succeeded in boarding the El Al jet.

Immediately after the Amsterdam takeoff these two tried to hijack the plane, demanding it be flown to Dawson's Field, now renamed Revolution Airfield. A security guard on the aircraft instantly shot and killed Arguello. Khaled had two grenades hidden in the cups of her brassiere but both failed to go off and she was overpowered by the plane's crew. In the shooting an Israeli crew member had been wounded, so the pilot diverted to London's Heathrow airport to get him medical treatment. The British arrested Khaled.

Three days later, the PFLP hijacked BOAC flight 775 from Bombay to London during a stopover in Bahrain. It too was flown to Revolution Airfield and the release of Khaled was added to the hijackers' demands.

During the next week, negotiations continued, with the Red Cross acting as intermediaries. The governments, with the exception of Israel, accepted from the outset that they would have to release the terrorists jailed in their countries and on the basis of promises made via the Red Cross, the PFLP freed 375 hostages but held on to 55 others.

On 15 September, fearing an attack by Israeli commandos, the PFLP evacuated the planes and in a spectacular display before the television cameras of the world blew them all up.

The operation resulted in the demands being met and all the terrorists held in Germany, Switzerland and Britain were released, including Leila Khaled who went on to become a leading propaganda figure for the Palestine Liberation Organisation, the umbrella group that claimed to represent Palestinians and was committed to establishing a Palestinian state in land occupied by Israel. Meanwhile King Hussein of Jordan had seen the hijack as a direct threat to his own authority, and so instituted an armed strike against PLO forces in Jordan; during what became known as Black September more than 7,000 Palestinians died. A commando of the Jordanian army found sixteen of the hostages hidden in the heavily-damaged outskirts of Amman. Of the others, thirty-two were released by the PFLO during the fighting and six had been handed over to the Red Cross. One, a Norwegian, was freed before hostilities began.

Skyjack Sunday served notice to the world that terrorism had arrived as a major political force. Of course, terrorism was not new. Over 900 years ago Al-Hasan ibn-al-Sabbah led a particularly savage band of terrorists that eventually gave him influence over territory that stretched from the Persian Gulf to the Mediterranean. Sabbah was born in Iran in the eleventh century and became leader of the dissident Muslim Ismaili group (themselves one of two divisions of the shi'ite sect). He set up headquarters in a hidden valley in Alamut in Northern Iran, giving rise to the legend of The Old Man of the Mountains.

After travelling all over the Middle East, preaching his particular faith and finding that peaceful persuasion failed to rally followers to his cause, like many who came later, he began a campaign of terror. He recruited men who were willing to die for their faith, and to reinforce their beliefs he built a beautiful garden in his hidden valley that was perfumed by rare flowers and watered by flowing streams. He would ply recruits with liberal quantities of hashish and when they were suitably stoned he would take them into the garden where, over the next few days, the hashish would be supplemented by food, wine and women – giving the recruits the understandable impression they had entered through the gates of paradise. Back in the real world, Sabbah explained to the recruits that what they had just experienced awaited them if they should die fighting for him. This early indoctrination technique helped to generate a wave of terror so great that no wealthy traveller in the region would consider moving without a substantial personal bodyguard. Sabbah called his followers fedai or fedayeen – adventurers or, as the PLO now refer to them, 'men of sacrifice'. To the people they attacked they were known by a chilling word that had derived from their use of hashish – assassins.

Even so, although acts of terrorism have regularly cropped up around the world, from the Thuggees in India to the Irgun in Israel, none of these campaigns has reached the proportions of that initiated on Skyjack Sunday in 1970.

That year, the US State Department reported that 302 terrorist acts occurred around the world.[1] Clearly, what has made the terrorism that began then and continues today so different from anything that occurred in the past is its broad base, and the vulnerability of modern society to attacks by limited numbers of highly-motivated people.

There is hardly a western democracy that has not been touched by terrorism in the past twenty years. The first generation of groups, such as the Baader Meinhof, the PLO and the Red Brigade, formed the vanguard of what appeared to many to be the beginning of a worldwide armed revolution. Fortunately, however, while many of the groups were from the political left, there was little firm evidence of a common hand directing them. Indeed, most of the groups had great difficulty agreeing a political view among themselves without confusing the issue by going across borders to deal with other national movements.

As terrorism developed, it became possible to break its perpetrators down into three distinct groups:

1. The revolutionaries. These, such as the Tupamaros in Uruguay, Action Directe in France and the Red Brigade in Italy, all want to see radical change in the society in which they operate. Of course, change is the aim of all terrorism, but the simple revolutionary defines the problem as one of overthrowing oppressive and unjust government (generally capitalist) and replacing it with a system more in keeping with the needs and wishes of the people – on behalf of whom the revolutionaries claim to be acting.

2. The Nationalist/Separatists. Led by the PLO, as the biggest and richest terrorist group, many of the most successful organisations, including the IRA, the Basque ETA, the Tamils in Sri Lanka and the Sikhs in India, all want to take for themselves a section of territory currently part of a larger country, in which they will set up a government of their own. This particular form of terrorism endures best, since it seems generally to find more support among ordinary people than revolutionary terrorism.

3. The right-wingers. These have emerged to counter the rise of left-wing terrorism and to remedy the ineffective nature of

existing legal systems in dealing with the threat. Although this form of terrorism seems to have declined in recent years, Italy, Turkey, Northern Ireland and several Latin American countries have experienced it. Furthermore, the most significant threat to United States stability today is judged to be from right-wing groups such as the Jewish Defence League and the Survivalists, who already have the arms and infrastructure in place to launch effective campaigns.

All these groups use many of the tactics that have been developed by counter-insurgency forces such as the SAS, the OSS and, more recently, the US special forces. The goal is to cause maximum chaos by hitting hard at society's political and economic infrastructure, and so they vary the methods and timing of their attacks, thus making an effective counter virtually impossible to devise. The main factor that distinguishes the terrorist from his more legitimate counterparts is his willingness to treat civilians as a legitimate target – indeed he accepts this as an essential part of his strategy. In the immediate aftermath of the 1980 bombing of the Bologna railway station in Italy when eighty-four civilians were killed and more than 200 injured, one terrorist was asked why he had caused such damage to innocent people. He replied, 'There are no innocents.'

Although these groups are generally small in number their attacks often affect millions. Terrorism in its modern form has been able to take advantage of the huge progress this century in communications, particularly since the arrival of television. The media, according to Britain's Prime Minister, Margaret Thatcher, provide the terrorist with 'the oxygen of publicity', and there is some truth in this view. Certainly, without a media obsession with terrorism, and the instant report of each terrorist act by television, newspapers and radio around the world, terrorism would have developed very differently.

If the media play their part in helping terrorism develop,

so too do governments. Beginning with Skyjack Sunday, governments have usually been prepared to capitulate to terrorist demands; until recently there has been no evidence of a common stand to meet the common threat; and the sharing of information that might be useful to all was, at best, an intermittent affair that depended on the whim of each country's intelligence agency. Thus terrorists have for the last twenty years held the initiative in a war marked by the reactionary nature of their enemies' counter-terrorist policies.

Recent key changes in the counter-terrorist strategy adopted by western nations have been forced on them by three different events: the assault by Palestinian terrorists at the Olympic Games in Munich in 1972, the rise of terrorism in Northern Ireland, and the hijacking of an aircraft to Entebbe in Uganda. Although these events spanned a number of years, they were the formative elements in the evolution of a comprehensive counter-terrorist strategy in the west.

10

The Hydra Strikes

Before dawn on 5 September 1972, eight terrorists belonging to Black September climbed over the six-foot-high wire fence that surrounded the village housing the athletes in the Olympic village in Munich. Dressed in track suits, the group was distinguished only by the AK-47 Kalashnikov automatic rifle each member carried. They burst in on the eleven Israeli athletes and their coaches. Two of them – wrestling coach Moshe Weinberger and weightlifter Yossef Romano – protested and were shot dead. The rest were held hostage in their apartment.

The West German police force were caught totally unprepared. The terrorists demanded the release of 234 prisoners held in Israel and members of the Red Army Faction held in West Germany, and an aircraft to fly them to Cairo. As on Skyjack Sunday, the West German government was prepared to concede to the demands while the Israelis remained adamant that there would be no negotiations.

After seventeen hours of talks, the terrorists and their hostages were flown by helicopter from Munich to Furstenfeldbruk military airport where they had been told they would board a Boeing 727 and fly to Cairo. In fact, as the terrorists left the helicopters at Furstenfeldbruk, snipers hidden on the roof of the terminal building opened fire. Two terrorists were killed and others wounded, along with two of the helicopter crew. Two of the snipers, even though they had terrorists in their sights, lost their nerve and failed to fire; the light was poor anyway, and the distances too long for accurate firing.

The disastrous result was that the remaining terrorists had time to reboard the helicopters, and when the Germans followed up their abortive sniper attack by launching a direct assault using troops and armoured cars, the Palestinians killed five of the bound and gagged hostages in one helicopter and blew it up. Such a slow and obvious German attack against terrorists who had clearly demonstrated their willingness to kill was the height of folly. As the firefight continued, the second helicopter with another four Israeli hostages on board also exploded. Although five of the terrorists were killed and three arrested, nine Israelis died and the entire rescue operation had been fatally bungled by an inexperienced army and police.[1]

The disaster had been watched live by television audiences around the world and the event did a great deal of damage to the credibility of the West German government.

The lesson was not lost on other politicians, however, with the result that specialist counter-terrorist units began to be formed. In Germany, the Grenzschutzgruppe 9 (GSG9) was set up as a special division of the Federal Border Guard. Under its charter GSG9 'is to be used in the carrying out of police missions of special significance. They may above all be employed in cases when the situation necessitates a single operation, whether openly or in secret, bringing to bear immediate force against violent criminals. This is especially the case when larger, organised groups of terrorists become active.'

The French followed the German lead and set up the Groupe D'Intervention de la Gendarmerie Nationale (GIGN), as a 54-man unit of the Gendarmerie Nationale that would be specifically employed to counter terrorism. The British SAS, too, was given the authority and the funding to establish a Counter-Revolutionary Warfare (CRW) wing which began with twenty men and was subsequently expanded to a full squadron of around eighty, designed to be a quick reaction force available twenty-four hours a day.

Special forces traditionally lead a precarious existence and the SAS are no exception. Before the Munich attack, with the dismantling of the British Empire and the conclusion of counter-insurgency campaigns in Malaya, Borneo and elsewhere, they had urgently needed a new role that would fully employ its special talents. As terrorism began to surface as a problem in the late 1960s it seemed to the SAS that they had a function at two levels: both countering threats directly and also gathering intelligence in areas not normally covered by the traditional agencies of MI5 and MI6. For both these agencies, the rise in sophisticated communications and intercept systems had radically changed the way they gathered their information. The previous dependence on the secret agent or human intelligence (Humint) had been replaced by signals intelligence (Sigint). It was felt that with the aid of monitoring devices that could pluck microwave telephone calls out of the air or listen to conversations in rooms using bugs the size of pinheads, the role of the man on the ground had ceased.

Northern Ireland provided the perfect opportunity to test this theory. When the IRA renewed their campaign there for a united Ireland in the 1960s, their campaign of terrorism won support among the Catholic minority who for many years had suffered discrimination at the hands of the Protestant majority. As sectarian violence increased, the British sent in the army to restore law and order. One of the first units to go was D Squadron of the SAS who were given an intelligence-style role controlling the flow of weapons from the Irish Republic to the Provisional IRA in the North. But this operation was cut short as the services of the SAS were needed in Oman to counter the activities of communist-backed rebels there.

For the next six years, intelligence gathering of all kinds was left to the British security services, the British army and the Royal Ulster Constabulary Special Branch. None of these was particularly suited to the task. They had very few good agents and inter-service relations ranged from poor to terrible. Besides, MI6 should not have been operating in the country at all, as its charter charges it with gathering intelligence outside the British Isles. It claimed involvement because of its role in Dublin during World War II countering the work of German agents. MI5 resented its presence, and the two agencies ended up competing with each other. Relations between the army and them were never good, and all three of them despised the RUC as a bunch of amateurs.

There were, of course, some successes. Perhaps the two most notable occurred early in the 1970s and began with the turning of ten IRA terrorists who agreed to work for the British. Run by the Parachute Regiment, the unit was known as the Special Detachment of the Military Reconnaissance Force or Freds for short, and proved useful in identifying IRA men and passing disinformation. The second operation of note was the setting up of the Four Square Laundry in the heart of Catholic Belfast, which acted as a secret forward observation post and intelligence centre. It was very profitable both economically and politically, and was shut down only when a former member of the Freds leaked its true nature to the IRA.

Although some individual members of the SAS went to Northern Ireland to help out on the intelligence side, there was no formal commitment of the SAS by the British government until January 1976. Certainly both the Catholics and the Protestants firmly believed that the SAS were already in the province (they had the nickname of the Special Assassination Squad), but not until a renewed outbreak of sectarian killing in 1975 did British Prime Minister Harold Wilson in fact decide to send the SAS over. The arrival of the Regiment in the province was not greeted with enthusiasm by the intelligence services already operating there. Inevitably they saw it as a criticism of their own performance. The exception to this was MI6 who, because of the SAS's extensive operations abroad, already had a good working relationship with them, one that continues today.

The SAS were very effective in the province. In the urban areas in Belfast and Londonderry and in the rural countryside of South Armagh their experience in setting ambushes and in intelligence gathering through lengthy surveillance operations was enormously useful, and their reputation among the terrorists grew. They were even falsely credited with orchestrating a widespread campaign of assassination against the IRA and with carrying out a series of operations such as bank robberies and train derailments aimed at discrediting the Provisional IRA.

While much of this was untrue, there is no doubt that the SAS interpreted their role in the province freely. They crossed the border into the South to snatch IRA men who were then reported to have 'strayed' into the North; others were brought north and left unconscious, whisky bottle in hand, for the local police to discover; there were also isolated incidents of killings of IRA men who could as easily have been taken into custody. And on one occasion, when a surveillance team learned that a pre-dawn bombing was going to be carried out by an IRA cell, they tampered with the alarm clock of the Provisional's driver, so that it failed to go off and he was late for his rendezvous. A small and apparently rather childish prank – except that British intelligence then leaked through their agents that the IRA couldn't even get to their own bombings on time, which gave further credence to the commonly-held belief in their military incompetence. In addition, the IRA subsequently shot the driver.

Propaganda value aside, the SAS had a real effect on the violence in the province. In South Armagh, for example, twenty-one people had died in the five months immediately before their arrival while only two were killed in the ten months after. Although Northern Ireland did represent a major departure for the SAS, since for the first time, they were operating in the British Isles and often in civilian clothes, something that their founder, David Stirling, had always opposed, the key to their success was their willingness to take the fight to the terrorists; to meet them on their own ground rather than passively wait for them to strike. This was a lesson that had yet to be learned by the special force commanders of most other countries.

The single exception to this was Israel. Under terrorist attack since the formation of the Palestine Liberation Organisation in 1964, Israel had maintained a consistently tough line when dealing with terrorists: not only would there be no negotiation but terrorists would be made to pay dearly for their attacks on Jewish targets. As terrorism gained momentum as a political force and the PLO fragmented, other groups outside the Middle East emerged which claimed common cause with the PLO. The result was a rash of attacks against Israel and Jews around the world.

On 27 June 1976, Air France flight 139 en route from Tel Aviv to Paris was hijacked following a stopover in Athens. Four terrorists, two Germans from the Baader Meinhof gang and two Palestinians from the Popular Front for the Liberation of Palestine (PFLP), seized the aircraft and flew it first to Benghazi in Libya where it was refuelled and then on to Entebbe airport in Uganda, where it landed before dawn the following day.

The 258 passengers and crew were taken at gun-point from the plane to the old terminal building at the airport, where they were met by another five terrorists who had landed earlier. There they were placed under guard by the terrorists. Additional security was provided by Ugandan President Idi Amin's own troops who surrounded the airfield.

In exchange for releasing the hostages, the terrorists demanded freedom for fifty-three of their comrades held in jails in France, West Germany, Kenya, Switzerland and Israel. While many of the European nations were ready to make concessions, the Israelis once more were not. From the outset, they considered military action but were unwilling to risk the possibly heavy loss of life that would be involved among civilians from other countries. But over the course of the next week all the hostages except 103 Jews were freed, thus unwittingly clearing the way for the Israelis to exercise the military option.

As soon as word of the hijack had reached Tel Aviv, Unit 269 of the Israeli paratroopers went on full alert. Similar in makeup to the Counter-Revolutionary Warfare group of the SAS, Unit 269 is Israel's quick-reaction counter-terrorist force. The Unit, commanded by Colonel Jonathan Netan-yahu, immediately began examining ways of rescuing the hostages.

Three options were considered: a parachute drop on nearby Lake Victoria followed by an amphibious assault on the airport; a conventional land assault from Kenya, with whom Israel had very good relations; or an airborne landing at the airport itself. Whichever option was chosen there were formidable obstacles. Entebbe was 5,000 kilometres from the nearest Israeli airbase at Ophira at the tip of the Sinai penin-sula. While there were aircraft with the range to get to Entebbe, they would have to find somewhere to refuel on the return journey.

The planners chose the third option, deciding it gave the best chance of reaching the airfield undetected and getting home again. The Israelis had two bonuses: unlike the West Germans in Munich four years before, they had specific training in hostage rescue, and Entebbe airport had originally been constructed by an Israeli firm and the plans of the terminal building still existed.

Unit 269 constructed a dummy Entebbe airfield complete with mock-ups of the terminal building. They practised again and again, until the first troops could reach the terminal exactly two minutes after leaving the aircraft.

The plan required that four Hercules transports would take off from Ophira and fly below radar level down the Red Sea, cross over Ethopia and land at Entebbe. They would be escorted by a Boeing 707 which would act as a command post, electronic warfare centre and aerial hospital in case of casualties. The Boeing would radio ahead of the Hercules to the Entebbe control tower that President Idi Amin was coming in to land and requesting the runway lights to be turned on. The first vehicle out of the first Hercules would be a black Mercedes, identical to the one used by the Ugandan president. If the bluff worked, five commandos in this car, followed by the 'presidential escort' in two jeeps, should get to the old terminal building before the alarm was raised.

The other Hercules transports held more troops, who had to secure the airfield, the new terminal and the control tower, and also had to destroy a squadron of Ugandan Mig–17 fighters which otherwise might well pose a threat to the assault force.

Prime Minister Yitzhak Rabin and the Israeli cabinet gave final approval for Operation Thunderball on 2 July. At dawn the following day the fleet of aircraft took off from Ophira and headed south. Despite meeting storms along the way, they landed at Entebbe at 23.01 that night, only thirty seconds behind schedule. The circling Boeing had done its job well and runway lights had been obligingly turned on for the 'president' and his entourage.

The Mercedes and its escort got to within forty metres of the terminal before they were challenged by two Ugandan soldiers. One was immediately shot but the other ran shouting towards the nearby control tower before he too was killed. The terrorists inside the terminal had been alerted therefore, but they still had no idea of the nature of the problem. Thus it was not until the first three men of the assault force burst through the glass doors into the terminal that the terrorists began shooting the hostages. Shouting through a loudspeaker to the hostages to lie on the floor, the Israelis found the standing terrorists easy targets, and they were swiftly killed. Three minutes later all the Israeli troops were deployed around the airfield to secure it against counter-attack by Ugandan forces.

Fifty minutes after the first Hercules had landed the freed hostages were airborne. They were flown to Nairobi, where the aircraft refuelled, and then on to Tel Aviv.

All the terrorists had been killed. Two hostages had died, one killed by the terrorists and one by accident by the Israelis, and seven were wounded. A further hostage, Mrs Dora Bloch, who had been taken from the airport to a nearby hospital for treatment, was later shot by Ugandan soldiers and her body dumped in a ditch outside Kampala. Only one Israeli soldier was seriously wounded in the attack but the commander of the operation, Colonel Netanyahu, was killed by a sniper while directing operations outside the terminal.

Given the enormous risks involved, the casualties were surprisingly light, and the Israeli action clearly demonstrated to the world that firm resolve in the battle against terrorism could acheive results. Highly-skilled special forces, trained to be used surgically to achieve a limited goal, were a valuable asset. The reaction among western governments, however, while publicly enthusiastic, was privately surprisingly unimpressed. Israel, after all, was expected to manage such feats. The true dimensions of the terrorist problem had still not been fully understood. That changed on 13 October 1977.

Armed with hand grenades, automatic pistols and explosives, four Palestinian terrorists two men and two women, bypassed the rudimentary security at Palma Airport in Majorca to board a Lufthansa Boeing 737 bound for Frankfurt. Immediately after takeoff, they hijacked the aircraft and flew it first to Rome and then, over the next five days, on to Cyprus, Bahrain, Dubai, Aden and finally to Mogadishu airport in Somalia.

The terrorists, who were acting on behalf of the Baader Meinhof group, demanded the release of the ten leaders of the group held in West German jails, including one of its founders, Andreas Baader, and two Palestinians held in Turkey, plus a ransom of fifteen million dollars. In exchange, they promised to release the eighty-six passengers and five crew held on the aircraft, together with the West German industrialist Hans Martin Schleyer, kidnapped six weeks earlier.

The West German government had established GSG9 as a

counter-terrorist unity after the attack at the Munich Olympics four years earlier, but it had not yet been used in action, and the government was still inclined to negotiate and, at the very least, to pay the ransom demanded. The unit was placed on alert at their base at St. Augustin near Bonn however. Much of their training had involved assaults on aircraft and they were already familiar with the Boeing 737.

In aircraft assault, the most difficult moment comes when the team has to gain entry into the aircraft which, if guarded properly, will have terrorists in the cockpit, the first class section and both ends of the economy class. The unit therefore has to attack a number of entrances simultaneously, blowing in doors or windows and overpowering the terrorists before they have an opportunity to kill the hostages or blow up the aircraft.

The SAS had given considerable thought to this problem and developed a new type of weapon known as a stun grenade or, more colloquially, a 'flash-bang'. About 15 cm long and 8 cm wide, the grenades at that time consisted of thousands of magnesium particles and fulminate of mercury. When thrown, the mercury detonates with an ear-splitting bang and the magnesium lights up, giving off the equivalent of 50,000 watts. Such a combination of light and noise is sufficient to deafen and blind anyone within range for a critical seven seconds. (A flash-bang that has now been developed and is in service today explodes like a firecracker six or seven times in four seconds. It is many times more effective than the original.) Men of GSG9 had visited the SAS at Hereford during training both to compare counter-terrorist techniques and to share information about equipment in service or under development; now they asked for SAS assistance and Hereford supplied Major Alastair Morrison and Sergeant Barry Davies, who came equipped with the required grenades.

The two SAS men joined up with the GSG9 commander, Ulrich Wegener, in Dubai where the hijacked aircraft had landed. The Germans hoped that the Dubai authorities would agree to an assault on the aircraft. A 26-strong GSG9 force was waiting on board a converted Lufthansa 707 jet, code-named Stuttgart, in Turkey. Dressed in T-shirts and jeans, the GSG9 men had with them a complete armoury including night sights, sniper rifles and Heckler and Koch sub-machine-guns.

In the event, however they had to wait until the hijackers left Dubai and landed at Mogadishu in Somalia before they could plan their assault. After that final journey, the terrorists shot the plane's pilot, Jurgen Schumann, and dumped his body on the tarmac at Mogadishu airport. Until then, the German government had been prepared to negotiate a peaceful end to the hijacking, and indeed had been following the aircraft around on its various stops with a steel box filled with the ransom money. But now the government was advised by the GSG9 psychologist that once the killing had begun it was likely to continue – unless the government completely capitulated and released the terrorists held in German jails, something West German public opinion would not have tolerated.

GSG9 was authorised to carry out an assault on the aircraft. At the same time, the terrorists were told that their demands were being met and that their comrades were being flown from Germany to Mogadishu.

At 17.30 on 17 October, the GSG9 aircraft landed at Moga-dishu and stopped 2,000 metres from the hijacked plane. At 23.52 Somali soldiers lit a wood fire 100 metres in front of the aircraft to distract the terrorists and hopefully draw them into the cockpit. The bluff seemed to work as two terrorists were spotted there. Under cover of the decoy, the GSG9 men approached the emergency exits over the wings and at the doors at the front and rear of the plane placed rubber-coated alloy ladders to the side. Seconds later the doors were opened, the SAS men threw their flash-bangs and GSG9 men poured into the aircraft.

As the hostages were evacuated out of the emergency doors, the terrorists fought a bitter but hopeless battle. One of the girls, Hind Alameh, opened fire from the first class compartment and was killed; the other, Suhaila Sayeh, was shot but captured alive; two grenades were thrown by the men in the cockpit before they too were shot and killed but the grenades fortunately exploded under seats, only slightly injuring some of the hostages.

Eight minutes after the operation began, Ulrich Wegener, who was directing operations from underneath the aircraft, gave the codeword 'Springtime' over his radio, signalling the aircraft had been secured. Only one GSG9 man was slightly wounded in the assault and four hostages were slightly injured.

Mogadishu was a textbook operation carried out by well-trained and determined men. At last Europe had clearly demonstrated its determination to fight back against terrorism. Since Mogadishu, whatever co-operation may be lacking at an official, political level, all special forces in the west have shared information, run exchange programmes so that officers and men can benefit from a different environment, and have given access to the extensive debriefings that occur after an operation. Also, if a major counter-terrorist operation is mounted by any country, such as the SAS attack on the Iranian embassy in London in 1980 or the planned assault on the liner *Achille Lauro* in 1985, most of the major western countries will send a special forces representative to observe the action and report back what is learned.

The terrorists, too, learned from Entebbe and Mogadishu. They recognised that hijacking, far from being a simple operation that almost always resulted in a bargain being struck, was now a high-risk venture. Not only did hijacking decline in popularity but, when it did occur, the hijackers showed a far greater sophistication. Any type of assault technique will, at best, only work once. After that the tactics need to be changed.

The evolutionary nature of terrorism was graphically illustrated nearly ten years later when poor counter-terrorist planning and unsophisticated techniques resulted in the bloodiest hijacking in aviation history.

On Saturday 23 November 1985, three terrorists armed with pistols and grenades boarded Egyptair Flight MS64 at Athens airport. It still is not known how they evaded security checks, although it seems likely they were handed their weapons by airport ground crew after being checked. Shortly after takeoff en route to Cairo, the plane was hijacked.[2]

Patrick Scott Baker, a 28-year-old American from Washington State was using up his savings flying the slow route to Bangkok. He gives a graphic account of what happened next.

'I was sitting in seat F. They were just ready to serve dinner and I was reading a book. The first I knew of the hijacking was when I looked up and noticed a guy with a grenade. I tapped the shoulder of the guy next to me who was reading a newspaper. (A Frenchman, Georges Briard). He looked up from his paper, rolled his eyes and went back to reading it. That's the sort of people that were on the plane; it wasn't like movie hysteria with people screaming.'

The co-pilot, Emad Bahey Monie, aged 27, was just as surprised. 'The hijacker kicked the cabin door open, very fast and very sudden. He burst in just like in the movies and said: "This plane is hijacked. Do whatever I say." I thought he was a friend of the captain; I thought he was joking. Then I saw he had a hand grenade in his left hand, and it was not a joke.'

The leader of the gang was 22-year-old Omar Ali Marzouki who had flown in from Belgrade to Athens on a false Tunisian passport three days previously. He had been joined by Mohamed Abu-Said Nur-El-Din, 23, and Salem Salah Chakore, 25, who were both using Moroccan passports listed with the CIA as having been stolen some months before. The two flew in from Tripoli in Libya the same day as the hijacking. The terrorists claimed to represent 'Egypt's Revolution'. In fact, US intelligence suggests they were under orders from terrorist Abu Nidal, the leader of a small gang of particularly bloodthirsty killers. But it still is not clear what lay behind the hijacking, since the group never made any demand.

Salem was given the job of moving through the cabins examining passports and segregating passengers by nationality. Two Israeli girls travelling separately were moved to the front along with Patrick Baker. When Salem approached another passenger, Medhat Mustafa Kamil, and asked for his passport, Kamil reached inside his jacket, pulled out a pistol, and shot Salem dead with one shot. Kamil, an airline security guard, then ducked down behind his seat and prepared to do battle with the other two hijackers. Outgunned, with terrorists in front and behind, he was shot six times. Although gravely wounded, Kamil survived. There were four other security guards on the aircraft but none of them supported him. Afterwards their pistols were found hidden under seats.

Ricochets from the gunfire pierced the cabin shell, causing the aircraft to lose pressure. After an emergency dive to 14,000 feet, the pilot, Captain Hani Galal, radioed Luqa airport in Malta that the plane was in danger of crashing into the sea. He was allowed to land there, and the plane touched down at 09.30. The terrorists immediately demanded fuel for the aircraft, but the Maltese authorities refused to supply this until the plane's ninety-eight passengers and crew had been released. One hour later two stewardesses were allowed off the aircraft followed shortly afterwards by eleven women. Fuel was still refused, so the terrorists promised to kill a hostage every ten minutes until the Maltese changed their mind. Patrick Baker describes what happened next:

'Omar asked for one Israeli girl to come forward. He took her outside to the platform. I heard her cry "Help" in English and a second later I heard a shot. Five minutes later they asked for another Israeli girl. They took her forward, where she was forced to lie on the floor for five minutes. Finally she was taken outside and there were two shots.

'Then Omar went through the passports again and singled out the American ones, of which there were three, and we were brought forward. We were tied individually with our hands behind our backs. I was the first to be shot. I was led outside and as soon as I was standing outside at the top of the steps, I thought of jumping over the side.

'If I was smart I would have dived off but it was too late. The bullet just grazed me, I think it bounced off my skull. The force of the shot pushed my head forward and for a second I was confused. A split second later I decided to play dead. I did a somersault down the stairs and landed about five steps down. Two people picked me up, dragged me back up the stairs and then rolled me over the side of the steps.

'I came out smelling like a rose. I hit the van that brings the steps and then rolled on to the tarmac and my hands, which were still tied behind my back, broke my fall.

'I had to stop myself from laughing. I was alive and it was my victory because the gunman hadn't killed me and I wanted to laugh in his face. I was on the tarmac for about two minutes then I ran under the fuselage about ten feet away, took a right angle back to the tail and ran for safety.'

Such ruthless violence was clearly designed to persuade the Maltese and the Egyptians, who had now joined them in the control tower, to supply fuel as the price for stopping the killing. But instead, the deaths provoked the Egyptians into a hasty and ill-advised assault on the aircraft.

As the aircraft was Egyptian, and carried twenty-two Egyptian passengers, the Maltese had given authority for the Cairo government to fly in 80 commandos, including 26 men led by Colonel Ismail Abdel-Mawgood of the Force 777 counter-terrorist unit. They had flown in on Saturday afternoon, on board C-130 transport aircraft.

The US had offered assistance but the Maltese, sensitive of their national sovereignty, turned it down. Nevertheless Admiral William Crowe, the chairman of the US Joint Chiefs of Staff, was telephoned at midnight on Saturday Washington time by General Wiegand, the head of the US Office of Military Cooperation in Cairo, who told Crowe that the Egyptians were sending in their commandos and that he and a small team intended travelling with them. He added that he thought they would be able to do the job.

When the jet carrying the commandos landed at Malta, the Egyptian Force 777 men disembarked wearing the jeans and T-shirts fashionable among special forces worldwide. The American team, however, were in full uniform and therefore instantly recognisable to the sensitive Maltese, who immediately complained to Washington about American interference.

Force 777 had been trained by the United States since 1981 and should, in theory, have been ideally suited to carry out the assault. But Washington had for some time been receiving reports that the Force was without the equipment it needed, and that its personnel were constantly being changed. Among the US training staff this had understandably raised serious doubts about their capability. And in fact a series of blunders doomed the assault from the outset. The Egyptians failed to use any sophisticated listening devices or infra-red surveillance equipment to discover the whereabouts and numbers of the terrorists; there was no serious debriefing of the hostages who had been released; the equipment used by the commandos did not include any disorientating devices such as the flash-bang grenades used at Mogadishu; no diversion was organised to distract the terrorists at the time of the attack; and finally the Egyptians compounded their errors by planning not only to enter the aircraft through the emergency doors but also by blowing a hole through the roof of the luggage compartment in the rear of the aircraft so that one commando had the slow entrance of scrambling up through the cabin floor, still intending to surprise the terrorists.

In the course of the evening the airport lights had been accidentally turned off. This had caused panic among the hijackers, who thought they were about to be attacked. When the lights were turned off a second time, therefore, they were convinced the first blackout had been a trial run and prepared themselves for the attack.

At 20.45 the attack began. One commando opened up the

rear luggage hold from the outside and placed an explosive charge on the roof, set the timer on the detonator and retreated. The charge was supposed to blow a small hole in the ceiling, sufficient to allow one man to crawl through, and to provide a signal for the commandos to enter the plane. Instead, a massive explosion ripped through the floor of the aircraft. So badly had the Egyptians misjudged the explosives required that six rows of seats were blasted from their anchorings. A wave of pressure and flame from the explosion smashed these seats against the ceiling of the plane, and killed six passengers instantly.

The rear of the aircraft filled with smoke and flames. To add to the confusion, several Force 777 men entered the front of the aircraft and threw smoke bombs. This ensured that the passengers couldn't see their way to the exits, and gave the commandos no opportunity to sort the terrorists from the hostages. Alerted well in advance, the terrorists met the attack with grenades and bullets from their automatic pistols. The co-pilot takes up the story:

'When the explosion happened the hijacker (Omar) was sitting in the captain's seat trying to see if there was anyone approaching. He immediately tried to stand up but the captain, who was behind him forced him back into his seat. They started to fight, the hijacker fired his gun but it only grazed the captain's head. The captain picked up the fire axe and hit the terrorist.'

(There is some doubt about the alleged heroism of the pilot. Subsequent investigation of the aircraft by Egyptian and American experts showed that there was no evidence of the axe ever being used and there was certainly no trace of blood, hair or tissue on it.)[3]

'Then about twenty things happened in three seconds. Bullets were coming through the instruments in front of me; I was shot in the knees; I took the escape rope that was in the cockpit; another big bomb exploded through the door of the cockpit – I think one of the hijackers wanted to kill

everybody. Then I jumped through the window. The rope
was rolled and I threw it, slipped down and jumped.

'I was trying to choose the safest way but I was surprised
by a group holding guns behind the wing; maybe they were
hijackers, I didn't know. I was confused for a few seconds. I
turned again to the nose and ran in front of it on to the grass
and that's when I got hit again. It was not bullets, it was a
grenade. I didn't feel pain then as I was running very fast
and then I fell on the grass and couldn't get up again.

'Lying on the grass I heard a strange noise. You know
when you hear a jet fighter, this was the same noise, it was
a bullet beside my ear. I laid down my head and stayed on
the ground for about ten minutes until the shooting stopped.
Then the fire engines and ambulances came but nobody saw
me on the grass for a while.'

The co-pilot's story is fairly typical. Those hostages who
were not burnt alive in the inferno following the explosion in
the rear of the aircraft, like him came under heavy fire from
Egyptian troops surrounding the plane as they tried to escape.

The contrast with the successful Mogadishu operation
could hardly be more marked. Fifty-seven passengers and one
terrorist were killed in an attack that was poorly planned and
appallingly executed by men with insufficient training.

Immediately after their bungled rescue attempt, the Egyptian government asked the United States for additional assistance in training Force 777. This was turned down. Instead,
four members of Force 777 are currently training with GSG9
in West Germany.

Terrorists, too, have learned a great deal. When hijacking
first became fashionable, they expected governments generally to give in to their demands. But as this changed, so a
new, tougher breed of terrorist emerged, one who was
prepared both to die for his or her cause, and to use the
killing of innocent civilians as a precise weapon, calculated
to keep counter-terrorist forces off guard and to maintain
maximum pressure on politicians.

'After Entebbe and Mogadishu the general public had an

expectation that they were all going to be like that,' explained one British counter-terrorism expert. 'But they were the exceptions and I will be very surprised if any hijacking in the future that involves an assault on the plane does not result in heavy loss of life.'

This view of the Luqa operation is echoed by a senior Pentagon official responsible for special operations. 'We knew there was going to to be a bloodbath but there was nothing we could do. Even if our own guys had gone in, we would have lost some people.'

If Mogadishu exemplified a successful counter-terrorist operation against a hijacked aircraft, it was Luga that provided the spur to the United States to improve their own capability to deal with any similar threat.

PART 5: AMERICA TO THE RESCUE

11

Charlie's Angels

In June 1962, Charlie Beckwith, then serving with the 7th Special Forces Group in Fort Bragg, was seconded to spend a year serving with the SAS at Hereford. This was part of an exchange programme set up in the late 1950s that still continues today. For Beckwith, used to the formality and bureaucracy of Fort Bragg, his time with the SAS was a revelation.[1]

There was little of the harsh discipline that he was used to and none of the rigid officer/other ranks distinctions that are so important to conventional soldiers. Instead, Beckwith found a unit that put a premium on initiative, intelligence and performance. He describes a custom of the SAS that perfectly illustrates the barrier between the two countries:

'Over pints of bitters (*sic*) in the Sergeants' Mess on those Saturday nights when the squadron was in Bradbury Lines, officers and sergeants would discuss freely situations that had developed during the week. The form here was that the regimental sergeant major would invite the officers in their Mess to come to the Sergeants' Mess. This was important. The officers would then literally run down the two blocks separating the Officers' Mess from the Sergeants' Mess. And it was in their Mess where it all happened. No one ever left before first light on Sunday morning. We stayed and drank beer all night. This was the opportunity for the officers and the sergeants to whittle away at traditional form and egotistical illusions.'[2]

Beckwith may have become a convert to the British way of doing things but his message was not well received either at Fort Bragg or by the Pentagon. Ironically, the commander of the Special Warfare Center at Fort Bragg at the time, General Williams P. Yarborough, had been made an honorary member of the SAS Regiment in the previous year in recognition of the training facilities he had provided for the SAS in the United States. Yarborough was therefore very familiar with the workings of the Regiment and admired them enough to co-operate with them, but he rejected Beckwith's recommendations for a similar US organisation. As a whole the Bragg community already thought they were pretty good at what they did and saw no reason to follow the lead of some foreign group with completely different standards and needs.

'I felt the US Army needed . . . to be able to go out in small patrols and blow up bridges and dams and railroad lines, to take out an enemy commander, say, like Rommel, to collect information for air strikes or for attacks made by conventional forces. The American army not only needed a special forces capability but an SAS one; not only a force of teachers, but a force of doers.

'The SAS had a very broad definition of what it does and remained flexible. The American Army was quite the opposite. We would go to a great deal of trouble to frame a Field Manual. . . . If it doesn't happen to be in the FM, no matter how good an idea it is, it won't get done. All our demolition recipes are recorded; all our communication procedures are spelled out. The Brits would never do that. They kept everything in their heads. If you aren't smart enough to keep it up there, they felt, you get your hat and go somewhere else to work.'[3]

The Vietnam War interrupted Beckwith's campaign. After serving with the special forces in Vietnam, Thailand and Cambodia, he returned to the United States in 1974, where he found the new commander of the renamed John F. Kennedy Special Warfare Center at Fort Bragg was General Bob Kingston, a supporter both of Beckwith himself and of unconventional warfare. The two put together a new paper which was submitted to General Edward 'Shy' Meyer, the Army's Deputy Chief of Staff for Operations and Plans.

In the two years of debate that followed, the idea gradually evolved of a small, highly specialised counter-terrorist unit, trained to deal with kidnappings and aircraft hijackings. In the trade-offs between roles already taken up by existing organisation such as the Rangers and the SEALs, this was the only realistic gap left that could be exploited.

On 2 June 1977, Beckwith was given preliminary authority to form the 1st Special Forces Operations Detachment – Delta (SFOD-D), more commonly known as Delta Force. The original organisation called for around 1,200 men commanded by a colonel and divided into sixteen-man troops that could break down into four four-man patrols, or even eight two-man patrols. The emphasis would be on flexibility and initiative so that men and units would be interchangeable. Each member of Delta would be required to be supremely fit, understand military and terrorist theory, and be competent in a wide range of skills, including parachuting, covert entry techniques, weapons and vehicles.

During the next four months Beckwith and his small team prepared detailed budgets, and found a home in the old Fort Bragg jail. The Stockade, a nine-acre site which was later expanded, included an Operations and Intelligence centre, a Selection and Training wing, a living area and a headquarters. The jail's former theatre and chapel were made into a briefing and conference room. The headquarters was redecorated so that a blue awning hung over the entrance, and a small rose garden was planted, reflecting Beckwith's enthusiasm for that flower. Formal authority, however, had still not been given. 'Shy' Meyer feared that the Army's Chief of Staff, General Bernard Rogers, had gone off the idea of Delta and, in the complex politics that are the hallmark of the US armed services, had preferred not to ask him directly in case he was formally turned down. Instead, Beckwith continued to work in limbo.

However, on the day GSG9 rescued the hostages aboard the Lufthansa jet, a memorandum was sent by President Jimmy Carter to the Joint Chief of Staff, asking if the US had a similar counter-terrorist capability. None of the Joint Chiefs knew the answer, but at the same time none of them was prepared to go to Carter and tell him the bad news. Rogers remembered the four-month-old Delta plan, summoned Beckwith and 'Shy' Meyer, and told them he now had full authority to activate Delta. Formal authority followed on 19 November 1977.

In theory that should have cleared the way for the new unit. In practice, the issue became stuck in petty rivalries between different army units and the army high command. The different units, such as the Rangers, saw Delta as competition for all their best talent and were therefore reluctant to co-operate with Beckwith's recruiting drive. This was a reluctance the SAS had encountered when it was first formed and diplomatic finesse had been required in order to overcome it. Beckwith, who was rightly nicknamed 'Chargin' Charlie', was not the right man for that particular job. His aggressive and acerbic manner succeeded in alienating almost everyone he contacted. His men became derisively referred to as 'Charlie's Angels', after a popular television programme, and his unpopularity led to a feeling that he was simply trying to build a personal empire that in fact had little military logic. At the same time, there emerged a fundamental difference in official opinion about the ideal make-up for such a group.

Colonel Bob Mountel, the head of the 5th Special Forces Group, also based at Fort Bragg, managed to convince senior officers that there was little point in setting up a new unit from scratch. He argued this would waste valuable resources, take an unnecessary amount of time, and that with some extra training the men were already available.

'There was a feeling that you didn't have to break everybody down, rebuild them and then start from ground zero and go from there,' explains one man who was serving with the 5th Special Forces Group at the time. 'We felt you could take latent special forces capabilities, the kind of mission profiles that already existed in what we called direct action missions or unilateral operation missions and add to that some of the things that came out of missions like the Son Tay raid.

'We were just saying there was a conflict in the approach that said this is going to be my personally controlled operation and I will build them in my own image, and another group that says this is just bullshit because we can do this perfectly well.

'I think there was an overcoat in the way Colonel Beckwith approached everything that governed how Delta first developed. It was basically a pastiche of techniques and backgrounds – some borrowed from the SAS, some borrowed from the Vietnam across-the-border operations – and all blundered into a macho whole that did not square with what I thought I knew about the requirements of counter-terror operations in the twentieth century.'

The result of this conflict was that Mountel seconded forty men from the 5th and set up Operation Blue Light. For nearly nine months, while Beckwith was establishing Delta, Mountel armed and trained a complete counter-terrorist force. In November 1977 Beckwith went to visit the SAS and GSG9, and early the following year Mountel did the same but added France's GIGN to his itinerary. This continued until General Bernard Rogers, and finally the President himself, heard about it. Both were astonished to learn that two units had been established when only one had been authorised, and Blue Light was cancelled.

Aside from internal rivalries, Beckwith also had to contend with attempts by the army high command to limit his freedom of action. Both the British and the West Germans had found by experience that a simple chain of command (in the SAS's case, if necessary direct to the British Prime Minister and in GSG9 direct to the West German Chancellor) was essential if the units were to respond to an often rapidly-changing terrorist situation. The US military, on the other hand, proposed that Delta should report first to the headquarters of special forces at Fort Bragg, then to XVIII Airborne Corps, then to Forces Command (FORSCOM), then to the Department of the Army, then to the Joint Chiefs and finally to the White House. This was a hopelessly cumbersome arrangement that would have severely damaged Delta's capability. After lengthy discussions over the following year, some of the intervening steps were bypassed so that at least Delta could now go straight to the Department of the Army. Although this represented an improvement the system was still seriously flawed as would shortly be realised.

Beckwith was given two years to get his unit fully trained and up to strength. One of his first recruits was Dick Meadows, who had played such a key part in the Son Tay raid. Meadows had just retired from the army but Beckwith valued his experience. He was to prove vital to the unit's first major action, Operation Eagle Claw, the attempted mission to rescue the US hostages in Teheran.

All recruits to Delta needed as a basic requirement to be of above average intelligence, to be physically fit, to have a clean record, to be airborne qualified or to volunteer for airborne training, and to pass a selection course. The course itself was loosely based on what Beckwith, Meadows (who had also served at Hereford) and others had learned from the British and the Germans. Inevitably they added their own refinements, most of which seem to have been concerned with physical fitness.

It is interesting to note that there is a marked physical difference between the men from Delta and those from the SAS. The vast majority of Delta men are superb physical specimens. By contrast, their SAS counterparts tend to be rather thin, wiry men.

All prospective Delta recruits had to pass a rigorous series of tests, some carried out at Fort Bragg and others in the Uwharrie National Forest in North Carolina, or at Camp Dawson in the mountains of West Virginia. According to Beckwith, 'The recruits were required to perform: a forty-yard inverted crawl in 25 seconds; 37 sit-ups and 33 push ups, each in a minute; a run-dodge-jump course transversed in 24 seconds; a two-mile run completed in not more than sixteen and a half minutes; and, finally, a 100 metre lake swim in which the recruits were to be fully dressed, including jump boots.' This was the minimum required to pass.[4]

This was followed by an 18-mile speed march during a set time carrying a 55-pound rucksack over thickly wooded countryside. To assess stress, the men were given an exhausting series of endurance trials. Beckwith again:

'The volunteers were asked to perform a series of individual, timed, land-navigation exercises that were conducted in the mountains. The length of each increased daily from 10 kilometres to 74 kilometres, with equipment increasing in weight from 50 pounds to seventy pounds. By the time the 74 kilometre exercise began, the candidates had reached a common level of physical exhaustion. They were totally pooped. We'd used up their reserves. The endurance march revealed clearly those candidates who had character – real determination, self-discipline and self-sacrifice – and those who did not.

'The 74-kilometre, independently executed march across rugged mountain terrain had to be completed in 20 hours. The man was given the co-ordinates of a rendezvous point some eight to 12 kilometres distant. He was not told on reaching the RV how many more remained, what route to take, or whether he was going too slow. He was not encouraged or discouraged, advised or harassed. . . . It was a matter of seeing what each individual could do.

'Around the twelfth hour, if the pace was sufficient to meet the requirement, the man would be, in the medical sense of the term, almost totally exhausted. He began to look for excuses to quit, to slow down, even to hope he would injure himself. Anything to allow him to stop. It was then, after the twelfth hour, that many men quit, or rested too long, or slowed to a pace that prohibited them from meeting the time requirement. A few others had the sense of purpose, the courage, the will, the guts to reach down inside themselves for that intangible trait that enabled them to carry on. Without that ability a man did not succeed. This was, perhaps a crude method of evaluation, but it was the one on which the British SAS had relied for 25 years.'

(This is slightly out of date. As a result of four casualties during similar endurance tests, the SAS have changed some of their training methods so that better account is taken of each individual's capability. For example, encouragement is given along the way and those who are thought to be genuinely exhausted are taken out.)

For those who survived the physical tests, a series of searching examinations both by senior officers and psychologists followed. These were designed to test the recruit's overall knowledge – including an examination on the meaning of Machiavelli's *The Prince*. He was also questioned on his willingness to kill and his moral standards.

Not surprisingly, such detailed tests weeded out the majority of applicants. The first thirty recruits had been personally selected by Beckwith and his staff and seven of them made the grade. The next selection course drew volunteers from other special forces units and the rangers, although there was still not full co-operation from some commanders who saw Delta as a leech feeding off their best men. By the middle of 1978, 185 volunteers had been assessed and fifty-three had been chosen. By the end of that year another course of seventy-nine volunteers had supplied Delta with a further twenty members.

For the next twelve months Delta trained and exercised to become capable of dealing with any act of terrorism aimed at American targets anywhere in the world. The basic training course lasted nineteen weeks (compared with twenty-six weeks for the SAS) and included the ability to 'hit a target; perform command and control functions; establish and maintain secure communications; move from position to position using appropriate techniques in support of assault operations; gain entry to a crisis point; manage hostages; stabilise an injured person for at least 30 minutes; properly employ and maintain optical equipment; operate selected machinery and wheeled and track vehicles; negotiate natural and man-made obstacles; navigate on the land from one point to another; protect hostages from the threat of explosive ordnance; perform selected maritime techniques; disarm and disable a hostile opponent.'[5]

In order to carry out this formidable list of tasks, Delta were supplied with a wide range of highly sophisticated gadgetry. Then as now they had the pick of the latest high technology. For example, the key to a successful counter-terrorist operation is getting the troops to the action. There are three ways of doing this, land, sea and air, and for each of these specialised equipment is available.

For parachuting, there are two principal methods in use, HAHO (High Altitude High Opening) or HALO (High Altitude Low Opening). Today the technology is available to drop a small team of parachutists from an aircraft at 35,000 feet. They can then parafly up to thirty-five miles and land with pin-point accuracy on the top of a building. This enables a team's delivery aircraft to stay outside radar range, or outside a country's territory, and still quickly and quietly reach a selected target.

At 35,000 feet the cold is intense and the wind chill factor possibly in excess of −50° Fahrenheit. If a parachutist were to hold his hands above his head in the usual descent control position for the thirty-minute duration of the flight, the poor blood circulation at high altitude would cause a serious danger of frostbite, so the parachute has a special control system that allows the operator to keep his hands at his side.[6]

Various aircraft have been developed that can covertly enter unfriendly airspace and, using the HALO system, a parachutist can open his chute just 500 feet above the ground. This is a highly risky venture as it requires split second timing and a very accurate altimeter.

For more conventional drops the principal system in use both in Britain and in the United States is TOPS (Tactical

Operations Parachute System). In this the parachute has a 550 square foot canopy that can take either heavy equipment or two men at the same time.

To enable Delta to bring equipment with them, another parachute has been developed, one with a guidance system that includes a miniature computer able to receive signals from a homing beacon and automatically guide the parachute to its landing point. Known as CADS (Controlled Aerial Delivery System), the parachute can handle loads up to 200 kilos. This system is also of value for acts of sabotage. Provided an agent can plant a homing beacon at the target, the CADS system provides a silent and virtually undetectable method of attack from many miles away.

Even a motorised parachute has been evaluated by Delta Force and other European special forces. Known as the Para-plane, it uses a parachute canopy to provide lift, has an endurance of about an hour and a half, and a range of around sixty kilometres.

While sea attacks are a particular speciality of SEALs, all Delta recruits are trained in underwater swimming, using rebreathing oxygen sets that leave no tell-tale trail of bubbles on the surface. Two nuclear submarines, the *Sam Houston* and the *John Marshall*, have been converted for special forces use. They can each carry up to fifty men.

But the most common method of penetration is by aircraft. Although this will be dealt with in greater detail in another chapter, Delta's favoured plane is the C-130. Special forces use a variant known as the MC-130E Combat Talon (shortly to be upgraded to the MC-130H) that has an array of sophisticated electronics including inertial navigation systems, forward looking infra-red radar, and electronic counter-measures that allow the aircraft to fly into and out of enemy territory without being detected.

The aircraft has the Fulton Surface to Air Recovery system (STAR), which allows a soldier to be plucked off the ground by the aircraft as it flies by. He releases a helium balloon from the ground with a wire attached. A V-shaped yoke is attached to the nose of the plane and, using on-board guidance systems, the wire goes into the yoke and is channelled to a winch at the rear of the aircraft. The wire then lifts the man off the ground as the aircraft flies over. This is a fairly hazardous procedure and not one relished by the men.

In addition, a wide range of helicopters is available, including UH-60 Blackhawks and Hughes 500 MD for shorter range missions. An extensive programme of upgrading all this equipment is under way and this will be dealt with in a later chapter.

All the Delta forces are required to be proficient with a wide range of weapons, from the ordinary rifle in service with Nato and the Warsaw Pact, to laser-sighted sniper rifles, grenade launchers and silenced machine-guns and pistols.

As a key role of Delta is to get hostages out either from an aircraft or a building, Fort Bragg has both an old Boeing 727 and a specially constructed building, known as the Shooting House or the House of Horrors, where such attacks are practised. The building – similar to one at Hereford known as the Embassy – has four rooms, each designed to present a different hostage situation.

The first room has a form of shooting gallery where silhouettes of targets representing both friend and enemy pop up, forcing the man with the gun to make split second decisions about when to fire. This relatively simple task becomes more complicated in the second room where a variety of scenarios are set up, all intended to simulate problems encountered when trying to clear a room full of terrorists and hostages.

In one case, the room is laid out like a normal living room with couches, tables and chairs, the seats occupied by dummies representing both terrorists and hostages. Before entering, the four-man team is briefed on the numbers of terrorists to expect (usually this information is inaccurate). The first man in the team blows the hinges off the door with a shotgun, kicks it in, and his three team-mates burst into the room, each heading in a different direction and placing two head shots into each terrorist.

(In 1984, a team of editors from British newspapers were taken down to Hereford to be shown around. The SAS were concerned that they had been receiving too much publicity and wanted to explain to those responsible that much of their usefulness depended on their methods being kept secret. Selected newspapermen were placed in a similar room at Hereford's training area and surrounded by terrorist dummies. The SAS men burst into the room and, in a convincing display, which terrified those present, managed to shoot the terrorists without injuring any of the journalists. The publicity given to SAS methods did indeed decline afterwards.)

The third room in the House of Horrors is set up for night fighting, to test the thermal-imaging sights that produce a holographic picture that turns night into three-dimensional day. All counter-terrorist units expect to carry out many of their attacks at night so a great deal of training time is spent wearing night vision goggles.

The final room is set up as the interior of an aircraft cabin. The room is sufficiently flexible for it to recreate different aircraft interiors. And for even more realistic assaults, Delta Force has the co-operation of airlines who will loan aircraft for training purposes.

In late October 1979 A and B Squadrons of Delta moved from Bragg to a 27-acre site in North Carolina, on a final exercise designed to test the efficiency and readiness of the unit. They were required to attack a building and an aircraft simultaneously to rescue hostages held in both. The aircraft assault began just before midnight on Friday 2 November. In less than a minute the aircraft had been assaulted and the hostages freed. At almost the same time, the doors of the bulding were blown off and Delta's troops went from room to room allowing seven seconds to clear each one. It was a copy-book exercise that had been carried out flawlessly.

Twenty-four hours later, on Sunday 4 November, Delta received notice of an event that would give them an opportunity to test their skills in the real world and would find them wanting.

12

Debacle at Desert One

On a rainy Sunday morning, 4 November 1979, some 500 militant Revolutionary Guards and students, followers of the Imam Ayatollah Khomeini cut the chain on the gate of the American Embassy in downtown Teheran and invaded the compound. Without a shot being fired the Iranian militants captured sixty-three staff working in the embassy, along with a vast quantity of top secret documents.[1]

The students demanded the return of the exiled Shah from his hospital bed in America to face 'revolutionary justice.' There was never any serious prospect of the Shah being returned and the US government began to look at alternative ways of securing the freedom of the hostages.

This was a dangerous time for Europeans in Iran. What appeared to be a popular revolution, but backed by many of the middle classes, had brought to power an ageing religious ascetic, a man who was expected to inaugurate a new era of freedom for a country long used to the despotic and at times tyrannical ways of the Shah. In fact, the Shah had been replaced by a religious zealot who would set new standards of oppression.

America, as the principle supporter of the Shah, was a focus of the Iranian revolutionaries' enmity. The United States was characterised as the Great Satan, the embassy walls were immediately plastered with anti-American posters and effigies of President Carter were regularly burned by the vast crowds that would gather along Taleghani Avenue outside the embassy.

In the midst of such violent public displays, however, Washington continued to get diplomatic signals from Teheran that no serious action was planned against US interests and that the lives of the hostages were secure. But for some in the US administration, men led by National Security Adviser Zbigniew Brzezinski, a political solution was never likely: the Iranian government was too fragmented for proper negotiations ever to get under way and the longer the affair dragged on the more important the hostages would become in internal Iranian politics. The alternative to negotiation was military action, and within two days of the takeover Brzezinski had told the military, through Defense Secretary Harold Brown, to prepare a rescue plan.

Charlie Beckwith sent three of his men (one of them Dick Meadows) to Washington to liaise with the Joint Chiefs of Staff who had formed an *ad hoc* committee to deal with the crisis. A separate co-ordinating committee had also been formed which included Brzezinski, Brown, Admiral Stansfield Turner, director of the CIA, and General David Jones, chairman of the JCS. This group met two or three times a week for the duration of the crisis. The remainder of Delta Force moved to a secret site away from Bragg where they would be secure from prying eyes.

The JCS put General James Vaught, a Ranger who had fought in World War II, the Korean War and Vietnam, in charge of the planning and co-ordination of this phase of the plan, codenamed Operation Rice Bowl. Vaught had a complex task ahead of him.

It had been made clear by the White House from the outset that operational security was of paramount importance. The Carter administration had been plagued by leaks and, with an election campaign now under way, the White House wanted at all costs to keep news of the possible rescue out of the press. This single order, given the military's paranoia about the media, was to cause many of the problems that dogged the operation.

Vaught placed Beckwith in charge of developing a military plan for rescuing the hostages. To the staff at Delta, there were three main problems. The first was the distances involved. Iran was remote from convenient US bases. Teheran is only 300 miles from the Russian border and surrounded to the north by Afghanistan, Pakistan to the east and the Gulf of Oman to the south and west.

The second problem was intelligence. The US government had relied for hard intelligence from inside Iran primarily on the Shah's own secret police, Savak, and those few CIA agents who had been left behind were now among the hostages. The result was that there was nobody available in Iran to carry out even basic reconnaissance, or to provide such fundamental details as the location and numbers of guards outside the embassy.

The third problem was the embassy layout. The embassy compound contained fourteen separate buildings in twenty-seven acres, and an assault would require a simultaneous attack on all the key buildings among these. In addition, the Chargé d'Affaires, Bruce Laingen, and two other officials were being held in a Foreign Ministry building some distance from the embassy, and they would have to be rescued at the same time.

For General Vaught the planning was further complicated by the fact that Delta had been designed to operate in friendly territory. It had always been assumed they would be operating in a country with the permission of the host government, and that they would therefore be able to get in position in advance of an assault, carry out an on-the-spot reconnaissance, refine a plan and only then attack. A number of plans were considered, therefore, including parachuting into the embassy compound or driving into the country across the Turkish border. At this stage the only thing that was clear was that an assault would need to be made on the compound itself. And as Delta had no air transport of their own, some would have to be found, along with pilots willing to fly across enemy territory, probably at night.

A scale model was built, followed by full-scale mock-ups of the key embassy buildings. The men of Delta Force practised scaling the walls, blowing out windows and eliminating the guards, so that they would be able to do the job silently, and at night, with complete confidence. In late November, thirteen black female hostages were released by the Iranians. Although they provided intelligence on the strength and arms of the guards inside the compound, this would very likely have changed by the time the assault began and could not be relied upon.

By mid-December a plan has been worked out that all felt might work. The rescue team would fly in helicopters to a desert site outside Teheran, refuel using enormous rubber bladders dropped at the site, and then fly on to a further staging post prior to assaulting the embassy the following day. The hostages and the rescue team would then be evacuated from another airport nearby.

Gradually the bare details of the plan began to be filled in. It was decided to use RH-53-D Sea Stallion helicopters which, although normally used against floating mines, could carry the necessary number of people and had the range. But nowhere in the US military were there pilots who had the experience required to fly this kind of low level mission at night. Vietnam veterans, who had extensive experience in covert operations, were mostly on the retired list and anyway the Sea Stallion had come into service after the Vietnamese war. Retraining a small group of veterans on the new helicopter would have been relatively simple but instead the Army chose to take Navy pilots (of all those available the men with the least experience of flying over land) and train them in the necessary skills.

Beckwith estimated he needed seventy of his men to do the job. If all the Delta Force were to be evacuated along with the hostages, that number would require six helicopters, which allowed for two breakdowns.

The first batch of navy pilots seconded to the mission were sent back to their units after they failed to reach the required standard. They were replaced by Marine pilots. From the start of training, however, there was considerable animosity between the pilots and Delta Force. The special forces men thought the Marines lacked commitment, while the Marines thought the Delta men were a bunch of gung-ho crazies, determined to get them all killed.

Nonetheless the planning lurched forward and it was decided next that, instead of refuelling the helicopters from fuel bladders, which proved unreliable in tests, KC-130 tankers would be made available at the first staging post, known as Desert One. That in turn required an airstrip that was secure and could take the weight of the aircraft – and if it was found, men would have to be made available to guard it. The numbers involved in the operation rapidly increased, finally reaching 120, which meant that an additional two helicopters had to be found and the pilots trained.

Intelligence began to improve. The Defense Intelligence Agency, using both satellites and SR-71 Blackbird reconnaissance aircraft, produced detailed graphics of the embassy and its grounds. By comparing each set of pictures, the intelligence staff were able to build up a detailed idea of the routine inside the compound. Since the CIA had failed to get any agents into the country to supply information, the Army therefore now began preparing their own team. Dick Meadows, with a cover story as an Irish businessman prepared for him by the CIA and with the codename Esquire, was sent into Teheran with two other Delta men and one Iranian exile. Using sophisticated satellite communications, they provided the only 'eyes on the target' intelligence available to the planners. (An earlier offer by Ulrich Wegener to infiltrate some of his GSG9 force into Teheran disguised as a German TV crew had been turned down by Vaught. This was an unfortunate decision as the GSG9 men could have provided very valuable on-site intelligence. Why the offer was turned down is not known.)

Photography of ground south-east of Teheran had revealed a desert strip alongside a one-lane unpaved road some 265 miles south of the city and 500 miles from the sea. As their contribution to the project the CIA organised a light plane to fly in to plant homing beacons and to take soil samples at the site to make sure the sand was dense enough to take the enormous weight of fully-laden C-130 transports.

The CIA team saw traffic on the road while they were on the ground, and intelligence reports suggested that the route was used fairly regularly by smugglers and by ordinary Iranians. Nonetheless, the planners were confident that they could deal with any casual passers-by.

By mid-January Operation Rice Bowl had a plan that had been agreed. Eight Sea Stallions would be launched fron an aircraft carrier, the USS *Nimitz*, which would be stationed off the Iranian coast. Flying at night at very low levels using inertial navigation systems, the helicopters would land at Desert One. A few hours earlier six C-130s would have taken off from Qena military airbase near Cairo in Egypt to a staging post on the airfield at Masirah Island off Oman, and from there on to Desert One, now codenamed Watchband. Three of these C-130s would hold the 100-strong Delta team, six Rangers who would secure Desert One, and an Air Force unit to control the logistics of refuelling the helicopters when they arrived and making sure all the Sea Stallions left on time. The remaining C-130s would be loaded with 18,000 gallons of aviation fuel.

After refuelling, the helicopters would fly to Desert Two, now codenamed Fig Bar, a hilly area 100 kilometres southeast of Teheran where they would be hidden under camouflage nets for the rest of the day. Six former supporters of the Shah's regime who had travelled with Delta would then drive into Teheran with Meadows to a warehouse he had rented, and Beckwith himself planned to drive into town for a personal reconnaissance. The following night, six 2.5

ton Mercedes trucks bought in Teheran by Dick Meadows and his team would be driven out to a third site where Delta had spent the night, collect them and head for the embassy.

A four-strong team would go ahead of the main convoy and, using silenced .22 rifles, would shoot and kill the guards overlooking the east wall of the compound that faced on to Roosevelt Avenue. Immediately the guards had been removed, seventy-five men from the Delta Force would use padded aluminium ladders to scale the walls and, after a brief pause inside to disperse to individual targets, a single bleep over each man's miniature radio receiver would be the signal to begin the assault.

At the same time, a thirteen-strong team would travel by Volkswagen bus to the Foreign Ministry. While the assault on the embassy compound was going on, they would scale the outside of the building using special suction pads, break in at the third storey, and rescue Bruce Laingen and his two colleagues. They would be collected in the Foreign Ministry car park by one of the six Sea Stallions from their temporary base in the hills south of the city. The remaining helicopters would fly to twelve designated 'bus stops', including the soccer stadium near the embassy, and scoop up the remaining hostages and the Delta Force and fly them to a disused airfield in Manzariyeh thirty-five miles south of Teheran. This was to be captured by a separate force of Rangers who would have flown in on C-141 Starlifters earlier that night.

During the evacuation two AC-130 Spectre gunships would circle over the stadium to prevent any Iranian military inter-ference, and fighters from the aircraft carriers Coral Sea and Nimitz would be on hand to shoot down any Iranian fighters that might be scrambled to meet the rescue force.

The whole operation would be controlled by General Vaught in Egypt. He would gain additional intelligence from an Airborne Warning and Control System (AWACS) aircraft circling over the Persian Gulf. This aircraft could simul-taneously track and target hundreds of aircraft and from its cruising altitude of 35,000 feet could see as far as Teheran.

At all times Vaught would be in contact both with the White House and with the assault force.

It was a bold but extraordinarily complex plan which required the faultless meshing of hundreds of cogs if its delicate mechanism was ever to work properly.

From the start, however, things began to go wrong. On the JCS staff at that time there were few officers with experience in covert operations or in unconventional warfare. Yet they chose to bypass the existing and proven system, and set up a new command structure of their own. It was decided, and Vaught agreed, that 'for reasons of security' a new team would be created from scratch. In reality, this team had more to do with satisfying individual services' wishes to be involved than it did with any operational requirement. Vaught drew on all the services, put together a team of men who had never worked together before, and from that shaky start the command and control of the operation never recovered. It was never clear who was reporting to whom or where the responsibility for key decisions lay. For example, three different individuals assumed responsibility for training the helicopter crews, all three thought they had the authority to do so, and it was never made clear to any of them who was in fact supposed to be in charge. For these basic failings, Delta Force would pay dearly at Desert One.

Then again, the obsession with operational security ensured that very few people involved in the training programme actually knew what was going on. Not only that, but poor command and control meant that all the players never actually worked together in a full-scale rehearsal of the attack and evacuation. Instead, the helicopter pilots practised from the Marine Corps base in Yuma, Arizona, Delta in Fort Stewart, Georgia, and the 8th Special Operations Squadron, who supplied the C-130s, from Eglin Air Force Base in Florida. The different groups did come together for periodic exercises but there was never a detailed analysis of performance by a central authority. The result was a group of individuals who had never worked as a team. Each could perform their separate tasks but no-one knew if together they could do what would be required of them.

Even the assault force was divided for training. It had been decided there were not enough Delta Force men to assault both the embassy compound and the Foreign Ministry building. For the latter, a thirteen-man team from the 10th Special Force Group at Bad Tolz was selected. Instead of training with Delta at Fort Stewart, operational security required they be kept separate. They did their training entirely in West Germany and were not to meet up with the main force until three days before the attack.

These training difficulties were exacerbated by an apparent need to involve as many of the branches of the armed services as possible. Certainly it is difficult to believe that in a small, highly secret operation such as this, it was really necessary to involve men from the Army, the Rangers, the Air Force and the Navy.

Beginning in January, the various elements spent the next four months training. Negotiations with Teheran, using Swiss and Algerian intermediaries, failed and President Carter gradually tightened the screws on the Iranian government, first using economic sanctions to freeze Iranian assets around the world and then cutting diplomatic relations and pressuring her allies to isolate the Khomeini regime. But the American public wanted more.

For week after week US newspapers and television had been full of the American 'humiliation'. The revolutionaries holding the hostages had become adept at manipulating the American media. Their press conferences would be timed so that the networks could make their satellite link-ups for the evening news; dispirited hostages would be paraded before the cameras; and a steady stream of embarrassing top secret material that had been painstakingly pasted back together after being retrieved from the shredder was released. This death by a thousand cuts was doing immense damage to the Carter presidency. His stock with the public was falling and unless he was seen to do something decisive his prospects for re-election later that year were slim.

On 16 April 1980 President Carter met with Vaught and Beckwith to be briefed on the prospects for the mission. Carter records that he was particularly impressed by the briefing and was reassured that there would be a minimum of civilian casualties. Beckwith, who clearly despised this civilian concern, remembers things rather differently.

'We were going to kill every guard in the four or five buildings and anyone who interfered in the assault. Any armed Iranian inside the buildings would be killed. We weren't going to go up and check their pulses. We would put enough copper and lead in them so there wouldn't be a problem. When blood began to flow, a lot of Iranians were going to turn and run for help, and when they did, Delta was prepared to hose them down. . . . Furthermore, I did not believe that the Iranians in the embassy would stand toe to toe and slug it out. Yes, there would be the odd person who would, because of his religion and beliefs, shoot to the death. We were prepared to help him reach his maker.'[2]

Later that evening Carter gave his permission for the operation to proceed.

Four days later, on 20 April, ninety-three Delta Force men left Fort Bragg and arrived in Qena, outside Cairo, via Frankfurt. Travelling with them were the six Iranians who would help secure the site at Desert One and help with translation, and two former Iranian generals – using radio equipment on board the C-130s, it was hoped that the generals would be able to tap into the Iranian command network and issue contradictory orders, thus creating chaos and preventing any concerted response once the force reached Teheran.

At Frankfurt they met up with the thirteen other special forces men who had been training separately at Bad Tolz for the assault on the Foreign Ministry building. At the same time, eighty-three Rangers took off from Savannah, Georgia. They joined Delta in Egypt, where their force was divided, six of them going on to Desert One and the balance staying in reserve to attack and secure the Manzariyeh airfield from which the rescue team and their hostages would eventually escape. The rescue team that was to land at Desert One now numbered 132, nearly double the seventy originally proposed by Beckwith.

Delta were all dressed in casual civilian clothes – jeans, sweaters, jackets with bullet proof vests underneath – with all identification removed. Yet they wore dog tags, and simply had tape pasted over the small United States flags that were sewn on to the shoulders of their jackets. This would be removed after the hostages had been rescued. No insignia were worn to distinguish officers and men, since it was thought all the participants knew each other. In fact, this was to cause considerable confusion later.

If the mission failed, the men were to escape overland via Turkey. Each man had been supplied with a basic escape and evasion kit including maps, a compass, and Iranian riyals. Survivors were to signal their whereabouts by making enormous signs on the ground with stones or vegetation. These would be identified by overflying satellites, a practice used with some success in Vietnam.

According to Beckwith, they were armed with Heckler and Koch MP-5 9mm sub-machine-guns, M-16s, M-60 and HK-21 machine-guns, a selection of grenade launchers and M-1911A1 .45 automatic pistols. Some weapons had silencers attached. Small charges of C4 plastic explosive were carried to blow out doors and windows. The most sophisticated equipment was the radios which would enable the Delta unit to be in permanent contact with General Vaught and, if necessary, with the White House.

Just before the assault force went in, Delta had a piece of luck. A Pakistani cook at the embassy had been given permission to leave Iran. Apparently quite by chance a CIA agent joined his flight during a stop over, and sat next to him. Quickly realising the prize he had, he took him in for a thorough debriefing. The cook was able to provide details of the locations of the hostages and the number of guards and their routines inside the compound. News of this coup only emerged after there had been some criticism in the post-raid analysis of the CIA's contribution to the intelligence gathering, and it is not clear if it was simply one of those happy accidents or if the CIA had in fact planned it.

On Thursday 24 April, after a prayer and a rousing chorus of 'God Bless America' that echoed round the Russian-built hangar at Qena airfield, Delta Force boarded their C-130s for the flight to Masirah. They arrived at 14.00, had four hours rest, and then took off again for Desert One.

The aircraft flew a route plotted from information supplied by the US intelligence community, who had monitored the Iranian radar transmissions of their ground stations for some weeks. There were huge gaps in the radar coverage, and the C-130s were able to fly a complicated zig-zag course that took advantage of those gaps. At 22.00 the first C-130 approached the landing site at Desert One. Beacons planted a month before by the covert CIA reconnaissance plane were activated, illuminating the landing strip and guiding the plane in. As the aircraft began its approach, its Forward-Looking Infra-Red System picked up traffic on the road running alongside the desert runway. The aircraft circled until the road was clear, and then came in to land.

First off the aircraft were the Rangers with their two motor cycles and a jeep. The motor cycles had two headlights specially rigged to make them look like trucks. Bandits were known to operate in the area, and it was felt that their vehicles would more willingly stop if the road appeared to be blocked by a truck rather than a motor cycle. This rudimentary disguise was put to the test almost immediately. As the men were still getting out of the aircraft and before the perimeter guard had been established. a large Mercedes bus full of passengers appeared, lights blazing. The bus refused to stop on command and only slewed to a standstill after several shots had been fired, one of which blew out a tyre, and a grenade had been exploded in front of it.

On the bus there were forty-two passengers, including women and children, the driver and his assistant. They were reassured that this was an Iranian military operation by Farsi-speaking and Iranian-looking Americans. After being searched they were made to sit on the sand under the watchful eye of some Delta Force men. The plan had allowed for this kind of contingency. After the men had left in the helicopters, the bus passengers – now hostages of a kind themselves – would be flown out on one of the C-130s and brought back two days later when the aircraft returned to pick up the assault team and the US hostages. For rural Iranian peasants it would have been a terrifying experience.

While the problem with the bus was being sorted out, another vehicle had appeared, this time a fully-laden petrol tanker. It too refused to stop and one of the Rangers rashly fired an anti-tank rocket at the truck, which immediately caught fire lighting up the night sky with an enormous pillar of flame, visible for miles. Immediately another, smaller, van appeared unexpectedly out of the night, and picked up the tanker's crew. The guard on the motor cycle nearest the blaze tried desperately to start his bike, but by the time he got it going the smaller van had disappeared.

The fast recovery of the tanker crew and their obvious reluctance to stop led the Delta team to conclude they were probably fuel smugglers, and therefore unlikely to raise the alarm.

Even with such early difficulties, nothing had yet happened to jeopardise the mission seriously. Further reassurance was provided by Dick Meadows. Using a radio with burst transmission that automatically compresses a signal to a very short squawk of sound and is very difficult to intercept he radioed: 'All the groceries are on the shelf', the signal that the holding sites outside Teheran were ready to receive the assault force and their helicopters.

All now depended on the helicopters. In mid-flight, the C-130s had received a radio message that all eight Sea Stallions had taken off from the *Nimitz* and were heading over the

desert for the Watchband rendezvous. They were to fly in
close formation and since the weather forecast indicated a
clear night, they would be able to maintain visual contact.
The helicopters had on board a number of navigation systems,
among them Omega and PINS (Palletised Inertial Navigation
System) that had been specially installed for the mission, but
unfortunately the pilots had not received enough training on
either system and therefore preferred dead reckoning navigation. To preserve operational security they were required
to observe total radio silence; although they were able to
receive messages there would be no communication between
helicopters or between them and mission control or with
Beckwith's team on the ground. This was an unnecessary
restriction as it was extremely unlikely that any Iranians
would be listening in on the correct frequency and, even if
they were, that they would be able to understand the coded
talk.

It also meant that the pilots never got to talk directly to
the weather men, and therefore they were never told that the
forecasters on Vaught's command team, who had done an
analysis of dust storms (haboobs) in the region, had identified
the likelihood of bad weather that night, including dust
storms.

Shortly after crossing the Iranian coastline, a warning light
began flashing in the cockpit of helicopter No. 6. It landed
and was followed down by No. 8. The warning light suggested
there was a failure that could result in one of the rotor blades
breaking up. The crew had no way of knowing if the warning
was genuine or if the light itself was faulty. In fact, in 38,000
flights of Sea Stallions not a single blade had fractured,
despite three cases of warning lights indicating trouble.
However, this information, too, had not been made available
to the pilots and they were left with little choice but to
abandon the helicopter. The crew of No. 6 boarded No. 8
and they continued the flight.

The incomplete weather forecast now played its part. Two
hours after crossing the Iranian coastline, the seven Sea Stal-

lions entered first one dust cloud and then another more than 200 miles across and 6,000 feet high. Astonishingly, the helicopters had not been fitted with special air filters, which are standard equipment for the Israelis. The pilots now entered a nightmare where visibility was down to zero. They quickly separated to avoid collision and flew the rest of the journey using dead reckoning navigation.

Poor visibility was compounded by the pilots' night vision goggles. In normal circumstances, because of their very restricted field of view, the goggles cause vertigo. As one person with experience of night vision goggles puts it: 'Using them one is considered legally blind because of their appalling field of view.'[3]

In the haboob all the crew began to feel very ill and for the pilots the journey became especially uncomfortable.

In the hope that the storm would blow over the flight leader of the helicopter unit actually landed, along with No. 2. Breaking radio silence he explained his position to Vaught, who ordered him to continue. At that stage no one knew that No. 6 had already aborted and the mission was down to seven helicopters. That became six when the commander in No. 5 was forced to abandon the flight and return to the *Nimitz* after his instruments failed. This reduced the helicopters to the minimum required to do the job. Now, as far as Beck-with's plan was concerned, nothing more could go wrong or the whole mission would have to be abandoned. However, to others this was a fundamental flaw in Beckwith's thinking. His task was to rescue the hostages and if that was achieved, the mission would be a success. And certainly one of the basic tenets of rescue operations is that they should be prepared to lose some or even most of their men, something Beckwith could not accept.

At Desert One there was increasing concern that the heli-copters were not going to arrive. Not being allowed to communicate with Vaught, Beckwith had no idea of the heli-copter pilots' troubles. As they stood around waiting, the

Delta Force's worst fears seemed to be realised: the Marine pilots had simply chickened out of the mission.

Then at 20.45, an hour and a half late and forty-five minutes after Delta should have taken off for Desert Two, the distinctive *whop whop* of the helicopters was heard. The first four came in from different directions. Refuelling started immediately. The commander of the Delta assault squad, Logan Fitch, personally ensured that explosives charges were handed out to the crews so that the Sea Stallions could be destroyed in the event of an accident.

He reports a conversation with the pilot of helicopter No. 2 whose hydraulic system had sprung a leak.

'Will you be able to make it?' Fitch asked.

'Don't look so worried. The primary system's down, but the back-up's fine. No problem,' the pilot replied.

The arrival of the first helicopters at Desert One had turned an already difficult situation into something close to chaos. To reduce the risk of engine failure, the C-130s were all sitting next to each other on the ground with their engines running. The helicopters, meanwhile, were obliged to move about the landing site in order to refuel. The result was a maelstrom of heat, noise and dust. Men were simply opaque shapes in the darkness, orders couldn't be heard, and visibility was so poor that individual recognition was virtually impossible. As a result no one knew who was in charge and the chain of command became hopelessly confused.

Two factors exaggerated the problem. There were actually four commanders on the ground at Desert One, one each for Delta Force, the air control unit, the helicopters, and the security team guarding the site. That alone was a recipe for confusion. But even those four people each had a separate short-range radio system and were unable to talk directly to each other. If Beckwith wanted to talk to the helicopter commander by radio he had to contact Vaught at head-quarters who would then pass the message on. Vocal and visual contact was therefore essential – but virtually imposs-ible in the prevailing conditions.

A few minutes later two more helicopters landed, Numbers 1 and 2. The commander, in No. 1, immediately went over to talk with the other pilots. As a result of that conversation he had to tell Beckwith that No. 5 had returned to the *Nimitz* as unfit to fly, and so the mission would have to abort. He did not explain how, if it was unfit to fly, it could still be flown back to the *Nimitz*, a longer distance.

Beckwith radioed Vaught with his recommendation that the mission be cancelled. Vaught in turn contacted the White House and spoke to President Carter. After some discussion – but no argument – Carter agreed and the mission was cancelled.

No plans had been made or practised for this particular evacuation. It was decided that the helicopters would fly out on their own after they had completed refuelling and the C-130s would take the assault force and the rest of the ground teams back to Masirah. Orders flew to and fro amid the noise and dust and after some confusion the men started climbing back into the aircraft.

Logan Fitch led his men aboard the C-130 at the northern end of the landing site. At the same time, a helicopter landed to join another at the C-130's rear to refuel from the 3,000 gallon bladder tank that was mounted on board the aircraft. As the helicopter lifted to manoeuvre closer, a sudden gust of wind blew its rotor into the C-130. Fitch takes up the story.

'When we boarded the fuelbird, its cargo space was dark, full of sweating, sand-caked soldiers and carpeted with a 3,000 gallon bladder that still contained some aviation fuel. My sergeant major and I stumbled over it, looking for an unaccounted-for man. Most of the soldiers were "tired, disgusted, and pissed off" as one put it – but they were accustomed to start-and-stop missions. And like me, they felt that bad luck surely wouldn't follow us on our second try.

'Our C-130 would be the first to take off – as soon as the two helicopters it had been refuelling repositioned themselves to avoid its prop wash. Screaming in warm-up, the turboprop engines made the airframe vibrate.

'Then two dull thuds shook the plane. I thought the nose-wheel had hit a depression. Suddenly, like fireworks, a spray of sparks lit up the entrance to the cockpit and the bulkhead, where most of the avionics were stored. The electrical fire, combined with one fed by aviation fuel, was turning the front of the plane into a murderous oven.

'I grabbed my weapon. We were obviously under attack. In one blink, it was clear we had no forward exit. Savage flames there were driving soldiers towards the rear.

'We had to answer the strike. The plane's crew chief began opening the door at my back before I could even ask him to. From its half-open position, it shot up on springs, but we were immediately using all our strength to slam it shut again before it reached the top of its ride, because the entire port side of the plane was a fireball, trying to reach in and consume us. Fierce heat scorched our faces. The cargo space reeked of burning wires, melted metal and aviation fuel.

'Opposite us, on the starboard side, the one remaining door was already open, and my men were leaping four or five feet down to the ground. And the rabid blaze that seemed certain to explode the fuel bladder before the next breath prompted unthinking panicked reactions. My men shouted, staggered, stumbled on to the hot bladder. They fell over and clawed one another in their urge to escape. Someone had to assert control and that came from the sergeant major who was responsible for the lives that would be saved.

'I had figured to be the last off but survival was my over-riding instinct. I entered the stream moving towards the door. I pulled myself up after being knocked down, then was flat on the floor again. At last I was out on the ground, this time knocked flat by men jumping on me. Down a second time, I finally got free of the jumble and ran off.'[4]

To another member of Fitch's command the occasion was even more startling. Actually asleep in the C-130 when the explosion happened he assumed that the aircraft had already taken off and had been hit by an air-to-air missile. When his turn came at the exit he assumed the parachuting jump position, without a parachute, and launched himself out of the aircraft, only to land face down in the sand.

Flames from the inferno were already reaching four hundred feet into the air. The night sky was crisscrossed by popping tracer ammunition and the occasional explosion of a Redeye rocket. Three of the crashed helicopter crew died in the blaze and all five of the crew on board the C-130. Several others suffered serious burns.

All the remaining personnel on the ground piled on board the other C-130s and headed back to Masirah. Contrary to orders, the Marine pilots left their helicopters intact, their engines running, and also boarded the transports. Thus when the Iranians arrived two days later they found a rich haul of intelligence material including codes, plan details, secure communications equipment, details of agents operating in Iran – and even some of Beckwith's own papers. Such information should never have been carried on board the helicopters and the first principle of operational security had been violated by one of its greatest proponents.

Back in the US, six days after the debacle at Desert One, a Los Angeles policeman stopped a car because he did not like the look of its occupants, both of whom turned out to be Iranian. In the back of the car was a cardboard box and inside the cardboard box was a large pile of documents. The curious policeman looked further and saw that the documents, which were in Farsi, included maps of the Middle East and Teheran, diagrams of what appeared to be routes into the city and drawings of buildings. He associated this with the aborted mission to rescue the hostages and called a friend in Santa Monica who is connected with covert operations. That friend suggested the Iranians should be arrested on a trumped-up charge and the documents confiscated. It turned out that the documents were an almost complete set of those recovered from the helicopters at Desert One which had been collated, translated into Farsi and shipped to some Khomeini supporters in the US, all within six days. The Russians, too, no doubt received copies. By contrast, it took the CIA eight months to translate into English Arabic documents they received from the Israelis after their invasion of Lebanon in 1982.

Operation Eagle Claw which had started out with the hopes of a beleaguered President and the American people ended in dismal failure. On 25 April it was Carter himself who announced the mission and that it had failed. He accepted full responsibility and said that the decision to abort was his.

Immediately, the recriminations began. The media, egged on by the politicians, saw it as a national humiliation: the greatest nation in the world was unable to organise an apparently simple rescue mission. Of course, the Iranians made all the political capital possible out of the affair, transmitting pictures of the downed helicopters and the dead American airmen and taking western journalists on a tour of Desert One.

Cyrus Vance, Carter's Secretary of State, resigned. Although he had been kept away from much of the planning of the mission as it was thought he would have opposed it, he now felt the honourable thing was to leave office. This was another blow to Carter whose image continued to suffer, particularly after the press began suggesting that he had cancelled the operation against the wishes of the service commander; in short, that he had lost his nerve.

For the military, the fallout was potentially much more serious. No one wanted to be blamed for the failure so a flurry of leaks to the press began, each service trying to place the blame on another's shoulders. The Marines leaked a report blaming the Air Force and the Army for poor planning and command and control. This prompted the Air Force to leak the story of the Marines abandoning their helicopters at Desert One.

Beckwith was the obvious scapegoat. He was wheeled out before a press conference on Monday 29 April and, obviously uncomfortable in the glare of publicity, was asked about his mission and the reasons for its cancellation. To Carter's relief he made it clear that the decision to abort was his alone. When asked if he couldn't have gone on with five helicopters he replied:

'I was not about to be a party to half-assed loading on a bunch of aircraft and going up and murdering a bunch of the finest soldiers in the world. I ain't going to do that. I have been in the army 27 years. I don't have to do that. I get paid for shouldering responsibility, and being a leader. I wanted to get the job done, but under those circumstances, it was a no-win situation.'[5]

This sounded fine but disguised the fact that Beckwith had no back-up plan once the first helicopters had gone down, and had placed a priority on getting his men out rather than on rescuing the hostages. Both were examples of poor leadership.

Meanwhile the army tried to salvage what they could out of the mess by trying to persuade the White House to authorise another attempt. Planning for a new mission, codenamed Operation Honey Bear and personally authorised by the President, began the day after the failure at Desert One. But as the hostages were moved from the embassy and put into a number of different houses all over Teheran immediately after news of the failed rescue mission leaked out, Honey Bear was never practicable.

However, the issue that needed to be resolved for the future was: could the original mission have succeeded? That is unlikely. Other special forces who have done their own separate analyses of the operation have concluded that success would have owed more to luck than skilful planning. Too many basic rules of covert operations were broken: the plan was too complex (21 different agencies or units took part, using 51 different radio frequencies, with more than 150 code words and call signs, and there were 17 different landing zones and airfields); many of the participants had never met each other nor trained together; the force was too large; much of the equipment was unsuitable; the command and control was unclear; and the forces planned to spend too long in enemy territory. Above all, the mission violated the first rule of all covert operations, known as KISS, or Keep It Simple, Stupid.

With hindsight, of course, it is always possible to suggest things that could have been improved. But, even at the outset, it should have been obvious the plan was dangerously flawed. For example, even if the helicopters had taken Delta from Desert One to Desert Two and if the assault on the embassy had succeeded, the pilots had still done no practice landings in anything resembling a soccer stadium. In that confined space and possibly under fire it seems likely that once again the mission would have been compromised.

Perhaps the most telling assessment of the mission came from Beckwith himself in testimony before Congress. Replying to a question from Senator Sam Nunn about what could be done to improve things, he replied:

'In Iran we had an *ad hoc* affair. We went out, found bits and pieces, people and equipment, brought them together occasionally and then asked them to perform a highly complex mission. The parts all performed, but they didn't necessarily perform as a team. Nor did they have the same motivation.

'My recommendation is to put together an organisation which contains everything it will ever need, an organisation which would include Delta, the Rangers, Navy SEALS, Air Force pilots, its own staff, its own support people, its own aircraft and helicopters. And give it sufficient time to recruit, assess, and train its people. Otherwise we are not serious about combating terrorism.'[6]

At that time Beckwith's views found few supporters. He was transferred to a staff job with JSOC producing training manuals. He then left the army to run a company in Texas called Security Assistance Services, a sad reminder of the group he tried so hard to emulate, the SAS.

To limit the political witch hunt, the JCS appointed a 'review group' under Admiral James L. Holloway III. Its six members had a narrowly defined task: simply to look at the operation and to list any deficiencies that might come to light. In its final seventy-nine-page judgement, known as the Holloway Report, produced in August 1980, the panel avoids all mention or criticism of the White House or the JCS, concentrating rather on the performance of the three services before and during the mission.

But Holloway did at least resist pressure from the military to tone down some of his criticism of their performance, both in the training for the mission and its execution. All the same, there was no suggestion of fault where the responsibility ultimately lay, with the JCS and the White House – even though it had been the JCS who insisted on such rigid rules for operational security, and who set up a new and untested command structure to deal with the crisis. It was from those two basic errors that the other failures flowed.

However, the Holloway Report did come up with two specific recommendations (both of which were ignored at the time) that some years later would form the basis of a new US strategy for handling covert operations. They are worth quoting in full. First:

'It is recommended that a Counter-terrorist Joint Task Force (CTJTF) be established as a field agency of the Joint Chiefs of Staff with permanently assigned staff personnel and certain assigned force.

Mission. The CTJTF, through the joint Chiefs of Staff, would plan, train for, and conduct operations to counter terrorist activities directed against US interests, citizens, and/or property outside the United States.

Concept. The CTJTF would be designed to provide a range of options utilising US military forces in countering terrorist acts. Such forces might range from a small force of highly specialised personnel to a larger joint force.

Relationships. The commander, CTJTF, would be responsible directly to the JCS. The CTJTF staff should be filled with individuals of all four services, selected on the basis of their specialised capabilities in the field of special operations of various types.

Forces. The organic forces permanently assigned to the JTF should be small and limited to those which have a unique capability in special operations.'

The second significant recommendation was 'that the JCS give careful consideration to the establishment of a Special Operations Advisory Panel, comprised of a group of carefully selected high-ranking officers (active and/or retired) who have career backgrounds in special operations or who have served at the CINC or JCS levels and who have maintained a current interest in special operations or defense policy matters.

'The purpose of the panel would be to review highly classified special operations planning to provide an independent assessment function, which might otherwise be lacking due to the absence of the echelons of service staff planners who normally review and critique JCS planning of a less sensitive nature.

'For example, the panel might consist of five to seven members, with a chairman and members representing the Army, Navy, Air Force, and Marine Corps, appointed to fixed terms not to exceed three years. Members of the panel would maintain current security clearances and meet at least annually for update briefings.

'When planning is initiated in response to a crisis, several members of the panel, depending upon individual qualifications and availability on short notice, would be organised to provide independent review. In this capacity, the panel members would not participate in the actual planning. Their function would be to provide the JCS with the most objective, independent review possible.'[7]

Such recommendations were anathema to the JCS who, already suspicious of unconventional warfare, had no wish to see a special command established which would give it legitimacy and would bring inevitable demands for funds, equipment and personnel.

A Review Panel was an equally uncomfortable concept. Outsiders, even if they were former military, should never be encouraged to interfere with the planning process. The JCS had already demonstrated that even when such a system was in existence as a sop to the unconventional warfare enthusiasts, they preferred to bypass it and take direct control of an operation.

It was hardly surprising, therefore, that both these recommendations were ignored by the JCS. This was to lead to exactly the same mistakes being made on a number of other occasions over the next five years, costing American lives and perpetuating the image of the United States military as a bumbling amateur, incapable of carrying out effective covert operations.

It is this image that has perhaps been the most lingering effect of the debacle at Desert One. The Iran operation had to be set against two great triumphs, one by the Israelis at Entebbe and the other by the West Germans at Mogadishu. To many politicians and certainly to the public at large an idea had developed that such covert operations were easy, which they clearly are not. The failure of the United States was contrasted against the successes of smaller countries who had triumphed in equally difficult circumstances.

No military commander ever likes to be associated with failure and after Desert One it was difficult to find a body of support for special operations outside the units themselves.

But, despite the misgivings of the military, unconventional warfare was eventually to be forced to centre stage by two events: the election of Ronald Reagan as President of the United States, and the Soviet invasion of Afghanistan.

PART 6: RUSSIA'S VIETNAM?

13

Assault on Kabul

On 24 December 1979 advance units of a Soviet invasion force began arriving in Kabul. Dressed in civilian clothes and numbering no more than one hundred, the men arrived on scheduled Aeroflot flights from the Soviet Union. Entering as 'advisers' or 'tourists', they left the airport and headed for the Soviet embassy.

At the same time, KGB agents from Directorate S of the 8th Department, operating inside the Afghan armed forces, began putting into action a plan that had been developed some seven months before. They persuaded two Afghan armoured divisions stationed at Kabul, one of them the Afghani President's personal guard, to hand over their ammunition and anti-tank weapons for inventory, and to remove their vehicle batteries so that they could be checked. Immobilised, neither of these key units were able to play any part in what was to come.

On Christmas Day, senior Afghan Army officers and government officials were invited to a reception at the Soviet embassy. After being plied with vodka they were shepherded to a downstairs room and locked in. At the same time, KGB agents broke into armouries around Kabul and sabotaged or removed weapons.

The following morning – a time carefully chosen to find western governments at their most vulnerable – the main Soviet invasion force moved in. Just after dawn, two Antonov transport aircraft landed at Kabul airport. On board were spetsnaz commandos dressed in Afghan army uniforms. In the belly of the planes were trucks and jeeps painted with Afghan army markings. The spetsnaz who had arrived two days before had already returned to the airport. Now, acting in concert, the two groups swiftly secured the control tower and the runway, planting beacons to guide the following invasion force.[1]

As the first of a vast transport fleet appeared over the horizon, the spetsnaz forces moved out along the dusty highway on their way to the city centre. These forces, bolstered by KGB men from the embassy and loyal agents from the Afghan secret service, were making for the Darulaman Palace of President Hafizullah Amin. Their orders were clear: Amin and all those inside the palace with him must be executed.

On the road in from the airport, the spetsnaz forces were stopped at a routine checkpoint. Surprised to see so many soldiers travelling along the road without prior notice, the Afghan troops gathered around the Russians. On command, the flaps on the armoured personnel carriers dropped, the stubby barrels of sub-machine-guns appeared, and the road to the palace was open.

The eight tanks guarding the palace were destroyed by anti-tank rockets, and the gates were rammed by an armoured personnel carrier – which unfortunately got stuck in the gap and delayed the assault. The attack was then further delayed by the unexpectedly stiff resistance put up by the presidential guard.

When the Soviet forces finally entered the palace they began a classic room-clearing operation, kicking down doors, lobbing in grenades and killing anything that moved after the subsequent explosions. President Hafizullah Amin was found at his private bar on the top floor. He was shot dead. A Soviet KGB defector claims he was with a beautiful woman who was also killed, but this is thought to be a romantic embellishment.

On the orders of the officer commanding the assault, KGB

Colonel Bayerenov from Directorate S, anyone attempting
to leave the palace was shot on sight. Soon afterwards Col
Bayerenov reportedly went outside to summon reinforcements, only to be shot and killed by his own men.[2]

At some time during or shortly after the attack, Lieutenant-
General Viktor Paputin, the commander of the special forces
and intelligence units died also. The exact cause of his death
is unknown. Since his obituary appeared without party
secretary Leonid Brezhnev's signature, a mark of disfavour,
he may either have been executed or have committed suicide.

Over the next two days, more than two hundred aircraft
arrived at Kabul airport, bringing regiment after regiment of
Soviet forces. And on 27 December two motorised rifle
divisions crossed the border, heading for Kandahar, the country's second largest city to the south. Within a week more
than 80,000 Soviet troops were inside the country, a total that
would eventually rise to around 115,000.

This overwhelming military force was immediately used to
round up and disarm those elements of the Afghan army
which continued to oppose the invading forces. The 26th
Afghan Parachute Regiment refused to hand over its arms
and was destroyed after a fierce battle. Using lists prepared
by KGB agents, spetsnaz toured the capital rounding up
senior officers and political figures: if they refused to support
the invasion or the puppet government of newly installed
President Babrak Karmal, they were executed.

As the Soviets had discovered in Czechoslovakia eleven
years before, the overwhelming use of force combined with
the thorough execution of a ruthless plan is very effective. In
fact, the similarities between the two operations are marked:
in both, extensive use was made of agents in place, deceptive
techniques ensured a surprise attack and undermined the
military's capacity to resist the invasion; KGB and special
forces were skillfully used; and the local political and military
command were eliminated.

A final similarity came about two days after the invasion.
Like the Dubcek government, the Afghan regime put out a

statement that appeared to provide some legitimacy for the Soviet action. Broadcast from Kabul, the statement read:

'Because of the continuation and expansion of aggression, intervention and provocations by the foreign enemies of Afghanistan and for the purpose of defending the gains of the Saur Revolution, territorial integrity, national independence and the preservation of peace and security, and on the basis of the treaty of friendship, good-neighborliness and co-operation dated 5 December 1978, the Democratic Republic of Afghanistan earnestly demands that the USSR render urgent political, moral and economic assistance, including military aid to Afghanistan.'[3] It seems unlikely that President Amin would have summoned Soviet troops so that they could come and kill him. The Kabul statement was clearly a propaganda exercise, and it fooled no-one.

The actual attack took western governments by surprise, even though preparations for an invasion, or at the very least limited Soviet intervention, had been evident for some months as Moscow saw its newly-acquired satellite slipping away from its control.

Since the days of the British Empire, Afghanistan had played a pivotal role in the geo-politics of the Near and Middle East. It provided a conduit from the Soviet Union and China through to India. And, more recently, it has gained additional significance because it is separated from the Indian Ocean by only around five hundred kilometres of Pakistan, a country that itself has been a regular subject of superpower rivalry. For the United States, Afghanistan was important both because Soviet expansion should in principle always be stopped, and also because a pro-west Afghanistan allowed access to the southern borders of the Soviet Union and to the western borders of China.

To both superpowers, therefore, Afghanistan represented a juicy plum in the strategic pie, and for many years various Kabul governments had been wooed with aid and advisers. This resulted in some ridiculous situations. For example, in the mid-1970s the quickest route from the Iranian border on the west to Kabul in the east was not directly across country but rather on a magnificent four-lane highway south-east to Kandahar, from where one drove north-east on another magnificent four-lane highway to Kabul. The first road had been built by the Americans, presumably for their tanks to move north, and the second road had been built by the Soviets, presumably for their tanks to move south. At that time, the only traffic in fact was hippies heading for the drug delights of Kathmandhu.

In the early and mid-1970s the Afghans, a fiercely independent people, had managed to steer a broadly neutralist line between their two suitors. Then, in April 1978, the People's Democratic Party of Afghanistan (a grouping of two separate political parties, the Khalq and the Parcham) seized power in a coup led by two Khalq men, Nur M. Taraki and Hafizullah Amin. The coup was supported by the largely Soviet-trained military, although there is still some doubt whether it was actually orchestrated by the Soviets. This doubt was sufficient to allow the US government to continue to accept Kabul's public line that it was a non-aligned nation. Aid poured into the country from the west, as well as from the east, even amid signs that the government was leaning increasingly towards Moscow.

President Taraki and Prime Minister Amin determined on sweeping reforms of the social, economic and political traditions of the country. To clear the way, they sent abroad as ambassadors leading members of the Parcham party. These were subsequently removed from their posts and ordered home. None chose to return. At the same time, there were widespread arrests of civil servants and leading members of the armed services who were thought to oppose the planned reforms. The government was attempting to remove centuries-old traditions of land ownership, abolish social customs related to marriage rites, and change many of the religious customs, including the wearing of the veil by women. All of these changes were deeply resented by conservative Afghanis, and none more so than the religious interference.

Afghanistan has an entirely Moslem population, swelled by refugees from the Soviet Union who had fled from that country's attempts to stamp out organised religion. They saw Kabul's efforts to change their customs as a direct attempt to impose a regime similar to that already existing to the north.

Encouraged by their religious leaders, the people began to protest, first peacefully and then with arms, after a Jihad or Holy War had been called against the godless communist government. By the middle of 1978, every one of Afghanistan's twenty-nine provinces was up in arms. As the security situation deteriorated, the government responded with increasing savagery. The result, in a foretaste of future events, was that they lost control of many of the rural areas and were forced to move around the country in convoys during daylight. Also, finding their ground forces unable to cope with the guerrillas, they used their air superiority to launch strikes against villages with bombs and napalm, an indiscriminate use of force which only alienated the people even further.

Then, in February 1979, the US ambassador to Afghanistan, Adolph Dubs, was kidnapped and held hostage by guerrillas, who demanded the release of some of their colleagues from Kabul's Pil-i-Charkhi prison. Despite intense pressure from the US government to negotiate and not to use force to free the ambassador, Afghan police stormed the Kabul hotel room where he was being held. They raked the room with machine-gun fire, killing Dubs and two of his captors. Soon afterwards the US government severely reduced its aid to Afghanistan, thus adding to the economic and political crisis.

The following month, Afghan army units deserted and joined forces with guerrillas in the western city of Herat. In an orgy of violence lasting several days, hundreds were killed. Special guerrilla assassination squads roamed the town searching for Soviet advisers and their families. Reports from the town say that many were flayed alive and others cut in pieces, beheaded, and their heads paraded on pikes around the city.[+]

Viewed from Moscow, this all had the characteristics of a western-sponsored campaign to destabilise a pro-Soviet government. To bolster President Taraki, the Soviets increased the number of advisers to 1,000, and supplied additional tanks and twelve Mi-24 helicopter gunships. None of this proved effective in reducing the violence.

As a precaution, in April the Soviets sent General Alexei A. Epishev, the head of the Main Political Administration of the Armed Forces, on an inspection tour with six other Soviet generals. Epishev had visited Czechoslovakia before the 1968 invasion, and since that trip he had become an outspoken advocate of military intervention. His April inspection tour was followed up with another, from August to October, by General Ivan G. Pavlovskii who was accompanied by eleven other generals and sixty-three officers. Pavlovskii had been the Commander-in-Chief of Soviet forces during the Czech invasion and there is little doubt he was on a reconnaissance mission to Afghanistan.

In the middle of the second visit by the generals, Taraki was summoned to Moscow for consultations. It seems clear that the Soviets gave him firm advice to do something about the economic and political situation. At the same time, they apparently encouraged him to get rid of his Prime Minister, Amin, who was seen in Afghanistan as the power behind the throne and more radical than the President himself.

On his return to Kabul on 14 September, Taraki asked Amin to consult with him at the palace. At first Amin refused to go, but after personal assurances for his safety from the Soviet ambassador he called on the President. A gun battle seems to have broken out between the two men and their bodyguards. Amin's life was saved by a Major Taroon, who flung himself in front of the Prime Minister and was killed. Amin himself escaped, but returned soon afterwards with a large contingent of troops loyal to him. Taraki was arrested and a month later executed and buried in an unmarked grave.

Amin claimed that Taraki was ill and that he had resigned on health grounds. After his assassination, it was officially announced that Taraki had died from the serious illness that had caused him to resign in the first place.

Amin declared himself President and immediately set about trying to ensure his own survival. He was aware that Taraki had been advised to get rid of him by the Soviets, and he therefore tried to win them over. In order to stabilise his country he announced a new era of religious tolerance, combined with changes in the planned economic and political reforms which would take account of local traditions. However, as Amin himself had been responsible for many of the original measures and for the conduct of much of the war against the guerrillas, his statements were greeted with scepticism by the tribesmen.

The Soviets, too, seem to have decided that Amin was a failure. Their original judgement of him, that he was too left-wing to make a credible leader, remained. The visit of the two generals, who were able to see for themselves the deteriorating military situation, must also have influenced the Politburo. It seems likely the report they brought back to Moscow was very pessimistic, predicting a total collapse of the Kabul government.

If this had happened, there were two strategic worries for Moscow. The west, if indeed they had been supporting the guerrillas (and there is no hard evidence for that), would install a puppet leader of their own in Kabul and once again Afghanistan would swing to the west. This led to a further concern. Iran, on Afghanistan's western border, had already undergone a fundamentalist Islamic revolution. The Khomeini regime had suppressed the communist Tudeh party in Iran and had already begun moves to export the revolution by funding and arming terrorists throughout the Middle East. This was an unwelcome development for the Soviets, with substantial Moslem populations in their southern republics who might easily be vulnerable to religious agitation. Also, more than a third of the Soviet armed forces would be Moslem by the end of the century, and their loyalty had to be assured.

If the Afghan rebellion was allowed to continue unchecked, and eventually overthrew the Kabul government, a huge tract of territory along the Soviet Union's southern border could fall into the hands of religious fanatics.

It is most unlikely that the Soviets ever expected a quick and easy victory in Afghanistan. Unlike in Czechoslovakia or Hungary, they were entering a country which was already gripped by civil war – and a civil war that had come about only in part because of the poor judgement of the Kabul leadership, but more importantly because the government was seen to be too close to Moscow. Therefore, in the short term an intervention by the Soviets was likely simply to exacerbate the situation and provoke the rebels to further attacks. There was also the risk that the rebels, at present split on a largely tribal basis, might unite against the Soviet invaders.

It was likely to be a long war. The Soviets had read their history books and were well aware that Afghanistan was a country that had maintained its independence against centuries of attempted interference from outsiders. There was every reason to suppose they would continue that tradition against any Soviet invaders. But, while the Soviets might have to pay a heavy price in the short term for an invasion – both through a lengthy military commitment to the country and through the loss of political prestige abroad through such an act of aggression – the potential long-term gains were substantial. The Soviets would acquire control of a strategically important country, and would be in a position to undermine the influence of Moslem fundamentalists inside the Soviet Union's own borders.

Preparations first became evident in August 1978, when 10,000 troops were airlifted from the Soviet Union to South Yemen and Ethiopia in what was obviously a dry run for the invasion. Over the next two months reservists living in Central Asia were mobilised to bring up to full strength the divisions along the Soviet border with Afghanistan, and US satellites picked up the movements of heavy equipment and pallets to airfields along the border. A command post for the invasion, headed by First Deputy Defence Minister, Marshal Sokolov, was set up at Temerz near the border.

In the middle of December, there was an attempt to assassinate Amin at his palace in Kabul. A guard and Amin's intelligence chief were wounded but Amin himself emerged unscathed – only to ask for the recall of the Soviet ambassador, whom he suspected of being behind the plot. When this last attempt at a solution short of military intervention failed, the invasion went ahead.

Despite the intelligence information that had been received over the previous three months, the invasion apparently caught the US government by surprise. The CIA, the Defense Intelligence Agency and the National Security Agency all had been putting forward reports that the Soviets were up to something, but the consensus seems to have been they were carrying out normal exercises, and it was not until a week before the Soviets actually moved that the White House felt an invasion might be imminent. Even then, no clear warning seems to have been given to the Kremlin. Instead, Carter and his advisers preferred to wait and see what happened. This apparent lack of concern may well have been interpreted by the Soviets as tacit US acceptance of their plans.

If that was so, it was a serious miscalculation. The invasion appears to have genuinely shocked President Carter, who thereafter was spurred to take a series of punitive measures against the Soviets, including trade sanctions and a boycott of the Moscow Olympic games, to signal his concern. In addition, Salt II, the key arms control agreement which at that time was due to go before Congress for ratification, was withdrawn. Internationally, too, the Soviets lost a great deal of ground. The invasion was the first time they had used massive armed force to intervene in a country outside the Warsaw Pact, and this lesson was lost neither on the developing nations nor on the western propaganda machine.

Damage to the Soviets was critical in two key areas: the Middle East and China. The Arab states saw the Soviet invasion as a possible prelude to an advance against their oil resources. The Soviets had always made clear they considered the Gulf oil wealth to be of considerable strategic importance and control of Afghanistan now put them in easy flying distance of the Strait of Hormuz, a choke point for sea-borne oil traffic leaving the Gulf.

The Chinese, on their part, felt that unless the Soviets were made to pay a heavy price for the invasion they might be encouraged to try the same thing again. And the next time, China itself might be the target.

Both views seem to be wide of the mark. The key factor influencing the Soviets was not the wish to gain better access to the Gulf (they already had extensive facilities in Aden, which was much closer to key oil states) but rather to curb the spread of Islamic fundamentalism and to get rid of a leader who was reducing to chaos a country that had previously been an ally. Nonetheless, the United States was able to play on these Arab and Chinese fears, and subsequently embarked on a campaign of support for the guerrilla movements in Afghanistan. In January 1980 Defense Secretary Harold Brown visited China and National Security Adviser Brzezinski went to Egypt and Pakistan. Both men were able to bring back promises of support for US policy in Afghanistan.

An extensive propaganda campaign was begun, aimed at showing the world the expansionist nature of Soviet foreign policy, and there was much talk in the US administration of 'making this Russia's Vietnam'. This has been a consistent theme of US foreign policy ever since, but, as we shall see, it was a wildly over-simplistic view and underestimated the resolve and resources of the Soviets.

Three days after the invasion, a meeting of the US National Security Council agreed to see what could be done to improve the supplies of cash and arms to the guerrillas. The CIA covertly began providing cash, with administration approval.

The mujahedeen cause was helped considerably when President Reagan was sworn in on 20 January 1981. To Reagan, who once described the Soviet Union as the 'evil empire', the invasion was a confirmation of a Soviet Union bent on an expansionist policy that had as its aim the communist domination of the world, a view that Churchill and Truman would have recognised. The resistance of the mujahedeen to the Soviets became a symbolic rallying point for the Republicans, who in turn felt that they themselves represented the wishes and aspirations of the free world.

It is hardly surprising therefore that the Afghan guerrillas have seen a substantial increase in aid and arms during the Reagan years. In 1983 that aid reached $25–30 million, and was well over $100 million by 1986. Saudi Arabia has contributed at least $25 million a year since the invasion began.[5] Other reports suggest that the United States and Saudi Arabia may each be sending $250 million a year to the Afghan guerrillas in arms, food and other supplies.[6]

Aside from simple cash, a network of international arms suppliers has sprung up, beginning with China and Egypt. Both countries helped arm and train the Afghans, using Soviet equipment. The arms network was later expanded to include Saudi Arabia and Israel, which passed on Soviet-supplied PLO weapons captured during their 1982 invasion of Lebanon – and eventually the United States itself began supplying arms directly.

There have been consistent reports that many of the arms never reach the guerrillas. The Pakistan government is responsible for the distribution of many of the weapons and they have used this as an opportunity to offload their older rifles and ammunition, thus replacing their own stocks for nothing. During the summer months, more than 80 per cent of the guerrillas, whose numbers vary between 50,000 and 85,000, are armed with captured Soviet equipment. Without doubt, there is a great deal of corruption among the guerrilla leaders based in Peshawar in Pakistan. As aid has increased so has the opulent lifestyle of some of them, who have build magnificent palaces for themselves in and around Peshawar.

Government officials, too, take their cut and there have been reports of arms intended for the guerrillas being sold to other groups, via the international black market.

Ahmad Shah Massoud, one of the most charismatic and successful guerrilla leaders, who has waged a successful campaign against the Soviets in the Panjir Valley for the past six years, claims he receives little or no support from guerrilla leaders in Pakistan. He buys most of his arms on the black market and pays for them with emeralds and lapis mined in the Panjir.

If the Soviets expected the invasion to remove the focus of rebel dissent in Afghanistan and bring peace to the country, they must have been sorely disappointed. Despite President Babrak Karmal's efforts to placate the people by scrapping some of the more unpopular reforms and releasing certain political prisoners from jail, the invasion had succeeded principally in providing the rebels with a common enemy, the infidel Soviet invaders.

14

Changing Tactics

Ironically, an immediate casualty of the invasion so skilfully carried out by spetsnaz units was the spetsnaz force that was arming and funding the friendly Baluchi tribesmen in Pakistan. Although the Baluch occupied territory in both Pakistan and Afghanistan, in the run-up to the invasion only the Afghan Baluch had been attacking Soviet forces. However, the invasion managed to unite Baluch on both sides of the border. According to US intelligence sources, at least two teams of spetsnaz were operating in Pakistan at the end of 1979, but unfortunately they had not been told of the imminent invasion and were captured by irate Baluchi tribesmen. All were skinned alive and killed.[1]

As in many wars, the early confrontations between the guerrillas and the Soviet forces were meetings of equal incompetents, the guerrillas being hopelessly divided and using ancient weapons, while the Soviets insisted on fighting a conventional campaign in what was clearly a counter-insurgency war.

The mujahedeen equipment was often fifty years old, some even dating back to the last century when it had been captured from the British, the last invader the Afghans had expelled. But, the guerrillas had one great advantage: their local knowledge of the territory. This, allied to an intelligence network that could pass information with great speed from village to village by word of mouth, gave them an early tactical edge.

But there were more than a hundred different guerrilla groups operating throughout the country at the time of the invasion, most of them structured on tribal lines which in turn were based on specific territory controlled by each group. Since in many cases these tribes had for centuries been at war, or at the very least in a state of armed truce, with their neighbours they were unable to move freely over large areas of territory as a guerrilla war demands, or to receive regular supplies from outside.

As fast as alliances were formed, therefore, others disintegrated. Since 1979 there have been at least six major alliances among the resistance movements, and the guerrillas seem to have basically divided into two groups, the moderates and the fundamentalists. Recently a core body has been formed, the Islamic Unity of Afghan Mujahedeen, which has a single spokesman appointed on a quarterly basis from the different groups. The fundamentalists are represented by Gulbuddin Hekmatyar's Hezb-e-Islami (Islamic Party); the Hezb-e-Islami faction of Yunus Khalis; the Jamiat-i-Islami (Islamic Society) headed by Burhanuddin Rabbani; and the Ittihadia (Islamic Unity) led by Abdul Rasool Sayyaf. The moderates are the Harakat-e-Inqelab (Islamic Revolutionary Movement) of Nabi Mohammedi; the Mahes-e-Milli (National Islamic Front) of Pir Sayyid Gailani; and the Jebh-e-Najat-e-Milli (National Liberation Front) led by Sibaghatulla Mojadeddi.[2]

Nearly all the groups operating inside Afghanistan have some links with this core body which acts as a co-ordinator for arms, cash and food to the guerrillas. Even so, there remain fairly basic differences of opinion among them, particularly concerning the nature of any post-Soviet government.

At the time of the invasion, the guerrilla leadership was based almost entirely on the traditional village. All the leaders were old and very few of the guerrillas, apart from the deserters from the Afghan army, had any military training. Over time, this has changed, and a new, younger generation has emerged to take command of the units in the field. Many of them have received some basic military training in the refugee camps in Pakistan and Iran and all have considerable experience of actual fighting. The result has been a marked improvement in the guerrillas' performance.

However, the same can also be said of the Soviets. Although special forces may have played a key role at the beginning of the war, they were swiftly replaced by conventional units of tanks, mechanised troops and ordinary soldiers, apparently on the principle that this was a standard military campaign where the simple deployment of substantial troops would be enough.

(They were not alone in this view. Two years after the war began, the US Joint Chiefs of Staff ordered a study done by a West Coast think tank into wars going on around the world. The group found there were fifty-five, of which only one could be classed as conventional (Iran/Iraq). The head of the study recalls: 'There was a big argument about Afghanistan, which the study classified as low intensity conflict, but which the JCs saw as a conventional war. So we told them that on that basis and knowing what we do about Soviet war doctrine, they would already have used tactical nuclear weapons.

'The JCS simply wanted the study to confirm that all wars are conventional and when the facts proved otherwise, they did not like it.'[3])

At the beginning of the Afghan war, if the Soviets had learned the lessons of counter-insurgency campaigns of the past forty years in countries as diverse as Oman, Algeria, Vietnam and Malaya, they would have embarked on an extensive hearts-and-minds campaign to win over the Afghan population, which at that time was almost wholly behind the guerrillas. But as we have already seen, the Soviets did exactly the reverse.

They accepted early on that the Kabul government's attempts to woo the population were going to fail, and that the Afghan army was at best a token force, suited to only limited operations. In fact, within weeks of the invasion widespread Afghan army defections to the guerrillas had taken place – sometimes whole regiments would defect, and take their arms with them, so that by 1983, the army had fallen from its pre-invasion level of around 90,000 to 30,000, a figure that has remained fairly constant ever since.

Instead of a hearts-and-minds policy to counter political and military weakness in the Afghan regime, the Soviets embarked on a wide campaign of terrorism. This had – and still has – two aims: to compel the population to stop supporting the guerrillas and to force over the borders into Pakistan and Iran those that refused to give in. To terrorise the population the Soviets have employed a scorched earth policy. Immediately after the invasion, this involved large units, perhaps including several hundred vehicles, sallying out from the cities, where they had large garrisons, into the countryside. They would capture and secure an area and then proceed systematically to burn and destroy everything inside it. They would then retreat again to their garrison cities.

These large formations of troops were also used at first against the guerrillas, but the Soviets quickly found that the mujahedeens' knowledge of the terrain combined with their support in the local community more than made up for their lack of modern tactical skills or weaponry. Again and again the Soviets were drawn into well-planned ambushes and by the time air cover or ground reinforcements could be summoned the guerrillas would have vanished into the surrounding hills.

Basic Soviet tactics have now changed, therefore, so that there is a much greater emphasis on air power. Helicopters armed with rockets or fighter-bombers, staying out of range of the guerrillas' air defence systems, bomb and strafe villages that are suspected of being part of the mujahedeen support network. For example, one visitor to the country trekking in-to the Panjir Valley in June 1985 reported: 'At about 100 kilometres from the valley mouth we reached the town of Dasht-i-Rewat which is one of the Panjir's biggest settlements.

Or was. What had been a busy, thriving community of maybe 15,000 was today a ghost town – a charred, blackened shell, fought over, bombed and systematically torched until not a single building remained undamaged. This was our first real taste of Moscow's prescription for non-Marxist Afghanistan: scorched earth. Total destruction.'[4]

Initially, too, Soviet problems had been made worse by their decision to use five reserve divisions made up of Farsi-speaking Tadjiks, Uzbecks and Turkomans, most of whom were Moslems. Not only were the divisions insufficiently trained for the campaign but there were regular reports of defections to the guerrillas. The Soviets may have calculated that the guerrillas would be unwilling to attack fellow-Moslems but they were mistaken. In fact it worked the other way around, and in January 1980 a report was received that an entire Moslem Soviet combat brigade had been executed for refusing to fight fellow-Moslems.[5]

These troops were swiftly replaced by better-trained forces that came from non-Moslem Soviet republics. This did not make the war any more popular with the Soviet soldiers, but at least cut down the desertions. Many of the new troops were employed in reinforced rifle battalions, a new development that produced a combined-arms unit of regular ground troops, a unit of tanks backed up with artillery, and air support. Previously, the Soviets had seemed to operate each part of the armed forces as a separate entity rather than each contributing to the tactical success of the whole. They also created the 40th Army with headquarters in Tashkent in Uzbekistan to fight the war in Afghanistan.

Other new tactics consistent with the Soviet aim of terror-ising the population began to come into operation. Helicop-ters were used more frequently to sow mines, to act as reconnaissance for the combat units, and to provide mobile firepower to take the fight to the guerrillas.

The United States started delivering Stinger shoulder fired missiles for the guerrillas to use against Soviet aircraft in 1986. They have proved highly effective and 600 Stingers were allocated for delivery in 1987. This will limit the Soviets' capability for ground attack by aircraft and will make them more dependent on special forces for ambush and assassination.[6]

The use of new types of mine, however, is a particularly deadly addition to the Soviet armoury. Some two million of them have been planted, disguised as pens, dolls or toys. The mines are not designed to kill but simply to maim. In a counter-insurgency war, an injured person is a burden on others and a visible warning to friends and family of the consequences of the war. And mines disguised as toys are aimed at children who, without hands and legs, may be a discouragement to future generations who might wish to enlist in the guerrilla army.

When spetsnaz were first inaugurated they were known as Guards Mine Layers, so it is appropriate that in Afghanistan they have pioneered the use of an acoustic mine newly developed to deal with the night convoys by which guerrillas move supplies around the country. Instead of a single mine going off when a truck or donkey touches the detonator, a whole string of acoustically detonated mines are planted. Only when a convoy is well into the minefield does the acoustic level get high enough, and then they all explode simultaneously.

Claude Malhuret, a French doctor who has visited Afghanistan several times, says that there is an economic side effect to the sowing of mines. 'When I arrived in Afghanistan, I was immediately struck by the number of goats and cows that had legs in splints made from bamboo sticks and tied with wire. The herdsmen explained to me what had happened: these animals had stepped on mines and been injured as a result of the explosion. But the greatest loss, the herdsmen told me, is not so much the ones with splints, but rather all those animals that were killed from secondary infections. And although the Afghans clear the mines from the roads to prevent more human deaths, the animals in the fields continue to get killed. Livestock in several regions of the country have been slaughtered in this way. The effect of this slaughtering of the food supply is clear.[7]

There have also been numerous reports of napalm and chemical attacks which have devastated whole areas. The use of such weapons is logical, given Soviet policy in the country. But western intelligence is particularly disturbed by the fact that Soviet survey parties spend considerable time in the areas where chemical agents have been used. Chemical warfare on the European front is a consistent preoccupation of allied planners. Chemicals are known to figure in Soviet tactics, so it may well be that in this area of weaponry, as in so many others, Afghanistan is proving to be an excellent operational laboratory.[8]

But perhaps the most significant change in tactics over the seven years of the war has been the renewed use of special forces. Relegated to a minor role immediately after the invasion, special forces re-entered the country in significant numbers in 1981, and now number 4,000, divided into two brigades based at Jelalabad and Lashar Gah. The Afghanistan men come from a total of only 25,000 spetnatz in the Soviet armed forces, and therefore, since the war began, the majority of spetsnaz will have seen combat – an extraordinary record that is unrivalled by any comparable unit in the west.

Although 70 per cent of spetsnaz forces in Afghanistan are conscripts, they are trained to a far higher standard than the regular troops, with a special emphasis on moving long distances over land and setting ambushes, particularly at night. Like their counterparts in the west, they can be deployed in teams of four (Vasaltnicki), although it is far more common for them to be used in numbers of fifty or even more, acting as a heliborne spearhead for a major attack.

Little distinguishes spetsnaz from the regular Soviet forces except their right to wear a prized blue-and-white striped T-shirt and paratroop wings on their uniforms (all spetsnaz are jump qualified). Three years ago, other soldiers started wearing the T-shirt and an order had to be issued by the Soviet commander in Afghanistan to stop them. Spetsnaz are also entitled to wear a blue beret, but this has not been seen often as they seem to prefer a more raffish bush hat.

Their equipment is quite different from that of the regular forces. They have used silenced 7.62 AKM rifles for night ambushes, AK-74 Kallikov and AKR Krinkov 5.45mm rifles, RPG-7, RPG-18 and under-barrel 40mm grenade launchers mounted on AK-47 Kalashnikov automatic rifles and AGS-17 30mm automatic grenade launchers. They also use subsonic rounds that have an effective range of fifty metres, a spring-loaded knife that can fire a blade about five metres and is sometimes mercury-tipped, thermal imaging for night vision, infra-red detection devices and R-350M portable radios with high speed transmission. They have also used laser guidance systems in concert with fighters to guide missiles to the more inaccessible guerrilla targets in caves and deep valleys.

Some equipment has been captured by the mujahedeen, however, and analysis in the west suggests that much of it is of poor quality. For example, the AK-47 uses a silencer that is of World War II technology which lasts for only 5–10 shots with subsonic rounds and does not work at all with the more normal supersonic rounds. The pistols they use are described as 'very poor' although the Dragonev sniper rifle is thought to be 'middling good'.[9]

If Afghanistan were a war being fought by special forces from a western country, much of their time would be spent infiltrating the guerrilla bands, capturing and indoctrinating the guerrillas or waging a hearts-and-minds campaign in the villages. But, as with the broader Soviet military effort in the country, spetsnaz have been used primarily as shock troops, to set and execute ambushes and on some occasions to try and assassinate rebel leaders.

A useful assessment of spetsnaz capabilities comes from Abdul Haq, the leader of the Hezb-e-Islami group of Yunus Khalis operating near Kabul:

'They specialise in ambushes, particularly at dawn, while the mujahedeen are praying. But now the danger is known,

and almost always the guerrillas have one or two of their
number on guard while the others pray.

'They are usually landed by helicopter at a distance from
the ambush site and cover long distances on foot to reach the
operational area undetected. They are used because they are
the only Soviet units who are able to take decisions for themselves and they are more effective and dangerous for the
mujahedeen.

'But they are trained to hit specific targets, gather information and carry out sabotage operations. But we do not
have a secret base with special planes or an infrastructure
they can hit or a power station they can blow up. Also, they
are trained to work in jungles or urban areas and the terrain
in Afghanistan is unsuitable for them.'[10]

That judgement may be overly optimistic. Other sources
suggest that spetsnaz have led every major assault by Soviet
forces in recent years and that they have also been behind
many of the covert attacks on guerrilla forces. For example,
guerrillas manning an observation post on a hilltop in
Nangarhar Province in March 1986 thought they had chosen
a site that was virtually impregnable. Behind them was a
sheer cliff that dropped hundreds of feet to a river and in
front of them a steep slope that was totally commanded by
the guerrillas. But shortly before dawn the outpost was wiped
out, apparently by spetsnaz commandos who had scaled the
seemingly unclimbable cliff to take the mujahedeen by
surprise.[11]

A typical night ambush occurred on 19 September 1985,
when a small party of guerrillas was travelling near the Kajaki
Dam, about fifty miles north-west of Kandahar. The
mujahedeen were accompanied by Charles Thornton, a
medical correspondent for the *Arizona Republic* and Peter
Schlueter, a photographer for the same paper. They suddenly
came under fire from hovering helicopters and from troops
hidden in the sides of the valley they were driving through.
The battle lasted all night and just before dawn the guerrillas
retreated leaving behind the body of Thornton, who had been

shot in the chest and neck. He was buried in a shallow grave at the site of the ambush and despite attempts by the guerrillas to reach the area again, the body has not been recovered.

Intelligence sources suggest that the attack was a classic spetsnaz night ambush. The attackers were well placed, supported by helicopters and, as the battle continued, reinforcements of regular troops were flown in by helicopters.[12]

Spetsnaz have also devised two new tactics that have changed the course of the war. the first has been the development of joint assaults, using Afghan militia. These are better-trained forces who operate in civilian clothes and who have as much knowledge of the local territory as the guerrillas themselves. These militia in some ways resemble the 'counter gangs' used by the British in fighting the Mau Mau insurgency in Kenya and the communist-backed guerrillas in Malaya and Oman. Moving in small groups and dressed like the mujahedeen, the spetsnaz militia forces have been able to infiltrate guerrilla groups, lay ambushes and carry out 'black' operations, such as the bombing or burning of mosques and villages, which will then be blamed on the mujahedeen.

The second tactic has involved the Soviets in establishing a string of outposts along known supply routes. These are well protected and can be swiftly reinforced by helicopter. Spetsnaz units acting as quick-reaction forces are deployed either from these garrisons or from a main base to attack convoys spotted in the area. This development has had a significant impact on the guerrillas' ability to resupply their groups operating far from the borders with Iran and Pakistan.

For example, in the Panjir Valley, beginning in 1984, the Soviets have gradually created a string of outposts that streches from Faisalbad near the Russian border to Nuristan in the south. The Soviets still do not control much of the surrounding countryside but their outposts make guerrilla communications with the upper Panjir extremely difficult. The most direct route requires nearly three weeks walking, crossing three passes higher than 14,000 feet. The numbers of supply caravans using this route have dropped by 75 per cent in two years and if the network of outposts combined with spetsnaz activity is developed the link could be completely severed.[13]

Extending that campaign one step further, the Soviets have taken the war over the border into the guerrilla camps. A campaign of bombings and assassinations began in Peshawar and in the refugee camps in 1984. Ninety-nine refugees were killed in these attacks in 1985, among them six prominent mujahedeen commanders. The majority of these attacks are carried out by the Khad, the 20,000-strong Afghan secret police set up after the Soviets invaded. Western intelligence believes that many of these agents are trained by spetsnaz.[14]

The importance the Soviets now attach to the influence of spetsnaz in the war was confirmed in July 1985, with the appointment of General Mikhail Mitrofanovich Zaitsev to command the campaign. Aged 63, Zaitsev is one of the new breed of generals who has helped to revolutionise the thinking of the troops under his control. He was previously commander of Group Soviet Forces Germany based in East Germany, and while there he oversaw the introduction of the concept of the Operational Manoeuvre Group which emphasises flexibility and speed in pressing home an attack.

Allied intelligence noted that while in East Germany Zaitsev introduced a whole new range of training techniques. Instead of the set piece exercises in which each participant knew and had rehearsed his part, Zaitsev insisted that such exercises be more realistic. There was greater emphasis on individual initiative and more junior officers were encouraged to make decisions on their own. An interesting illustration of Zaitsev's thinking comes from an article on tactics which he wrote in 1982.

'Tactics. To a military man the very sound of the word means movement, changes in a situation and constant mental effort. And that is what tactics really are – an integral part of military art: ever developing, reacting sensitively to changes in technology, in armaments, in means of control, in the enemy's methods of operation. Tactics and routine are poor bedfellows. . . . To learn how to fight, to learn what is necessary in battle means to possess a whole variety of tactical skills, and always to bear in mind that it is only he who relies on prowess rather than numbers in a battle and who is capable of creativity and initiative who will win through in the end.'[15]

In Germany, Zaitsev's thinking and the strength of his personality made him into something of a cult figure among the military. With admirable impartiality, one of his colleagues, writing in a Soviet army journal, describes him:

'Nature perhaps was the reason why he joined the ranks of fighting men, having been endowed with a tall physique, huge powerful shoulders, herculean strength and an iron will. But this is not all; he has developed and strengthened a natural instinct and the character of a commander. Purposefulness, ability to organise and lead. Furthermore, during moments of acute tension . . . you would never hear him utter a coarse word or oath.'[16]

This apparent paragon has taken the Soviet campaign in Afghanistan to its most commanding position since the war began. From a military standpoint therefore, there is no reason to suppose that Soviet resolve in fighting the war is weakening.

A further example of the importance the Soviets have attached to the spetsnaz operations comes from allied intelligence. Many Soviet radio transmissions are routinely intercepted both by satellites and listening posts in Pakistan and Turkey, and are routinely decoded by America's National Security Agency and Britain's GCHQ. This information has led western intelligence to believe that since the deployment of spetsnaz forces in Afghanistan the KGB has developed a new covert unit of its own. No doubt piqued by their old rivals the GRU getting so much of the action, the KGB has set up an active measures unit to rival them.

This is an interesting departure and marks a significant

change from the early 1970s when the active measures units in the KGB were cut back. In 1971, the KGB had its own extensive active measures section known as Department V. Then an attaché with the Soviet Trade Delegation in London, Oleg Lyalin, defected to Britain. He brought with him documents which supplied clear proof of Soviet KGB plans for sabotage and assassination in Britain. Included in the documents were photographs and detailed maps of landing sites for saboteurs around Liverpool; a scenario to assassinate Prince Charles at his investiture as Prince of Wales; and plans to drop radioactive isotopes into the water at Holy Loch in Scotland to poison submariners and workers responsible for Britain's nuclear deterrent.

In an operation codenamed Foot, Sir Alec Douglas-Home, the British Foreign Secretary, expelled or barred 105 Soviet officials, working from a list supplied by Lyalin. The result of the purge was that Department V was downgraded to the S Directorate of Department 8. However, it now appears that the KGB are looking for a share in the kind of sabotage and assassination tasks currently undertaken by spetsnaz.

Governments and the media in the west tend to regard the Soviet campaign in Afghanistan falsely, in simple ideological terms. As one US intelligence analyst puts it: 'The temptation among western commentators increasingly has been to surface the Vietnam analogue, with images of a giant superpower bogged down by primitive yet determined insurgents. This may be comforting but it is wide of the mark. Afghanistan, while costly, is viewed by the Soviet military as the first operational laboratory since World War II.'[17]

More than 60,000 officers have now seen service in Afghanistan, the majority of Soviet special forces have been in action in the country and, increasingly, the Soviets are using troops who would normally be deployed against Nato forces.

Western governments place a great deal of emphasis on the poor fighting quality of Soviet troops in Afghanistan and the fact that there is evidence of extensive drug-taking and disenchantment with the war, Much of this is exaggerated.

It is true that there have been some desertions but given the size of the Soviet commitment to the country these are not even approaching the problems the Americans experienced in Vietnam. Drug-taking and alcoholism exist, but neither in their scale nor in their effect on the war can they be seen as particularly significant.

Morale among Soviet troops seems to vary widely. It has certainly improved since better-trained forces were introduced to replace the predominantly Moslem forces that came in after the invasion. Afghanistan is a miserable country to fight in especially when faced with guerrillas of the skill and brutality of the mujahedeen. It is hardly surprising there is some unhappiness among the Soviet forces but it does seem to have been kept within reasonable bounds. An interesting personal insight into the life of a Soviet soldier comes from an article written by Captain S. Dyshev in November 1985:

'What is the most difficult thing about service in Afghanistan? Ask those who have been there and they will tell you. They will tell you about the heat, about the dust storms, about the gloomy silence of the mountains outside the window of your tent. They will impart tales of the difficult life in the field, when you suddenly begin to pine acutely and hopelessly for things which used to be very ordinary. Of course, they will tell you about the insidious Dushman ambushes which can be lying in wait for you in the most unexpected places. Waiting is very difficult, they will tell you. Waiting for that coveted, and yet seemingly so unrealisable distant meeting with your nearest and dearest.

'But, all the same, the most difficult thing of all is to find yourself without your comrades in a tricky situation, without their help and support. Everyone who has been even just once in the mountains far away from his unit will tell you this.'[18]

All things considered, when military successes are combined with their scorched earth policy and the comprehensive indoctrination of Afghan youth, the Soviets seem in a stronger position than ever before. Speculation that they are anxious for a face-saving agreement so they can withdraw from a too-costly war shows a basic misunderstanding of Moscow's resolve and strategic considerations. The Soviets originally invaded Afghanistan because they feared the rise of an independent regime in Kabul that might be used as a base for Moslem extremists. This possibility remains, and therefore, until a Soviet-approved regime is solidly established, the Soviets will not leave. Meanwhile, an apparent Soviet willingness to discuss withdrawal is useful propaganda to undermine foreign criticism. The war may be expensive in cash and manpower, but Moscow will never sanction a withdrawal that would leave Afghanistan open to the mujahedeen.

Furthermore, should the Soviets leave it seems likely that Afghanistan would swiftly collapse into the kind of civil war that was already taking place before the invasion. It is true that a united front between the moderates and the fundamentalists has been formed and seems to be holding together. But it is a fragile alliance that only exists while they have a common enemy, and anyway does not include the Shia guerrillas who are operating out of Iran. All the more reason then for the Soviets to stay.

Meanwhile, the Soviets are still looking for a political leader who will be acceptable to the Afghan population. Babrak Karmal was an abject failure and was removed, and in May 1986 General Najib, the former head of the Afghan secret police, was appointed General Secretary. In a style that must have been personally approved by Mikhail Gorbachev, the new Afghan leader has criticised the corruption and poor economic performance of his countrymen. However, this is unlikely to have much impact among the population at large who still, correctly, see the Soviets as the real government in Afghanistan

In several years of war as many as one million Afghans may have been killed and another three to five million forced over the border into Pakistan and Iran as refugees in what has become known as 'migratory genocide'. At the same time, more than 10,000 young Afghani people have been taken back to the Soviet Union for indoctrination. Clearly Moscow hopes that a combination of scorched earth, genocide and indoctrination will, over a long period, eliminate opposition and produce a population willing to embrace the Soviet way of life.

For their part, the Soviets have lost 10,000–15,000 killed and perhaps 30,000 wounded out of an occupying force of roughly 115,000. They have also lost around 1,000 aircraft and several thousand vehicles. These losses are perfectly tolerable when placed in the context of previous Soviet campaigns, where they have demonstrated a single-mindedness and a ruthlessness unthinkable in the West. For example, in a 10-year campaign of nationalist suppression in Lithuania, ending in 1956, the Soviets had 80,000 army casualties and about 5,000 civilian officials were killed.

It is also significant that no critical media exists inside the Soviet Union to whip up public concern about the war, and no electorate is eager to go to the ballot box to express their disapproval of government policy. The Soviet leadership can do what it likes for as long as it likes, and therefore it is their narrow judgement alone that will decide the course of the war.

The withdrawal of six regiments of Soviet forces in November 1985 should be seen in the overall context of the war. The Soviets emphasised that this was a major concession and a conciliatory gesture. It was nothing of the kind. It was simply an opportunity to remove conventional anti-aircraft and tank units that were a wasted asset in what had become a truly unconventional war.

Despite a new Soviet sophistication, however, the guerrillas too have improved their capabilities. Communications between many of the groups remains fragmented but there is some common leadership. More arms and equipment are being supplied, particularly by the United States – although it is unclear how much of that is filtering through the web of corruption, which includes a growing drug network, that surrounds the guerrilla movement. As the Soviets have made more use of helicopters, so the guerrillas have received their first Stinger missiles from the United States, which they are using to good effect.

Most importantly, a new generation of leaders has emerged in the guerrilla movement. Many of these men are in their twenties, have had rudimentary training in guerrilla warfare, and are proving formidable opponents.

But, in a war marked by brutality and incompetence on both sides, a victor is unlikely. The best either protagonist can hope for is stalemate when – as the British have found in fighting the IRA in Northern Ireland – violence is reduced to a level tolerable to both sides.

In the meantime, the Soviets are using the lessons learned in Afghanistan to devise new tactics for their forces in Europe. In 1986, Nato intelligence has watched new training methods in operation at the secret spetsnaz base at Furstenberg in East Germany. As a testing ground Afghanistan is being put to good use.

PART 7: THE BRITISH EXPERIENCE

15

Attack at Princes Gate

On 20 January 1981, two minutes after Ronald Reagan had been sworn in as President of the United States, Ayatollah Khomeini released the hostages held at the US embassy in Teheran. The timing of their release was a further humiliation to former President Carter, who would attribute his failure at the polls to the debacle at Desert One.

His fate was not lost on the new Republican administration. They fully understood the vulnerability of American power and prestige to the actions of a few determined individuals, whether sponsored by governments or acting independently.

Terrorism around the world was on the rise and Americans seemed to be a favourite target. At the same time, the influence of communism around the world appeared to be growing with the establishment of a communist government in Nicaragua, the Soviet invasion of Afghanistan, continued Cuban involvement in Angola, and signs of Soviet-supported action against the South African government by the African National Congress.

To President Reagan and his close advisers this seemed to confirm their worst fears: that communist subversion was undermining the free world and endangering western democracies, in particular the United States. And in a world of black and white, with no grey shading, it was up to the United States to stand up for what was right. This simplistic view of the world, so different from Carter's pragmatism and obsession with detail, was to colour every aspect of the administration's foreign and military policy.

During the early part of his first term, therefore, the President evolved a policy that eventually became known as 'the Reagan Doctrine'. As we have already seen, at its most basic level this involved US support for right wing, preferably democratic, governments or for groups that wished to establish such governments or, to put it another way, Reagan had decided to take on the Brezhnev Doctrine which talked of the 'irreversibility of socialist gains' around the world. At first this policy was one of containment, of stopping Soviet expansion wherever possible. But, as the policy evolved it changed to concentrate on rollback, or forcing the communists out of countries where they had won influence. This was a fundamental tenet of the Reagan administration and vital to an understanding of the importance they placed on special forces which were seen as the spearhead of this movement.

At the United Nations, President Reagan stated that one American objective was 'the elimination of the foreign military presence and restraint on the flow of outside arms' to troubled nations where the wars were 'the consequence of an ideology imposed from without, dividing nations and creating regimes that are, almost from the day they take power, at war with their own people.' The President argued that change should, if possible, come through negotiations but 'until such time as these negotiations result in definitive progress, America's support for struggling democratic resistance forces must not and shall not cease.'[1]

But the administration had seen an America made to appear impotent by Iranian revolutionaries holding US hostages, and by an aggressive Soviet Union invading the free country of Afghanistan. So, if it was agreed that more should be done, the question was what tools would be suitable for the job? A revitalisation of US special forces was seen as a key part of this more assertive policy. This idea had many detractors in the political and military establishment, but while the first revitalisation steps were being taken, a number of events occurred that were to endorse perfectly the arguments of its supporters.

At 11.15 on the morning of 30 April 1980, six days after the failure of the American rescue mission in Iran, the telephone rang at SAS headquarters in Hereford. On the line from London was a former SAS NCO, Dusty Gray, who had left the regiment to join the Metropolitan Police as a dog handler. He was, he explained, outside the Iranian embassy in Princes Gate, London. It had been taken over by terrorists, and he felt that the SAS should know they might be called in.[2]

Without any further notice, the Counter-Revolutionary Warfare unit from B Squadron 22 SAS loaded up their special Land Rovers and headed up the M4 motorway to London. The SAS have an arrangement with the police that allows for the outside lane of the motorway to be closed to all traffic so they have a clear run to the site of an emergency, but on this occasion, as they were acting without authority, they did not take advantage of this.

Control of the SAS works at two levels. During a crisis, particularly one involving acts of terrorism, a special unit is chaired by the Home Secretary and includes representatives from the Ministry of Defence, the Security Service (MI5), the Foreign and Commonwealth Office and the SAS. This unit, known as COBRA after the Cabinet Office Briefing Room in London's Downing Street where it meets, dictates both the military and political response to the crisis.

For actual operations, a special cell within the Ministry of Defence, called the Joint Operations Centre or JOC, which includes members from the regiment, the Foreign Office, Home Office and the intelligence services, is responsible for activating the SAS either at home or abroad. On 30 April formal authorisation for the move from Hereford came from the Home Office via the Ministry of Defence cell some six hours later, after it had in fact arrived in London.

Earlier that morning, five terrorists, who claimed to be members of a previously unknown group, the Democratic

Revolutionary Front for the Liberation of Arabistan, backed by Iraq, had forced their way past the police guard on the Iranian embassy door. The leader of the group, Salim Towfigh, also known as Oan, demanded a plane to take his band, their twenty-six hostages and an Arab ambassador to an unnamed Arab country.

All the hostages were Iranian, with the exception of Police Constable Trevor Lock, the embassy police guard, and Sim Harris, a BBC sound recordist who had been at the embassy to arrange for a visa.

In keeping with long-standing policy, the British began to negotiate. The intention was to wear out the terrorists and at the same time allow a relationship to build between them and their hostages and between them and the negotiator. It had been learned in the past that the longer a hostage situation lasts, the more likely is a peaceful outcome. Invariably a terrorist and his hostage draw closer together, both fearful of what the authorities might do, and this makes the terrorist increasingly reluctant to kill his hostage. At the same time, the negotiator, through careful use of what bribes he has – usually food and water – can build a Pavlovian relationship between himself and the terrorist leader. The negotiator becomes the friendly figure holding off the brutal forces who want to kill the terrorists. His persuasive powers can often result in the terrorists surrendering. In this case five of the hostages were in fact released in exchange for food in the course of the negotiations.

From the outset, the SAS assumed that they would have to go in to rescue the hostages. At a nearby barracks they first constructed a small scale model of the embassy and then a full scale replica. They managed to plant a number of very sensitive listening devices from the next-door building and drill tiny holes in the embassy wall, which allowed cameras with lenses no bigger than pinheads to be inserted. These devices helped build up a picture of exactly who was where inside the building and what sort of routine the terrorists were keeping.

The picture was not good. The embassy had fifty rooms and the terrorists were located on three floors with the hostages mostly kept to one floor, but in two different rooms. Any assault would have to be fast enough to simultaneously bring fire to bear on every room that held terrorists and hostages. Any delay would put the lives of the hostages in jeopardy.

On Monday 5 May the patience of the terrorists finally ran out. Infuriated by the endless delays in deadlines for the aircraft to be provided, their leader Salim killed the press attaché to the embassy, Abbas Lavasani, and rolled his body down the front steps in front of the waiting television cameras.

On the direct orders of the Prime Minister, Margaret Thatcher, the SAS were commanded to attack. On these occasions, authority is still preserved in the civil power, the police, being only temporarily handed over to the SAS. Immediately after the action, the police once again take over and an exhaustive examination is undertaken to make sure there has been no wrongdoing, i.e. an excess use of force resulting in unnecessary deaths.

This is a key aspect to the position of the SAS. On no occasion do they act independently of the civil power, instead they are there solely to provide military advice, and assistance if required.

On this occasion, it was made clear to the SAS that they were to take no prisoners. The government recognised that captured terrorists tried in British courts and sentenced to long terms in British prisons would simply make the country a more prominent target for terrorists wishing to force the release of their comrades. As one Ministry of Defence source puts it: 'There would have been a degree of awkwardness about too many survivors.'[3]

There was some concern at these instructions, and assurances were asked for and given that, provided the SAS followed the rules of engagement allowing for the use of force in self-defence, there would be no comeback from any subsequent police inquiry.

Just before 19.00 on 5 May the assault began. One group of SAS men abseiled down from the roof while another team made a frontal assault, using shaped charges to blow in the embassy's armoured windows. The operation nearly degenerated into disaster when the main assault team burst into a room where they thought there would be both terrorists and hostages, only to find neither – and also no way of getting access to the rest of the embassy. This critical planning failure gave the terrorists time to shoot a hostage and wound several more before others of the SAS assault teams, preparing their way with flash-bangs, were able to reach the critical rooms.

Some of the terrorists did manage both to fire their guns and throw a grenade in the first few, vital seconds causing injuries to at least three hostages. But, as soon as the terrorists realised they were outnumbered and outgunned, they threw down their arms and mingled with the hostages. Nonetheless, all except one of them were killed. According to one former member of the SAS, one terrorist had eighty-two bullet wounds, a surprisingly high figure, given the SAS emphasis on minimum force.

Afterwards there were allegations, particularly from some of the hostages, that the SAS had executed the terrorists after they had surrendered. While there was undoubtedly a feeling that the best terrorist is a dead terrorist, the SAS are trained to kill all those who are clearly identified as a threat and to get any hostages out of the building as fast as possible. This particular operation took eleven minutes from start to finish and during that time there can have been little opportunity to ask a clearly identified terrorist whether or not he was armed, or was really surrendering.

Uniquely for a counter-terrorist assault, the whole operation was watched live on television by the British public. Although television cameras had been officially banned from the immediate area, one had been smuggled in and even recorded the actual assault.

The SAS learned important lessons. They had been practising for seven years for just such an assault, but now that the terrorists, along with the general public, had seen their perfected techniques in action, new ones would have to be devised. The next time around, terrorists will not keep their hostages in one place but will constantly change their location and vary the numbers of hostages in each group. They will also be aware of the surveillance techniques available against them and can be expected to take precautions.

A second lesson is connected with television coverage. As one former SAS officer puts it: 'It could all so easily have been a disaster. If the terrorists had been watching television at the time, they would have known we were coming and it would have had a very different ending.' Next time, television can perhaps be exploited, possibly by broadcasting a pre-recorded cassette showing peace and quiet around the building as the assault begins.

The Iranian embassy assault was the first of its type to take place on British soil. It was a vindication of the CRW wing and the importance the British government had placed on developing a counter-terrorist capability. But the SAS had equally important roles both in the event of war and in projecting the influence of the British government overseas. In the space of two years both were to be tested.

16

Three Men and a Coup

Modern communications have made life very difficult for secret armies. For those who really wish to operate in secret, as opposed to the guerrilla armies who actively seek publicity, secrecy can often help success while the unwelcome attention of the media can often bring failure.

But, even in a country as open as the United States, where public accountability is a cornerstone of the democratic system, the special operations forces have frequently managed to operate away from the public. In Britain, where secrecy is a national tradition and governments are used to suppressing unwelcome information, operations run by the SAS and the SBS have continued almost uninterrupted by the attentions of the media or by scrutiny from elected officials.

This freedom has allowed the special forces to fight in foreign countries with a freedom unthinkable in the United States. One such operation, which has never before been revealed and which is still not officially admitted by the British government, occurred at the end of July 1981.

The wedding of Prince Charles to Lady Diana Spencer on 29 July 1981 provided the perfect opportunity for Libyan- and Cuban-backed rebels in the tiny west African country of the Gambia to attempt a coup. While the Gambian president, Sir Dawda Jawara, was sitting in Westminster Abbey, a 500-strong rebel force moved to seize the country's radio station, the palace, and the airport, and to take hostages from among the cabinet and the President's family.

News of the attempted coup reached the British Foreign Office in London on 30 July. The British ambassador in the country's capital, Banjul, reported heavy fighting and that the radio station had been taken over and was now broadcasting Marxist propaganda in the name of a National Revolutionary Council. The broadcasts said that the council would introduce a 'dictatorship of the proletariat' led by a 'Marxist-Leninist party' to promote 'revolutionary socialism.'[1]

The Gambia had received its independence from Britain in 1965, but ties between the two countries remained close. Although it covers an area of only 4,361 square miles with a population of 600,000, it had become popular with British tourists and was held up as a fine example of a working democracy in Africa. Opposition parties were allowed in its parliament and the leader of the main opposition party was paid a salary by the government. Free elections were held and as there was no effective standing army there was little interference from any military clique. All of this made a persuasive argument for Britain doing its best to quell the attempted coup.

The Foreign Office consulted France, which had very good relations with Gambia's neighbour, Senegal, then spoke to Washington, who were known to be very concerned about any Libyan-backed expansion in the region, and finally telephoned to Hereford, the headquarters of the SAS.

The call was taken by Major Ian Crooke, then second-in-command of 22nd Regiment of the SAS. He in turn alerted his commander, who was walking with his two children in the Welsh hills. Responding to his bleeper, the commander found a telephone, spoke to Crooke, and ordered him to take whatever he needed and get out to Banjul by any means possible.

Crooke and two colleagues took a flight to Paris with bags filled with rifles, grenades, explosives and a satellite communications system so that he could keep in constant touch with Hereford. The fastest way to Banjul was by Air France which had a plane leaving that same day. The problem of the bags filled with explosives and other dangerous items was overcome by Crooke making a call to a diplomat he knew at the British embassy in Paris who in turn knew an employee at Air France who arranged for the three men to bypass all the normal security checks and board the flight carrying their dangerous cargo (this subsequently caused a major diplomatic row between Paris and London).

Events in Banjul had meanwhile become very confused. The French, in consultation with London and President Jawara, had sent in French-trained paratroopers from neighbouring Senegal who had secured the airport, and the President had returned there from London. But the rebels had consolidated their hold on the capital and were known to have taken twenty-eight senior officials including Lady Thielal N'Diaye, one of Sir Dawda's two wives, and her four children hostage, and neither the President nor the Senegalese had any clear idea about how they should proceed. The hostages were being held at the headquarters of the Gambian Field Force in the village of Bakau, seven miles west of Banjul.

Kukli Samba Sanyang, the rebel leader, said on the radio that he was ready to kill the President's family unless the Senegalese troops withdrew. 'Jawara can't frighten me. The country is with us and I hold . . . the power to execute the prisoners – the Jawara family and the members of the government.'

After a meeting with the President, the SAS men were given a free hand to do whatever they felt was necessary to liberate the hostages and put down the revolution. Crooke then moved through the Senegalese lines around the airport, through the rebel lines that surrounded them, and arrived at the British embassy in Banjul. To his amazement, he found the ambassador hiding under a table, although the sporadic mortar fire at the time hardly seemed to justify such precautions.

From sources at the embassy, Crooke learned that the President's wife had been moved, with one of her children, who had a fever, to the Medial Research Centre in the capital.

The three SAS men, whom eyewitnesses reported as being in civilian clothes but festooned with weapons and grenades, headed for the hospital. The guards posted on the gates were distracted by Crooke, a white man, walking up to them apparently unarmed. His two colleagues moved behind and overpowered them. Inside the hospital, a British doctor persuaded the guards looking after the President's wife that their guns were distressing the other patients and after some argument they laid them down outside the ward. The SAS men then freed Lady Thielal and took her and her child back to the British embassy.

Meanwhile, Senegalese troops had made an attempt to break through the rebel lines and relieve Banjul. Their attack was poorly planned and co-ordinated, however, and they were beaten back. The three SAS men therefore returned through the rebel lines to the airport, rallied a small group of the Senegalese troops who had received counter-terrorism training, and launched an assault that not only quickly broke the rebels' hold on the airport, but four days later led to the total collapse of the coup and the arrest of all its leaders – with the exception of Kukli Samba Sanyang, who fled to Cuba.

Throughout the action, two other sideshows had been taking place. The US State Department, wanting to play a part in quelling the Libyan-supported coup, had authorised a team of Delta Force counter-terrorist specialists to fly to Dakar, the capital of Senegal. However, State then got cold feet and Delta were in fact never allowed to go into action. Similar nervousness was exhibited by the British Foreign Office, which demanded regular updates on the whereabouts and plans of the SAS men from their headquarters in Hereford. But, not wanting political interference once the operation was running, Hereford firmly claimed that it had lost all contact with the men: they were known to be heading for the Gambia but any further details were unobtainable because of poor communications. In fact, however, Crooke was in regular contact with his headquarters via his portable satellite communications system.

The Gambia intervention was a classic example of the effective use of special forces. A very small number of highly-trained specialists were able to achieve more than two battalions of regular soldiers could have, and with a great deal less political damage. As it was, the revolution was put down in a week, the outside world never heard of Britain's covert involvement, and the Gambia continues to be a peaceful, democratic country.

A similar but less successful mission began on 23 July 1982, when six tourists – two Americans, two Britons and two Australians – were kidnapped by guerrillas in Zimbabwe. They were taken from their truck about fifty miles north of Bulawayo and dragged into the bush.

Both the British Foreign Office and the US State Department were concerned that the troops of Prime Minister Robert Mugabe were not sufficiently qualified to hunt down the kidnappers. Within hours, a Delta Force team had left Fort Bragg in a C-141 Starlifter transport aircraft on the long journey to Zimbabwe. At the same time three SAS men left Hereford, took a scheduled flight from Britain and arrived in Bulawayo on 29 July. For the next few weeks, the SAS men stayed in the country trying in vain to track down the kidnap victims, who were never seen again; Delta Force got as far as the air base on Ascension Island in the Southern Atlantic and remained there for some days before returning to Fort Bragg.

'They couldn't even get overflight clearance, never mind permission to land in Zimbabwe,' said one US official involved in the mission. 'Our effort was hailed as a great triumph. We had shown an ability to move at a moment's notice but the fact remained we didn't get there so the whole exercise was pointless.'

The Zimbabwe affair demonstrated how widespread the use of special operations forces has become. This was no war or revolution but simply the kidnapping of some British and

American citizens in a foreign country. It seems likely that increasingly groups like the SAS and Delta Force will be used outside what are seen as their traditional roles of countering terrorism and fighting wars to go wherever lives or property are at risk.

17

Operation Corporate

On 2 April 1982 the commanding officer of 22 SAS (the same man who had commanded the assault on the Iranian embassy) was in bed listening to the early morning news on BBC radio. The broadcast led with news of the Argentine invasion of the Falklands and added that the Royal Marines had been put on alert.

D Squadron was immediately placed on stand-by and a call put through to Brigadier Julian Thompson of the Royal Marines to offer the services of the SAS.[1]

The Falkland Islands lie in the South Atlantic about 400 miles from Cape Horn and some 8,000 miles from Great Britain. Sovereignty of the islands had been a matter of dispute for nearly four hundred years and for much of this century the Argentine government had claimed the Falklands, which they called the Malvinas, as their own. Negotiations had sputtered on through different governments in both countries, but with few signs of progress. The islands were of little strategic or military importance to either country and if the British could have found a convenient way of passing them over to the Argentine, they would probably have done so. However, the islands were occupied by 1,800 people, the vast majority of them sheep farmers, British citizens who wished to remain British. They commanded a forceful parliamentary lobby in London, far out of proportion to their size, and had so far managed to undermine any deal with Buenos Aires.

Finally, at a time of great unpopularity for his government, the Argentinian leader, General Galtieri, decided to assert Argentine sovereignty of the islands. Invading with over-whelming force, the Argentines overcame the token British Royal Marine presence at Port Stanley, the country's capital, and on the outlying island of South Georgia. In the following few weeks, the invading army was reinforced to a strength of 12,000.

The British response was swift. Operation Corporate was devised, a plan to take back the islands. A task force was immediately assembled, and only three days after the invasion the first ships set sail for the South Atlantic.

In many ways the campaign that followed was a special operations forces war. The SAS, the SBS, the Royal Marines and their Mountain and Arctic Warfare Cadre, and the Para-chute Regiment were all sent with the task force. Although the story of the war itself is well known, the precise activities of the SAS and the SBS have never been fully described and they will not be here. However, new details of their role have emerged, and these can now safely be revealed.

The same day that the task force sailed, sixty-six men of D Squadron, commanded by Major Cedric Delves, flew out from RAF Brize Norton to Ascension Island accompanied by fourteen signallers and 50,000 pounds of equipment kept permanently available by the SAS, already packed in pallets, for just this type of emergency. The previous day a squad from the SBS had left Faslane in Scotland aboard the submarine HMS *Conqueror*. Both teams would join up in two weeks' time for Operation Paraquat, the retaking of South Georgia.

The status of the SAS and SBS in the forthcoming war was quickly decided. On 3 April Lieutenant-Colonel Michael Rose the commander of 22 SAS met with Brigadier Julian Thompson, the commander of the ground forces during the landing and early part of the operation, and Major General Jeremy Moore, who was to command the final stages of the land battle. It was agreed that both the SAS and the SBS commanders would be integrated into the planning group and that their headquarters would move to HMS *Fearless*, which was to be the planning centre for the landing. In theory this should have made the chain of command quite clear. But the SAS also had direct contact via their satellite communications system with their headquarters at Hereford and via a relay direct to the task force command headquarters at Northwood, and in practice some senior officers, particularly Jeremy Moore, came to resent this freewheeling attitude: in his view they frequently operated without authority.

The SAS were fortunate that Brigadier Thompson had worked with them before, while serving in Northern Ireland. They were not so fortunate with Major-General Moore: he treated them with suspicion and showed little knowledge of their capabilities.

'Moore quite evidently had no understanding of special operations,' said one SAS officer with the task force. 'He kept asking people why they were doing certain things, although he never seriously questioned what we were doing because he quite clearly didn't understand it.' This may be an overly harsh assessment – Moore had seen action in both Aden and Northern Ireland, had the Military Cross and bar for bravery, and had considerable experience of unconventional warfare.

The special forces' role was underlined at a key planning meeting on board the task force flagship, HMS *Hermes*, on 16 April. Chaired by the Commander-in-Chief (Fleet), Sir John Fieldhouse, the purpose of the meeting was to generate a general discussion on the problems and options associated with an invasion of the islands. More than a hundred officers gathered in the briefing room and, after a preliminary speech which underlined the political resolve that supported the task force, the discussion was opened to the floor. A clear definition of the special forces' role in the operation was set out as: 1 – intelligence gathering, and 2 – interdiction before and possibly after the landings. The operation to retake South Georgia fitted the defined roles exactly.

In the context of the main invasion, South Georgia was a sideshow. Situated one thousand miles south of the main

Falkland Islands, the island possessed only an old whaling station at Leith, which had been occupied by Argentine scrap merchants early in March, and a British Antarctic Survey station at Grytviken. Otherwise the island was uninhabited, and even for that part of the world was unusually inhospitable. High cliffs, glaciers and a constant bitter wind, often combined with driving snow and freezing temperatures, all ensured that even the most hardy traveller gave it a wide berth. But the retaking of the island was considered by the government in London to be an important demonstration of political will. If successful, it would once again show a British presence on the islands and reassure Britain's allies of her determination.

In theory such an assault should not have been particularly difficult for highly trained special forces, but the inhospitable surroundings, combined with appalling weather, created severe problems. The operation was commanded by Major Guy Sheridan of the Royal Marines, who had sailed on the County class destroyer HMS *Antrim* with M Company 42 Commando on board and the Type 12 frigate *Plymouth* providing escort along with the nuclear submarine HMS *Conqueror*. The tanker *Tidespring* and the auxiliary *Bramblelea* completed the force. It was to the SBS and the SAS that he turned for early reconnaissance. There was almost nothing known about the disposition of the Argentine force on South Georgia, so Sheridan asked the SBS to investigate Grytviken, and the SAS Leith.

In a classic covert operation, the SBS were successfully inserted into Hound Bay, in observation range of Grytviken. All the men landed safely and immediately began filing intelligence back to the small naval task force waiting over the horizon.

The SAS were not so fortunate. In order to ensure their landing went undetected, and against the repeated advice of the experts who believed the weather too cold to permit prolonged exposure, the SAS insisted on attempting to land on the Fortuna Glacier. On 21 April, after two helicopter approaches over the glacier north-east of Leith had been aborted because of the appalling weather, a third attempt was finally successful. However, the men of 19 Troop, commanded by 29-year-old John Hamilton, immediately found themselves at the mercy of weather that allowed them to move only 500 metres in the first five hours. The wind was blowing in excess of 100 m.p.h., driving snow and ice off the surface of the glacier and cutting visibility to a few feet at best. The advance across the glacier had to be made with the men roped together, the lead man probing ahead for crevasses.

After an exceptionally uncomfortable night huddled in a shallow depression, the men asked to be withdrawn before some of them died from the cold. Three helicopters were launched from the fleet and, guided by a homing beacon, landed on the glacier. After takeoff, the lead helicopter headed safely away down the glacier towards the sea, as did the third, but the second helicopter was hit by a sudden snowstorm which immediately cut visibility to zero. The pilot lost his horizon and the aircraft fell two hundred feet, onto the ice. Fortunately, just before the crash the pilot had pulled the helicopter up so that the tail rotor hit first. Injuries to the men were slight and they were able to transfer to the other two helicopters that returned for them. Now heavily over-loaded, these took off. Exactly the same sequence of events occurred. The lead helicopter flew out safely, while the second crashed into the glacier, again without any serious injury. Major Guy Sheridan takes up the story:

'Now we had thirteen men ashore who needed rescue pretty quickly if they were to survive the dreadful conditions on the glacier. It was not possible to fly off until the afternoon came when Ian Stanley and Chris Parry (his co-pilot) again took off. We all thought there was little chance of anyone coming out alive. About half an hour later Ian radioed to say he had found them and was picking them up. What we didn't realise was that Ian had assessed that this would be the only chance and that to take half the survivors would leave the rest out for the night and everything that meant. So he put the whole lot in on top of each other and flew back to *Antrim* sixteen men up! Quite unbelievable, and what a daring and skilful pilot Ian Stanley is.'[2]

Despite Stanley's bravery (for which he was awarded the DSO) the operation had been a complete failure.

The next day, 23 April, 17 Troop tried a different approach. Five Gemini rubber boats were launched from the naval task force. But they were powered by notoriously unreliable Johnson 40 outboard motors, three of which broke down on the way to the shore. One of the three-man boats was swept out to sea and, after an uncomfortable night bobbing about in the Antarctic Ocean, was rescued the following day. Another managed to paddle to shore, landing on the southernmost tip of the island in the shadow of Mount Carse, where they spent five days holed up before radioing for help. The third boat was towed to shore by the remaining two. Once they were ashore, however, wind-driven ice splinters punctured the ballast tanks of the Geminis, rendering them useless and tying the reconnaissance force to the landing site, some distance from the Argentine positions.

The SBS force at Grytviken reported the next day that an Argentine submarine was in the area. Unwilling to risk his ships, the task force commander dispersed them and withdrew HMS *Endurance*, the commando support vessel, 200 miles from South Georgia. Then, the following day, the weather improved, and with it the luck of the assault force.

On the morning of 25 April a Wessex helicopter spotted an unidentified radar contact moving on the surface out from Grytviken harbour. The task force immediately launched Wasp anti-submarine helicopters which made contact with an Argentine Guppy class submarine, the *Sante Fe*, and attacked with torpedoes, depth charges and machine-gun fire. The submarine was badly damaged and returned to the harbour.

Guy Sheridan was anxious to press home his advantage but his commandos were still out of range of the island and by the time their ship had sailed within striking distance the opportunity would have been lost. Sheridan and Major Delves gathered together all the available men from *Antrim* and produced an assault force of seventy-five, made up of Marines, SAS and SBS. That afternoon, after a preliminary bombardment from naval frigates, the first of the assault force was helicoptered ashore. Corporal Davey, a member of D Squadron, recounts what happened next:

'All SAS troops were helicoptered ashore, landing on an area of flat ground known as the Hesterleten, two kilometres south-east of the British Antarctic Survey. The Troop formed up in all round defence to await the arrival of some thirty men from M company, 42 commando, and the commander of the operation, Major Sheridan, Royal Marines. . . . Having shaken out for an advance to contact, we engaged likely enemy positions, and by this time naval gunfire was supporting our advance.

'In the area where the Brown Mountain ridge line joined the coast we saw what appeared to be men in brown balaclavas among the tussock grass. They were engaged by GPMG (General Purpose Machine-Gun) fire from approximately 800 metres and by naval gunfire. Captain Hamilton and I also engaged a possible enemy position on the top of Brown Mountain with Milan (shoulder-fired anti-tank missiles). Advancing across open ground towards the ridge line we discovered that the balaclava'd enemy were in fact seven or eight elephant seals, which were now somewhat the worse for wear. The enemy position on Brown Mountain had been a piece of angle iron on which we had scored a direct hit.'³

Softened up by the heavy naval bombardment, the Argentine garrison of 140 men put up no resistance either at Grytviken or Leith. The Union Jack was run up the flagpole outside the British Antarctic Survey building and South Georgia was once again back in British hands.

The taking of South Georgia was a very costly military operation that had been pursued solely because of the political imperatives driving it. Nevertheless, both the SBS and in particular the SAS had insisted on landing men when they had been clearly told the weather was unsuitable and the conditions on the island extremely dangerous. The result was the loss of two helicopters, which were in very short supply to the task force, and the fact that there was no heavy loss of life was due solely to the exceptional bravery of one helicopter pilot.

Nevertheless, four SAS operations are worth highlighting as they clearly demonstrate the versatility of such a force when working in support of conventional forces.

The Argentine soldiers were commanded by Major-General Mario Menendez who had decided early on in the campaign to concentrate them around Port Stanley. He established well-fortified outposts at every point in the island where he thought a British landing was likely. As soon as an approaching force was spotted he planned to reinforce the relevant outpost with troops from Port Stanley, using Chinook, Huey and Bell helicopters. Realising how vulnerable these were to artillery or air attack, he moved them each night and camouflaged them during the day. Undeniably, therefore, his forces were both superior and highly mobile, and why he never took advantage of them has been a previously unexplained mystery of the war.

At the beginning of May however, when G Squadron of the SAS had joined the task force bringing the SAS contingent up to 125 men, a four-man unit from G Squadron, commanded by Captain Aldwin Wight of the Welsh Guards, was inserted to the Port Stanley area by a helicopter launched from HMS *Hermes*, 120 miles away. For twenty-six days Wight and his team followed Menendez's helicopters around East Falkland. Each night they had to evacuate their hastily dug 'scrapes' in the ground, pack up their camouflage netting and trek across the island through minefields and the Argentine lines to find the next site where the helicopters had been hidden. Three times Wight called in an air strike. Twice the strikes failed because, by the time the Harrier bombers reached the grid reference, the helicopters had been moved.

But the third strike was successful and the majority of the
helicopters were destroyed. Wight's reconnaissance operation
was a quite extraordinary feat of courage and endurance, and
it had a critical effect on the outcome of the war. When the
British landings began on 21 May the Argentines were unable
to oppose the landings from the battalion-strength force at
Goose Green ten kilometres away because they had no helicopters. Also, even when the BBC actually announced an
impending attack by the British at Goose Green on 28 May,
Menendez still had only two helicopters left with which to
reinforce. If he had had his total fleet available the outcome
of the San Carlos landings, the battle at Goose Green, and
indeed the whole war might have been very different.

The citation in the *London Gazette*, which announced the
award of the Military Cross to Wight, said in part:

'Inserted by helicopter . . . he positioned his patrol in close
proximity to enemy positions, cut off from any form of rescue
should he have been compromised. This position he maintained for twenty-six days. During this time he produced clear
and accurate pictures of enemy activity in the Stanley area,
intelligence available from no other means, which proved
vital in the planning of the final assault . . .

'In spite of his exposed position, vulnerable to air and
ground search and the Tactical Direction Finding of his
communications, his intelligence reports were detailed and
regularly updated. The conditions in which he and his men
existed were appalling with little cover from view or the
elements. The weather conditions varied from freezing rain
to gale force winds with few clear days.'[4]

If helicopters for troop reinforcement were one worry,
ground attack aircraft that could do considerable damage
to British forces after the landing were another. The main
concentration of Argentine aircraft in the Falklands was on
Pebble Island, a rocky outcrop to the north of West Falkland.
On the airstrip at Pebble Island was a concentration of eleven
Pucara ground attack aircraft. These are specifically designed
for counter-insurgency and, loaded with napalm or firing their

extensive armament of rockets and machine-guns, they can do immense damage to troops on the ground.

On the night of 11 May eight men from D Squadron were landed by helicopter on West Falkland from where they intended to paddle by canoe to nearby Pebble Island. The weather was too rough that night to launch the fragile canoes and so it was not until the following night that they were able to make the crossing. They reported that a group of some one hundred Argentines was guarding the airfield.

On the night of 14 May the main British assault force of forty-eight men, commanded by Major Cedric Delves, was flown in by helicopter to land five miles from the airfield. They met up with the advance party from D Squadron and walked across the island to the airfield. The Argentine barracks were some half-mile from the airfield and it wasn't until the attackers started pouring machine-gun fire and 66mm rockets into the aircraft that the enemy was alerted. The SAS men moved swiftly among the planes planting explosives, and then began to withdraw.

The Argentines launched a half-hearted counter-attack which petered out when the SAS shot and killed the officer leading it. However, they detonated a mine by remote control injuring one SAS soldier, and another took a bullet in his leg. The party were withdrawn by helicopter, leaving eleven aircraft and a fuel dump totally destroyed.

It was a classic SAS operation, the daring and success of which did as much to raise spirits among the friendly forces and hit the morale of the enemy as similar actions had done in the war against the Axis forty years before.

The air threat had not been entirely removed by the attack on Pebble Island, however. There remained a strong Argentine air force of Mirage and Skyhawk fighters, supplemented by the French-built Super Etendard fighter armed with Exocet missiles, operating from three air bases, at Rio Grande near Ushuaia on the southern tip of Argentina, Rio Gallegos in the south-east, and Commodoro Rivadavia in the north-east. Even though the distance to the Falklands was such that they would be operating at the extreme edge of their range, all these aircraft were threatening to the task force – and none more so than the Super Etendard. The Exocet missile has a range of more than forty-five miles and can travel at super-sonic speeds. The British fleet had no real protection against this kind of modern system, and if the Argentine Air Force were allowed to operate with impunity the task force would suffer heavy losses.

Opposing the Argentine Air Force were the limited surface-to-air missile systems of the frigates, destroyers and carriers, some hand-held missiles such as Blowpipe and Stinger, and the heavily outnumbered Sea Harriers. The problem of Argentine air superiority was therefore acute. An armed attack on bases on the Argentine mainland was ruled out, however; it would be seen by the world as an escalation of the war by Britain who was anxious to portray herself as an aggrieved innocent party under assault by expansionist Argentines. (This is also why suggested attacks on leading political and military figures on the mainland if the war should go badly for Britain were also ruled out.)

But, within those constraints, timely intelligence was never-theless vital to the task force if it was to present an adequate defence to the Argentine Air Force and therefore, by the middle of May, it had been decided that special forces units should be inserted into Argentina to provide intelligence on Air Force movements and, if possible, to deal positively with the Exocet threat.

Under normal circumstances this would have been a natural task for the SAS, but G Squadron was already heavily committed on other reconnaissance missions and D Squadron was about to attack Pebble Island. It was decided, therefore, to send units from both the SAS and SBS.

During the night of 17 May, two Sea King helicopters, numbers ZA 290 and ZA 292, fitted with night vision equip-ment and navigation equipment to allow night flying with pin point accuracy, transferred from the aircraft carrier *Hermes* to the *Invincible*. With the Type 22 destroyer HMS *Broadsword*,

Invincible immediately broke away from the task force and headed west at twenty-five knots. Both ships observed total radio silence and navigated with their radars shut down, in order to avoid any possibility of being picked up by overflying Argentine aircraft or shore-based detection systems.[5]

At 03.15 on the morning of 18 May, ZA 290 commanded by Lt. Richard Hutchings, Royal Marines, with Lt. A.R.C. Bennett and LACMN P.B. Imrie as crew, took off from *Invincible* and headed west. On board were men from the SAS. The helicopter was spotted by two different Argentine radars, but the triangulated fix suggested that it was headed for a farm owned by a German named Braun, thirty kilometres from Rio Gallegos, which was used as a fuel store by the Argentines. Several hundred troops were therefore moved to the area to counter the perceived threat. In fact, the SAS men were dropped off undetected many miles away, within striking distance of Rio Grande, from where they supplied valuable information for the rest of the war.

The helicopter then either crashed or was landed and was destroyed by its crew on a beach at Agua Fresca, eleven miles south of Punta Arenas in Chile. The helicopter and its equipment cost around £4.5m but was willingly sacrificed. The crew gave themselves up to the Chilean authorities a few days later and were flown back to Britain. Hutchings and Bennett were awarded the Distinguished Service Cross and Imrie the Distinguished Service Medal.

Other reconnaissance units are believed to have been put ashore by submarine to cover the airfields at Rio Gallegos and Commodoro Rivadavia, where they spent the remainder of the war huddled at the end of the runways, sending back information on the numbers, armament, course and take-off times of Argentine aircraft. This information gave the task force vital minutes in which to prepare for attacks.

Although the information sent back by the SBS was valuable, it could undeniably have been better if they had had completely up-to-date communications equipment. Neither they nor the SAS had portable radios that allowed for burst transmission or the condensing of lengthy signals into a single 'squawk' that is virtually impossible to intercept. Instead, they were using equipment that had normal voice transmission, and in consequence each broadcast had to be kept to the barest minimum.

Immediately after the war both the SAS and the SBS tested and purchased a new pocket-sized transmitter that has a highly sophisticated burst facility and is able to broadcast enormous distances. The British special forces have bought four hundred of the PRC 319 manufactured by MEL and in 1987 the US special forces will test the same units.

Once the landings had taken place and the advance inland had begun, both the SBS and the SAS reconnoitred the island giving advance intelligence of Argentine positions and, when required, attacking Argentine rear areas to help demoralise the occupying forces. One of the more significant intelligence contributions by the SAS occurred at Mount Kent, a critical position that, if properly manned, could have brought massive firepower to bear on the British forces advancing towards Port Stanley. Astonishingly, SAS patrols reported that the mountain was lightly defended, if guarded at all.

The SAS commander, Mike Rose, therefore, proposed to Julian Thompson, the commander of 3 Commando Brigade, that they send a team forward by helicopter to secure the mountain top. Mount Kent was well ahead of the British front line and the attack would be a high-risk gamble, but Brigadier Thompson agreed. In a memorable forty-mile dash in fading light on 31 May, helicopters flew in advance elements of K Company of 42 Commando to meet up with the SAS who were already in position. The journalist Max Hastings had managed to hitch a lift on the helicopter with Mike Rose and recounts how he shouted to Rose during the flight that the Argentines were bound to shell their position as soon as dawn broke. In a moment of pure theatre Rose grinned and shouted back: 'Who dares, wins', the motto of the SAS.[6]

In the event, the expected artillery barrage never happened

and the commandos held Mount Kent for the rest of the campaign.

While all the special forces operations helped to reduce casualties and contributed to the overall success of the campaign, perhaps the one that did the most to shorten the war falls into the category of psychological operations, a vital part of special forces work.

The SAS had consistently been reporting from their reconnaissance missions into the Argentine lines that morale among the enemy troops was very low. At the beginning of the war this proved overly optimistic and in consequence caused some resentment among the regular British forces. However, once the landings had begun and the advance inland was under way, and certainly by the time Port Stanley was surrounded, it was estimated that morale really had reached a new low.

The task force had a particularly useful asset in Rod Bell, a Royal Marines Captain, who had been born in Costa Rica and spoke fluent Spanish. Bell was a tough Marine of considerable experience but, because of his background, he also had sympathy for the Argentine position in the war. His voice of understanding had been a lonely one among his colleagues, but now proved invaluable.

Beginning on 6 June a telephone line was opened to Port Stanley, using the network that already existed on the islands and which had been kept open by the medical staff on both sides. In an initial conversation Captain Bell spoke to Alison Bleaney, a doctor working at Stanley Hospital. She could not get any Argentine officer to come to the phone but nonetheless Bell, and Mike Rose who had initiated the operation, were convinced that the conversation was being heard by a wider audience. Every day for the next week, as the British forces pushed the Argentine forces back to Port Stanley, Bell broadcast a message encouraging the Argentines to surrender to save further loss of life 'as the honourable thing to do.'

The conversations between Bell and Dr Bleaney had in fact been listened to by an Argentine staff officer, Melbourne

Hussey, who was relaying Bell's remarks to Menendez. Finally, on 14 June, Hussey himself came to the telephone and told Dr Bleaney that Menendez was prepared to talk. Later that afternoon, Rose and Bell boarded a Gazelle helicopter with a white flag draped underneath and flew to a prearranged rendezvous at the Government House football field. The helicopter missed the rendezvous, landing some quarter of a mile away, and Rose and Bell were obliged to walk openly through the lines of Argentine soldiers, hoping that no one would break the truce.

The two men met with Menendez and began a two-hour negotiating session which eventually resulted in the Argentine agreement to surrender all their forces in West and East Falkland.

In fact the last of the special forces units did not leave the Argentine until seven weeks after the war ended. Even though a peace treaty had been agreed there was concern in London that hostilities might break out again, and so selected units were asked to stay behind to gather intelligence and give early warning of any new attack.

The Falklands War was a unique campaign, and in most ways it was unsuited to Britain's lean fighting machine designed almost entirely to meet a Nato commitment on the central European front. Certainly no war plans existed that required such a large force to fight so far away over such inhospitable territory. In the event, however, the British forces acquitted themselves remarkably well – somewhat to the surprise of many of the senior service staff who believed the losses might have been much higher.

But for the special forces the Falklands War presented a fine opportunity for them to test their performance in a combined operation. For some, it was undoubtedly an uncomfortable experience. The Royal Navy, for example, had not worked with the SAS in recent times, and found their apparently undisciplined behaviour and often scruffy appearance difficult to handle.

Nevertheless, at an operational level the war justified all

the investment that had been made in special forces since 1945. It proved that special forces did have a clear role outside of counter-insurgency or counter-terrorist work, and that they could work in support of the conventional forces, acting as a force multiplier in a wide range of areas. For example, on 21 May SAS from D Squadron launched a diversionary attack at Darwin in the south-west of East Falkland, while the main landing force went ashore at San Carlos Bay. Such was the volume of mortar, missile and machine-gun fire put down by the SAS that the Argentine commander at nearby Goose Green felt he was being attacked by a full battalion.

On a number of occasions, the SAS and the SBS were able to carry out night attacks that would have required many more conventional troops. At the same time, the intelligence produced by the special forces was crucial to the planning of the landings and the subsequent advance across the island. The emphasis that both the SAS and the SBS place on initiative, endurance and teamwork during training was also justified.

Amid all the successes there were mistakes made and lessons learned. Casualties in the fighting were surprisingly light: two injured during the assault on Pebble Island; one officer wounded and then killed after staying behind to cover the withdrawal of his signaller during a limited engagement on 10 June in the hills above Port Howard; one man killed in a tragic accident when two special forces units mistook each other for the enemy. The 'blue on blue' incident occurred near Estancia House west of Mount Kent when an SAS unit opened fire on some SBS men. It turned out that the SBS were 3,000 metres to the north-west of their agreed patrolling zone. There was never a clear explanation for the mistake and although such things happen in war there are a number of SBS men who, perhaps unfairly, still lay the responsibility for their colleague's death at the door of the SAS.

The biggest loss of life occurred on 19 May when members of D and G Squadrons were being flown by Sea King helicopter to the assault ship *Intrepid*. The majority of the squadron had been safely moved when 19 Troop, who had already survived South Georgia and Pebble Island, boarded the helicopter. Shortly after takeoff, the Sea King struck an albatross, the body of which was sucked into the engine intake, immediately causing the helicopter to lose all power. Corporal Davey was on board:

'Suddenly and without warning there was an extremely violent impact at the front of the helicopter, near to where I was seated. Immediately the cab filled with water. All I remember was being thrown about under water and in complete darkness. I don't know how I got out but assume it was via the front passenger exit. The journey to the surface seemed to take for ever. Once on the surface, coughing and vomiting AVTUR and sea water, I looked back towards the helicopter but saw only one wheel which was by now only just above the surface. I became aware of a group of men around a small life-raft and swam towards it. . . . We spent a most uncomfortable half hour or so awaiting rescue. The majority of us had a life jacket of some sort and had managed partially to inflate them, but without the one-man aircrew raft we would have really been in trouble.

'By the time the rescue helicopter came we were all very close to unconsciousness . . . a dinghy from HMS *Brilliant* also arrived on the scene. We were hauled aboard. I must have lost consciousness at this stage as the next thing I remember was waking up in the sick bay wrapped in blankets several hours later.'[7]

The accident killed eighteen members of the SAS. The loss in numbers was bad enough, but the average age of those who died was thirty-four – above the overall average for the army – and they had been an average of sixteen years in the squadron. 'It was an enormous loss of collective experience that will take many years to replace,' said one former SAS officer.

The special forces equipment, with the exception of the portable radios and the outboard motors on the Gemini boats, performed well. The special forces have their own budgets and weapons research section but Fort Bragg helped the SAS by supplying American night vision equipment which proved invaluable.

Perhaps the biggest failing was in command and control. The SAS, used to going their own way, acted too independently for the ground commander, Jeremy Moore. He found their habit of carrying out reconnaissances without consultation frustrating and dangerous. He blamed the SAS for the death of the SBS man because he claims that, unlike the SBS, the SAS had failed to inform him where they were operating. After the war Moore wrote a highly critical report on the performance of the SAS that personally attacked their commander, Michael Rose, and used language unusual in such a report.

But, for their part, the SAS insist that not a single operation was launched without the full knowledge of headquarters and never without their approval.

Further down the command chain there was also considerable resentment among some officers with what they saw as inadequate command and control of special operations and intelligence-gathering. For example, a senior officer in the 2nd Battalion, Parachute Regiment, claims that 'at the outset we went in with very little intelligence. Either it was not gathered or not available. We just heard off-the-cuff comments like 'Hit them hard and they will fold', and it didn't quite work out like that.

'Also, we were never clear just who special operations people thought they were working for, the commander on *Fearless* or headquarters back in London.'

There is no doubt that initially some SAS observation posts did send back over-optimistic reports about the morale of the Argentine forces. They saw and heard a largely undisciplined force which they felt would have little stomach for a fight. Their judgement had been coloured by the experience of South Georgia and Pebble Island. In the former, a force outnumbered two to one forced the occupying troops to surrender almost without a fight. In the latter a small force had done considerable damage despite the presence of a guard that hugely outnumbered it. Both these early engagements suggested that when the full weight of the British was brought to bear the Argentine army would crumble. This was undoubtedly a mistake.

In the minds of the staff planners, too, some confusion was created because the SAS were known to be in regular contact with their headquarters at Hereford and with the Fleet headquarters at Northwood. They had their own separate satellite communications system that actually worked much better than that of the fleet and allowed individual officers to discuss problems of logistics and plans with other experts in England. It also allowed Rose to talk frequently with the SAS director, Brigadier Peter de la Billiere.

A story that has gained wide currency suggests that after the San Carlos landings, when Julian Thompson refused to advance until he had his logistics train on the shore, Rose personally telephoned Prime Minister Thatcher to say that the commanders on the ground seemed to be losing their nerve and, by not advancing, were giving the Argentines ample opportunity to reinforce and then attack the British while they were still trying to establish a bridgehead.

It is true that there was a great deal of concern about the delay in breaking out from the beachhead following the landings on 21 May. Among the politicians in London, aware that every hour of delay meant the likelihood of attacks by Argentine aircraft and heavy British losses, and that continued positive news to give to the public was necessary to counter the loss of life among the British troops, there were serious fears that support for the war would rapidly disappear. On 23 May Peter de la Billiere called the SAS commander, possibly at the behest of Downing Street, to find out the reasons for the delays. Rose spoke to Thompson who explained his problems with shortages of stores, particularly ammunition. The message was passed back with a recommendation that the advance be delayed. This was ignored and the order given to break out of the beachhead.

This order was the one fundamental error of the war. The army were instructed to move south and capture Darwin and Goose Green to give a quick victory to the politicians. Militarily it made no sense as both targets were far off the line of march to Port Stanley, the ultimate goal, which lay due east. Also, SAS advance units reported that Goose Green was defended in battalion strength by a force that was well dug in. There were no helicopters or ships available for any troops to attack from an unexpected angle – instead, they would have to go in exactly from the direction the Argentines had prepared for.

There remains some confusion about the intelligence supplied by the SAS for the assault on Goose Green. The SAS claim that a two-hour briefing was given to Colonel H. Jones of 2 Para during which the strength and disposition of the Argentine forces was laid out in great detail. Admittedly D Squadron of the SAS withdrew from Goose Green the day before the Argentines reinforced the garrison, but even so the SAS appear to have considerably underestimated the strength of the defending force (although they claim that they estimated exactly the number of combatants and that the higher totals were made up by administrative and logistics staff).

Any SAS mistakes were compounded anyway by a failure in communication between London and the task force. The complete order of battle of the Argentine forces on the islands was known in London because of interceptions of signals traffic which had been made by the American National Security Agency and passed to GCHQ in Cheltenham, but this information was never passed on.

It is the nature of warfare that such intelligence failures and communications problems occur. However good the planning and training, mistakes are made and those on the spot have to adapt to unexpected circumstances. The British were fortunate in having an effective body of special forces on tap, and well-trained general forces. With the one exception mentioned above, the failures were only those that occurred in the heat of battle and, while improvements can always be made, they were not in areas that could reasonably have been foreseen.

However, in the field of psychological operations, the British were found seriously wanting. It is recognised by every nation today that such operations can play a critical part in any war. Both the United States and the Soviet Union have invested money and men in developing an effective civilian and military capability to run psychological operations. In the Falklands, however, the British were unable to take advantage of the fragile morale of the Argentine forces. Although the SAS invented their own version of Psyops on the spot, there was only one fluent Spanish-speaker with the whole task force, the ubiquitous Rod Bell, and his effectiveness underlined how important this aspect of warfare can be. This lapse in capability is now being addressed.

Perhaps in the long term one of the most significant lessons to be learned from the Falklands War was the degree of overlap that exists between the SAS and the SBS. Originally the distinction between the two forces was clear: the SBS would take care of reconnaissance and sabotage at ports or on the high seas while the SAS would take care of the land. But the development of new and sophisticated detection devices using microwaves and ultra sound has forced the SBS to change their tactics. Instead of attacking under water at the target they now more often will covertly approach the shore and go inland before coming at the target from the rear. This new emphasis has forced them to hone already capable skills for operating on land.

For their part, the SAS have always had the capability of operating underwater and are as capable in boats as they are in aircraft. In fact, both SAS and SBS were needed to retake South Georgia and to carry out sabotage and reconnaissance in the Argentine and both operated all over the Falkland Islands.

There remains a reluctance to discuss in any detail the special forces operations in the Argentine. All special forces work in a foreign country is politically sensitive, especially when, as in this case, the British were committing a serious escalation of the conflict. After all, there was never any suggestion that Argentine commandos were planning to assault any bases in Britain. Even the United States, which was otherwise co-operating very closely with Britain throughout the conflict, was kept in the dark about SAS-SBS operations in Argentina.

The special forces themselves are reluctant to discuss such matters as they have no wish to betray special forces operating techniques in wartime, which are seen as quite different from their counter-terrorist or counter-insurgency role. 'We may need to use some of them again and we do not want our enemies to know how we do what we do,' said one intelligence source with special forces experience.[8]

A closer relationship between the SAS and the SBS seems inevitable. For many years they have been kept apart by the natural rivalries that exist between the Royal Navy and the Army, but operational requirements now make it necessary for them to work more closely together, perhaps with a view to eventually merging.

The first indication that this may happen came in March 1987, when it was learned that a joint SAS-SBS Headquarters Group was to be established in London. It will be commanded by an SAS member with the title of Director of Special Forces with an SBS deputy. These are logical steps, actually suggested by the special forces themselves without either the civil servants or the senior military commanders at the Ministry of Defence being involved initially.

In the space of two years, the British have demonstrated a clear capability in the counter-terrorist role and in conventional war. Just as the lessons learned by them during the period of unconventional warfare in the 1950s, 60s and 70s led to renewed interest in special forces, so the example of the British has combined with a newly assertive American spirit in the 1980s to create a renewal of international interest in special operations forces.

PART 8: THE SNAKE EATER RETURNS

18

The Snake Bites Back

One month after the end of the Falklands campaign, an important article appeared in the June issue of the influential Soviet journal *Military Affairs*. Written by Colonel A. Tsvetkov, the article was titled 'Special Purpose Troops' and provided an unusually detailed account of Soviet perceptions of western special operations forces. Anything other than conventional forces are rarely discussed even in specialist military journals and so this article marked a new departure. It was obviously designed to increase the significance of western special forces in the minds of serving officers and clearly demonstrated the importance the Soviets believed the west attached to special forces. It is worth quoting at length.

'Under the cover of the notorious myth of "Soviet military threat" imperialist states are continuing to follow a dangerous course toward aggravation of international tension and confrontation with the Soviet Union and other countries of the socialist fraternity. To implement their aggressive designs, they have included in their arsenal for the struggle against communism – in addition to political campaigns and ideological sabotage – active subversive operations conducted by agents and by special reconnaissance and sabotage formations.

'Imperialists are making a broad practice of such actions, called special operations in the west, in many regions of the world. Sending off cut-throats from "special purpose" units to suppress the liberation movement in El Salvador, US President Reagan impudently declared that their mission had exceptionally important significance to "ensuring the security of the USA and other Nato countries".

'So-called "special purpose" troops have been formed in the capitalist states for the conduct of subversive actions. Such formations have now been formed in the USA, FRG, Britain, France, Italy and some other western countries.

'The following basic missions are assigned to "special purpose" troops: acquisition of information on the enemy's most important objectives, and their annihilation; organisation of sabotage and terror; creation of insurrectional detachments out of groups of the population dissatisfied with the existing regime to one extent or another; conduct of ideological sabotage; participation in the suppression of national liberation and partisan movements in their rear and in dependent countries.'[1]

The paper goes on to list in considerable and accurate detail the composition, equipment and training of special forces in the USA, West Germany and Britain. As is common with such articles, the opportunity for the odd propaganda dig at the enemy is not lost.

'The reconnaissance-sabotage sub-units contain many déclassé elements who had fled their countries after committing political or criminal offences. "In the operations which we are now waging against international communism," declared the American General W. Jackson, "we do not display any special scruples and we are prepared to use any gangsters and cut-throats that we can find to achieve our end goal."

'The saboteur training programme is extremely intensive according to the foreign press. It includes brainwashing and generalised special training. The idea that the capitalist system is superior to the socialist system is constantly suggested to the personnel, and a savage hatred of communism, of the labourers of socialist countries and of peoples fighting for their national liberation is instilled. Creation of an atmosphere of suspiciousness, mutual shadowing, coarseness and brutality, advertisement of the horrors of the "communist prison" and simultaneous advancement of the myth that the "special purpose" troops are an élite make the overwhelming majority of the trainees capable of all crimes, even going as far as murder.

'Personnel of the "special purpose" troops regularly participate in various exercises of the ground troops and naval forces, and in so-called punitive actions in "hot spots" of the globe: for example, they were involved in the attempt to liberate American hostages in Iran in April 1980, in the bloody raid of a group of Green Berets in Laos in early 1981, in the reprisals conducted by the Pentagon cut-throats against the peaceful population of El Salvador and so on.

'Having lost all sense of reality, the ruling circles of the imperialist states, headed by the USA, are making increasingly more overt preparations for aggressive war against the Soviet Union and other countries of the socialist fraternity, in which they devote an important role to their "Black Guard" – the "special purpose" troops. Soviet soldiers must oppose the intrigues of Nato saboteurs by high revolutionary alertness, honed military proficiency and constant combat readiness.'

Such an open assessment of the capabilities of western special forces undoubtedly reflected the increased attention being paid to them by the Soviet high command. As is often the case in defence matters, their concern was in response to increased US attention in the same area. Both west and east had begun a process where each side perceived in the other a new and disturbing threat. To meet that threat both began developing new and better weapons and tactics, with specially-trained people to use them effectively.

The US government had initiated an important shift in tactics towards the end of the Carter administration, when the US Army announced a new concept of operations known as Airland Battle. This was a response to the Soviet development of the Operational Manoeuvre Group (OMG) which was an evolution of German blitzkrieg tactics used in World War II. The OMG was basically a highly mobile attacking force that could exploit any weaknesses exposed by a Warsaw

Pact advance on a broad front. The Airland Battle strategy was designed to blunt the OMG by attacking deep into enemy territory and destroying the second echelon forces before they could be committed to the battle.[2]

To strike deep behind enemy lines not only needed new 'smart' weapons systems fitted with laser sights and other sophisticated technology but also required special operations forces to work deep in the enemy rear, committing widespread acts of sabotage. When the Reagan administration came to power, they swiftly recognised that the men, money and equipment to fight that kind of war were simply not available.

At the same time, the Americans had come to believe that one of the major threats to world peace was the aggressive and expansionist nature of the Soviet Union. The White House saw a Soviet hand in many acts of terrorism and most insurgency movements in the world. Fred Ikle, the Under Secretary of Defense for Policy, has been an articulate exponent of this view.

'These small wars in many regions are not just a collection of self-cancelling insurgencies, of meaningless coups and counter coups, or border skirmishes that randomly shift national boundaries hither and yon.

'There is a driving organising force behind it all: here it stirs up and feeds an insurgency, there it exploits a coup d'état, here it instigates terrorism to weaken a democratic government, there it provides police forces and praetorian guards to perpetuate a regime beholden to it. Two steps forward, one step back, it diligently, relentlessly expands its dominance throughout the world.

'It was Lenin who created this new force, on the crumbling foundations of Russian imperialism that had been steadily expanding Moscow's rule for at least three centuries. . . . We in the west thought that the Atlantic Alliance had checkmated the Soviet expansion of the Cold War period. But the Leninist expansion continued by advancing into other regions – primarily into the so-called Third World. Thus the Cold War was followed by insurgency warfare and other small-scale warfare in many regions.'3

While there are many historians and intelligence analysts who might disagree with this interpretation of history and current events, such simple views have clearly guided the Reagan administration.

The military, too, were being given very much the same kind of message, although stripped of the political dogma. For example, a study commissioned at the beginning of the Reagan administration for the Army Training and Doctrine Command, suggested that until the end of this century wars will mainly fit into the pattern of low intensity conflict which included 'coercive diplomacy, special intelligence operations, psychological operations, terrorism and counter-terrorism, various levels of guerrilla warfare, and Soviet-proxy limited conventional war.'4

The study identified four reasons for the concentration on low intensity conflict:

'1.   The Soviets will gain and maintain a solid reputation for strategic nuclear parity, if not actual superiority. . . .
      This . . . will accelerate Soviet political-military adventures viewed by the Soviet leadership as relatively low cost and low risk operations with high geostrategic payoffs.

'2.   Soviet leaders will not be predisposed toward conventional war in Europe; the high risks of nuclear escalation would outweigh any possible benefits and, given progress by alternative means, would be unnecessary.

'3.   The Third World will be an increasingly attractive target for Soviet political-military initiatives in the 1980s. There will be skyrocketing population pressures, especially in urban areas, and food, water and wood shortages. Cross-border refugee flows will create severe political problems. Competition by the industrialised nations for increasingly scarce energy and mineral resources will continue to drive up prices and the costs of development capital; these shortages may foster conditions of intra- and interstate violence that the Soviet Union will seek to exploit.

'4.   If the United States does not make . . . decisions on

doctrine, equipment, organisation, and training
appropriate for LIC, the nation will be left with
conventional military forces that, although formidable,
the Soviets will view as inadequate to counter their various
options in the Third World.'

One of the first priorities of the Reagan administration, in its overall commitment to improve the capabilities of the US armed forces, was to invest in special forces. In 1981 Defense Secretary Casper Weinberger issued a Defense Guidance to service chiefs which outlined a five-year strategy to enhance special operations. In fact, the administration was planning on lasting the full two terms and they had already developed approximate goals for special forces through to 1990.

Weinberger instructed all four services to develop a special operations capability. 'We must revitalise and enhance special operations to project US power where the use of conventional forces would be premature, inappropriate or unfeasible. . . . The US must be able to defeat low-level aggression both to prevent the step-by-step expansion of Soviet or surrogate influence and to prevent escalation to a higher level of conflict. The US must be able to achieve these objectives when to its advantage without direct confrontation.'[5]

This was the first time that the terms 'special operations' or 'Special Operations Forces' had appeared publicly in an official document, although a policy of revitalisation had really been in force since President Reagan took office. But the Defense Guidance served clear notice on all four services that the administration attached a high priority to the area. Weinberger underlined this by demanding that the services produce, as a matter of urgency, Special Operations Force Master Plans to outline their programme goals.

To give the directive some muscle, in March 1981 the administration appointed Noel C. Koch to be the Principal Deputy Assistant Secretary of Defense for International Security Affairs. Koch, a former special assistant to Presidents Nixon and Ford, was to become the administration's link with all special operations and counter-terrorist activities carried out by the military. This was underlined in June 1983 when Koch was appointed head of the Special Planning Directorate, which was designed to improve co-ordination and co-operation between all the agencies dealing with special operations.

During Koch's first month in the job, the Reagan administration had an opportunity to demonstrate the capability of US special forces. On 28 March an Indonesian airliner was hijacked and forced to land in Bangkok. The five terrorists on board demanded the release of eighty-four people held in Indonesian jails whom the hijackers described as political prisoners. Negotiations continued for two days and on 30 March Thai officials announced that the Indonesian government had agreed to the hijackers' demands.

Since an American had been shot and wounded during the hijacking the US government was taking a close interest in the case. In fact, unknown to the hijackers, the Thai government had asked the Americans for assistance and a team from Delta Force had flown out to Bangkok, arriving on 30 March. Early the following day, they stormed the aircraft with the help of local commandos, killing four of the terrorists and capturing the fifth. It was a successful and unpublicised mission that had been personally authorised by President Reagan just before he himself was wounded by John Hinkley.

Original administration goals were across-the-board increases in special services manpower, readiness and equipment. In 1981 there were 11,600 men and women in US special operations units. By 1985 the Army would add 2,900, the Navy 200 and the Air Force 200, bringing the overall total to 14,900. By the end of the decade the Army would add a further 3,300, the Navy 1,000 and the Air force 1,700, bringing the total of special operations forces up to 20,900 nearly double the total when Reagan became President. With the addition of reservists, the US would have a total of around 30,000 special forces available.

It was the intention that new units would be established,

including two Green Beret Special Forces Groups, one Ranger battalion, one Ranger Regimental headquarters and HQ company, a Psychological Operations Battalion, two SEAL teams, the 23rd Air Force and the First Special Operations Wing.

Complete modernisation of the equipment available to special forces was also planned. This would include new aircraft, both helicopters and the revolutionary JVX Tilt Rotor, enhancements of the existing C-130 and C-141 planes, purchase of MC-130H transport aircraft, six submarines dedicated to the covert delivery of SEAL teams, new surface craft and a wide range of the latest communications and night vision devices.

The budget for SOF would rise from $441 million in 1981 to $1,693 million in 1987, and that year the government requested $2.5 billion for 1988 with a $330 million supplemental for FY '87. It was expected that the budget would drop back down to $2 billion in '92 once the revitalisation was complete.

The armed forces greeted these changes with something less than enthusiasm. Among the special operations community, of course, government interest in their field was welcome news. But among the service chiefs, with their budget constraints and preoccupation with conventional warfare, there was less enthusiasm. If funds were made available, they were happy to recruit more people – the Army hired an additional 1,200 men in 1982 against a 1981 total of 6,200 – as the additional billets could be used as an argument for more cash the following year. Beyond that, however, the services reacted with some classic bureaucratic manoeuvring. They simply created a number of high-profile, high-sounding new commands to make it appear a great deal was being done.

On 1 February 1982 the Air Force set up the 1st Special Operations Group to monitor all covert operations in the Air Force. Its responsibilities included suggesting improvements in training and equipment as well as acting as a point of contact between the special forces and the JCS. In fact, the organisation was created in name only and although it did have a small staff it was never an effective operation.[6]

On 1 October 1982 the Army set up the 1st Special Operations Command (SOCOM) based at Fort Bragg under the command of Major-General Joseph Lutz. SOCOM was to act as a centralised doctrine and training unit for all army special operations forces. As Lutz described it:

'In the 1st Special Operations Command we are not sitting around patting ourselves on the back because our value has apparently been recognised. On the contrary, special operations forces will never be more than modest in size. To accomplish the mission set before us, however, our soldiers must be extraordinarily professional. We are working at the business of integrating all elements of the new command into a cohesive professional force.'[7]

In the same year, largely in response to the Holloway Commission report already mentioned, which after the Desert One affair had severely criticised the command and control of the operation, the JCS established the Joint Special Operations Command headed by Brigadier-General Richard Scholtes. Also based at Fort Bragg, the command was a 'joint headquarters designed to study special operations requirements and techniques of all services to ensure standardisation. Special operations are supporting operations which may be adjuncts to other operations and for which no service has primary responsibility. Examples include: training of indigenous forces in guerrilla warfare, counter-insurgency operations, and unconventional warfare missions in enemy held or controlled, or politically sensitive territory. The JSOC may, on occasion, participate in overseas exercises. JSOC is under the operational control of JCS.'[8]

In theory these changes should have gone some way to improving US capability in special operations. In fact, little changed. Additional layers of bureaucracy and an increase in numbers disguised a lack of willingness in the JCS and senior service commanders to divert the money from other projects necessary to fund the training and equipment that would give real muscle to the new commands. Thus, with consummate political judgement, the JCS used every opportunity to publicly proclaim their support for special operations. So, in their 1982 annual statement on military posture, the JCS were able to say:

'The current special operations forces levels reflect a serious shortfall in the number and types of units to meet requirements now and in the remainder of the decade. To offset this critical shortfall, a measured expansion of special operations forces is required.'9

Aside from the increase in mere numbers, the single area where there was a significant increase in actual capability was in intelligence gathering. During the Desert One episode there had been considerable frustration with the performance of the CIA in placing agents on the ground to pass back timely intelligence. In the event, the Delta Force team had inserted their own people under Dick Meadows, a special forces veteran who had retired from the army. The unit, known as the Forward Operating Group (FOG) was so successful that the army determined to build on that small team to develop their own intelligence gathering capability. (In the Soviet Union, this problem would not have arisen. Spetsnaz teams control their own agents and have their own intelligence gathering capability that is controlled by the GRU and kept separate from the KGB.)

The US military were keen to develop their own intelligence agents because they felt that none of the existing agencies had any interest or ability to feed them the information they required. But at the very time that the military was expanding its covert capabilities, the intelligence agencies were operating under very different priorities.

The CIA's original charter had allowed the Agency a free hand in virtually any aspect of covert warfare, including intelligence gathering. After a series of fiascos such as the Bay of Pigs, however, Congress introduced restrictive legislation to curb the Agency's paramilitary excesses. At the same time, sophisticated technology was developed that allowed many of the espionage activities normally undertaken by the Agency gumshoe, or covert intelligence agent, to be taken over by computers and satellites. The CIA purges carried out during the Carter administration cleared the last of the undercover warriors from the Agency's ranks.

The CIA, helped by the Defense Intelligence Agency and the National Security Agency, had the most high-powered computers in the world on which they could produce analyses on anything from the future grain harvest in the Soviet Union to the impact of delivery of Stinger missiles to the Afghan mujahedeen on Soviet foreign policy. But they no longer had the wish or the manpower to send out an agent to bring back information from a potential area of conflict.

This is a critical need for the military, and one that is not satisfied simply by sending a satellite over the area concerned. It was in that climate that General Shy Meyer, then Chief of Staff, Army, and a strong advocate of special operations, gave the authority for FOG to continue under the code name Intelligence Support Activity (ISA), with an initial budget of $2 million. This had risen to $6 million by 1983 and in excess of $10 million by 1986.[10]

Meyer's stand was backed up the following year by General Richard Stilwell when he was appointed Deputy Under Secretary of Defense for Policy, with a brief that included intelligence responsibilities for the Secretary of Defense.[11]

Stilwell in fact wanted to see a broader emphasis on intelligence gathering and wanted to set up a whole new agency under the code name Monarch Eagle to gather Humint. The CIA opposed this, arguing that there would be a conflict between its own efforts and those of the new agency, so the ISA continued as a covert compromise.

On 4 December 1981 the Reagan administration issued Executive Order 12333 which set out for the first time the distinctions between special operations and intelligence gathering, described as 'special activities'. The definitions and thrust of EO 12333 are important as they mark the limits of freedom of action available to special operations forces and their intelligence gathering apparatus.

Special activities are described as 'activities conducted in support of national foreign policy objectives abroad which are planned and executed so that the role of the United States Government is not apparent or acknowledged publicly, and actions in support of such activities, but which are not intended to influence United States political processes, public opinion, policies, or media and do not include diplomatic activities or the collection and production of intelligence or related support functions. Special activities, which are approved and authorised by the President, are conducted by the Central Intelligence Agency, unless the President, in accordance with EO 12333 specifically designates the Department of Defense as the lead agency. . . . The lead agency is responsible for informing the House and Senate Intelligence Committees of the special activity.'[12]

In fact, for a year this presidential order was ignored by ISA who operated with total freedom and without any form of official sanction. There was no presidential finding to justify its existence and the House and Senate Intelligence Committees were not informed.

Thus the existence of the ISA was kept secret from the Pentagon, the CIA and the White House and it only surfaced at all after a private mission to rescue some American soldiers reportedly held as prisoners of war in Laos went badly wrong. The issue of American prisoners missing in action (MIA) in South Asia is one filled with emotion for many Vietnam veterans, and for those families who have never given up hope of their lost sons one day returning home. It has been argued that the American government has not done enough to trace those MIAs still believed to be held somewhere in South Asia.

Under Congressional pressure, the government directed the Defense Intelligence Agency to set up a task force to look at the problem. Since then, the DIA has attempted to trace 2,497 Americans still unaccounted for since the fall of Saigon

in 1975. The DIA collected reports of sightings from thousands of refugees and investigated hundreds of those reports.
That work is still going on.

In February 1979 Lieutenant-Colonel James 'Bo' Gritz was
approached by two retired officers and asked if he would
resign his job as chief of congressional relations for the
Defense Security Assistance Agency, so that, working as a
private individual, he would be able to carry out his own
investigations into the MIA question, to determine once and
for all if there were still any Americans being held prisoner.[13]

Gritz was a good choice for the job. He had extensive
special forces experience and had carried out over a hundred
missions behind enemy lines during four years' service in
Vietnam. He accepted the assignment and as a cover was
given a job with Hughes Aircraft Co. that allowed him to
travel all over South Asia.

By the middle of 1980, two possible prison camps had been
identified, one in South Vietnam and one in the North. Then
in December 1980 Gritz was told that an SR-71 spy plane
had come up with a more promising site in Laos, close to the
border with Thailand. The aircraft photographed a rice field
which appeared to show – based on the size of the shadows,
thought to be too long for Asians – that up to thirty Cauca-
sians might be working in the field. Also, they were grouped
in such a way that they seemed to spell out 'B52'.

Gritz hired twenty-five former special forces men with
Vietnam experience and began training them in Florida for
a mission, codenamed Velvet Hammer, to take place in late
April before the monsoon season. Gritz was supplied with
equipment including cameras and secure radios to help them.
All of this led him to believe he was being officially supported
by the US government. In fact, it was an entirely freelance
effort with the support of some former special operations
people in the Pentagon.

As word of the pending mission leaked out, there was
official concern that such an operation could be very embarrassing if it went wrong and Gritz and his team had to shoot

their way back home. Gritz was summoned to Washington and told his mission was not to proceed as it would conflict with other, more official, ventures already under way. It is not clear whether any such missions actually took place but word of Gritz's mission was out and with it the existence of ISA.

News of the ISA first surfaced in 1982 when 'Bo' Gritz was giving testimony to a Congressional committee about his plans to resuce US prisoners in Laos. He mentioned that he had received intelligence and support from 'the Activity' an organisation that Congress had never heard of before. The Deputy Assistant Secretary of Defense for East Asia and the Pacific, Richard L. Armitage (who was later to oversee the special operations forces) had never heard of them either and told his boss Frank Carlucci, who initiated an investigation. Officials in the Pentagon were told to produce the dossier on ISA.

'When he saw what they had been doing he went nuts,' said one Pentagon official in on the meeting with Armitage. 'He saw they had been operating all over the world. They had things like a hot air balloon and a Rolls-Royce bought from the Drug Enforcement Administration which they said they needed to do their job. Armitage didn't believe them and wanted them disbanded.'[14]

Armitage discovered that in theory ISA was responsible to the Army Intelligence and Security Command (INSCOM) but in reality it operated wherever it saw fit. (It had originally been suggested that ISA come under JSOC but General Scholtes wanted nothing to do with them as this would have given JSOC an intelligence gathering capability which in turn would have automatically brought it under the scrutiny of the intelligence oversight committees.) Operations that ISA were initially involved in included sending a 20-strong team to Italy to help the Italian police search for American General James Dozier, who had been kidnapped by Red Brigade terrorists in December 1981 (it has been rumoured that these men were from Delta Force but in fact they were ISA). The

General was released the following month after police received a tip-off from an informer. They also operated for three years from 1981 on behalf of the CIA and on their own initiative in Nicaragua and El Salvador to gather intelligence that was passed back to the Agency and then on to the Contra rebels fighting the Nicaraguan government, and they traded arms and bullet proof vests with an unnamed African country in exchange for information about military deployments.

General Richard Stilwell argued that ISA was too valuable to lose and that if it were disbanded there would be no organisation that had a similar capability. This argument won the day. In 1983 President Reagan issued a secret finding that authorised the ISA, and for administrative purposes it was placed under the control of the DIA at Arlington Hall Station, near the Pentagon in Washington DC. Still there today, they are directly responsible to the Secretary of the Army and administered by the Assistant Chief of Staff for Army Intelligence.

As Congressional and Army higher command interest in the ISA grew, so the opponents of unconventional warfare saw an opportunity to investigate both ISA and Delta Force in the hope that one or other of them had exceeded their briefs. This coincided with a complaint made by subordinates of Lt.-Col. Dale C. Duncan, an ISA member, that he had diverted secret funds for his personal use while running an ISA front company called Business Security International, based in Annandale, Virgina, in an operation codenamed Yellowfruit.[15]

An investigation began in 1983, codenamed Task Force Catalyst Maker. It revealed that not only had both organisations been operating outside their charters but there had been widespread corruption. Through the expenses filed by members of both organisations, Army investigators discovered a series of unauthorised operations that had been carried out covertly.

In early 1982, in Operation Seaspray, the ISA purchased a King Air aircraft through a front company, Shenandoah

Aerolease, fitted it with electronic surveillance equipment and flew it from a Honduran airfield. The crew posed as civilians taking aerial photographs but in fact they gathered intelligence on Salvadorian rebel forces, including the pinpointing of rebel radio transmission sources. This information was fed back to the National Security Agency, who then passed it on to government forces in Salvador.

A widespread illegal intelligence-gathering operation had been mounted both in the United States and abroad. This included bugging a room used by a Soviet official on the West Coast, an Arab airline office in West Germany and the conference room of a Central American head of state.

But the most damaging evidence came from the financial records of both organisations. Admittedly, what to the conventional military might look like a nightmare of fraud and abuse with dummy companies, false accounting and poor record-keeping, to the special forces operators was often simply sensible security: if you were working undercover abroad, keeping receipts or staying in a hotel at the required army per diem rate might not be sensible. On the other hand, investigators found that operators had been travelling first class all over the world, and that there had been significant double accounting, enabling agents to pay one sum and file expenses accompanied by a forged receipt for a much larger amount. Also, contracts for equipment and services had been given out by senior officers to friends without there being any opportunity for competitive tender.

The most serious charges were made against the man who was the cause of the initial investigations. Lt.-Col. Duncan. In 1985 he was indicted on seven counts, including accusations that he had submitted expenses for $56,230 for electronic equipment that had already been paid for, and that he charged for an airline ticket that had been given free through a frequent-flyer programme. According to Congressional sources Duncan bought a red Porsche 911 SC-Targa for his wife with some of the funds.[16]

Duncan was found guilty of fraud in 1986 and is appealing.

Special Forces during World War II

Above: Informality in the desert, January 1943: Corporal Bill Kennedy of the Royal Scots Grays sits behind the twin Lewis machine guns that were so effective for the Long Range Desert Group.

Left: Otto Skorzeny, also known as Scarface, seen both in wartime and as he was in 1973, modelled the methods of the German special forces in World War II on Britain's Special Air Service.

Below: The Long Range Desert Group, pictured in May 1942, were an early example of the effectiveness of special forces working deep behind enemy lines to attack strategic targets such as airfields and fuel dumps.

US Special Forces

Above left: Snipers, working in pairs, rely on effective camouflage to remain hidden from the enemy. These US special forces would more usually carry thermal imaging or laser sights rather than the traditional telescopic sight pictured here.

Above right: All special forces in both the West and East train extensively in unarmed combat and various forms of silent killing.

Below: The Fort Bragg Stockade in North Carolina, headquarters of the US Delta Force.

The Mission that failed

Above left: Colonel 'Chargin Charlie' Beckwith, the commander of the abortive mission by Delta Force in April 1980 to rescue US hostages held in Tehran. He is pictured here in Vietnam in 1968.

Above right: The body of a US crewman lies beside one of the American helicopters that crashed at Desert One during the rescue attempt. Other helicopters were captured intact with secret documents relating to the mission.

The horribly burned body of a US serviceman lies amid the wreckage of an American helicopter that crashed and caught fire during the 1980 mission.

West Germany's Counter-Terrorist force

Above left: Members of Germany's counter-terrorist force, GSG9, return home to Bonn after their successful 1977 mission to free hostages held at Mogadishu in Somalia. In an eight-minute operation, the 26 members of GSG9 rescued 91 passengers and crew, killed four of the terrorists and captured a fifth. One GSG9 man and four hostages were slightly wounded.

Above right: GSG9 use specially-tuned Mercedes 280SE cars when deployed inside West Germany. The cars are not armoured; speed – they can move at 145mph – rather than security is paramount. Each car is fitted with three different scrambled telephone systems. The men are armed with Heckler and Koch MP5 sub-machine guns.

The Entebbe Mission

For their raid to free 258 passengers and crew held hostage by gunmen from the PFLP, Israeli commandos from their elite Unit 269 relied on deception to give them a vital few seconds of surprise. The commandos, who had flown direct from Israel, pretended they had on board Ugandan President Idi Amin. To maintain the fiction, they drove from their transport aircraft in a convoy led by a Mercedes car identical to that used by Amin.

Soviet Special Forces

Above left: At Furstenburg in East Germany, the Soviet Special forces –
Spetsnaz – have a secret training facility complete with mock-ups of Nato
aircraft, cruise missiles and other weapons that would be prime targets in the
event of war. This drawing was prepared by America's Defence Intelligence
Agency from satellite photographs and other intelligence sources.

Above right: Allied intelligence claim that Spetsnaz are obsessed with unarmed
combat and place far more emphasis on training in martial arts than their
Western counterparts.

Below left: This unique photograph was taken secretly by Western intelligence
in the bazaar in Kabul. It shows three Spetsnaz soldiers in civilian clothes. The
soldier on the left is holding a 7.62mm AKMS assault rifle with a folding stock
for easy concealment.

Below right: Spetsnaz exercise extensively in East Germany where this
photograph was taken by allied intelligence. The soldier is wearing camouflage
and carrying a 7.62mm AKMS assault rifle.

The SAS

The SAS first hit the headlines in May 1980 when members of the Counter-Revolutionary Warfare unit drawn from B Squadron 22 SAS launched their spectacular assault on the Iranian embassy in Princes Gate London in May, 1980. Four terrorists and one hostage were killed in the attack. Another terrorist was captured and 24 hostages freed. The face of the soldier on the right has been deliberately retouched to disguise his identity.

To the outside world, the attempted coup in the Gambia in July 1981 was a purely African affair. This picture shows troops from neighbouring Senegal entering the city of Banjul on 2 August 1981. However, behind the scenes three men from 22 SAS were secretly waging and winning their own war which resulted in the collapse of the revolution.

The first action by special forces in the Falklands War was a near disaster. Against advice, the SAS insisted on landing on the Fortuna Glacier in South Georgia by helicopter. During a later evacuation, in appalling weather, two Wessex helicopters crashed.

In May 1987 one of the SAS's most successful undercover operations resulted in the deaths of eight IRA men, who mounted an attack on the police station in Loughall, County Armagh, Northern Ireland. The SAS kept the area under surveillance for six weeks prior to the attack and the local IRA unit was wiped out when they walked into the ambush.

The Grenada Fiasco

This is the only existing photograph of one of the Delta Force helicopters being shot down during the Grenada invasion. Confusion over the timing of their mission meant that Delta launched their attack during daylight, instead of at night.

Below left: The US found a warehouse filled with Cuban supplied weapons on Grenada after the invasion. However, contrary to US intelligence estimates there were insufficient trained troops on the island and the weapons were never uncrated.

Below right: Fox Company of the US Marines prepare to assault the Grenadan town of Grenville. Intelligence predicted that Cubans and Grenadan militia might number 3,000 and be armed with tanks. In fact, there were only 50 Cubans with military training and 2,000 local militia. The marines took Grenville without firing a shot.

He was sentenced to seven years jail by an army court martial on similar charges the same year. Trials are still pending against two other officers.

Within Delta, the Army investigation found evidence of more than $200,000 of double billings on expenses. These mainly related to a three-year period from 1981–3 when eighty members of the unit were assigned overseas to protect US ambassadors. Their mission was paid for by the State Department but the Delta men also billed the Army for their lodgings.

As a result of the investigations, Delta was reorganised. The then commander, Colonel Sherman H. Williford, was promoted to Brigadier-General and transferred to Fort Drum, New York State. He was replaced by Colonel William Garrison who had previously commanded the American contingent of the Sinai peacekeeping force.

'Garrison is one of the finest military commanders I know,' said one Congressional source with extensive special operations experience. 'Financial irregularities will not be tolerated any more and there is a big shake-up going on to sweep those guys involved in lying about their expenses out of Delta.'[17]

The fact that any corruption at all was allowed to occur is a reflection on America's current ineptitude in this field. It is notoriously easy to use secrecy as an excuse to launder money to personal accounts or accept bribes for passing lucrative contracts to friends and contacts. The CIA, for example, which has a long history of covert operations, has a great deal of experience in handling corruption among its employees. (The most famous example is Edwin Wilson who became a millionaire while running covert operations and dummy companies on behalf of the Agency during the 1960s and 70s.) The Agency has improved its oversight capabilities in the last ten years, and the Army too has now learned that an effective system of oversight is as important a part of covert operations as training the operators to kill silently or bug a telephone.

The investigations into the irregularities of Delta and ISA

were just the latest in a list of troubling aspects to special operations forces. Despite Weinberger's 1983 directive to all four services to produce master plans for the future of special operations, all were slow to do so. While the numbers of special forces personnel were increasing, there was concern that training and equipment were not being developed to meet these increases, and that in fact all four services were doing everything they could to delay the revitalisation effort.

In January 1983 a meeting was held in the Pentagon with Weinberger, Under-Secretary for Defense, Paul Thayer, the Secretary of the Army, John Marsh, the Secretary of the Air Force, Vern Orr, the Under-Secretary of the Navy and Noel Koch, the Principal Deputy Assistant Secretary of Defense for International Security Affairs, who was in charge of overseeing the revitalisation effort.

The meeting had been called at the instigation of Weinberger, Thayer and Koch, who were concerned that the revitalisation was proceeding in name only; that the military were taking all the money but had nothing of substance to show for the investment. Some of those in the meeting recall that it began amicably with the military assuring the civilians of their total co-operation. However, once it had been made clear that action, not words, was required the military, while publicly still adopting a supportive posture, were consistently obstructive.[18]

Previously Weinberger had been arguing to his aides that spelling out the requirements for an enhanced special forces in the Defense Guidance document would be sufficient. However, he realised now that further action was necessary, and agreed that a classified memo should be sent to the JCS, spelling out exactly what was needed. Simultaneously, an unclassified version of the memo would be circulated. This would ensure that the JCS would be pinned down by Congress and other officials and made to deliver the detail spelled out in the classified memo.

In February, Weinberger told the JCS to come up with a new command structure for the special operations forces, to be delivered to him by July. Drafts of both the classified and unclassified version went back and forth between the JCS and the civilians over the next few months. John Vessey, the chairman of the JCS, Jack Merritt, the Director of the Joint Staff, and Art Moreau, a Special Assistant to Vessey, were controlling the military response. In April the classified letter was accepted but the unclassified version remained the subject of serious disagreement.

Meanwhile, the study on the command structure for special forces requested by Weinberger had been completed, but for some reason the JCS sat on the results. The solutions to the command of special operations forces had ranged from leaving things as they were to creating a unified command under Readiness Command (REDCOM) at Fort McDill, with the latter being preferred as it ostensibly created a new command but effectively left it powerless under REDCOM.

Nine months after Weinberger had told the JCS that an unclassified letter spelling out force goals should be agreed, and eight months after he had asked for details of a new force structure, neither had been delivered. A 6 October meeting was scheduled between him and the JCS in the Tank, their secure briefing room in the Pentagon. The previous Friday, 3 October, while Weinberger was out of town, Noel Koch met with Paul Thayer over the heads of the service chiefs, and persuaded him to sign and release what was, in effect, simply an unclassified version of the classified letter that had already been agreed with the JCS.

By the time Weinberger returned to Washington the following Monday, the letter had been distributed. The JCS, who found their blocking manoeuvres undercut, were furious and relations between the military and the civilians were soured even further.

The letter from Thayer to the JCS was circulated to the Assistant Secretaries of Defense, the Directors of the Defense Agencies and the Secretaries of the Military Departments. His letter was entitled 'Special Operations Forces' and read: 'US national security requires the maintenance of Special

Operations Forces (SOF) capable of conducting the full range of special operations on a worldwide basis, and the revitalisation of those forces must be pursued as a matter of national urgency. Therefore, I am directing that the following steps be taken:

'1.   Necessary force structure expansion and enhancements in command and control, policy, training, and equipment will be implemented as rapidly as possible and will be *fully* implemented not later than the end of Fiscal Year 1990.

'2.   Collateral activities will be enhanced as necessary to provide fully effective support to the planning and execution of special operations.

'3.   Each service will assign SOF and related activities sufficient resource allocation priority and will establish appropriate intensive management mechanism to ensure that these objective are met.

'4.   Resource decisions for current and programmed SOF, once made at the Secretary of Defense level, will not be changed or reduced by OSD or Service staffs unless co-ordinated by the Principal Deputy Assistant Secretary of Defense (International Security Affairs) and the Assistant Secretary of Defense (Comptroller) and approved by the Secretary of Defense.

'By 1 March 1984, each military department and Defense Agency will submit a time-phased master plan for achieving these objectives for review by the Principal Deputy Assistant Secretary of Defense (International Security Affairs).

'You should disseminate this memo as widely as possible within your organisation to ensure that the priority attached to this programme is clearly understood.'

This was a clear declaration of war by the politicians against the military structure. But, before the service chiefs could respond to this opening salvo, a war of another kind broke out that was to take special operations off the drawing board and into the firing line. On 25 October 1983 the United States invaded Grenada.

19

Operation Urgent Fury

The Secretary of the Army, John Marsh, told the House of Representatives Appropriations Committee on Tuesday 26 February 1986 that the US invasion of Grenada 'was a great success. I think as a combat operation it was a success.' This view was supported by General John Wickham, the Chief of Staff of the Army, who added: 'I think they did a whale of a good job.'[1]

If success is judged by the ability of an overwhelming military force to subdue a few lightly-armed militia, then the Grenada invasion was a success. Judged on any other military basis including intelligence capability, command and control, communications and special forces operations, it was a failure. And a failure made worse by the military's consistent subsequent refusal to acknowledge shortcomings or take steps to make sure the same mistakes were never repeated.

The Grenada operation is important because it was the first time that a combined US force of all four armed services had fought together since Vietnam. Although artificial in the sense that so few out of America's total military were committed to the invasion, it was real in that actual combat was involved. It was also the first time special forces had been deployed on any scale since the announcement of the revitalisation programme two years earlier.

The ground for the invasion of Grenada was laid in 1979 when Maurice Bishop successfully led a peaceful coup against the country's unpopular Prime Minister Eric Gairy, who had

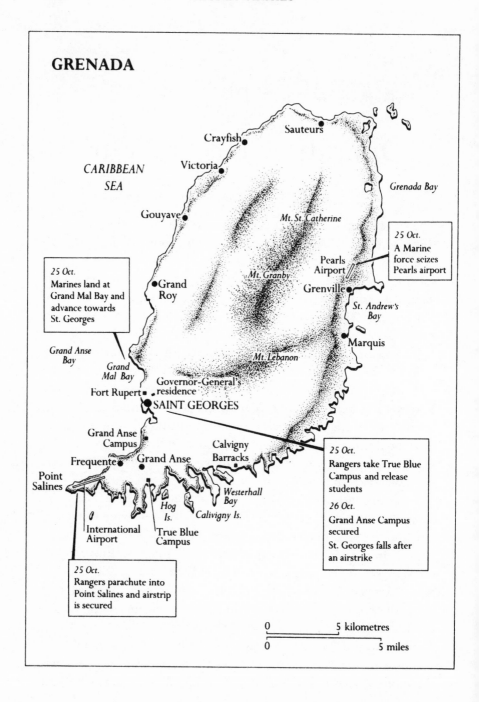

GRENADA

CARIBBEAN
SEA

Crayfish•

Sauteurs•

Victoria•

Grenada Bay

Gouyave•

Mt. St. Catherine

25 Oct.
A Marine
force seizes
Pearls airport

25 Oct.
Marines land at
Grand Mal Bay and
advance towards
St. Georges

•Grand
Roy

Mt. Granby

Pearls
Airport

Grenville•

St. Andrew's
Bay

Grand Anse
Bay

Grand
Mal Bay

Mt. Lebanon

Marquis•

Governor-General's
Fort Rupert• •residence
•SAINT GEORGES

Grand Anse
Campus

Frequente• •Grand Anse

Calvigny
Barracks

25 Oct.
Rangers take True Blue
Campus and release
students

26 Oct.
Grand Anse Campus
secured

St. Georges falls after
an airstrike

Point
Salines

Westerhall
Bay

Hog
Is.   Calivigny Is.

International True Blue
Airport   Campus

25 Oct.
Rangers parachute into
Point Salines and airstrip
is secured

0   5 kilometres

0   5 miles

been firmly pro-west. Bishop promised to introduce economic and political reforms to turn the country into a modern democracy. But, after only a few months in office, he consolidated his power in his own party, the New Jewel Movement, and effectively muzzled any opposition, either political or religious.

To the alarm of the United States, already worried by Soviet advances in Central America, Bishop established close ties with the Soviet Union, North Korea, Vietnam and, above all, Fidel Castro's Cuba. According to US government sources the first shipment of eastern-bloc manufactured arms arrived from Havana within a month of Bishop taking power. This included 3,400 rifles, 200 machine-guns, 100 heavier weapons and ammunition.[2] Shortly after this the Grenadans began construction of a new airfield at Point Salines that would be capable of handling the latest and largest Jumbo jets. Although Bishop repeatedly said that the airfield, which was being built with British and Cuban help, was simply to encourage tourism, the Americans insisted it was designed as a military base.

It is difficult to justify these alarmist assessments. Grenada, a sleepy island of 110,000 people with tourism as its main industry, is an improbable hot-bed of revolution. Certainly the British, whose former colony Grenada is, took a much more relaxed view of Bishop's left-wing tendencies than did the Americans.

In July 1981, amid the general anti-communist fervour that was gripping the new administration, the CIA put up a plan to the Senate Intelligence Committee for the destabilisation of Bishop's government through a propaganda campaign, a reduction in aid and other measures to cause him economic problems. This campaign was very similar to one used against Castro when he came to power and, as had happened then, its effect would undoubtedly have been to push its victim even further into the communist camp. The Senate refused to give authority for the plan, believing that Grenada did not rate so much attention. However, the CIA did manage to continue with a propaganda effort drawing attention to the left-wing nature of the Bishop government.[3]

The war of words took a different turn when Bishop himself was placed under house arrest by a newly-formed People's Revolutionary Army on 13 October 1983 in a coup organised by Bernard Coard, a left-winger from Bishop's own party who thought he had become too moderate. That same day an inter-agency group met in the State Department in Washington to discuss the situation and see if any action was necessary to protect the lives of the estimated 1,000 American citizens living and working on the island. Around 300 of them were residents, and the balance were medical students living at a US-owned school.

On 14 October the National Security Council ordered the JCS to begin planning an evacuation of Americans from Grenada. The JCS passed the instructon on to Admiral Wesley McDonald, the Commander-in-Chief Atlantic (CINCLANT) for action.

On 18 October the US sent a formal note to the Grenadan government asking for assurances of the safety of the Americans on the island. The Grenadan Ministry of External Affairs replied the next day: 'The interests of US citizens are in no way threatened by the present situation in Grenada which the Ministry hastens to point out is a purely internal matter.'[4]

Washington found this brief response less than reassuring – even though it seems unlikely, in the chaos on the island at the time, that any official would have had the time to draft a careful reply that would have taken care of all the diplomatic niceties. Certainly, there is no evidence that at this stage, or indeed at any other time, lives of Americans were threatened in any way.

Bishop was freed on 19 October by thousands of supporters. Along with some members of his cabinet, the chanting demonstrators marched on Fort Rupert in an attempt to free a cabinet colleague, but members of the People's Revolutionary Army then separated Bishop, three members of his cabinet and two labour leaders from the crowd, took them inside the fort and summarily executed them. The troops also opened fire on the crowd, killing at least fifty and injuring many others.

That same day, Ambassador Bish, the US ambassador in Bridgetown, the nearest American diplomatic post, sent a message to the State Department that said: 'There appears to be imminent danger to US citizens resident on Grenada due to the current deteriorating situation which includes reports of rioting, personnel casualties (possibly deaths), automatic weapons being discharged, Soviet-built armoured personnel carriers in the Grenadan streets, and some loss of water and electricity on the island. Embassy Bridgetown recommends that the United States should now be prepared to conduct an emergency evacuation of US citizens residing in Grenada.'[5]

It is not clear on what the ambassador was basing his extremely alarmist cable, but it galvanised an already concerned State Department into action. Some preliminary meetings involving senior military officials had taken place over the preceding three days. In addition, because it was expected that a 'non permissive evacuation' (in State Department jargon) might be involved, JSOC at Fort Bragg had been alerted and asked to come up with a rescue plan.

The National Security Council had, naturally enough, been keeping a close eye on the matter. In particular, a Lieutenant-Colonel Oliver North was producing memoranda suggesting that a military assault on the island was the only way forward. While North's fairly lowly position on the NSC should not have given his views undue influence, he was seen as the President's point man on military and counter-terrorist matters. To many, it was North's enthusiastic endorsement of an armed response that pushed the plan forward.

On the morning of 20 October the JCS met to discuss what should be done. At this stage the assessment of the military strength of the Grenadans on the island was sketchy but it was thought that there might be about 250 Cuban construction

workers with military training and arms and around 300
Grenadans.

In the view of JSOC the presence of such a small and
poorly-trained opposing army presented a perfect opportunity
for the special forces to carry out the entire operation. Two
plans seem to have been advanced, one devised by JSOC that
simply involved special forces, and another by CINCLANT
that suggested using only Marines. In an apparently stormy
meeting of the JCS on 20 October, both plans were discussed.
Each of those present demanded a slice of the action, with
General Paul X. Kelley, the Marine commander, being
particularly vociferous. The result was a compromise: in the
initial assault, the special forces and the Rangers would take
the southern half of the island and the Marines would take
the north.

The operation would not be run by JSOC, although it had
been specifically designed for this kind of emergency. Neither
would it be run by the Commander-in-Chief of the Cuba
Caribbean Contingency Joint Task Force, in whose operational area the action would occur – indeed he was not even
informed of the impending invasion. Nor would the Joint
Deployment Agency based at MacDill Air Force Base in
Florida be involved, even though the JDA had been set up
in 1979 specifically to co-ordinate the rapid deployment of
forces. JSOC was not used because the operation now
included more than special forces, and the JDA was kept out
because the service chiefs were worried that it was insecure.
Instead, the JCS asked the US Atlantic Command at Norfolk,
Virginia to set up an *ad hoc* planning group. CINCLANT
would have overall command of the operation.

Once the decision to produce detailed plans had been
taken, the JCS imposed total operational security (OPSEC).
In after-action reports, the JCS justified this by arguing they
were worried that details of the operation might leak out to
the Soviets, who would have told the Cubans, who would
have alerted the Grenadans. That might have resulted in
some of the Americans on the island being taken hostage.

They were also concerned that the media might get wind of the plan.

The JCS set a fine example in OPSEC. They met every day for the next five days and none of them even took their notes out of the meeting room in the Pentagon, because they were so concerned about leaks.

These may have been genuine fears but the result of the OPSEC obsession was inadequate planning and considerable confusion for all those involved. In many ways this mirrored what had happened in the Desert One mission four years previously, and it is astonishing that the JCS appeared to have learned nothing from that failure.

News of the planned operation was confined to the JCS, the White House, senior officials in the State Department and CINCLANT's planners and JSOC. The two exceptions were the Marine Amphibious Unit (MAU) that two days earlier had set sail from the US for the Lebanon, and a carrier group, led by the USS *Independence*, that was on its way to the Mediterranean.[6]

At 03.00 on the morning of 21 October, the Marines received a signal to divert to a grid reference off the coast of Grenada. The message added that if no further instructions were received by midnight on 24 October they were to resume their journey to Lebanon. The group was also instructed to immediately adopt EMCON, a total shutdown of all communications, including the radar that operated the helicopters. From now on, the Marines were not allowed to query any orders received from CINCLANT. The same orders were given to the carrier battle group.

Beyond the simple order to move to a new map reference, the Marines had no idea what they were supposed to be doing. They had no orders to prepare for an assault on the island. However, all of them listened to the BBC World Service later that day which had news of a coup in Grenada and speculation that the US might be about to launch a military operation to rescue US citizens on the island. They assumed this would be a single-service operation and the following day all the commanders met on board the command ship *Guam*. Unable to get any clarification from CINCLANT, the Marines decided on a simultaneous helicopter and landing-ship assault on Grand Anse Beach, near the capital St George's, and on the airfield of Point Salines.

Over the next few days, the Marine commanders, under the radio shutdown, actually found it quicker and more efficient to communicate with each other by Aldis flashing light rather than by ship-to-ship radio. 'You could get an answer back in an hour rather than a day which is how long it took a radio message to get through the bureaucracy,' recalled one Marine officer.[7]

On 22 October two officials from the US embassy in Bridgetown reached Grenada. The report they sent back appeared to confirm Ambassador Bish's alarming cable of two days previously: a 24-hour shoot-on-sight curfew had been imposed, a number of officials and journalists had been arrested and jailed, the airport was closed and telephone and telex links had been cut. Also, the officials reported that more than 300 American citizens wanted to leave the island. Whether these were students or residents was not made clear, but certainly the vast majority of the students were not contacted before the invasion.

The next day, following a meeting of the Organisation of Eastern Caribbean States, a message was sent to the US, Jamaica and Barbados in the names of Antigua, St Lucia, St Vincent and the Grenadines, Montserrat and Dominica asking for assistance in restoring order in Grenada. This plea for help was reinforced on 24 October when the Prime Minister of Barbados, Tom Adams, said he had received a letter form the Governor-General of Grenada, Sir Paul Scoon, asking for assistance.

This was welcome news for the American administration which needed every legal justification if the operation was not going to be seen as an aggressive invasion rather than simply the rescue of beleaguered American citizens.

Sir Paul Scoon's role in this affair was important. Since the independence of Grenada from Britain in 1974, the Governor-General acted as the representative of Queen Elizabeth on the island, and the Queen herself is still recognised as the official head of state there. It was she who appointed him in 1978, and it was to Britain that Scoon owed allegiance. It is extraordinary, therefore, that Scoon should have asked America for help before turning to Britain, especially since he had no reason to suppose that the British would not have come to his aid.

The letter that Scoon was supposed to have written to Adams was only revealed on 27 October, two days after the invasion and after the Governor-General had been in US hands for some time. In his letter Scoon said: 'I am requesting your help to assist me in stabilising this grave and dangerous situation. It is my desire that a peace-keeping force should be established in Grenada. . . . In this connection, I am also seeking assistance from the United States, from Jamaica and from the OECS.'[8]

It was certainly convenient for the US that this letter surfaced after the invasion, asking for US assistance in exactly the terms that the Americans themselves had been portraying the operation. There are many in the British government who regard the letter with deep suspicion.

Even before Scoon's invitation, however, momentum behind the invasion plans was gathering. CINCLANT had now allowed JSOC to devise a special operation plan that would involve both Delta Force and SEALs. Where necessary they would be flown to the island by Task Force 160.

TF160 had been set up by the Army in the wake of Desert One, to provide the special forces with their own highly-trained helicopter pilots (and the Army with a share of the glamorous special forces pie). Known as the Night Stalkers, the unit is based at Fort Campbell, Kentucky, and uses Black Hawks, Hughes 500-MD, Chinook and other helicopters, all of which have special equipment including terrain-following radar and night vision devices.

This would be the first time the TF160 had seen combat.

In training they had a high accident rate, seventeen deaths
from five crashes in 1983 alone, but many of these were
accounted for by the 'edge of the envelope' flying practised
by all the pilots in the unit. 'The majority of those deaths
had been completely unnecessary,' said one source who had
reviewed the circumstances. 'They were flying missions that
had more to do with macho than operations.'[9]

Delta had been specifically set up for rescuing hostages in
foreign countries. On this occasion there were no hostages to
rescue but JSOC was still determined that Delta, rather than
other Green Berets, would be involved in the assault. In part
there was a feeling that Delta still had to make up for the
Iran affair, and in part there was a need to justify the massive
investment that the Reagan administration had begun to
pump into special forces. The SEALs, on the other hand,
were trained to carry out just the kind of unconventional
operation that JSOC had in mind, and their deployment
therefore had some military logic.

A five-man joint JSOC/CINCLANT team flew first to the
carrier *Independence* and then to the *Guam* to brief the Marines.
In a conference on 23 October the Marines were told that
the operation had been expanded to take in roles for the
Rangers and the special forces. The draft plan gave the special
forces and the Rangers the south of the Island, and the
Marines the north. (In fact, the Marines never received the
final plan because of a communications failure. Of course,
they were unable to query this because of OPSEC.) The
Marines were told that they would attack before dawn on 25
October.

The headquarters team brought with them just one map
of the island with a scale of 1:50,000. With 125 officers in the
Marine Amphibious Unit, additional maps were required so
that planning and operational assignments could proceed.
The only photocopier on the *Guam* was a reducer that copied
the map perfectly but made it so small that it couldn't be
read. The staff team flew back to the *Independence*, promising
to send more maps. None arrived until after the invasion. All

the Marine planning was done using a single 8in. by 5in. map taken from a tourist brochure that happened to be in the library of the *Guam*. The planners on the *Guam* were actually using a map that had last been updated in 1895.[10]

It has to be said that the special forces of most other nations are rather better equipped.

On board HMS *Fearless*, for example, one of the British Royal Marine assault ships, is a fully computerised mapping system. In its database is every single beach in the world that has been surveyed by the SBS. With the right information the computer can print out a detailed and up-to-date map within seconds.

The US difficulty was only solved on the afternoon after the invasion had begun, when some Grenadan army troops were captured with maps.

This was only the first of many intelligence mishaps that were to bedevil the operation. After the JCS meeting on 20 October a message was sent to the CIA asking for any intelligence they had on the island. Despite the fact that they had been running a propaganda campaign against the Bishop government for nearly three years, the CIA did not have a single agent in place. Their only operative was a local businessman on a small retainer, who happened to be off the island when the crisis blew up. When contacted by Langley, he refused to return. The CIA then claimed they had no agents available to put in to the island and, despite further entreaties from the JCS, throughout the operation they were unable to develop a single Humint source. This was extraordinary: not only is the world's second largest community of Grenadans in New York City, but there were anyway 300 Americans resident on the island and several hundred more there as students.

Of course, this was exactly the kind of operation that ISA had been created for. However, General Richard Scholtes, the JSOC commander, had an intense dislike of ISA – he privately described it as 'a bunch of Delta rejects'. His antipathy could be traced back to an exercise ISA had run the previous year in Las Vegas, which had gone wrong. In the course of the practice, ISA aroused the suspicion of the local police and were arrested. When questioned they claimed they were members of Delta Force and, much to Scholtes's disgust, he had to get the men freed, and then suffer the political fall-out. ISA were never deployed in Grenada.

After the Defense Intelligence Agency were asked to provide information on the numbers, arms and whereabouts of troops on the islands, a number of overflights of the island by SR-71 or TR-1 reconnaissance aircraft were authorised. The data they brought back was analysed by the DIA, and the reports were passed on to JSOC. But the information never reached the men who actually attacked the island.

As one commander of the invasion force put it: 'Ninety per cent of the intelligence I had before we went ashore came from the BBC.'

The result of the inadequate intelligence was that the invading force had no clear idea of what exactly they might be facing. Initial intelligence on which the planning was based suggested they would be met by 1,200 troops of the Grenadan People's Revolutionary Army, 3–5,000 local militia and 2–300 Cuban construction workers. The strength of the Cubans was revised upwards to 700 just before the invasion and then during the course of the first day was revised once again to 5,000, a figure out of all proportion to reality. As well as being criminally vague about numbers, the planning teams also had no idea what arms the Grenadans had, nor where the troops were on the island.

The CINCLANT plan specifically banned any advance reconnaissance of the island by members of the invasion force. The Marines, for example, had their own SEAL team on board but they were not allowed to send any of their own men ashore in advance of the landing; that was to be left to the men from Fort Bragg.

On the afternoon of Sunday 23 October the CINCLANT plan was put before the JCS. According to General John Wickham, the Army Chief of Staff, the JCS had received some new intelligence that suggested a larger Cuban and Grenadan military presence than had previously been thought. It is unclear exactly where this information came from (no intelligence agency had people on the island and photo reconnaissance had not produced that kind of information) and in any event, it proved to be completely wrong.

The JCS now decided to double the size of the invasion force. The Rangers would be backed up by the 82nd Airborne, and the invasion would take place using elements from the Army, Navy, Air Force, Marines and special forces, giving all the services a slice of the action.[11]

Authority for the assault to proceed was informally passed down the chain of command from the White House on the morning of 24 October. That evening the British government and Congress were informed of the planned attack. Despite a personal telephone call from President Reagan, in London Prime Minister Margaret Thatcher was furious to hear of the American plans. She saw the US action as being in contravention of international law and a gross interference in another country's internal affairs. London's assessments of the Grenadan situation were very different from Washington's: it was acknowledged that there was instability but no indication was seen that US or British lives were in danger. Thatcher attempted to persuade Reagan to abandon the plan but failed, and the President gave formal approval that evening.

To the US government, Grenada appeared to provide a perfect opportunity to demonstrate the strength of their determination to combat the communist menace. Until then, the Reagan administration had concentrated their efforts on El Salvador and Nicaragua, both of which, they argued, were being destabilised by Cuba and the Soviet Union. Now Grenada was going the same way, and had the added attractions of being a small target, with US citizens in place to rescue.

Admiral Wesley McDonald placed Vice-Admiral Joseph Metcalf, the commander of the US Second Fleet, in charge of Joint Task Force 120 which would oversee the assault on the island, now code named Operation Urgent Fury. Metcalf was based on the *Guam*.

The final plan had three aims:

1. To neutralise the People's Revolutionary Army and any other armed forces on the island;
2. To establish conditions which would allow the people of Grenada to regain control over their own government;
3. To evacuate Americans and other friendly foreign nationals as required.

To do this a highly complex plan had been devised. During the night of the 24/25 October special forces elements would be placed on the island. They would have five principle tasks:

1. Landing by parachute before dawn on 25 October, Delta was required to secure the airfield under construction at Point Salines. Overhead reconnaissance had shown that after the day's work the partially-completed runway was littered with debris and construction vehicles that could cause serious damage to aircraft trying to land. Delta must secure the airfield perimeter and clear the runway for the Rangers and the reinforcements of the 82nd Airborne.
2. Another Delta unit should attack the Richmond Hill jail to free the civil servants and other citizens who had been imprisoned over the previous few days. It is unclear why this was given such a high priority as there were no prisoners of great political significance being held. It is possible that the planners considered the freeing of prisoners would be a welcome gesture to the population at large.
3. A SEAL team was to assault the residence of the Governor-General Sir Paul Scoon, and take him off the island. As the Queen's representative, his endorsement of the US action was important, and there was concern that he might be held hostage by the Grenadans. There was no intelligence to support this fear.
4. The SEALs would also attack Radio Free Grenada, the single radio station that covered the island. The planners

felt that if it was allowed to broadcast during the course of the invasion, it might rally the thousands of Cubans and Grenadans against the American forces.

5. Two other four-man SEAL teams would reconnoitre the landing strip at Pearl's Airport and the beach near Grenville where the Marines intended to land.

All these attacks would take place during the night in advance of the conventional forces. JSOC would control the special operations and the transport aircraft from a C–130 aircraft circling over the island.[12]

The Rangers and the Marines were told that the special forces had 'selected targets in the St George's area'. No details were supplied and in fact all tactical plans prepared by the Marines and Rangers included assaults on Delta and SEAL targets.

Two days before the invasion, the 1st Ranger battalion had been airlifted from their base at Fort Lewis, Washington, to Fort Stewart, Georgia, where they joined up with the 2nd Ranger battalion. In the early stages of the planning, it was decided that the battalions would go in separately, led by the 1st. However, in the jockeying for action that followed, it was agreed that elements of both 1st and 2nd Battalions, combined into a single unit, would go in the first wave. Thus, skilled teams of men were broken up, as was the command and control network, producing a force that had never even worked together, let alone fought together.

The combined force, totalling 600 men, would leave the US in the early hours on 25 October, landing at Point Salines shortly after dawn. The plan called for the Rangers to follow the Delta parachute force in, using C-130 transports. They would then secure the airfield for the next contingent of Rangers which would be flown in by those same aircraft.

Later on the first day the Rangers would be relieved by the 82nd Airborne who would fly in a brigade of 3,000 men from Fort Bragg. Another brigade would be waiting in reserve to fly in if necessary.

At the north end of the island the Marines divided their Battalion Landing Team of around 800 men into three companies, Fox, Echo and Golf. Echo and Golf would seize Pearl's airfield, and Fox would assault Grenville Port. The Marines planned to then move south eventually to link up with the Rangers.

The American force that was eventually committed to Operation Urgent Fury totalled 6,500, including reserves, against intelligence assessments of a total opposition force – including Cubans, People's Revolutionary Army and reservists – of 11,200 at their most pessimistic. It is unclear just how these figures were arrived at. If the staff planners actually believed them, then the force the US was sending to Grenada was far too small. For an invasion of this type, the assault force should outnumber the defenders by at least three to one. What seems more likely is that, although nobody really believed the opposition was anything like so strong, the figures were bumped up in order to justify sending more troops.

On the evening of 24 October the Marine commanders were briefed about how they were to deal with the local people once they were ashore. Their commander told them they should say: 'We are here to neutralise the People's Revolutionary Army, to evacuate Americans, and to restore peace to Grenada. We do not want to have to hurt anyone but will certainly kill anyone who resists us. Remain in your homes, do not gather in large groups, and do not take any hostile action towards us.'

In the final briefing for the Marines on board the *Guam*, they received their first hard intelligence from photographic reconnaissance: namely that the airfield at Pearl's was defended by anti-aircraft guns, probably Soviet-supplied ZSU-23s. It was decided that the Marines would switch their landing site from Pearl's to a nearby racetrack, which close examination of the tourist brochure had revealed. 'We had no intelligence on that and had no idea whether it was defended or not,' admits one Marine officer.

In the final hours before the first mission, a number of

serious gaps in the planning of the operation began to appear. In two critical areas, fire control and logistical support, OPSEC requirements ensured that none of the key people had been consulted during the planning of the mission. The Rangers had decided to fly in without their own mortars, and instead they would rely on fire support from the Navy. But, until forty-eight hours before the operation began, no teams trained in co-ordinating Navy fire for ground forces were involved in the planning. Even when they were notified, the teams did not arrive at Fort Bragg in time to deploy with their host units. When they eventually did link up they did so without any of the codes, frequencies and call signs that were needed to communicate with the Navy ships offshore.[13]

Subsequently in the fighting, the co-ordination of fire from ships and aircraft was a shambles. The land forces had radios that couldn't talk to the Navy operators, and even when they managed to make contact they had no codes to authenticate commands. They resorted to ham radios, sent couriers with verbal orders by helicopter and in one case used a credit card to place a call on a civilian telephone to Fort Bragg to get a request for fire support relayed back to the flagship.[14]

OPSEC also ensured that the JCS's own Director of Logistics was kept out of all the preliminary planning for Urgent Fury. In fact, the first any expert in logistics knew about the operation was twenty-four hours before the assault began, when CINCLANT's logistics specialist, Rear-Admiral Neil Ferraro, was given a preliminary briefing. The result of such poor planning was that the Rangers and the Airborne arrived on the island with one day's food, no drinking water, no transport and a serious shortage of ammunition.[15]

Even when urgent supplies were required, the system was unable to cope. Requests for jungle boots resulted in a huge supply of diet soda, a misunderstanding that is perhaps understandable when it is realised that goods were being sent from depots all over the United States by Express Mail or Express Freight to Fort Bragg, and each order took an average of twelve days to fill.

As planned, Operation Urgent Fury began with a pre-dawn Delta Force parachute drop on to the airfield at Point Salines. It was to be one of the very few things that did go right on that day. Delta had arrived in Barbados on 24 October aboard C-130 transports and giant C-5 transports which carried dismantled Black Hawk helicopters for the other Delta team.

Soon after the Delta parachutists landed, they were spotted by a Grenadan airport guard who raised the alarm. They quickly came under heavy rifle and machine-gun fire and were pinned down in a small ravine by the airfield, surrounded by Grenadan and Cuban soldiers. In the dark they were unable to summon assistance. Eventually, after dawn had broken, an AC-130 Spectre gunship came overhead and put down devastating covering fire. In four hours of fighting six men from the Delta unit of thirty-five were killed and sixteen wounded.

The Delta Force team's assault caused the alarm to be raised all over the island. Key points were reinforced as local army and militia men prepared for the US invasion.

As Delta was approaching Point Salines, a SEAL team had attempted a night attack on Radio Free Grenada. But by the time they reached the beach in their boats east of Point Salines, the alarm had already been raised and they walked straight into an ambush, losing two men killed and two others wounded out of an eight-strong party. They evacuated without getting within range of the radio station, which continued to call the Grenadan forces to arms all morning.

Two other SEAL teams met with disaster as they attempted a complex and dangerous night landing from a low-flying C-130 transport aircraft. According to the historian Richard Gabriel, the teams used a system known as LAPESing (low altitude parachute extraction system), which uses a parachute to drag men and equipment, including inflatable dinghies, out of a low-flying aircraft and put them down on the water. The first team of four was apparently knocked unconscious and drowned. The second team reached the water safely and was heading for the shore when a fishing boat happened to emerge from nearby Grenville Port. They cut the outboard engine on the dinghy to avoid being discovered, but by the time the fishing boat had disappeared into the darkness the engine was flooded and the dinghy was swept away into the night. They were picked up eleven hours later by a Navy helicopter.

The Marines were alerted that they would now have no advance intelligence on their targets. The MAU therefore decided to put its own SEAL team ashore, and did so just before dawn.

H-Hour for the Rangers was 04.30 and for the Marines 05.00. Neither of these deadlines would be met. As far as the Rangers were concerned, they had been alerted in the course of their flight from the mainland that the airport at Point Salines had not been secured. It was decided in mid-flight that they would parachute in rather than doing a normal landing. The time required for the troops to rig the aircraft for a jump meant that they did not get over the airfield until much later, after first light.

The first two C-130s approached the runway and were met by small arms fire from the alerted ground force. The two aircraft, radioing they were under 'heavy fire', turned away from the jump zone having released just twelve Rangers, who for a few terrifying minutes found themselves unsupported on the ground. Then the third aircraft, which contained the commanders and their support teams, completed its mission and dropped its cargo.[16] The command unit immediately came under fire from the defending forces. They were surprised to find themselves alone on the airfield. The Delta force was still pinned down in its ravine. The seven C-130s coming in behind them were widely spread out as they had expected to land one at a time rather than execute a massed parachute drop, and it was several minutes before the next aircraft appeared with troops to relieve the ground commanders.

It took two hours to land the first wave of Rangers, about

four times as long as any realistic war plan should have allowed. Once on the ground, the units seem to have been afflicted by something close to panic. This might be explained by the fact that only eight or nine men out of the whole Ranger battalion had any combat experience. Rather than immediately advancing to clear out the small enemy contingent that continued to fire on them from the eastern end of the runway, and then, moving on to the nearby True Blue Medical campus where the students were supposed to be, the Rangers dug in at the western end and awaited reinforcements.

The signals that Admiral Metcalf had been receiving on the *Independence* seemed to confirm all the worst intelligence fears. The Rangers had evidently met massive opposition and urgently needed support. The original plan had called for the ten C-130s that had dropped off the first batch to return to Fort Stewart to pick up the balance of the 1st and 2nd battalions. After that, the C-130s would head for Fort Bragg to help airlift the 82nd Airborne in to Grenada.

That plan was now changed. The C-130s were diverted directly to Fort Bragg to lift in the 82nd. Within an hour of the attack on Grenada beginning, therefore, the whole Airborne division had been committed. The balance of the Ranger battalions, however, never did get to war.

At the northern end of the island the Marines had fared rather better. At 02.00, their commander had received a coded radio message 'Walk Track Shoes' from the SEAL team reconnoitring the beach. This meant the beach was passable to shallow draft landing vessels but not to ordinary boats. He therefore planned to land Golf company at the beach next to Pearl's airport, with Echo landing by helicopter on the airfield. Immediately the airfield was secured, Golf would head south to take Grenville. Fox company would be held in reserve.

Over the next two hours, the plan was changed twice. First the surface assault was cancelled, forcing all the Marines to land by helicopter. Fox company now landed at Grenville and Echo at the landing zone next to the airport, with Golf held in reserve. Then there was confusion over landing zones, but finally it was decided the assault would begin at 04.00 while it was still dark enough for the helicopter pilots to use night vision goggles. Delays with getting the helicopters airborne and finding the landing sites meant that the Marines did not actually begin landing until 05.20, just as dawn was breaking, when the night vision goggles were starting to blur in the first light of day.

Echo company found that their landing zone was marshy and dotted with palm trees. Again poor intelligence had failed to spot these obvious hazards. The first CH-53 transport helicopters to land began to sink into the spongy ground and had to unload very rapidly. The first jeep loaded with TOW anti-tank missiles to come out of the helicopter sank into the marsh and turned over.

The Marines came under scattered fire but fortunately none of it was effective and there were no injuries. Cobra helicopter gunships attacked some anti-aircraft positions at the end of the runway and destroyed them. Within thirty minutes the airfield was secure. A group of enemy soldiers manning a .50 machine-gun post was spotted on the hill to the north of the airfield and a platoon was ordered to capture the ground and the gun. They ran up the hill without firing a shot and the enemy soldiers ran down the other side. As one Marine recalled:

'The troops' fire discipline is actually too good in this case, as they probably could have killed several but tried to catch them instead. Burdened with packs, flak jackets and helmets, they have no chance. The heat and humidity are already intense and the terrain is really steep.'

Fox company had landed at Grenville and encountered no opposition of any kind.

At 06.30, the Marines were astonished to see flying over them nine Black Hawk helicopters belonging to Task Force 160. Five hours late, they were at last on their way to assault Richmond Hill prison: at their Barbados staging post it had taken much longer than expected to put them together.

(Others, less charitably, have put the delay down to the fact that different elements of the Task Force were operating in different time zones. The orders were given out simply with a time written on them without specifying Eastern Standard Time, Greenwich Mean Time or some other time. This has been impossible to confirm.)

Rather than cancel the operation or move to an alternative plan, JSOC allowed Delta to attack Richmond Hill five hours late, during daylight, several hours after the alarm had been raised, and an hour and a half after the conventional attack had begun. Not surprisingly, they ran into trouble.

Task Force 160 were known as the Night Stalkers because they specialised in night flying using special goggles that allow them to see in the dark. For three years they had been practising this technique and yet on this first major operation they found themselves attacking in daylight. This was also the first time that the use of a new type of helicopter, the Hughes 500, was confirmed, when one was shot down and the incident captured on film by a Grenadan resident.

One Black Hawk was shot down crossing over the coast and a second dropped out of the assault force to circle overhead until help arrived. This would seem to be in clear breach of normal practice for special forces where the mission takes precedence over the lives of a few of those involved.

The Richmond Hill prison is built on the site of an old fort and overlooks the town of St George's. The prison itself is dominated by Fort Frederick, then an important garrison for the People's Revolutionary Army, which sits on a slightly higher hill. Between the two runs a valley and it was into this valley that the remaining seven helicopters flew.

The plan was for the machines to hover over the prison while the men with full packs let themselves down ropes hanging from each helicopter. Two different techniques can be employed. The first, abseiling, uses a special harness with a spring clip attached to the rope, and requires about eighteen seconds to reach the ground from forty metres; the second, and more dangerous, is known as 'fast roping' where the men simply slide straight down the rope in under seven seconds from fifteen metres.

Neither technique was used, however, since the helicopters immediately came under heavy fire as they flew up the valley under the guns in Fort Frederick. It was an obviously empty gesture to have attempted the assault in such circumstances and not surprisingly the attack failed. Some confusion exists concerning the number of helicopters that were lost in the attack. A sergeant from Delta Force, who was wounded in the attack, was later debriefed on the *Guam* and claimed that only one Black Hawk had been shot down and another had crashed after running out of fuel. On the other hand, Richard Gabriel maintains that five helicopters were shot down, one turned away from fire and another abandoned the assault after taking some hits. Either way, the Delta men were pinned down for the rest of the day and the assault on the prison was abandoned.

An air strike was called in on Fort Frederick later that morning which missed and levelled the island's mental hospital three thousand yards away, killing twenty-one civilians.

Shortly after the Night Stalkers had flown overhead, the Marines on the airfield received word from the *Guam* that a SEAL team was pinned down under heavy fire. The Marines were not told that the SEALs' mission had been to evacuate the Governor-General, Sir Paul Scoon, and his staff from his residence in St George's. The SEAL team commander was patched through to the Marines and he simply told them that eight of his thirteen-strong team had been wounded and they were surrounded.

Two Cobra helicopter gunships were diverted from Pearl's airport to go to the rescue of the SEALs. It was known that anti-aircraft units were in the area and it was thought the helicopters might be very vulnerable. However, the message from the SEAL team was so urgent that the risk was taken.

This was a serious tactical mistake. Both Cobras were shot down and three Marine pilots were killed (the only Marine fatalities of the operation). When a Marine force eventually relieved the SEALs the following day, they found no wounded at all in a party of twenty-two which included the Governor-General and his staff. 'In fact, they had not been surrounded but had simply panicked and lied to get help,' recalled one officer.

To the commanders on board the *Guam*, things seemed to be going from bad to worse: the Rangers were pinned down at Point Salines, the special forces operations had been a disaster, attempts to extract the Governor-General had failed, and there were reports coming in from special forces and the Rangers of enormous enemy concentrations on the island.

For Vice-Admiral Metcalf the next few hours brought radical changes to the initial plan. Significantly, he had on his staff the MAU operations officer, Major Ernie von Huss from Tennessee. Von Huss was a military historian, a lover of Stonewall Jackson, and a man with a long memory for slights against the Marine Corps. He recalled the invasion of Okinawa during the World War II when, in a similar joint operation, the Army had taken all the prestige targets and left the Marines without any of the glory.

His first thought when at the original briefing he had seen the map of Grenada divided in two with the northern (red) half given to the Marines and the southern (green) half to the Army, was that Urgent Fury was going to be a re-run of Okinawa. So, during those critical first few hours when Urgent Fury began to go badly wrong and Metcalf kept turning to his staff for advice, von Huss spoke up every time and recommended the Marines advance, and every time Metcalf accepted the recommendation. The result of this little ploy was that the Marines with twenty per cent of the force ended up occupying eighty per cent of the island and von Huss became a hero to his friends and colleagues.

By mid-morning the first contingent of the 82nd Airborne began to arrive at Point Salines airfield. But the reinforcement quickly became a shambles. The Airborne expected to arrive at an airfield that had been captured by the Rangers. In fact, they found the Rangers at the west end, while the Cubans and Grenadans at the east end fired everything they had at each aircraft as it flew in to land.

The problem was made worse by the small size of the airfield and the complete lack of planning that had gone into the reinforcement operation. The runway could only take one aircraft at a time and each aircraft was obliged to spend at least thirty minutes on the ground. But C-130 and C-141 Starlifters were being sent in a continuous wave, so that they had to spend more time circling over the island than they had flying from the US. Some even had to return to Puerto Rico to refuel.[17]

In the midst of the chaos at the airfield, there was a moment of farce when JTF120 received an order from CINCLANT that no Army helicopters could be refuelled by the USS *Guam* because inter-service funding arrangements had not been worked out in Washington. The order came at a most inconvenient time when there was intense pressure on the helicopters, in particular to evacuate the wounded. Fortunately, the officer in charge of aircraft on the *Guam* disregarded the order on his own initiative.

The Rangers now joined up with the Airborne and together they attempted to break out of the airfield and head towards St George's. For the next five hours, the combined might of the assault force was thrown at the Grenadan and Cuban forces. Strikes by A-7 Corsair and helicopter gunships were called in as the ground forces moved at a snail's pace east towards the capital. By the end of the first day, the Rangers and the Airborne had advanced approximately one mile, and the Cuban barracks next to the airfield had not been secured. The US troops dug in for the night.

Intelligence had reported that the medical students, in whose name Urgent Fury had been carried out, were housed in the True Blue campus of the medical school, near the eastern end of the runway. This campus was finally reached just after dark on day one and the students there were ferried out the next morning.

Only when they were questioned did it emerge that another 224 students were staying at the Grand Anse campus four miles north-east of the airfield, a further 202 were at Lance-aux-Epines south-east of St George's, and some thirty-five others were lodging in private houses in the town. Using numbers supplied by the rescued students, the Rangers telephoned to their homes in the United States to get the local numbers of the students who had boarded out. They were then telephoned and asked to describe their whereabouts. Once again intelligence had been laughable. At no time before or during the course of the fighting had any Grenadan or Cuban made any threat of any kind against the students.

To relieve pressure on the beleaguered Rangers and the SEALs at the Governor-General's house, Metcalf now decided to move the reserve Marine company, Golf, by ship around the island to land at Grand Mal Bay. A second company would then fly from Pearl's to link up with them.

Throughout Urgent Fury, ship-to-shore communications varied from bad to hopeless and in consequence these decisions could not be relayed to the Marines on the island. The Army and the Marines both used UHF, but the frequencies were incompatible so they were unable to talk to each other. JTF120 on board the *Guam* had radio equipment that could communicate separately with each ground unit, but it had been designed to be used only when the ship was stationary – an unlikely occurrence at sea. Every time the ship turned, all communications were lost until the radio antennas had been manually readjusted.

Because of the poor communications, the Marine battalion commander, Lieutenant-Colonel Ray Smith, was unable to get details of Metcalf's plans to move Golf company round to Grand Mal Bay. When Smith arrived on the *Guam* to find out for himself, he was told by the JTF120 intelligence officers that photo reconnaissance showed enemy tanks and armoured personnel carriers about to counter-attack on Pearl's airfield. As there were no roads or bridges in the area that would hold a tank or an APC, such intelligence seemed unlikely.

Nevertheless, over the next half hour, he and Admiral Metcalf received intelligence that Grenadan and Cuban tanks were already moving on to the airfield. The news caused panic in the operations room. No tanks at all had been reported on the island in advance of the invasion; furthermore, the Rangers and the 82nd Airborne were bogged down and no other reinforcements were available to send to Pearl's. Fortunately, the Marines on the ground saw no tanks or APCs all day. It was all a false alarm.

Golf company had already been sent around the island on board the USS *Fort Snelling* and the USS *Manitowac*. They had been given an assault time of 16.00. At 15.40 the operations room realised that the Marines had not been briefed about their mission once they were ashore. The landing was hastily rescheduled for 18.30.

Smith wanted to join Golf company before the assault and therefore picked up a helicopter to take him via Pearl's where he planned to collect his radio operators. It took thirty minutes to find a helicopter so that by the time he landed at Pearl's it was already 18.20. Smith then hitched a lift in a CH-43 helicopter to fly on to the *Manitowac* but, immediately after they left the shore in the gathering darkness, the helicopter lost all its communications and navigation aids. For four hours, they searched for a ship to land on and finally chanced on the USS *Trenton*. Smith eventually returned to the *Guam*, but the delay made him 'so frustrated [he] could barely see.'[18].

By 23.30, Captain Bob Dobson, Golf company commander, had brought his men ashore and the airlift of Fox company to Grand Mal had begun. The MAU SEAL team leader had gone ashore in broad daylight in a dinghy and reported the all-clear, but neither Fox nor Golf had in fact yet been briefed on what they were supposed to be doing.

Arriving from the *Guam*, Smith and his command team had to wade ashore from the ramp of their CH–53 as the landing zone off the beach could only take one helicopter at a time and was already occupied. A beachside conference was hurriedly held with the Fox and Golf commanders. Intelligence apparently generated by special forces teams and Sigint filtered from *Guam* suggested that the Marines were confronted by at least a battalion between the beach and St George's, and another battalion in the area around the radio transmitting tower north of Grand Mal.

As Fox was still on its way to Grand Mal, a platoon of Golf company was told to dig in to the north in case of a counter-attack by the battalion facing them. The remainder of Golf company advanced along the road towards St George's with the aim of relieving the beleaguered SEAL team, capturing Fort Frederick and the Richmond Hill prison.

During the night Golf advanced into St George's unopposed except for some occasional small arms fire which did no damage. At no time was there any evidence of the two battalions that were supposed to have been confronting them. Again, this seems to have been a wild exaggeration based on very unreliable intelligence.

It was not until 03.00 on 26 October, nearly twelve hours after the Marines were ordered in to relieve the SEALs, and nearly twenty-four hours after Urgent Fury began, that the Marines were told that the Governor-General was inside the building where the SEALs were. The SEALs were rescued along with the Governor-General's party and evacuated by helicopter just before dawn.

During the course of this second day the Marines consolidated their position and took Fort Frederick. That evening their commanders were briefed on board *Guam* to attack southwards and seize the three remaining strategic points, Forts Lucas and Adolphus and the Richmond Hill prison. They were also told to move on to the Ross Point Hotel where intelligence suggested four hundred Canadians were taking refuge. The Marines were instructed to have control of Fort Adolphus by 10.00 'even if it has to be reduced to rubble'.

Richmond Hill prison was secured at 08.00 without a shot being fired. By then it was empty and unguarded. Captain Dobson reported that a strange flag was flying over Fort

Adolphus and he was ordered to advance cautiously but to be prepared to bring TOW and .50 fire to bear if attacked. In fact, Golf received a warm welcome in Fort Adolphus from the staff of the Venezuelan embassy sheltering there. The Ross Point Hotel was captured by Fox Company without incident and twenty-four Canadians, not four hundred, were found inside.

The following morning elements of the 82nd Airborne also arrived at the hotel. Despite the fact that the Marines had received written orders two days previously to link up with the 82nd Airborne, the soldiers, the Airborne company commander, and the battalion commander had not been told of the Marines' likely presence there. The Airborne forces had been briefed instead that the Ross Point area was a free-fire zone and they had been prepared to carry out reconnaissance by fire, in other words to level the area and then advance over it. 'After all,' the Airborne battalion commander told the Marines, 'what you kill you don't have to carry.'

Later that day, a mass evacuation of the capital began as the local population responded to threats by the 82nd Airborne that they intended to 'blow the town away'. The Marines made strong representations to Admiral Metcalf for him to try to get some control over the invasion force.

It seemed that, in the general chaos and worry over massive enemy counter-attacks, the fate of the students had been forgotten. Certainly a message from JTF120 that other students were elsewhere on the island had failed to reach the Rangers and the Airborne. The first they had heard about it was when one of the students telephoned them on the morning of 26 October to say that they were surrounded and asking to be rescued. In fact, the main batch of 224 students were not rescued from Grand Anse until 16.14 on that day, nearly twenty-four hours after the invasion began. Another 202 students were evacuated from the Lance-aux-Epines campus the next day.

Only the assault on Grand Anse involved any real drama. Intelligence reported that the enemy had dug a defensive line in front of the campus, which backed on to the beach. It is unclear just how many enemy forces were supposed to be in place but a complicated plan was agreed, involving a land assault by Rangers and Airborne and a sea assault by Marine helicopters to handle the evacuation.

Heavy air strikes by fighters from the *Independence* were called in on the enemy positions. These levelled most of the buildings in the area, including two motels. The marine CH–46 transport helicopters, commanded by Lieutenant-Colonel Granny Amos, then flew in to the beach. One was shot down and one severely damaged in the rescue. One senior Marine claims that the only fire taken by his helicopters was friendly. 'I am absolutely convinced the only people firing at us were our forces and that is what shot us down,' he said.[19]

In the aftermath of that rescue, the Army were convinced that the Marine pilots, who were also responsible for ferrying the Rangers to the campus, had veered off when they came under small arms fire. However, all the students were taken off without injury.

One of the final actions of the war took place at Calvigny Barracks, on the south-east of the island. This was believed to be a Cuban stronghold housing as many as six hundred troops. The Rangers were briefed for the assault and in the course of air strikes by Cobras and A-7s, backed up by Navy guns and 155mm, the barracks were severely damaged. Three helicopters with Rangers on board moved in to occupy them. The first helicopter had just landed when the two hovering immediately above him crashed into each other. One landed in the middle of the Rangers who had just disembarked from the helicopter already on the ground and four men were killed. Whirring blades took off the arms and legs of several other soldiers.

It turned out that the barracks had been evacuated some time before and the only fire at the helicopters or at the ground forces was some long range and intermittent rifle fire.

At 10.00 Admiral Metcalf stepped ashore for a tour of St George's which was now quiet, and the following morning

CINCLANT and the chairman of the JCS, General John Vessey, flew in to survey the territory that had been won. They returned to Washington confident that America had at last stood up for freedom and shown the world that, in President Reagan's words, the US was 'walking tall' once again.

It was certainly true that the people of Grenada greeted the American forces as saviours. All the troops were impressed by the cheerful welcome they received. Local people plied them with food, drink and often very useful intelligence on the dispositions of enemy forces. To the extent that the United States had committed an act that was popular with the vast majority of the Grenadan people, Operation Urgent Fury was justified.

The Reagan administration was swift to point out, too, that the Grenada government had close ties with Moscow and indeed had concluded agreements that would have given Soviet and Cuban aircraft and ships landing and berthing rights on the island. Considerable stocks of ammunition were found and a number of eastern bloc advisers discovered during the mopping-up operations. All this supported Washington's theory that Grenada would have posed a threat to the security of the Caribbean and possibly of the United States itself if America had not intervened.

It is questionable whether, because a particular government favours Moscow, military invasion is justified. Furthermore, the medical students, in whose name Urgent Fury had been carried out, emerged from the island unscathed despite being left at the mercy of the Cubans and the Grenadans for between twelve and forty-eight hours after the invasion began.

But it is in the context of a military operation that the Grenada invasion should be closely examined. The United States military has placed a great deal of emphasis in recent years on two aspects of its planning: special operations and rapid deployment overseas. In neither of these can Urgent Fury be considered as anything other then a failure.

On the available intelligence, the US prepared to meet a force of up to 11,200 well-armed and trained Cuban and

Grenadan troops. The invasion force was configured accordingly. It had available to it the full panoply of American military might: state-of-the-art satellite communications, a carrier battle group, a Marine amphibious force, highly trained special forces, élite Ranger and Airborne troops and the latest helicopters and small arms. These were deployed in overwhelming force.

They actually met a force of some 784 Cubans, of whom only fifty had received any military training, and around 2,000 Grenadan troops. The fighting was done almost entirely by the Grenadan People's Revolutionary Army and even they had been told to lay down their arms and don civilian clothes by 04.00 of 26 October.

Within hours of the landing in the south of the island more than 600 of the Cubans were captured, leaving only very light opposition, and yet it took the Rangers and the Airborne three more days to move only four miles. As one officer recalled: 'The failures of the Airborne must have made the Cubans look ten feet tall in the eyes of the Third World.'

The United States lost twenty-nine killed and had 152 wounded in the fighting, while 110 Grenadan and seventy-one Cuban troops were killed. Forty-five civilians died and 358 were injured. These casualties have to be considered high, given the short duration of the conflict and the poor calibre of the oppostion.

Operation Urgent Fury demonstrated serious flaws in the command and control system operating from the JCS down. The obsession with OPSEC kept key figures out of the planning of the operation. For example, Major-General Edward Trobaugh, the commanding general of the 82nd Airborne Division, was briefed only forty-eight hours before the first men under his command landed on the island. CINCLANT did not have available to him sufficient Army, Marine or Air Force staff to advise him on joint working procedures. As a result there were very few and they mostly did not work.

Intelligence was a disgrace. Not a single one of the units involved on Grenada received adequate intelligence. The CIA actually refused to send any agents to the island and the single agent they had in the area refused point blank to go there. JSOC would not use ISA because of a personality clash, and intelligence gathered by the DIA was not passed to those who needed it.

Grenada was the first real test of the revamped special forces since the Iran raid. It was also the first test of JSOC which had been specifically set up to handle command and control of special operations. Both were found wanting on the day.

With the exception of the mission to rescue the Governor-General, the special operations given to the Delta and SEAL teams were of little relevance to the main campaign. They seem to have been designed to show the military command that special operations were viable rather than that they had a valuable tactical or strategic role. A more sensible use of the resources would have been to get Delta and the SEALs to rescue the students. After all, they were supposed to be in danger, and that would have been exactly the kind of operation for which those units had been trained. JSOC allowed them to be used in roles that were not suitable and even after the mission started to go wrong, such as the delayed assault on Richmond Hill Prison, the plan went ahead. This showed serious weaknesses in the command structure at JSOC.

None of the special operations went according to plan and there is some evidence of poor intelligence being passed by Delta and SEAL to other commanders. Also, if the account of the siege of the Governor-General's residence given by the Marines is correct, some SEAL officers should be court martialled.

Many of the men involved in the planning and execution of the operation consider it to have been little short of a military disaster. As one senior intelligence officer puts it: 'It was Ollie North's charade. Whatever was screwed up was the fault of North, the Navy and the gutless JCS. JSOC should not have been used and their performance was absolutely horrible.'[20]

It would not be fair, however, to blame all these failings on either JSOC or the special operations forces themselves. They were forced to work in an environment and to a plan imposed on them by the JCS. As the JCS clearly had so little understanding of the abilities and purpose of special operations forces, it is hardly surprising that their integration into the overall plan was woefully inadequate.

Sadly, the JCS insist on portraying Operation Urgent Fury as a great military success. In a number of reports, they have accepted some criticisms but have generally put the mistakes down to 'the fog of war'. There has never been a joint critique involving all the services so that each can learn from the mistakes. 'We are a zero-defect orientated military and we simply cannot accept that any mistakes could have been made,' commented one officer.

This is supported by the fact that in the months following the invasion, the Army awarded more than 8,612 medals to the soldiers who had taken part, even though no more than 7,000 ever set foot on the island.

Among those officers who fought on the ground in Grenada there is unanimity that there are many improvements that could be made to prevent the same kind of errors from happening next time. However, further up the military command structure self-criticism is regarded as bad for the service and bad for the career. This has produced considerable frustration among those men who saw action and who have since been unable to institute any changes. As one puts it:

'I can no longer say that I have not seen the big picture. I have and it is sickening. It has made me bitter and cynical.'

Both Congress and the administration exhaustively examined the Grenada invasion in an attempt to learn from mistakes made. For them, it is not so much that Grenada itself was such a shambles that matters. To them the issue is: what would have happened if this had been the central front in Europe and the opposition had not been some poorly-armed and badly-trained Caribbean islanders, but had been crack Soviet divisions? There are many who feel that if the military refuse to learn from Grenada, the lessons should somehow be forced on them.

20

Congress Bites the Bullet

On 23 October 1983, three days after the Marine Amphibious Unit on its way to Lebanon received orders to divert to Grenada, the unit it was to relieve was destroyed. At 06.15 that Sunday morning a yellow Mercedes truck, licence number 508292, turned into the car park outside the headquarters of the Marine Battalion Landing Team outside Beirut airport.

Lance-Corporal Eddie DiFranco was standing at guard post Number 6, just inside a row of barbed wire 235 feet from the car park entrance. He looked up when he heard the racing of the truck's engine.

'I kind of stared for a couple of seconds and then started to load my weapon. When my weapon was loaded the truck had gone through this fence and was on its way towards the gate . . . out of range to do anything effective to the truck. . . . The magazine was in at the time [when the truck was closest to him] but not locked and loaded. . . . I got a round in the chamber after the truck was already through the gate. . . . I knew what was going to happen so I just went back into the bunker. I was going to call the guard shack at that time, but by the time I was ringing it up and getting ready to call, I thought, well, why call, he must see the truck coming. So I let the phone down and the truck just crashed in and blew up a couple of seconds later.'[1]

Fifty metres away, Corporal Michael Petit was lying in bed contemplating the quiet Sunday stretching before him.

'The texture of that moment will remain with me always: the soft methodical breathing of those sleeping around me; a beam of early morning sunlight sparkling with dust motes slanting into the room from the doorway; the smell of dank air.

'In a split second my mood went from complacency to trepidation. The explosion was tremendous. Deafening, the deep rumble shook the building to its foundation and catapulted me from my cot. The air was full of choking dust that made it almost impossible to see and breathe.'

In the first few minutes after the explosion, the Marines believed they were under attack and took up defensive positions. But, when no rockets or bullets came their way, they began to look for the source of the explosion.

'I sprinted around the corner of the main command post. . . . I stopped running when I saw the lines of cots with the twisted bodies of Marines piled upon them. The semi-nude men were partially covered with ponchos and bloodied blankets. Arms and legs dangled grotesquely. We've got to get them medical attention, was my first frantic thought. It did not occur to me they were dead.

'I rounded the bushes and saw the carnage for the first time; the four-storey Battalion Landing Team building had been reduced to a smouldering heap of rubble no more than fifteen feet high. I couldn't believe what I was seeing. Cedar trees on the hill overlooking the building were broken and stripped of greenery. The heavy, acrid smell of explosives hung in the air. The ground was covered with pieces of building, and a grey pallor of dust hung over everything like a shroud. Boots, seabags, scraps of paper, running shoes, torn sleeping bags, parts of uniforms, and shredded mosquito netting were strewn everywhere. Jeeps had been crushed and tossed about like children's toys. The plywood outhouses twenty metres from the building were splintered, and macabre streamers of toilet paper fluttered from the trees.

'Everywhere I looked I saw bodies sprawled in gruesome positions. One Marine, still in his sleeping bag, hung from a tree. The decapitated body of another was under a jeep, his arms twisted at an impossible angle. The legs of yet another jutted from beneath a huge slab of concrete. The screams of agony from those still living seared like a red hot knife. I stared at the building feeling helpless and numb.'[2]

The explosion killed 241 men and wounded more than 100 others. It was a devastating act of terrorism that achieved exactly what was intended: the withdrawal of American forces from the Lebanon.

Following the attack, Defense Secretary Caspar Weinberger set up a commission to conduct an independent inquiry into the incident. The commission was chaired by retired US Navy Admiral Robert L. J. Long. Several specific criticisms of the command and control and intelligence capabilities of the Marine Corps and the US armed services were made by the Long Commission, and by Congressional investigators who launched parallel inquiries.

One of the Long Commission's most significant statements was a general assessment on the role of terrorism today.

'The systematic, carefully orchestrated terrorism which we see in the Middle East represents a new dimension of warfare. These international terrorists, unlike their traditional counterparts, are not seeking to make a random political statement or to commit the occasional act of intimidation on behalf of some ill-defined, long term vision of the future. For them, terrorism is an integrated part of strategy in which there are several well-defined political and military objectives.'[3]

It was the view of the Long Commission that terrorist acts such as the Beirut bombing can no longer be viewed as isolated incidents but have to be seen as part of a long term strategy. That analysis seems to be borne out by the result of the bombing, which was the withdrawal of US troops from the area. Thus, by committing a single act of extreme violence, a small group (in this case Moslem extremists backed by Syria and Iran) were able to force the United States to change its policy in a key area of the world.

If terrorists and their sponsors have moved beyond random

bombing and isolated assassination, it is obviously important that western governments should be aware of the changed nature of the threat and be prepared to counter it effectively.

Yet investigations into the circumstances surrounding the Beirut bombing revealed exactly the same shortcomings that have bedevilled US military opérations since World War II: poor intelligence, flawed leadership and a basic misunderstanding of terrorism today.

In the immediate aftermath of the bombing, the Marine commander, General Paul X. Kelley, instead of trying to find out what went wrong and why, attempted to cover up the clear failings that had resulted in the deaths of so many of his men. He had visited the Marines in Beirut a month before the bombing and he had made no recommendations about the security at the base. In testimony to the House Armed Services committee in November, Kelley said that the bomber drove his truck at 60 m.p.h. over and through a number of obstacles that had been specifically placed in the way of such an attack. Kelley also said that the two armed guards had been killed by the bomb.

The committee found that 'many of the details of the attack upon the BLT as related by General Kelley were erroneous'. A map supplied to the committee by the Marines was found to be inaccurate, and other testimony was 'often inaccurate, misleading and erroneous. Thus, the first explanation provided [to] the Congress and the American people presented a false picture as to what actually took place.'[4]

There were in fact no effective obstacles in place to foil this kind of attack; although the guards were armed, their weapons were not loaded; moreover, the guards had not been killed and their evidence was critical in exposing weaknesses in the defences.

Also what was not revealed during the inquiry was that almost six months previously, in the aftermath of the bombing of the US embassy in Beirut on 18 April, a complete intelligence assessment had been carried out.

That bombing had killed seventeen Americans, all of them

either from the military or the CIA. Robert C. Ames, the CIA's National Intelligence Officer for the Middle East, had just arrived in Beirut with members of staff as part of a tour around the region. All the Agency's men in the country had been in the embassy to meet him when the bomb went off. At one stroke, the CIA's capability in the Lebanon had been crippled. (There were suspicions that were never proved that the CIA had a major security leak and that the terrorists knew in advance of Ames's visit.)

To maintain a curious fiction that the bombing had killed only State Department people, a US Air Force jet with senior State Department officials on board came to claim the bodies and fly them back to America. Also on board were Pentagon officials and, when the aircraft stopped in Frankfurt to refuel, it picked up Colonel William Corbett, the Special Assistant for Security Matters to the Deputy CINC Europe. Corbett had long experience in unconventional warfare and he, too, was asked to see what could be done to improve security.

After the aircraft returned to the United States, it had been decided to send a team from the Intelligence Support Activity to Lebanon to look at security at the embassy and to find out what had gone wrong. Working separately, both ISA and Corbett had made a number of recommendations regarding the embassy and the military presence.

Security at the embassy was tightened and, because Corbett was an Army officer, he was able to persuade the Army units to move out of vulnerable buildings and take a number of steps to secure the perimeter of their base. However, since Corbett was of the same rank as the Marine commander, Colonel Geraghty, he had been unable to order any major changes, and those of his recommendations which passed through the Marine chain of command were ignored.

The ISA had produced a report that clearly warned of a possible attack and also suggested concrete measures to improve security. That report, too, was passed to the Marines and to service chiefs in the Pentagon, but the information never reached anyone actually responsible for the Marines' presence in the Lebanon. The feeling among those involved in the ISA was that the information had been ignored because it was generated by people with 'special operations associations'.[5]

Such a wilful disregard of basic security in an unconventional environment should not, perhaps, have been that surprising. For more than a year prior to the first Beirut bombing Pentagon officials with responsibility for counter-terrorism had been unable to make an appointment to brief the JCS on the nature of the terrorist threat to the military and on steps that could be taken to combat it.

Both Congress and the Long Commission made it clear that poor intelligence gathering and analysis was the single most important factor contributing to the disaster. Although the commander on the spot, Colonel Timothy Geraghty, had been made aware of more than a hundred car bomb threats made against his men over the previous few months, he had not been warned that a truck attack was possible. He had no independent capability for analysing the raw intelligence he received.

Most of the information available to him came from Sigint and photographic reconnaissance and there was very little reporting from agents on the ground. For example, although the DIA had prepared maps of Beirut that listed every single house in the city, the occupants and the threat they represented, this valuable resource was never passed on to the Marines. Besides which, that kind of information needs to be supplemented by regulars reports from agents inside the different guerrilla and terrorist movements, and as the Long Commission pointed out: 'The USMNF (US Multinational Force) commander did not have effective US human intelligence support. The paucity of US-controlled Humint is partly due to US policy decisions to reduce Humint collection worldwide.'[6]

The terrorists undoubtedly recognised that weakness, and were able to exploit it. Their task was made easier by failures in the Marine and other service commanders to understand the risks involved in basing US forces in such a vulnerable area.

General Bernard Rogers, the commander of US forces in Europe, had sent a team of counter-terrorist specialists (including members of Delta Force) to Lebanon in April 1983 after that first bombing of the US embassy in Beirut. That team made a number of recommendations about improving embassy security, but they did not look at the security of the Marine compound – despite the fact that Rogers's own security experts had predicted a follow-up to the embassy attack, probably on the Marines.

The significance of the second Beirut bombing was that it once again demonstrated that the US military was unable to meet the challenge of operating in an unconventional environment. The same failures that run through all the operations from Desert One onwards occurred in Beirut. There is no evidence that the military accepted any responsibility for them and it is interesting to note that none of the senior commanders with responsibility for the Beirut disaster was reprimanded.

The deaths of the Marines once again brought Lieutenant-Colonel Oliver North to the fore. He and National Security Adviser Robert McFarlane were so shocked at the tragedy and at America's apparent inability to do anything about it that they decided to respond themselves. They found out that responsibility for the bombing lay with Hezbollah, a shadowy Iranian-supported terrorist organisation with bases in Lebanon. North encouraged the Lebanese Deuxième Bureau to find and arm some Lebanese Baha'is who on 8 March 1985 planted a bomb intended to kill one of Hezbollah's leaders. The bomb missed its target, however, and killed eighty innocent civilians.[7]

To the administration and to the supporters of special forces in Congress, the Beirut affair proved once again that more needed to be done to oblige the military to take effective control of special operations, not simply by taking money but by putting in place an organisation that actually worked.

The next attempt by the military to put its house in order came on 1 January 1984, with the formation of the Joint Special Operations Agency (JSOA). The JCS had announced the planned formation of the Agency on 19 October 1983, just before the invasion of Grenada, as a direct result of the Thayer letter issued two weeks previously urging the JCS to move more quickly on SOF reorganisation. Although presented as a service initiative, it had in fact been forced on the military by civilians in the Pentagon who remained concerned at poor co-ordination in the revitalisation of special forces.

'The services did not want it established,' recalled one senior Pentagon official. 'If you have JSOA then you have accepted that special operations forces are needed, which of course they did not want. Once they accepted that Special Operations Forces was the way of the future, the whole rationale behind the huge tri-service investment in conventional systems was brought into question.'[8]

According to its charter, JSOA is 'charged with advising the JCS in all matters pertaining to special operations and the military activities related thereto, including national strategy, planning, programming, budgeting, resource development and allocation, joint doctrinal guidance, exercise and readiness evaluation, and employment of force.'[9]

The underlying functions of JSOA are identified by the charter as: 'providing the JCS with comprehensive objectives, independent analyses, and evaluation of US policies, proposals, and programmes, existing or tentative, in the entire field of special operations plans, operations, and special activities related thereto; and second, [to] develop and submit to the JCS joint strategic plans, policies and recommendations on current and future strategy, organisation, doctrine, research and development, exercises and training and on the planning, programming and budgeting systems concerning special operations matters.'

JSOA, with a staff of sixty-one, would have no operational control over special forces but would co-ordinate all the different groups in an attempt to give a national direction to what was then a very dispersed programme.

This looked impressive on paper, but from the start the JCS attempted to undermine the influence of JSOA by placing a two-star Marine Corps general, Wesley Rice, in charge. All generals on the JCS staff were of at least three stars, and in the status-conscious service hierarchy, this difference was considerable. 'Rice sat well below the salt and had no clout at all,' said one Pentagon official.

The appointment was made despite a memorandum sent to Weinberger on 23 December 1983 in which the Special Operations Advisory Group strongly recommended that the JSOA Director must be a three-star flag or general officer. This was considered necessary since 'key elements [of Special Operations Forces] – JSOC, 1st Special Operations Command and 23rd Air Force – are all commanded by two-star general officers,' and any JSOA director could 'more effectively orchestrate the joint aspects of Special Operations with benefits of superior rank.' The memo also suggested that unless the JSOA director were of sufficient rank he 'could well be overwhelmed by the joint system.'[10]

Weinberger took the criticisms seriously enough to write a memo to the JCS suggesting that if Rice was as good as the JCS claimed, he should be promoted to three-star. The JCS ignored this suggestion.

Administration officials continued to find evidence that the services were trying to frustrate their efforts to rebuild the special forces. Money that had been allocated to specific programmes suddenly turned up in different accounts, being spent on projects high on the services' list of priorities but low on the administration's. On 2 March Weinberger issued a classified directive to service chiefs in his annual Defense Guidance which once again stressed the importance of Special Operations Forces (SOF).

For the first time the question of developing a strategy for

SOF was raised. The Defense Guidance suggested that the service chiefs devote some thought to the problem and come up with a broad rationale for SOF that would give them clear roles both in peace and war. But to have developed a strategy would have meant the JCS clearly accepting that there was a genuine need for SOF, and so no strategy has yet (June 1987) been written.

Weinberger also stressed the need for the services to put more effort into the revitalisation programme. 'The modernisation goal is a joint SOF capability, quantitively and qualitively manned, trained and equipped to react swiftly to conduct a wide range of special operations missions worldwide, across the full spectrum of conflict and crisis,' Weinberger wrote.

'This capability must be founded in comprehensive joint doctrine, inclusion of SOF in all joint plans and, wherever feasible, in joint exercises and the provision of dedicated and augmenting units forward deployed in, or immediately deployable to, all unified commands.'[11]

The mid-term requirements spelled out in the Defense Guidance included: to develop sea and air infiltration capabilities – to include the purchase of more C-130 aircraft; to remedy the existing severe inadequacies in secure communications and electronics equipment that 'debilitate our ability to conduct strategic reconnaissance and unconventional warfare missions'; to develop a way of bringing out special forces operating up to 1,000 miles behind enemy lines, and to improve the helicopter capability; and to investigate the need for a new aircraft to replace the ageing C-130.

Weinberger's suspicion that the military might not be fully behind this revitalisation seemed to be confirmed by Noel Koch, the Pentagon official responsible for special forces, during testimony before the House Appropriations Committee on 10 April 1984.

'Human nature resists change, and the case at hand is no exception. And, of course, when defense policy changes, defense budgets also change, and anytime one reallocates resources vested interests and the status quo are challenged.

'We cannot yet meet all the requirements for SOF established by the unified commanders. SOF units remain multiple-tasked and, thus, face conflicting requirements imposed by the unified commanders. We lack sufficient means of infiltration to deliver Navy SEALs and Army special forces, and we have too few special forces to conduct assigned wartime missions.'[12]

With that preface to his remarks, Koch went on to set out four main areas of concern that were still unresolved, even after four years of effort:

1. Readiness. As special forces will be among the first to be sent to war, they have to be at a constant high state of readiness. Yet, Koch pointed out, the strength of the Army's special forces groups was 12 per cent below authorised wartime requirements; also, although all groups should be at the highest readiness level, known as ALO-1, the operational A-Detachments were at ALO-3 and the military intelligence companies were at ALO-6, the lowest level. The army planned to reach a level of ALO-2 but even that still remained below the ideal. (In fact to ensure that SOF trainees reach ALO–2, standards have been lowered, thus artificially improving the ratings. For example, there is now very little cross-training in a 12-strong A-team, something that used to be considered a necessity.)

2. Equipment. Special forces typically require small quantities of specialist equipment not in service with other units. The procurement system was not capable of handling such items and the flow of new equipment to the special forces was very slow. In the perhaps extreme case of the PRC-70 radio, for example, it took seventeen years from the day it was ordered for it to be delivered to the special operations forces for which it was intended. By that time it was already some ten years out of date.

3. Languages. In the early days of the Green Berets, many recruits came from Eastern European countries that had been taken over by the communists. It was common for

each A-Team to have half of the team fluent in another
language, often their mother tongue. In recent years that
source of recruits has dried up. In 1984, the predominant
language, other than English, was Spanish. 'But, in regions
of the Third World in which other languages predominate,
we can deploy *no more than one* fully language-qualified 12-
man special forces A-Detachment to defend our interests,'
said Koch.

4. Promotion. Special forces have traditionally been the
graveyard for a service career. In the past, no officer with
a career in the special forces has been promoted beyond
brigadier, and even that rank is very rare. In consequence,
ambitious officers stay in special forces for only a short time.
'If we are to attract and retain the highly qualified
personnel we need for special operations, their career
opportunities must be comparable to those of their peers
in other branches of military service,' Koch told the
subcommittee.

This testimony, plus the critical nature of all the reports on
special forces actions since Desert One, finally forced
Congress to act. In May 1984 they fired the opening salvo in
what was to become a long running battle with the Pentagon.
The Readiness subcommittee of the House Armed Services
Committee formed a Special Operations Panel with the
Florida Democrat Earl Hutto as its chairman. The Panel was
intended to act as a watchdog over the Pentagon and the
military to make sure that funds allocated by Congress were
actually spent on the projects that had been authorised – and
at the required speed.

As if to underline the need for Congress to intervene, in
that same month the Air Force proposed handing over all
SOF rotary lift capability to the Army. The scheme was
dreamed up by General John A. Wickman, the Army chief
of staff, and General Charles A. Gabriel, the Air Force chief
of staff. Known as Initiative 17, the agreement had thirty-
one clauses that detailed how the Army would take control of
long range reconnaissance and the infiltration of SOF behind

enemy lines. This was a clear attempt by the Air Force to kill a programme it didn't want. 'Putting long range infiltration and exfiltration in the hands of the army is like putting the space shuttle programme in the hands of Chad,' as one critic put it.[13]

From the start of the SOF revitalisation programme, the Air Force had in fact been the most reluctant participant of all the services. Even though it had been clearly demonstrated during the 1980 Desert One operation that there was insufficient trained pilots with the right aircraft available to the Air Force, nothing had been done. In theory the Air Force had made a commitment in 1981 to buy twelve new MC-130 Combat Talon aircraft and in 1983 the Department of Defense had added another nine to the programme, but in fact the Air Force still had exactly the same number of MC-130s – and their seven HH-53 Pave Low helicopters were two fewer than in 1980. This was not even enough to carry out counter-terrorist tasks: using the existing war plans, the Air Force had five times fewer Combat Talons than required, and there was also a serious shortage of reconnaissance aircraft.

All the services had put SOF equipment into the programme, but then had been guilty of letting it drop off the bottom as other systems took precedence. Even so the Air Force seemed especially reluctant to give SOF the priority demanded by Weinberger.

'The Air Force has a fighter pilot mentality: unless it's above the speed of sound they don't want to do it,' commented one Pentagon official.[14]

In their budget for 1985 for example, the Military Airlift Command (MAC) placed the SOF airlift programme 59th on their list of priorities. Numbers 53 and 54 were for travel for senior Air Force officers and officials, and number 60 was a programme to modernise Ranch Hand aircraft that had been used to spray Agent Orange in Vietnam.[15]

The longer the delays in implementing a programme, the more expensive the programme becomes. At the start of the revitalisation initiative, the cost of a new MC-130 Combat

Talon was around $20 million. In 1986, that figure had risen to $60 million, around four times the cost of an F-15 fighter.

News of Initiative 17 came as a complete surprise to Weinberger and his staff. By transferring the helicopter requirement to the Army, the Air Force clearly hoped that funds intended for special operations would be freed for use elsewhere. But both the administration and Congress feared that the move would simply result in a shuffling of an inadequate pack to further reduce the capability, and the Initiative was stopped from going through. However, in its final compromise in April 1986, the DOD simply told the Air Force they could not transfer the mission until the Army was capable of handling it. 'This was a perfect Pentagon solution,' said one official. 'This allows the Army to construe this as they want and the Air Force to say that in their view the Army is capable. All that means is that SOF will be less effective than before.'[16]

This pessimistic view was supported by a letter written on 4 February 1986 by the chairman of the House Defense Appropriations Committee, Joseph Addabbo, to Weinberger. 'Transfer of rotary wing assets from the Air Force to the Army appears to be taking place. In some cases these transfers are taking place despite the objections of the very theatre commanders-in-chief who must deploy these forces. . . . While the committee has no predisposition as to whether the Army or the Air Force should operate SOF rotary wing assets, I am concerned that such action appears to be taking place piecemeal, in violation of Congressional language, and without sufficient consideration of the needs of SOF commanders and theatre CINCs.'[17]

Aside from the transfers, Addabbo had evidence that the Air Force was engaged in widespread disbanding of SOF helicopter units. Four UH-1N helicopter gunships based in Panama were deactivated against the wishes of the local Army commander; six H-3 helicopters based in Arizona were being transferred to the Coast Guard for search and rescue; and two HH-53 Pave Low helicopters which were the key to the long range delivery of SOF forces had been switched to the search and rescue role.

While the Air Force were quietly undermining the revitalisation programme, the service chiefs were publicly going along with the requirements set out in the 1983 memorandum from Paul Thayer. In July 1984, three years after being asked, the Army, Navy, Air Force and Defense Agencies completed their master plans for the revitalisation of special operations forces and submitted them to Weinberger. These plans were little more than a formal acknowledgment of the administration's already announced investment in SOF, but at least this was the first time the services had formally committed themselves to the project.

Setting out their policy with regard to SOF did not, of course, mean that any of this policy would be reflected in their procurement programmes. Also, there was still no doctrinal basis laid down for SOF, so to the conventional military they still had no clear reason for existing.

But to the politicians the problem of fighting unconventional warfare was getting more urgent by the day. A new alliance of anti-Nato terrorist organisations had sprung up in Europe. It included terrorists from France, West Germany, Belgium, Portugal and the Netherlands and one of its declared aims was to concentrate on American targets as a symbol of the Nato alliance. Terrorism worldwide continued to grow at around 15 per cent a year and to the Reagan administration's eyes much of that was sponsored by the Soviet Union. In Central America the US was firmly committed to opposing the government of Nicaragua, and the policy of merely containing the perceived expansionist aims of the Soviet Union was evolving into a new policy of rollback, of aggressively persuading countries in the communist camp to switch sides. All of these projects required the deployment of special operations forces.

In August 1984, Delta were called on by the government in the Netherlands Antilles for help during the hijacking of a Venezuelan DC-9 airliner to the island of Curacao. The two hijackers, a Dominican and a Haitian, demanded $5 million in ransom for the release of the seventy-nine hostages.

A 12-man Venezuelan commando unit, trained in the United States, flew to Curacao, and a small team of Delta Force flew on board a C-130 transport to the island of Bonaire, east of Curacao, with nine crates of sophisticated surveillance devices, including microphones and infra-red sensors. These were transferred to a light plane that flew on to Curacao and landed on a racetrack at the eastern end of the island. A final hop by helicopter was made to Hato International Airport, eighteen miles away. During the subsequent storming of the aircraft, both hijackers were killed and the hostages released unharmed.[18]

Four months later, on 4 December, Delta Force were deployed again after a Kuwaiti airliner had been hijacked during a flight from Kuwait to Karachi, by terrorists that the US government believed were from the Islamic Jihad, a terrorist group based in the Lebanon and sponsored by Iran. The aircraft was flown to Teheran where the terrorists demanded the release of colleagues held in Kuwaiti jails.

Two Americans from the 155 passengers were killed during the hijacking and for the next six days negotiations were stalemated. Iran put pressure on the Kuwaiti government to release the jailed terrorists but they refused to do so.

As soon as news of the hijacking had reached Delta Force at Fort Bragg, a counter-hijack team had flown first to Turkey and then to Masirah Island, off Oman, which had also been the staging post for Desert One. Delta never planned to go in to Teheran to free the hostages but was ready to assault the aircraft if the terrorists had ordered it flown to another country. In the event, Iranian commandos finally stormed the plane and captured the four hijackers.

With few opportunities for the SOF to convince the military sceptics of their worth, revitalisation continued to lurch forward. For Noel Koch, the job of persuading the military to carry out the policies of the administration had proved lonely and frustrating. He found himself unable to force the powerful bureaucracy in the Pentagon to move at anything like the speed demanded by Weinberger. Instead of keeping his battle with the Pentagon inside the system, Koch decided on the extraordinary step of going public.

In a series of interviews with the media, Koch criticised the delaying tactics employed by the services in the revitalisation effort. 'We've got [military] bands in higher states of readiness than some of our special operations assets,' he told the *New York Times*.[19] In testimony to the Special Operation Panel on 6 September Koch said that the pace of revitalisation had been 'agonisingly slow' despite the fact that the SOF budget had averaged only one-tenth of one per cent of the DOD budget since 1975.[20]

Such criticisms came in the wake of two more terrorist acts that had had a dramatic effect on US public opinion, and they further served to convince Congress that an enhanced SOF capability was vital. The first of these, the hijacking of a TWA aircraft, had taken place in June and the second, the assult on the *Achille Lauro*, in October. Both had been specifically aimed at the United States and in both cases major action by special forces was thwarted by the terrorists.

On 14 June TWA Flight 847 was hijacked after a stopover at Athens airport by two Arabs carrying false Moroccan passports in the names of Ahmed Karbia and Ali Yunes. A third hijacker, Atoua Ali Tourenda, had not been allowed to board the aircraft as it was full, and because of his suspicious behaviour he was subsequently arrested by the Greek police.

The two terrorists had managed to smuggle on board a 9mm pistol and at least two hand grenades wrapped in glass fibre which successfully concealed them from the airport's security system. One of the two men was later identified as Mohammed Ali Hamadi after he had tried to enter West Germany in January 1987 carrying wine bottles filled with explosives. His fingerprints matched those found aboard the aircraft.[21]

The hijackers forced the aircraft with 145 passengers and a crew of eight to fly to Beirut. After reading a list of their demands, which included the release of more than 700 Shi'ites being held in Israeli jails, the terrorists released seventeen women and two children and then took off for Algiers. Over the next four days, the aircraft flew back and forth between Algiers and Beirut four times. On the second stop in Beirut, the terrorists brutally beat and then shot a 24-year-old American Navy diver, Robert Dean Stetham, and dumped his body on the airport tarmac.

The hostages were gradually released until just thirty-two Americans were left. Then after seventeen days of negotiations that involved the governments of the United States, Syria, the Lebanon, Algeria and Israel, these hostages too were released. Without much prodding from the hijackers, the Greeks freed their accomplice in Athens and flew him to Algiers. But, under intense pressure from the US government, the Israelis also freed 735 Shi'ites from their jails. This represented a major victory for the terrorists, especially as they walked away free.

Within hours of the hijack, however, members of Delta Force had boarded aircraft in Fort Bragg for the long flight to a British RAF base at Akrotiri in Cyprus. Once Robert Stetham had been killed, for Delta the assault was simply a matter of waiting for the right opportunity. That came during the second night, while the aircraft was in Algiers.

Although the terrorists had taken on ten reinforcements during the previous day's stopover in Beirut, now that the aircraft only had thirty-two hostages on board a rescue attempt was thought worth the risk. The State Department had sent along a representative from the Office for Combating Terrorism to liaise with Washington, and he sought authority for the rescue.

It was a difficult decision as the Algerians had made it clear they would prefer a negotiated settlement and the US did not want to upset officials who had played a key role in the negotiations that had resulted in the freeing of the hostages held in the American embassy in Teheran. But Secretary of State George Shultz personally gave the order for Delta to go in. Unfortunately, the order was not believed by an official in the Crisis Management Group at the State Department and for some hours officials tried to find Shultz to get it confirmed. By the time this was done the window of opportunity had gone, the plane was on its way back to Beirut, and soon afterwards the hostages were dispersed in secret locations around that city.

During the seventeen-day ordeal, the hijackers demonstrated a remarkable knowledge of US counter-terrorist techniques. Until then, the expected pattern had been for terrorists to stay in one place after negotiations began. Thereafter, if the terrorists began killing hostages, negotiations would stop and an assault to rescue the remaining victims would begin. But the TWA hijacking conformed to none of this.

For one thing, the terrorists kept moving the plane from Algiers to Beirut. Then again, even after they had killed, they never gave the Delta Force time to mount an operation, negotiations continued and a peaceful settlement was reached. In all this the terrorists had clearly been enormously helped by the kidnapping and torture in March 1984 of the CIA station chief in Beirut, William Buckley.

Formerly in charge of Middle East intelligence gathering at the CIA, Buckley had been a major catch, as he knew a wealth of detail about US counter-terrorist contingency plans, which he revealed after being brutally tortured. It was directly because of Buckley's intelligence that the terrorists knew to keep moving, to reinforce the aircraft as soon as possible, and to disperse the hostages to secret locations in Beirut.

Three months later, a far more audacious terrorist operation unfolded in the Mediterranean. Just before lunch on Monday 7 October, four members of the Palestine Liberation Front, a militant group in the PLO, left cabin number 82 on board the Italian luxury cruise liner *Achille Lauro*. The gunmen, armed with pistols and machine-guns, burst in on the passengers beginning lunch in the ship's main dining room. Shooting wildly, they injured two people and then separated the 427 passengers and eighty crew into national groups, putting twelve Americans and six Britons on deck surrounded by oil drums which they threatened to ignite.[22]

Once again, Washington ordered counter-terrorist units to the area. This time, because the act involved the hijacking of a ship, both Delta and the Navy's specialist counter-terrorist unit, SEAL Team 6 based at Dam Neck, Virginia, were flown out. The responsibility was primarily the SEALs', commanded by Carl Steiner.

A crisis management team met in the State Department, and included representatives from the Pentagon and the Office for Combating Terrorism at State. A senior member of that office flew immediately to Rome to co-ordinate with the Italian government.

'Our first requirement was that the ship was kept at sea,' explained one official involved in the operation. 'That way we would have a chance of the assault being successful.'

At the beginning, things seemed to be going America's way. The Syrians, who are often directly involved in such terrorist acts, denied any foreknowledge and refused to allow the ship to berth at the Syrian port of Tartus. In fact, the Syrians told the Italian ambassador that they *would* allow the ship to· dock, so that negotiations could begin, but only if both Italy and the United States officially requested it. The Italians wanted to go along with that but Washington, which was playing a deeper game, refused to agree.

On Tuesday, the *Achille Lauro* headed back for Port Said. By this time, the American forces were in position for a strike. A plan had been drawn up with the Italians. A night attack had been agreed: SEAL Team 6 would approach by sea, using small boats with specially silenced engines. Two separate Italian units were involved, the Commando Raggruppamento Subacqueri ed Incursori, or Frogman and Raiders Group known as COMSUBIN, and the Gruppi Interventi Speciali or Special Intervention Group (GIS). COMSUBIN are a highly trained underwater sabotage and reconnaissance team, similar to the regular SEALs, while GIS specialise in counter-terrorist work. Since neither group had any experience in assaulting a ship moving at sea, however, it was decided that the main attack would be carried out by the American forces who would disappear once the ship was secure, leaving the Italians to take the glory.

The Americans gathered on the amphibious assault ship *Iwo Jima* and prepared to assault the *Achille Lauro*, now lying off Port Said, on Wednesday night. However, Yasser Arafat, the PLO chairman, sent two of his men, one of them Abu Abbas the leader of the PLF, out in a tug to the *Achille Lauro* to help negotiate a peaceful end to the hijack. They took with them guarantees from the Mubarak government of safe passage out of Egypt for the hijackers, provided there had been no killings on board the ship.

At 16.30 that Wednesday afternoon, the hijackers left the ship, landed at Port Said and disappeared out of the country – or so the Egyptians said. The US and Italian special forces were stood down and some of them even began to head home. Then, over the next twelve hours, two items of news emerged that were to change everything.

That evening, after a trip out to the *Achille Lauro*, the US ambassador to Egypt, Nicholas Zeliotis, learned that a 69–year-old American Jew, Leon Klinghoffer, had been killed by the hijackers. Confined to a wheelchair after a stroke five years previously, Klinghoffer had been taken from his cabin on Tuesday morning and shot. He and his wheelchair were dumped overboard. When Zeliotis heard the news he sent an uncoded radio message to his embassy in Cairo that ordered: 'You tell the Foreign Ministry that we demand they prosecute those sons of bitches.'

It seemed to be too late. The Egyptian government maintained that the terrorists had already left. Then, later that night, Washington received hard intelligence from inside the Mubarak government that the terrorists were in fact still in Egypt and planned to fly out the next morning in an Egyptian Boeing 737.

The news reached Lt.-Col. Oliver North, the man on the

National Security Council charged with overseeing the counter-terrorism effort. He had been co-ordinating the planned assault on the *Achille Lauro* (and the previous abortive TWA assault) and was bitterly disappointed when, yet again, it had to be abandoned and the terrorists freed. But now North approached John Poindexter, the deputy staff director on the NSC:

'Do you remember Yamamoto?' he asked Poindexter, referring to the Japanese admiral whose military transport had been intercepted and shot down by American fighters during World War II. Poindexter was nervous about shooting out of the sky an aircraft belonging to a friendly country, but North proposed diverting the plane to the US Air Force base at Sigonella in Sicily.[23] Poindexter gave provisional approval to the idea and a detailed plan was drawn up which involved intercepting the Egyptian 737 using fighters from the USS *Saratoga*, which was then cruising off Greece. President Reagan was contacted during a tour of the Sara Lee bakery in Deerfield, Illinois, and gave his provisional approval but wanted more work done on the likely casualties and political consequences.

Weinberger, who was out of town, was also told of the impending mission and objected to it with some force. His views were disregarded.

The following morning the US received hard intelligence indicating the Boeing was about to take off from the Al Maza Air Base outside Cairo. By the time it had done so, President Reagan had given formal authority for the mission.

The Egyptair Boeing 737 was refused permission to land at Tunis (Washington had already blocked that) and Colonel Qadaffi swiftly refused it Tripoli. As the aircraft turned towards Athens, four F-14 Tomcat fighters from the *Saratoga* came alongside and ordered it to follow them to Sigonella.

Radio traffic intercepted by the National Security Agency was relayed to the crisis management team at the Pentagon. A garbled message apparently read in part '707 on board the 737'. This made no sense until it was understood that the

Egyptians had actually sent members of their own élite unit
Force 777 on board the aircraft with the terrorists. Further
information suggested there were four men from 777 on board.
It is a measure of the distrust between the Egyptian and
American governments at the time that the 777 men were
expected to side with the terrorists in any confrontation with
US forces. It was therefore decided to take certain additional
precautions.

Before the Boeing landed at Sigonella, an aircraft loaded
with SEALs had arrived at the base. As soon as the Boeing
came to a halt, it was surrounded by the US forces who in turn
were encircled by Italian Carabinieri. Evidently overawed by
the massed firepower around the aircraft, the Egyptian 777
commandos played no part in what followed.

There was immediate confusion over who had jurisdiction
over the hijacked plane, with the Italians arguing it had come
to a halt in their part of the airfield and the Americans
believing it was under their jurisdiction. The official of the
State Department's Office for Combating Terrorism listened
to the conversation between the SEALs and the Italians from
the security of the Rome embassy.

'It was a crazy situation. At one time we heard the Texas
drawl of one of the SEAL officers discussing whether he
should order his men to open fire on the Italians. That would
have been very embarrasing,' said one man in the embassy.

The impasse was resolved when US Secretary of State
George Shultz ordered his men to back off after the Italians
had given an assurance that the terrorists would be tried for
murder. It was decided that to avoid further confusion the
terrorists would be flown to Rome. The SEAL commander,
Carl Steiner, didn't trust the Italians and suspected the terrorists would be released as soon as they were out of sight of his
men. He therefore boarded a plane with a small SEAL unit,
shadowed the terrorists' aircraft all the way to Rome, and
landed immediately behind, claiming his plane had engine
trouble. The Italians kept to the letter of the agreement,

although they released the PLF leader Abu Abbas, who was also discovered on the aircraft.

The successful interception of the Egyptian aircraft did a great deal to restore American morale in the fight against terrorism, as did the attack on Libya in April the following year. But neither of them gave American special forces an opportunity to show their mettle, and this was very frustrating to all the men concerned. They had trained hard for each eventuality, had been deployed to the scene of the action, and then had been stood down at the last minute.

This frustration was being mirrored in Congress and amongst some Pentagon officials. They felt that unless firm action was taken the service chiefs would continue to avoid implementing many of the measures called for in the revitalisation programme, and if nothing substantial was done by the time of the 1988 presidential elections, and the Republicans failed to get re-elected, then the whole initiative might have been wasted.

In August 1985, Dan Daniel, the chairman of the House Armed Services Readiness Committee, suggested that all special operations should be placed under one command, thus creating a sixth service. He gave seven reasons why he felt this was necessary:

'1.   Philosophy: . . . SOF have always been peripheral to the philosophical core of the military. They have historically been the target of mistrust and suspicion, and their capabilities and requirements are poorly understood. If they are to become truly effective, they must have their own intellectual and professional core around which they can coalesce, evolve and mature.

'2.   Professionalism: As things stand, special operators have one foot in the SOF camp and the other in the parent service camp and, thus, have divided loyalties. In the best of times, service in SOF has been a ticket to be punched, which is fine from a career perspective but not so fine for building a long-term core of professionals. In the worst of times, SOF service has been a career-killer, which means that those

who choose to stick with it must do so out of pure
dedication. If we are to develop a true SOF professionalism
and reward honourable service in an equitable way, SOF
must have a professional home.

'3. Budgets: Special Forces compete against M-1 tanks,
     SEALS against carrier air wings . . . for a slice of the
     individual Service's budgetary pie. . . . Under a single
     service, Special Forces, SEALS and Combat Talons
     would compete among themselves in a self-regulating
     process.

'4. Continuity: The history of the last 40 years shows that the
     health of SOF is directly proportional to the degree of
     political emphasis placed on the programme. . . . A Sixth
     Service would be subject to the same de-emphasis, but
     the way in which the lumps were taken would preserve a
     balanced (if diminished) force that could be restored in
     orderly fashion the next time the country discovered that
     it needed an effective SOF capability – as it inevitably
     would.

'5. Unique Solutions to Unique Problems: So long as SOF
     reside in the individual services, we face a choice between
     relying on support mechanisms that are ill-structured to
     respond (and respond quickly) to unique, low-cost, low-
     density SOF requirements, and skirting those mechanisms
     by establishing special off line procedures. As a Sixth
     Service, SOF would have its own support systems that
     would make sense to no one but special operators – but
     they would work.

'6. Advocacy: The "SOF Mafia" will never capture control of
     their parent services. Thus, while they may be beloved
     by their civilian masters and the military leadership may
     sincerely champion their cause, they will never be
     admitted to the inner circles of power. . . . The creation of
     a Sixth Service would carry with it the presumption that
     a vital, unique national capability should have a
     commensurate place in the workings of the national
     security apparatus.

'7. Relationship with the National Command Authorities:
     Special operations are inherently high-risk, high-payoff,
     and . . . have a large political dimension. A Sixth Service

would give the NCA a "ready to go" command structure
and military capability they could turn to immediately in
those situations in which the good of the country
outweighs personal political risk.'[24]

This was the opening salvo in a battle between the House,
the Senate, the service chiefs and Pentagon officials that went
on for the next year. At issue was a reorganisation of SOF
designed to address some of the complaints about funding,
equipment and command and control that had been raised
repeatedly since the revitalisation programme began.

The House proposed a bill (HR.5109) that would establish
a National Special Operations Agency within the Department
of Defense which would operate in the same way as the CIA
or the DIA. All SOF would come under the new agency whose
Director would report directly to the Secretary of Defense and
the President.

This radical proposal was opposed by the Senate. In
another bill (S.2453) they in turn suggested setting up a
Defense Special Operations Agency which would operate
within the existing structure. Its mission would be to prepare
for and conduct joint special operations, and a companion
organisation within the Office of the Secretary of Defense
would be charged with making policy for special operations.
Command and control of special operations would be exercised through a subordinate joint command. All SOF from
the Army, Navy and Air Force would be assigned to this
command during peacetime.

To the House, the Senate proposals were too tame and
could be seen as simply setting up another bureaucratic layer
to be manipulated and undermined by the JCS. To the
Pentagon, on the other hand, both proposals were unsatisfac-
tory. Anything that suggested an alteration in the existing
boundary lines between the services or, worse still, taking
budget money from one slot and putting it in another, caused
the JCS to adopt a strongly defensive position. In the horse-
trading that is so much a part of Pentagon life, new structures

do evolve, but only as part of complicated trade-offs between senior officers and officials where everyone benefits. What was being proposed by Congress cut across all these traditional and cosy relationships.

Instead, the Pentagon proposed the creation of a new Special Operations Force Command controlled by a three-star general. The general would report through the JCS to the Secretary of Defense, and oversight of the SOF would continue through the existing office of the Assistant Secretary of State for International Security Affairs. However, Congress felt that a three-star general would not have enough authority to take on the JCS. It also noted that Noel Koch had resigned on 5 May 1986, leaving no strong advocate for special forces on the civilian side in the Pentagon.

In a formal hand-delivered note to Weinberger, Koch simply resigned without giving any reasons. But, after Weinberger asked him to stay, he wrote another, longer, letter giving the reasons why he was leaving. In part, his letter dated 7 May reads:

'To the extent that internal events were determinant, it was far more the management of the SOF lift issues, and the report to Congress, than any other single factor that convinced me I should proceed with plans to leave. I have no great difficulty supporting a decision with which I disagree, but I do have trouble supporting one that I can't even understand, which is arguably no decision at all and which, in any case, is indefensible in light of the Department's own priorities – economy not least. In addition, to put it plainly, I don't believe the matter was managed honestly, in good faith. It stinks of duplicity. Now it's finished – or my part in it is, and I intend to be silent on it.'

Koch's replacement was Larry Ropka, an Air Force colonel with no special forces experience apart from helping with the planning for the Son Tay raid. He was not a firm advocate of SOF and was hardly the man to do battle with the generals and admirals in the Pentagon.

The service chiefs had added a further wrinkle: 'SOF would

be assigned to the command after achieving certain skills at the level of individual or team training which would continue to be a service responsibility.'[25] In other words, nothing would change as individual services would be able to decide if and when their SOF units could be seconded to the new command.

Some civilian officials in the Pentagon, led by Richard Armitage, Ropka's boss, also opposed the Congressional plans. Armitage saw the proposals by Congress as a clear attempt to undermine the influence of his office: 'It would be far better for DOD to solve the problem than for Congress to impose a legislated solution. One inescapable reality is that regardless of how we ultimately reorganise SOF, they will remain a part of DOD and, more specifically, they will continue to rely on their parent services for their lifeblood. While the impact of S.2453 would be essentially identical to that of the DOD initiatives, I am concerned that such an imposed solution will serve to reinforce the subliminal wall between SOF and the rest of the military that we have been laboring over the last five years to dismantle. . . . In deriving a solution, I want to reiterate that our objective must be to insulate, not isolate, SOF.'[26]

These arguments did little to influence Congress, and by November 1986 a compromise between the House and Senate had been worked out which was attached to the Defense Authorisation Bill. Ironically, it was the secret testimony of General Richard Scholtes, who had been in charge of special operations in Grenada, that finally swayed the Senate. Scholtes was highly critical of the way special operations had been conducted and argued for radical reform.

Congress agreed that a new Unified Command for Special Operations would be established that would embrace all existing SOF forces. The command would be controlled by a four-star general or admiral, and a new post of Assistant Secretary of Defense for Special Operations and Low Intensity Conflict would be created. The command and control of all SOF would therefore be taken out of the existing service and civilian structure so that SOF would have its own budget, command and control system and direct access to the Secretary of Defense.

The commander of the Special Operations Command was charged with responsibility for

1. Developing strategy, doctrine and tactics.
2. Training assigned forces.
3. Conducting specialised courses of instruction for commissioned and non-commissioned officers.
4. Validating requirements.
5. Establishing priorities for requirements.
6. Ensuring combat readiness.
7. Developing and acquiring special operations-peculiar equipment and acquiring special operations-peculiar material, supplies and services.
8. Ensuring the interoperability of equipment and forces.
9. Formulating and submitting requirements for intelligence support.
10. Monitoring the promotions, assignments, retention, training and professional military education of special operations forces officers.

Special operations activities included direct action, strategic reconnaissance, unconventional warfare, foreign internal defence, civil affairs, psychological operations, counterterrorism, humanitarian assistance, theatre search and rescue, and 'such other activities as may be specified by the President or the Secretary of Defense'.

To ensure that the new command was recognised and used properly by the planning groups, Congress also directed that a Board for Low Intensity Conflict be established within the National Security Council and that the President should appoint his own Deputy Assistant for National Security Affairs for Low Intensity Conflict.

This radical reform went to the heart of all the problems that had bedevilled special operations since World War II. Not only had Congress removed from the service chiefs all control of special forces, but they had also built a civilian structure that ensured regular access to the White House and the Defense Secretary. Command and control would be improved, and with their own budget, SOF would have the opportunity to develop their own equipment plans.

Neither the service chiefs nor some civilians in the Pentagon welcomed the changes. Immediately attempts began to undermine the spirit of the Congressional amendment. A series of unqualified and weak individuals were proposed by Richard Armitage for the position of Assistant Secretary of Defense for Special Operations. His intention was to devalue the post so that it would continue to be subordinate to the existing structure. At the same time, the Pentagon found they had no qualified four-star general or admiral able to head the special operations command. Several retired senior officers were considered for the post.

In addition, the Pentagon proposed housing the new command at Fort MacDill in Florida, far removed from the Pentagon building, and the Assistant Secretary's staff was to be located in Rosslyn outside Washington, in a building where the lease expired in eighteen months.

The Pentagon response moved several members of Weinberger's Special Operations Advisory Group (SOPAG) to write to him in protest. On 9 March General Dick Stilwell wrote a memo to Weinberger which said in part:

'We consider the overall tenor of [the Pentagon's] report to be disappointingly tentative. . . . Certainly outsiders can reasonably conclude that the Department is not moving out with customary efficiency to implement the Congressionally mandated reorganisation. Compliance with the letter of the legislation is one thing; acceptance of its underlying rationale is quite another. And the evidence does suggest that your components have not yet re-evaluated the significance of the Special Operations role in the execution of national security policy.' The letter goes on to describe the proposal to locate the command at MacDill as 'fatally flawed' and to urge immediate action to appoint key staff.[27]

Larry Ropka, whose job it is to implement the Congressional legislation and who is supposed to be a supporter of SOF, passed a copy of Stilwell's letter to Richard Armitage with a handwritten note which reads in part: 'Selection of key staff are high on his mind. He will not get his way so long as I have anything to say about it. At any rate let's not make a fuss about this. I invited him to lunch today . . . and I will attempt to cool his passion.'[28]

In April 1987, President Reagan appointed General James Lindsay to head the new Special Forces Command. Lindsay, who has considerable experience in the Rangers and with special forces in Vietnam and Thailand, was seen as a sensible appointment by the special forces community and by Congress. However, at the time of writing (June 1987), no Assistant Secretary for Defense to oversee special operations has been appointed.

There is no doubt that Congress is determined to give the Reagan administration's SOF revitalisation programme the teeth it has been so obviously lacking. Since the initiative began in 1981, there has been a 284 per cent increase in funding for SOF and its forces have nearly trebled. Yet Air Force Chief of Staff General Charles A. Gabriel, Jr. told the House Armed Services Committee in February 1986 that Air Force Special Operations units are 'slightly less' ready than they were in 1981.

Of course, there have been improvements. Delta Force and SEAL Team 6 represent a new and potentially effective counter-terrorist strike force. But they have yet to see effective action and doubts remain about some of their training and the command and control system used to deploy them.

Overall, the US undoubtedly has an improved capability for engaging in low intensity conflict. But until an effective structure is in place it seems doubtful that the capability will ever be used to its best advantage. There remains embedded within the defence establishment a mentality that sees all unconventional operations as threatening to the existing organisation. There remains the general and contradictory perception both that SOF are a bunch of thugs and that they cream off the best talent from regular units.

Yet, even with the structure in place and the right equipment, insufficient work has been done on developing a strategy and a doctrine for special forces to ensure that they are used correctly. In recent years, they have either been used as a reactive force to counter a terrorist act that has already been committed, or else in support of conventional forces. Both are essentially tactical purposes and in a real war would have little effect on its overall conduct – a key test for SOF actions.

As Noel Koch pointed out in testimony before Congress: 'First and most importantly, we must build a solid strategic and doctrinal foundation for the most wide-ranging capabilities inherent in SOF. The Joint Special Operations Agency has already begun this process. But, what we have to keep in mind is that there can be no purely "military" solutions to the challenges that confront us. This is especially true in situations short of declared war.

'If we are to meet the challenge, we must undertake a concerted national effort. In turn, this will require a strategy that fully accounts for the political-military nature of low intensity conflict and, in the implementation of that strategy, a mechanism for bringing the efforts of the various components of our government into a coherent, cohesive whole. In short, low intensity conflict is a problem that is too big for DOD to handle alone.

'By the same token, the CINCs are integrating SOF into our strategy and planning for major conflict. During the 1970s the contribution SOF could make to conventional defense in a major war was routinely ignored. That is changing.'[29]

But the changes are barely perceptible to many inside the US special forces community. Today, the normal exercise still has SOF attacking minor targets in support of the conventional force. The CINCs, who remain responsible for deploying SOF in wartime or in low intensity conflict, still do not understand the capability they have at their disposal.

There is little point in the United States investing billions of dollars in SOF only to see them deployed by the military in a conventional, unimaginative, and inefficient way.

However much JSOA or other bureaucratic bodies work to improve this situation, nothing will really change until more SOF officers are promoted through the system to two-, three-, and four-star rank. Until then there will only be suspicion and misunderstanding and the misuse of force.

Yet it has been clearly demonstrated in Britain, West Germany and Israel, among other countries, that an effective SOF capability can in fact benefit all the armed forces if the aim is to improve a nation's ability to fight wars rather than just to win bureaucratic skirmishes.

PART 9: TRAINING AND EQUIPMENT

21

Targeting the West

Some months before Cruise and Pershing nuclear missiles were first deployed in Europe in 1983, US reconnaissance satellites detected new construction work beginning at a secret Soviet training base at Furstenburg, in the centre of the East German plain, seventy-five miles from the West German border. Over a period of weeks, replicas of both Nato missiles, plus their transports, were constructed, and Soviet forces were later seen practising attacks on them.

The dummies were a useful addition to the mock-ups of Lance missiles, nuclear-capable Nato artillery, and nuclear storage dumps that had been in place for a number of years.

The complex of wooden buildings and parachute towers at Furstenburg is the centre for Soviet special forces training in Europe. It lies in the middle of one of the largest restricted areas in East Germany and despite agreements between Nato and the Warsaw Pact allowing for inspection of training areas, the spetsnaz base is kept strictly off limits – even to conventional Soviet forces. It is duplicated at Kirovograd near Kiev and in every Warsaw Pact country.[1]

Spetsnaz are controlled by the 2nd Chief Directorate of Soviet military intelligence, the GRU. The vast majority of the estimated 25,000 spetsnaz troops that pass through the training schools are conscripts who have been creamed off from the regular forces during the selection process. All recruits need to be politically reliable, physically fit, to have above average intelligence, and to demonstrate initiative. In addition, unusual security measures apply: they are forbidden emigration and all references to them in the general media are banned.[2]

Most spetsnaz recruits are selected from the Komsomol, the Soviet communist youth organisation which is considered politically reliable, or from the DOSSAF, a voluntary organisation that carries out preparatory training for the armed forces. The DOSSAF has a number of flying clubs and parachute schools, and in the spetsnaz any airborne qualifications are particularly welcome.

The spetsnaz mission is to conduct what the Soviets call 'Special Reconnaissance' (Spetsialnaya Razvedka). According to the *Soviet Military Encylopaedia*, this is defined as:

'Reconnaissance carried out to subvert the political, economic and military potential and morale of a probable or actual enemy. The primary missions of special reconnaissance are: acquiring intelligence on major economic and military installations and either destroying them or putting them out of action; organising sabotage and acts of subversion; carrying out punitive operations against rebels; conducting propaganda; forming and training insurgent detachments, etc. Special reconnaissance is . . . conducted by the forces of covert intelligence and special purpose troops.'[3]

Training is done in brigades and is organised by regular officers. Ordinary soldiers receive three months special training, and the officers six months. Each recruit spends two months at jump school and then goes on for more general training. Unlike their western counterparts, there is very little cross-training in the spetsnaz, so each unit of from four to ten men will have a radio operator, an explosives expert and other specialists, but no one will be able to do the other's job. Such specialisation is very inefficient and in part accounts for the large number of spetsnaz.

During training, which is far less stylised and regimented than that of their conventional colleagues, the spetsnaz recruits will be taught:

a. Covert infiltration and exfiltration of target areas. It is
   expected that special forces will arive by road, rail, air
   and/or sea. Many spetsnaz officers are required to carry
   out personal reconnaissance of the area where they will
   operate in the event of war. Therefore they arrive in Europe
   and the United States disguised as tourists, long distance
   lorry drivers or aircraft flight crew. As many of them will
   be deployed in advance of hostilities, covert infiltration
   using standard civilian routes will be preferred.

'It is astonishing that they still do this when more
detente and trust are being demanded,' said Peter Kurt
Wurzbach, the state secretary at the West German
Ministry of Defence. 'This is being done in a time that is
not one of war.'[4]

In January 1986 it was reported by the magazine *Jane's
Defence Weekly* and others that women spetsnaz teams had
been permanently based outside the Greenham Common
Cruise missile base in Britain since the first missile was
deployed in 1983. The Greenham site had become the focus
of a women's protest against Cruise missiles and a
permanent peace camp had been established alongside the
perimeter fence. It was reported that a number of spetsnaz
teams had rotated through the camp, although none was
present by the time the report appeared.[5]

Exhaustive inquiries in Europe and the United States
suggest that this report was wrong. Allied intelligence has
no evidence to suggest that any spetsnaz forces have been
based at Greenham or at any other Cruise missile base.
As one senior intelligence officer said: 'As far as I am
concerned, there has been no evidence that Soviet special
forces have attempted to infiltrate here either in exercises
or at Greenham Common.'[6]

However, Cruise missile bases are high on the list of
spetsnaz targets, so the Soviets will probably have agents
in the area and will certainly have detailed satellite
reconnaissance of every base readily available.

Spetsnaz also train in HALO (High Altitude Low
Opening) and HAHO (High Altitude High Opening)
parachute techniques. They favour the UT–15 parachute
which is a development of a civilian sporting type. During

training, most jumps are done between 400 and 1,000
metres. Heavy loads can be dropped on pallets from An-
12, An-22 or IL-76 aircraft. Two telescopic poles
approximately four metres long hang down from the pallet
and, on striking the ground, trigger a retro rocket pack that
reduces the pallet's rate of descent.

b.   Sabotage methods. These include the use of explosives,
     incendiaries, acids and abrasives. More importantly, since
     one of the spetsnaz tasks is to spread panic behind the
     enemy lines, it seems likely they will make extensive use
     of chemical and biological agents to poison the water
     supplies of major cities and disable or kill large numbers
     of people in key areas. Biological agents placed in the New
     York City water supply to create acute dysentery for one
     week would disable one of the US's most important centres.

c.   Hand-to-Hand combat. 'Spetsnaz seem to be obsessed with
     the martial arts and spend an inordinate amount of time
     learning Karate and Kung Fu,' says one western
     intelligence analyst.[7] 'By contrast we do very little in that
     area.' Silent killing is obviously an important part of their
     job, and the techniques are certainly taught to their
     western counterparts.

d.   Clandestine communications. Spetsnaz carry high speed
     burst-capable radio transmitters and generally each unit
     will also have portable radio direction finding kits. These
     are used to locate enemy bases. As spetsnaz are expected
     to operate up to 1,000 kilometres behind enemy lines, the
     radios they use are smaller and with longer range than
     those available to the regular forces.

e.   Survival. Units are expected to survive for several weeks
     without resupply and are taught to live off the land.

f.   Identifying and locating targets. Some units are now
     equipped with laser designators to guide in air strikes;
     others are trained in placing radio beacons to guide
     bombers.

g.   Languages. All personnel receive training in the language
     and customs of the target country and every officer is
     expected to be fluent in at least one foreign language. Ethnic
     Germans from the Soviet Union and other Warsaw Pact
     countries may well be able to pass themselves off as native

West Germans. Those whose language would not deceive
native speakers might still hope to be able to fool Nato
soldiers of a different nationality. It is not clear just how
successful this tactic would be. In the paranoid atmosphere
of a time of armed international tension soldiers and
civilians would see spies and spetsnaz everywhere and
anyone seeming out of the ordinary would be arrested.
However, this would encourage uncertainty and chaos,
which would be to the Soviets' advantage.

h. Weapons. Spetsnaz train with a wide variety of weapons,
both Warsaw pact and Nato. A large number of them will
operate in civilian clothes or Nato uniforms and will carry
Nato weapons and use transport common to the Nato
forces. Each unit is equipped with camouflage smocks and
a good range of personal equipment including folding
spades, wire saws, silencers for guns; survival kit including
fishing hooks and line, a compass and maps. Each team
will generally carry RPG-7 grenade launchers and perhaps
anti-tank weapons, a wide range of mines and explosive
devices, passive night vision devices and target designators.

According to Nato intelligence sources, the primary targets
given to spetsnaz are listed below in the priority given to
them by the Soviets themselves:

1. The physical incapacitation and, if possible, actual
   destruction of Nato nuclear and chemical warheads,
   means of delivery, and related command and control and
   guidance systems – both strategic (Trident and Polaris
   nuclear submarines) and tactical (Lance, Cruise and
   Pershing).
2. The interruption and disruption, from the very highest level
   downward, of Nato political, strategic and tactical
   command, control and communications elements. This
   includes the destruction not only of equipment and
   organisations (radio antennae, field headquarters, civil
   radio and television stations) but also of personnel in key
   political and military appointments, especially those in the
   nuclear chain of command.
3. The physical incapacitation of some but not necessarily all

electronic warning and reconnaissance equipment; radar;
early warning systems; air defence equipment of all types.
Even supposing they were able to destroy all such systems,
some method of communicating with the enemy must
remain in place to discuss peace terms, exchanges of
prisoners etc.

4. The capture of key airfields and ports to prevent
   reinforcement or redeployment, particularly by the US; and
   the destruction or neutralising (by mine or other explosives)
   of airfield and port facilities not required intact by the
   USSR, and of railway and key road junctions important in
   mobilisation plans.

5. The disrupting of key industrial targets and facilities –
   power stations, oil refineries, military-electronics industries
   etc.

6. The destruction of troops in garrisons.

7. The destruction of logistic installations, e.g. fuel supply
   terminals and fuel and ammunition dumps.

8. The destruction and interruption of transport systems,
   traffic control posts, road and rail intersections, bridges
   and tunnels.

9. The seizure of dropping zones and tactical landing zones
   for subsequent larger landings.

10. The seizure of key areas of terrain – river and coastal
    bridgeheads, defiles, commanding ground, canal sluice
    and lock gates, bridges etc. – essential for the continuation
    of a rapid advance by enemy forces.

11. The capture of prisoners for interrogation and of documents
    or items of equipment for examination and intelligence
    gathering.

Soviet military doctrine has a single concept of putting troops
behind enemy lines known as Desant. While this may include
the use of regular airborne forces, which mirror their western
counterparts, it is more likely that Desant forces will mainly
be composed of spetsnaz.

While directly commanded by the GRU, Soviet military
intelligence, the spetsnaz are organised as follows:

a. Army. Each army has an independent company of 110–120
    men.

b. Front. Each Military District and Group Soviet Forces
    Germany has an SPF brigade with a fighting strength of
    1,000–1,300 men and its own intelligence unit. Unlike their
    western counterparts who rely on centrally-organised
    intelligence, each front runs its own agents in enemy
    territory and is therefore able to work up-to-date
    intelligence directly into their own tactical plans.

c. Fleet. Each Fleet has a naval SPF, although very little is
    known about their tactics apart from their apparent use
    of midget submarines (see below).

d. Strategic. Spetsnaz regiments of between 700–800 men are
    directly subordinated to the GRU Central apparatus.
    These are both pure intelligence-gathering units and units
    which will engage in offensive action.

e. Warsaw Pact. Each non-Soviet army in the Warsaw Pact
    has its own special forces of around 800 men.

f. KGB. Although strictly an intelligence-gathering and
    counter-intelligence organisation, the KGB's Department
    8 does have units trained for special forces work. It is
    believed they will mainly carry out assassinations of senior
    political and military figures.

g. Fifth Columns. Unconventional warfare operations are
    supported by large agent networks in target countries that
    fall into two basic categories:

    First. Intelligence gathering. These networks are active
    in peacetime and provide details on the enemy's order of
    battle, equipment, plans and any other details that might
    provide a tactical advantage. They are primarily KGB
    although the GRU are specifically tasked with gathering
    intelligence on technological developments in the west.

    Second. Intelligence and sabotage agents. These are
    recruited and controlled by the spetsnaz themselves. They
    not only provide target information during peacetime but
    also will provide safe houses and possibly be a source of
    pre-dropped arms and explosives in the event of war.

Accounts of Soviet special forces in action are extremely rare.
There have been defectors, but these still remain closely

controlled by western intelligence services. The only recent
account of spetsnaz training appeared in the Soviet Union in
a paper written by Evgeny Mesyatser and translated into
English by the Soviet Studies Centre at Sandhurst. It is worth
quoting at length as it gives a fascinating first-hand account
of training, techniques, likely targets and equipment.[8]

'Day One:

'We get up and turn to face the distant space below us.
Our hands grip the rings controlling the parachutes.

'The green light – we are off . . .

'The grey and yellow dome obscures one half of the sky. . . .
The ground is not more than 500m away – one can see a
forest with some cuttings in it and a stream. One hundred
metres. The air current has unfurled the parachute and I now
descend with my back towards the ground. . . . A rough blow
below the belt, a headstand, a somersault, a fall on a moss-
covered hummock and I am being dragged towards the edge
of the clearing. . . . We run into the forest leaving the space
open for those who jump after us. They crash into the tall
grass or slide off the trees. "Secure your weapons. . . . Check
your haversack."

'The loaf of white bread and two hefty tins of stewed meat
and some fish have to be tucked away further so that they do
not press against one's back. Poncho, cam-suit jacket, spare
footcloths, mess tin, spoon, a small net, hooks, a fishing line,
matches, a wire-saw, packets of explosives, cartridges, a torch,
bandages, cotton wool and tubes of disinfecting tablets have
to be placed in separate sections of the kit bag. The flask of
water, the folding spade, the small axe are hitched on to the
belt. On the right hip – the pistol. We also have AKMs with
silencers; a machine-gun, two RPG 7Ds, two radio sets and
a set of batteries, a set of flares, magnetic and other mines,
special instruments and devices for their destruction.

'Silently we go through the dark forest leaving hardly any
traces behind. The air is stuffy and humid. The mosquitos
sing their boring tune, dry twigs crack softly under foot. In
fifteen hours we have to cover more than 50 kilometres.

'Day Two:

'The devil himself would not find our new hiding place. Each one of us has his own position; a fallen tree, an uprooted tree stump, a thick alder grove, a willow thicket. A dull ache of cramp in my feet, the soles have swollen and are burning; I have no strength to get up.

'At three in the morning we come out of the wood on to a sandy cart track. We pass a village; a cock crows, dogs whine, a cow breathes heavily. Suddenly people are heard and the unit's scout imitates the call of a quail as a signal for the group to hide off the trail. We then approach a guard post . . .

'Safety catches on the AKMs are off, the RPGs have been loaded . . .

'Dawn is breaking. We move stealthily along the bottom of an overgrown gully in the direction of the guard who is whistling in a low key. When he becomes silent we hold our breath.

'A twig cracks loudly on the other side of the road – this is the work of Korchagin. The guard has raised his AKM. As if shot forward on a spring, Glotov dashed from behind a bush. Vashurkin hurls himself at the feet of the enemy soldier, seizes him by the knees and with a shoulder hits him below the belt. One huge hand closes the mouth and holds back his head. The other hand grabs his throat – Glotov at once gags him.

'I am looking at this lad – information is pouring from him like water from a tap. . . . Galtov seems to be reading my thoughts; "according to the rules of training, the prisoner of war should play the game . . . If the 'enemy' captures me, my part has come to an end and I will have to answer all their questions . . ."

'Glotov is preparing a raid against the battery. We cover the 400 metres in one swift movement. The caterpillar truck is standing by the wattle hurdle on the edge of the village; four men leap like cats into the cab, grab the driver who seems to have gone mad and pin him to the ground, and Glotov and I look for the Major.

'He was stretched out blissfully under the vehicle in a sleeping bag. The Major wakes up, raises his hands and then quickly turns over on to his stomach and tries to reach his belt. The Lieutenant kicks the belt away with the toe of his boot.

'So far we are lucky. . . . We have a good rest on the bank of the stream in the wood. In the stream there is a lot of fish and crayfish but they are not for us. We must be ready at all times either to defend ourselves or to carry out a raid. At the end of the day, we study mines of various types, we are reminded how to make the simplest form of detonating fuse and how to obtain from almost nothing a powerful igniting fuse or blasting charge. The first drops of rain fall on our weapons.

'Day Three:

'For some time now we had been soaked to the skin; our boots swelled with water and felt like penitentiary chains. Huddling against the pine trees and the aspens, hopping mad with anger, we curse goodness knows whom for the fact that no waterproof tobacco has been invented specially for us . . .

'Towards three in the morning the rain abated. A warm wind woke up; the forest began to rustle, to whisper and to creak. The new sounds made it difficult for us to hear the birds which warn us of danger. The lead scout gave the signal: "Stop" . . .

'A burst of automatic fire from behind. We throw ourselves to the ground grabbing our weapons as we do so. Gunfire from both right and left – an ambush.

'Glotov shouts the words of command: "Do not return fire."

'We run through the wood and then towards the stream. We make our way through the marshy ground holding our weapons and the blasting charges above our heads; four or five kilometres along the sandy bottom of the stream will definitely cover up our traces. At last Glotov looks at the map for the hundredth time and orders us to make camp. I immediately sink into oblivion.

'Reveille at half past seven. I have a headache: it is a bad thing to sleep at sunset. The radio operators intercepted an enemy radio transmitter. The portable direction finders are tuned into enemy signals. The indicator points at the village N – some ten kilometres from us. It is precisely in the place that our air reconnaissance had seen the traces of caterpillar tracks. There is no reason for tanks to be there. Are they rockets? Perhaps there are artillery dumps near the village?

'We reached the area of particular attention at 23.15 hours.

'Day Four:

'In the village everything is quiet and peaceful. To avoid all risks we go round it by way of garden allotments and on the moist clay of the road we soon find the expected traces of caterpillar tracks. They lead us to a solitary barrier with an iron notice board: "Out of Bounds". From here stretch two lines of barbed wire, watchtowers, several long, low vaults. Dumps. Their walls and roofs are covered with camouflage patterns – this is why our pilots found nothing here except those tracks.

'The AKM's bayonet and its scabbard are converted into a pair of cutters with which we hack through the barbed wire. Three sappers equipped with a blasting charge move to the other side of the fence. The remainder of us take aim at the watchtowers with our weapons. Forty minutes later the sappers return with empty hands. . . . Powerful mines will go off activated by a radio signal which will be passed on to the detonators at the right moment by our distant headquarters.

'Day Five:

'The anxious morning brings with it low cloud and drizzle. The water reserves are exhausted and we are forced to drink the tasteless rainwater which drips from the stretched surface of the ponchos.

'And then Glotov thinks up something else for us to do. How to recognise a minefield quickly, how to cross it without leaving any traces and how to make the enemy fall into its own trap. And then a show begins. Two men throw a third one into the air. He makes a somersault and just before reaching the ground and landing on his feet or falling into the mud, he fires a cartridge clip on to a target. They are doing the same using knives and sapper's spades . . .

'The exercise continues for another twenty days as the unit scouts an army camp and an airfield, relaying the information it gathers back to headquarters in advance of a major assault.'

Another account, this time of a winter exercise, comes from a Soviet defector, Aleksei Myagkov, who served both in spetsnaz and in the KGB:

'Once the sabotage group which I commanded was ordered to take part in an exercise which involved being dropped by parachute in the woods of Belorussia some 400 km from our base to destroy the opposition's communications centre, even if it were to cost the lives of the whole group to do so. The group was then to destroy two railway bridges, start a forest fire, attack some population centres and make its own way back to base. The targets were guarded by motorised infantry, and, of course, we were forbidden to cause any casualties during the exercise. It was winter and we had to cover some 800 km on skis.

'We were allowed 24 hours to prepare for our mission, and were issued with special explosives, incendiary materials and radio equipment; the latter known as the radiogram is able to shoot the message to the centre in just 8–10 seconds. Our machine-guns were designed to fire silently and without showing flashes. We were issued with dry rations for three days, but on my order took only enough for one day in order to carry more ammunition. We paid particular attention to the skis which were to be dropped separately in protective wrapping containing a small radio transmitter.

'Each paratrooper carried a tiny receiver which emitted a homing signal in his earphones when he faced the transmitter so that the group could assemble as quickly as possible on landing. Using models and maps we planned our operation down to the last detail, including contingency plans for possible problems such as the transmitter failing to function.

'The night of the operation was dark and cloudy and snow

was falling thickly. At 10 p.m. we jumped from the aircraft and 15 minutes later the whole group had assembled, looking like ghosts in their white camouflage. By 1 a.m. we had covered the 18 km to our target. The six guards were easily overpowered and tied up. The doors and windows of the barracks were booby-trapped with quantities of explosives sufficient to give a nasty fright to the 20 men inside without causing injuries. At the same time, mines were planted on the communications building. We could hear the explosions as we set off. By midday we had covered about 70 km and, concealed among the trees, slept for four hours, lying in pairs for greater warmth.

'We continued to operate at night and sleep during the day, stealing provisions from the peasants until we had carried out all our tasks. At one time we were spotted from the air and were soon surrounded by ground troops who were gradually tightening the noose around us. We decided to seize an armoured troop carrier from the opposition to escape from the closing ring of troops, but these normally carried 10–15 men – too many to be easily overpowered by our small group. We waited for a command vehicle, which usually carries only two or three men.

'When one appeared a soldier dressed in clothes stolen from a peasant waved it to a halt. When the officer got out to investigate, we seized him, his driver and the armoured vehicle in which we then made our escape and returned to our base, looking more like unshaven forest bandits than regular soldiers.'[9]

Western intelligence organisations concentrate their assessments and analysis on the threat posed by Soviet spetsnaz operating on land. This in part is because so much more is known about them and because they operate in much larger numbers, and in part because the threat is easier to recognise. However, the Soviets have also invested men and equipment in developing and training a naval surface and sub-surface threat. Like their western counterparts, the naval spetsnaz are expected to carry out acts of sabotage and disruption against coastal targets, including civilian ports and military installations.

Examples of their training techniques are hard to come by. The most recent and detailed training over the past ten years seems to have occurred in the waters off Sweden and Norway. Spetsnaz operations first came to the attention of the world's press with the grounding of a Whisky Class submarine on the rocks outside the Swedish naval base at Karlskrona in October 1981. This episode, inevitably dubbed Whisky on the Rocks by the media, was just the latest in a long series of violations of Swedish territorial waters.[10]

Exactly a year later the wake and periscope of another submarine was spotted by two Swedish soldiers inside the Stockholm archipelago. Helicopters and patrol boats immediately gathered in the area and there was sufficient evidence of sonar contacts for an extensive hunt to be launched. Over the next month, the full resources of the Swedish navy and air force were brought to bear; depth charges, mines and torpedoes were used against possible targets. On 5 October, following the dropping of twelve depth charges, air bubbles and an oil slick came to the surface but no boat followed them.

The search was abandoned at the beginning of November. As a result of sonar evidence and a search of the sea bottom by divers, the Swedish government is convinced that six submarines were involved, three of which were midgets. The divers reported that two different types of midget submarines had been used. One had two propellers and a reinforced keel; when it had moved off from resting on the bottom, the wash from its propellers had disturbed the sand and left distinct marks. The second type had a single propeller and twin caterpiller tracks to enable it to crawl along the bottom.

The Swedish government's report of the incident concluded that one conventional submarine, acting as a mother ship, had been sent to operate with its mini-sub in the middle of the Stockholm archipelago. After decoupling from its mother ship, the mini-sub had penetrated the inner archipelago.

This mini-sub made its way into Stockholm harbour during the last week of September; the mother ship returned to a holding area near Sandham, where it was later to reconnect with the mini-sub (this mother ship was observed during the evening of 4 October near Sand Island, where it was attacked with a depth charge); then, after the mini-sub rejoined the mother ship, both vessels left the area during the second week in October.

The other two mini-subs and their mother ships had missions in the southern area of the archipelago; on 1 October both mini-subs entered the area of Haarsfjaerden; one submarine left a week later and the other, which might have been damaged, was picked up by its mother ship on 12 October.[11]

Dozens of further sightings off the coasts of both Sweden and Norway have since occurred. But despite improvements in sonar and anti-submarine weapons made by both the Swedish and Norwegian navies, there have been no successful attacks. This has puzzled analysts in the United States and Britain who have looked in vain from defectors and other sources for confirmation of spetsnaz activity in the area. 'We cannot be specific about spetsnaz involvement,' says one western intelligence analyst. 'Certainly the Swedes are convinced.'

Despite the lack of conclusive evidence, it seems logical that the Soviets would regularly practise sub-surface attacks in the Baltic. Their own war plans place a great deal of emphasis on securing Norway in the early stages of any war, so that they can control Nato's northern flank. A key to that operation would be the disruption of port facilities in order to make reinforcement more difficult. Soviet exercises around neutral Sweden are less easy to explain, but it is possible that the Soviets calculate that if they ever attacked Norway, the Swedes would shelve their neutrality and join Nato. With a capable navy Nato could pose a serious threat to Soviet naval forces, particularly to Russian submarines, which would be trying to break out through the Greenland/Iceland/UK gap to control the North Sea and the Atlantic.

Tracks identical to those found in Swedish waters have also been discovered off Japan. In September 1984 divers found tracks within three miles of the Hokkaido coast in the Soya and Tsugaru straits. These are two of the three straits through which Soviet warships based at Vladivostock must pass in order to reach the Pacific Ocean. There have also been reports of midget submarines operating off the coast of Alaska close to the oil terminals.[12]

On the basis of the information gathered from these incidents, the naval spetsnaz units apparently have two principal targets: carried in pairs on the hulls of specially converted India class submarines, the midget submarines with two propellers will infiltrate ports and naval bases to plant mines and destroy ships and facilities. The midget submarines with tracked keels will be used either to cut or tap communications cables on the bottom of the ocean.[13]

Inevitably, the Soviets will not limit their attentions to Sweden and Norway. They will also target vital installations such as the British nuclear submarine base at Holy Loch in Scotland, Norfolk Virginia, headquarters of CINCLANT, and Cherbourg, a key port for the reinforcement of Europe by the US. And yet, apart from Sweden and Norway who have both invested substantial sums in the past five years re-equipping their navies with a more effective anti-submarine warfare capability, no country appears to take this threat seriously. Instead, the west's focus has been on land-based spetsnaz operations, or on detecting the larger Soviet submarines which operate in mid-ocean.

This is a serious omission. There is little point in protecting land bases if the communications and supplies going to those bases remain vulnerable to a different form of surprise attack.

The most comprehensive testing of western defences against spetsnaz attack occurred in the autumn of 1985, when 65,000 British troops took part in Exercise Brave Defender designed to test Britain's defences against spetsnaz operations. The nationwide exercise for the first time involved the police and civil authorities along with United States forces based in Britain. Eight thousand troops were infiltrated from Germany to act as the enemy, while SAS and SBS troops attempted to penetrate defences to key buildings and sensitive bases.

The exercise showed up serious weaknesses in Britain's defences. Almost all the targets attacked by the SAS and SBS were successfully penetrated, detection and surveillance equipment for early detection of intruders was not available in many cases, and the 2,500 Home Guard units were too few to do an effective job – particularly as in wartime it is unlikely that reinforcements from regular units would be available. The British government has agreed to increase the Home Guard force to 5,000 men, but some senior officers believe this is still only a fraction of the numbers required.

General Sir James Glover, the Commander-in-Chief of UK Land Forces, reported that the Soviets had tried to penetrate Brave Defender. The number of Warsaw Pact cargo and fishing vessels off the British coast rose from a seasonal average of forty to seventy-six, and it proved impossible to keep track of the Soviet sailors coming ashore on leave. (This illustrates a situation very worrying to allied intelligence. In Britain, for example, 40,000 Soviet seamen come into the United Kingdom each year. They do not require visas and are seldom checked.)

'Obviously in time of tension we must regard Soviet merchant ships as an extension of the Russian Navy right inside our ports,' said Glover. 'We must now consider that, apart from mining, there could be pre-arranged scuttling at exits and entrances to strategic harbours. Surveillance could have gleaned valuable information about the way local army units and the police would respond to spetsnaz intruders.'[14]

Serious gaps were exposed also in the defences around nuclear power stations, both during Brave Defender and in a series of other exercises carried out over the past three years. The SAS and the SBS are used to test nuclear security and, as a result of their demonstrations, it had been decided to

increase the number of guards and install a wide range of
sophisticated detection devices.

A more comprehensive approach to attacks on nuclear
facilities is taken in the United States. In 1973, the Defense
Advanced Research Projects Agency commissioned a study
to examine the risks of a Soviet paramilitary attack on US
nuclear forces on the American mainland. The report is still
secret but one of the conclusions points out:

'The possibility of moving paramilitary units through
Mexico, into the US and to their targets, without detection,
seems serious when one considers the limited effectiveness of
the US internal security forces in stopping illegal traffic in
aliens and narcotics. The probability of a paramilitary unit
being detected or captured prior to the attack could be further
minimised by maintaining the independence of the units and
limiting their interaction with each other and with the US
populace. The usual procedure of limiting the detailed knowledge of any unit to that required for performance of its precise
mission would severely constrain the information that might
be obtained from a paramilitary unit, which might in turn be
interrogated by US authorities. A judicious choice of the time
and conditions for the attack . . . would further reduce the
credibility of any defecting or captured unit. In addition, the
Soviets would probably delay and confuse any US reaction
by disguising the attack under a cloak of US terrorists or
fanaticist activity. As a result it might be weeks before the
US could establish the credibility required to take serious
action. . . . We conclude that the threat of a Soviet paramilitary attack on the US and Nato nuclear forces may be
comparable to the threat of direct nuclear attack.'[15]

Ironically, it was the civilian nuclear authorities that
responded most strongly to this and to other reports that
sounded the same clear warning. The US Department of
Energy has a $700 million budget for safeguarding nuclear
weapons and facilities under its control and employs 4,500
guards. Many of these men are former SOF and are armed
with equipment that ranges from armoured cars, through

sophisticated perimeter defences, to surface-to-air missiles. These are in fact required if a nuclear facility is to receive an operating licence from the government. They are constantly tested by private firms who use ex-Delta Force and SEALs in actual operational conditions.

Nevertheless, the ability of the US armed forces themselves to deal with an unconventional threat on the American mainland remains weak. During World War I, 100,000 men were used to protect vital facilities, and during World War II, 300,000 men. Today, as General Wallace H. Nutting, the Commander-in-Chief of the United States Readiness Command (USREDCOM) has made clear: 'We . . . do not have a single soldier, airman, or sailor solely dedicated to the security mission within the US. I question the advisability of this practice.'[16].

The lack of resources is not because the nature of the threat is misunderstood. 'The current assessment of the land threat . . . is that posed by the Soviet Union's unconventional warfare forces. Soviet doctrine calls for forces to operate far behind enemy lines for extended periods of time and to be capable of operating throughout an enemy's homeland. These forces are composed of KGB infiltration teams, possibly in-place agents and . . . spetsnaz. Soviet unconventional warfare forces are tasked to perform acts of sabotage and assassination deep in the enemy's base. Additionally, land infiltration could become a future concern along the porous US-Mexican border. . . . These infiltration teams and in-place agents could be targeted against key command and control centers, nuclear capable assets, critical lines of communication and other targets critical to their war effort. Their overall goal would be to degrade or destroy the US war-waging capability.'[17]

Even so, although the increased threat posed by spetsnaz has been used in part as a justification for the revitalisation of US special forces, there has still been no serious attempt to educate either military or civilian agencies in the dangers posed by unconventional warfare on the American mainland. All the training that currently goes on is directed at countering terrorism, and while many spetsnaz techniques are similar to those used by terrorists, these men will be better trained and should have a much higher success rate.

Soviet strategy places considerable emphasis on surprise and a quick victory. In previous campaigns, for example the invasions of Czechoslovakia and Afghanistan, spetsnaz were used to cripple the chain of command and secure key targets such as radio stations and centres of government. It is likely that any Soviet attack will use the same proven and successful tactics again.

There remains, therefore, a serious gap in US defences which the Soviets must have discovered. This gap is acknowledged by senior US military officers, but few believe anything will ever be done to plug it. In the constant trade-off between cash and resources, the money will always go on the front line projects that have a high profile – the new fighter, tank or state-of the-art electronics. Guarding the rear is low profile and, until the shooting starts, of no demonstrable benefit.

The United States has yet to experience a major attack on its territory either from terrorism or during any conflict since the Civil War. But in World War III the American mainland will be a prime target, and the short-sighted approach to defending the home territory currently being demonstrated by the service chiefs could prove critical to America's ability to fight that war.

As far as Europe is concerned, western war planners assume that there will be a period of international tension that may last days or even weeks before World War III actually breaks out. The 'bolt from the blue' scenario which envisions a pre-emptive nuclear strike or massive surprise conventional invasion of Europe is actually considered the least likely eventuality.

It is during this time of tension that spetsnaz forces will convert their training to action, and the focus of their attacks will be on undermining the morale of the armed forces and the civilian population. Two likely methods will be the comprehensive use of chemical and biological agents to disrupt the civilian population, and widespread bombings and assassinations which will be conveniently blamed on indigenous terrorist groups. At the same time, agents in place in trade unions, the civil service and the armed forces will be activated to cause maximum disruption.

'The whole security system in Nato will become so over-loaded that it will break down,' said one intelligence officer. 'Even when they fail in a mission they will still spread rumour and lower morale. It is a very cost-effective method of waging war.'

The timing of spetsnaz operations will be critical. If they occur too soon, the value of surprise will be lost; too late and their effect will be insufficient. There is disagreement among intelligence analysts as to exactly when spetsnaz forces will begin infiltrating, but some experts believe they will move in up to a week before hostilities break out.

As one senior Nato intelligence officer puts it: 'We have intelligence as well as deduction that brings us to question the Soviet Union's capacity for surprise. If you are going to have a preparatory programme of sabotage, how then can you keep surprise for the main attack?'

If spetsnaz should begin their attacks too early, the Nato allies already have a sophisticated warning system in place that should sound the alarm. For example, there is a list of key Nato officials, such as heads of intelligence and those in the nuclear chain of command, whose disappearance would trigger the system. It seems likely that industrial action and sporadic acts of 'terrorism' might occur some days before the outbreak of war in a limited attempt to disrupt reinforcements. But the real campaign would happen during a very compressed few hours just before the Warsaw Pact moved its troops forward on the Central Front. As with all Soviet plans, it is helpful to look at the past to get an idea of what they might do in the future. Students of spetsnaz operations repeatedly cite the Manchurian Operation against the Japanese in August 1945. At the start of that operation, the theatre commander deployed some twenty airborne assaults, each of between thirty and forty men. The troops were dropped close to Manchurian cities with the task of causing as much disruption as possible by sabotage and raids against strategic points, and military and industrial targets. At the same time, boats landed small teams of frogmen in North Korea with responsibility for disrupting ports through sabotages and diversions.

The teams did not achieve a significant level of destruction in the Japanese rear – but they did create panic among the authorities, which greatly increased the effect of the massive surprise attack which followed shortly after.

As one Nato intelligence assessment puts it: 'We consider this is a valid historical model for the initial employment of diversionary troops in any future war. The actual damage that a small team of men could accomplish might, with luck on their side, be moderate but would probably only be slight. However, the shock to national morale of an attack made on, say, the Ministries of Defence in Bonn, the Hague or London, or of the assassination in their own homes of senior politicians, industrialists, financiers etc. in the very first hours of the war would be disproportionally great in comparison to the small cost of attempting such an operation.'

The window of opportunity available to spetsnaz is narrow enough to have provoked debate among the allies as to how effective they will really be. In the British army, for example, General Jimmy Glover believes spetsnaz could do immense damage and has consistently argued for greater home defence. His background entitles him to some respect, as he served in Malaya, Cyprus and Northern Ireland where he gained considerable experience in dealing with terrorism and unconventional warfare.

However, other senior officers disagree with him. As one of them said: 'In terms of capability there is a reasonable risk of Soviet Special Forces (SPF) threatening vital installations. But it is easy to exaggerate the amount of penetration the KGB and the GRU can do in peacetime.

'You have to ask yourself just how these people will get here. Will they land by submarine on the Norfolk coast and hike inland, or will they drop in by parachute? And when they are here just how much can they achieve? It just isn't as easy as all that.'

Opinions within the intelligence community in fact only really differ in degree. Everyone recognises that spetsnaz form a vital part of the Soviets' preparations for war. By using them simultaneously throughout the Nato alliance, the Soviets will hope so to create panic and undermine morale that Nato's ability to repel a massive Soviet attack will be severely reduced.

Of course, the opposite also applies. If the allies develop sufficient resources to defend the home territory against spetsnaz attacks and if these therefore fail, then allied morale will be unaffected – and that would have a considerable deterrent effect on the Warsaw Pact planners, and in their eyes would lessen the likelihood of a swift resolution of the war.

Intelligence assessments suggest that in a long conventional war the Warsaw Pact would swiftly disintegrate, leaving the Soviets to fight on their own. Isolated and with very extended lines of communication, they would have considerable difficulties and would either resort to nuclear weapons or sue for peace. The performance of spetsnaz could therefore prove critical to the course of any conventional war in Europe.

22

Preparing for Conflict

Above the entrance to the corrugated building at the heart of Camp Mackall inside the Fort Bragg complex is pinned a 20 ft. by 2 ft. sign that spells out the word SURVIVAL. Next to each letter is a short phrase to remind the recruits what their training is all about: Size up the Situation; Undue haste makes waste; Remember where you are; Vanquish fear and panic; Improvise; Value living; Act like natives; Learn basic skills.

Mackall is part of the two hundred square miles of territory inside Fort Bragg where special forces begin the Basic Skills phase of the three-part qualification or Q course that all special forces take.

The Green Berets provide a useful example of how special forces everywhere in the world are trained. However they may be recruited, all special forces must become physically fit, highly-motivated individuals who understand teamwork and discipline, yet are able to operate on their own initiative. Every member of special forces is also expected to be competent in a wide range of skills, from communications to small arms to hand-to-hand combat. Differences between national training schemes are only in emphasis. The SAS have a more lengthy selection process divided into six phases that last nearly two years. Both the Green Berets and Germany's GSG9 have much shorter courses – seventeen and thirty-two weeks respectively – while the Ranger course only lasts fifty-eight days.

The purpose of all this training is to prepare SOF to operate in five specific roles:[1]

1. Unconventional military operations in conventional war. SOF are often used, particularly by the US armed forces, as a support element for conventional forces which is a misuse of their talents. The SAS have responsibility from forty to four hundred kilometres behind the enemy lines, while US SOF work outside the corps area, or a hundred and fifty kilometres plus.
2. Peacekeeping. The UN has been the most frequent sponsor of these missions but they can be undertaken unilaterally. As the US army training command points out: 'A peacekeeping mission may present situations that are often ambiguous and may require force to deal with extreme tension and violence in the form of terrorism, sabotage, and minor military conflicts from known and unknown belligerents.'
3. Combat Rescue Missions. This is an essential role for counter-terrorist forces, primarily the rescue of hostages.
4. Paramilitary operations. The Soviet invasions of Afghanistan and Czechoslovakia began as paramilitary operations, as did the US invasion of Grenada.
5. Counter-insurgency. This has become a major focus for the US administration to counter what they see as increased Soviet activity. It includes civic action and civil affairs programmes and training assistance as well as psychological, political and economic warfare.

The SOF of every western nation co-operate and share information on training and tactics with other friendly countries. Yet there are marked differences in capability between the organisations and a different approach to basic training.

To an outsider, the US course appears a mixture of sadism and self-torture that places more emphasis on brutality than brains. It successfully destroys any semblance of individual identity, after which the recruit is reformed into the special forces mould.

'Everywhere else in the Army we work on a buddy system

where guys look after each other. On this course we deliberately set out to break that down, to see how each person
performs as an individual,' explained one Green Beret
instructor.

Individuals are actively encouraged not just to compete
against each other but to do anything possible to undermine
the success of others. At the end of an exercise involving
competitive patrols Green Berets are encouraged to spend
five minutes shouting insults at each other. Foreign special
forces, such as the British and the Germans who visit the
Bragg training course, find it baffling. 'If we did the kind of
thing that goes on at Bragg, we would be in jail,' said one
British officer. However, the course does turn out some exceptionally able individuals.

On the first day of their thirty day introductory tour at
Mackall, volunteers are given a two-hour show by the Gabriel
Team, a twelve-strong unit able to show exactly what can be
accomplished with the skills the new men will learn. The
show begins with an introduction to the heart of special
forces operations, the A-Detachment. The unit consists of two
commissioned officers, a captain and a first lieutenant as
executive officer and ten non-commissioned officers, and is
required to have people qualified in one of five basic SOF
skills:

1. Each unit has an expert in heavy and light weapons. He is
    expected to be able to fire and strip eighty foreign weapons
    within specific time limits, even in the dark.
2. The senior non-commissioned officer, a master sergeant,
    and his assistant are responsible for planning all operations,
    training and intelligence.
3. An engineer and his assistant are trained in the construction
    of sabotage devices.
4. A medical expert and his assistant are trained in first aid,
    minor surgery, dental care and the running of a field
    hospital. They are trained in surgery and mending broken
    bones using live goats on a course nicknamed 'Peticuts'.
5. A radio operator and his assistant are trained to handle

secure communication in UHF, VHF and morse at
eighteen words a minute.

Each A-Team has at least one qualified sniper who is generally one of the weapons experts. As they normally operate in
pairs, another member of the team will also be qualified.

All A-Teams are cross-trained so that at least two other
members of the team duplicate any one skill. All the members
also receive some language training. In theory every A-Team
has to have one man who is fluent in the language of the
country they are expected to operate in and all the others
need a working knowledge. However, the current level of
language knowledge is below standard and the Army is in
the middle of a five-year programme to have three out of
the twelve team members speaking a foreign language to
elementary level – 'just good enough to read the sign on the
men's room' as one Congressional critic puts it. There has
also been discussion at Fort Bragg about allowing foreign
nationals to join the SOF, and they are considering adopting
the British SAS method of encouraging a language capability.
After basic instruction, the SAS member receives a monthly
payment that is based on his proficiency. It is left to the SAS
soldier to acquire and maintain the language and no formal
instruction is provided.

At Mackall, after being introduced, the Gabriel Team gives
demonstrations of parachuting, bridge building, sabotage,
trapping, hand-to-hand combat and helicopter rescue. Suitably inspired, the raw recruit moves on to the second day of
his training, which begins at 05.00 with a three mile run
carrying weapons. This has to be completed in twenty-four
minutes and is followed by two parachute jumps from a
helicopter and then another three mile run, this time with a
45lb rucksack. During the Phase 1 course there will be thirty
such marches with the rucksack increasing in weight each
day to a maximum of 65lb. The students must average a 14-
minute mile during the twelve mile run on the final day.[2]

The students are also expected to navigate the obstacle

course several times during the month. The 1,800 metre course has twenty-eight obstacles with nicknames like 'Tarzan', the 'Whopper', the 'Grunt' and the 'Dirty Name' and if any student fails three obstacles he is dismissed from the course.

Once the run and the obstacle course have been successfully negotiated, the average 240-man recruiting class is divided between the three committees that make up the Basic Skills Course:

1. The General Subjects Committee teaches hand-to-hand combat, using ropes for rapid descent from helicopters or buildings known as rappelling, ropes and knots, river crossing and survival.
2. The Land Navigation Committee teaches basic map and compass reading and land navigation.
3. The Patrolling Committee teaches the duties and responsibilities of every person in an A-Team, danger areas, raids and ambushes.

Seventy-five per cent of all applicants pass the Phase 1 course. The units are then divided into their five specialisations for the next eight weeks after which they come together for a final five weeks of team training including unconventional warfare, air drops, ambushes, night operations and escape and evasion.

The preliminary twenty-one-day selection course for Delta Force adds additional requirements, among them an IQ of at least 110 and the ability to march 30 miles in 12 hours with a 55lb rucksack. Once selected, Delta men receive training in assassination techniques from the Secret Service at their Beltsville, Maryland, training centre. They also refine the techniques of sabotage, reconnaissance and counter-terrorist work at a special compound on Mott Lake near Fort Bragg.

Every week, all the Delta men are required to pass a physical that includes an all-fours 40 yard run in 24 seconds, a run-dodge-and-jump dash through log gates and over a six foot pit, 32 situps in a minute, a two mile run in boots in 19 minutes, a swing down a 35-rung horizontal ladder in 60 seconds and a 100 yard swim in full uniform.[3]

The training effectively prepares each individual A-Team to perform a wide range of functions, and much of it is done in isolation from the other services, who simply provide aircraft or ships to get the SOF to their targets. It also extends far beyond the basic outline given above. For example, in the final phase of all special forces training, considerable emphasis is placed on what is known as SERE or Survival, Evasion, Resistance and Escape. The course is self-explanatory but is designed to test as far as possible in the peacetime environment the ability to resist interrogation.

In Britain these simulated exercises are carried out by the Intelligence Corps, and back during the Malayan campaign they reached appalling levels:

'Just to try the chaps out; and it was quite amazing, off the record, how many of our big tough soldiers in fact weren't quite so tough under the skin. No physical violence whatsoever, it was purely mental. For example, you'd sit a chap down in a chair and you'd put a latrine bucket over his head, and a chap would sit there going bong, bong, bong with a spoon for about half an hour, and then he'd be taken outside and tied to a tree that had been smeared with jam, with ankle cuffs and wrist cuffs, so he had to keep away from the tree, because the ants were pouring up and down it, red ants. All sorts of lovely tortures they devised, these chaps. They would take a bicycle wheel with the spindle still in the centre, and put it on the ground and make you kneel on the rim, kneel inside the rim on the spokes, with your hands behind your back tied to a rope over the ceiling, and you had to keep this bicycle wheel absolutely flat. You can't do it, because you get cramp in the ankles and knees, and every time you moved, you got a jerk on the wrists and it was very painful. It didn't leave any mark or sign, you weren't actually beaten up. And they wouldn't give you any sleep for thirty-six hours or no food, you just didn't get a thing, and they'd put you in solitary confinement, and you'd be in this little cell all on your own with a board on the floor to sleep on, and every time you got on the board somebody would open the door and throw a bucket of water over you. Or they'd put you in a pit and surround you with guard dogs and turn the hose on you from time to time just to keep you cooled down. It was great fun and it gave everybody a very good insight into the sort of chaps you had. You picked out then the really good and you picked out the doubtful ones.'[4]

While some of these practices have changed, the SAS still place a great deal of emphasis on SERE. On the other hand, the US Navy course lasts just four days and 'realism stops well short of cruel treatment and it is forbidden to subject students to torture or excessive personal indignities.'[5]

At Fort Bragg the Green Berets are given a twenty-six-day course that includes a drop in the middle of North Carolina's Uwharrie National Forest where they must travel forty kilometres over the rugged ground while being hunted by dogs and aggressor teams from the 82nd Airborne.

As a result of experience in Vietnam, the old rule about prisoners only giving name, rank, service number and date of birth has been changed: soldiers are now taught that they are to avoid 'to their utmost ability' answering any questions harmful to US or allied interests. This important shift is intended to allow the prisoner a degree of latitude so that he will be more likely to survive. Several officers and men were killed in Vietcong camps for refusing to give anything but the official minimum of information.

The survival training given to special forces varies widely but all are expected to live off the land and their wits for considerable periods. The best indication of SOF survival capabilities comes from John Wiseman, a twenty-six-year veteran of the SAS who in 1986 produced an extraordinary book called the *SAS Survival Handbook*. In its 287 pages is an impressive catalogue of tips on how to survive in anything from a tropical rain forest to the icy wastes above the Arctic circle.[6]

There are useful tips on diet: 'Ants quickly gather round

the merest scrap of food, where they can be collected, or you can break into a nest. Take care. Most ants have a stinging bite and some large jungle ants can inflict one that will lay the victim out for twenty-four hours. Go for the smaller ones. Some ants . . . have a distended abdomen full of nectar . . . they make much better eating. Some ants have a bite that feels like a nettle sting. Some fire formic acid. Ants *must* therefore be cooked for at least six minutes to destroy the poison. They are then quite safe to eat.'

There is an explanation of soapmaking. Two ingredients – an oil and alkali – are needed to make soap. The oil can be animal fat or vegetable but not mineral. The alkali can be produced by burning wood or seaweed to produce ash. 'Wash ash with water. Strain and boil with the oil. Simmer until excess liquid is evaporated and allow to cool. This soap will clean the skin but is not antiseptic. Adding horseradish root or pine resin to the brew will make it antiseptic.'

There is a tip for navigation: 'Razor Blade Compass. A thin flat razor blade can be used as a compass needle because it is made of two metals bonded together. It can be magnetised simply by stropping with care against the palm of the hand. Suspend it.'

The increased emphasis on SERE, which plays very little part in Soviet training, underlines one of the key roles of allied special forces. While Nato plans do call for strategic reconnaissance and even selective assassination it is assumed that the allied front will be swiftly overrun, so that men must be prepared to work deep behind enemy lines. Some special forces, such as 21 SAS, have a specific stay-behind role, to harry the enemy rear and to interrupt lines of communication and resupply. Others, such as 22 SAS, will be directed at specific strategic targets.

Both Nato and the Warsaw Pact carry out extensive reconnaissance on each other's territory. Under an agreement with the Soviets, Britain, France and the United States maintain military liaison missions in East Germany, and the Soviets maintain their equivalent in the west. They were originally set up so that both sides would have early warning of a surprise attack but have now become a form of institutionalised spying. Mission staff on both sides invariably carry cameras and notebooks to record what they see.

US SOF based at Bad Tolz are sent on detachment to the military mission in Berlin where they are expected to reconnoitre their area of operations. One former member recalls that in the late 1970s the Berlin mission had a file six inches thick that detailed all the routes into the eastern bloc and the hiding places that would allow the SOF to go to ground as soon as war began. 'We would regularly go east through the sewers or underground tunnels to survey the other side and to check the routes were still open,' he said.[7]

Extensive reconnaissance of Soviet bases has been carried out by British and American submarines which routinely operate inside Soviet territorial waters. They gather intelligence not only on the movements of Soviet shipping but also on potential targets for special forces in time of war.

Both Russian and Nato forces play a high-risk game with their opposite numbers in the military missions, involving car ramming and night chases at high speed to prevent too close an inspection of sensitive installations. In May 1985 a member of the US mission in East Germany, Major Arthur Nicholson, was shot by a Soviet guard while trying to photograph the latest T 80 Soviet tank hidden inside a building.

There was a brief flurry of diplomatic protests after the incident, but it is in neither side's interests to make too much of it. The spying produces valuable intelligence for all concerned.

In theory, the US special forces are charged with raising guerrilla forces in enemy territory, but this is hardly practical in Europe, given the planning assumptions for a war that will last a maximum of thirty days and, more probably fourteen days, before tactical and then strategic nuclear weapons are released.

Every year, Nato special forces take part in an exercise code-named Flintlock, which is controlled by Special Operations Command Europe. Using airfields like Machrihanish

in Scotland, US special forces deploy to Europe and are joined
by other Nato members. In 1986 every Nato ally, with the
exception of Greece, took part for the first time; in 1987
Greece was also expected to join. As the command briefing
for an earlier Flintlock exercise points out: 'In order to make
the Flintlock setting as realistic as possible, a notional scenario and master incident list will be used reflecting a large
scale general war as well as appropriate contingency
situations.'[8]

Flintlock practises fighting the unconventional side of
World War III. A series of other exercises has taken place,
designed to increase co-operation between the counter-
terrorist forces in European countries. Counter-terrorist units
such as Delta Force and the SAS have always shared information and technology. But in recent years, as terrorism has
grown and tactics have changed, there has developed a need
for joint training and perhaps joint action.

During the TWA hijack, US forces were based at RAF
Akrotiri in Cyprus; during the hijacking of the *Achille Lauro*,
the US SEALs received help and advice from the British SBS;
and during the hijacking of the Pan Am jet in Karachi in
September 1986, the flying time from Fort Bragg to Pakistan
was such that Delta was not able to arrive in time to influence
the assault that – perhaps in consequence – resulted in the
deaths of twenty-two passengers. All these events illustrate
logistic difficulties in countering terrorist attacks. There are
other difficulties: for example, many terrorist actions take
place in one country, against a building or aircraft used or
owned by another. Often a number of different nationalities
are held hostage by the terrorists. In both cases the issue of
sovereignty arises: who is responsible for trying to free the
hostages or capture the terrorists?

The issue of national pride is a difficult one. In the case of
the Malta hijack it meant that neither the Maltese nor the
Egyptians would allow the participation of Delta Force. Such
chauvinist concerns play into the hands of the terrorists, and
a number of schemes have been proposed in an effort to

overcome this problem, one of which includes establishing a multi-national counter-terrorist force. To date, however, no two countries have agreed on exactly what constitutes terrorism and what should be done about it, so it has been impossible to reach a consensus on forming a joint counter-terrorist force.

Instead, there have been regular exercises involving the joint deployment of European and US groups. In November 1986 GSG9, Delta Force and the SAS joined forces in an exercise to test communications between the different groups. The US has been pushing hardest for international co-oper-ation, since its own Delta Force usually has to travel very long distances to reach the site of a hijacking or kidnap. 'While they are in the air, the situation on the ground may have changed radically and the information they may get from our embassy people or others is often very unreliable,' said one State Department counter-terrorist expert.[9]

For much of 1986, the US looked for a Delta forward base that would be closer to the Middle East. RAF Akrotiri was considered but rejected as the British were unhappy about the high profile Delta was given during the TWA hijack. A plan to set up a tripartite unit in Jordan with the SAS was abandoned after it was recognised both that King Hussein might find the presence politically embarrassing and that the Delta team would themselves be vulnerable to terrorist attack. Finally, it was agreed that a twelve-strong advance unit would move to West Germany. They can now provide early intelli-gence from the site of a terrorist act to the rest of Delta on their way from Fort Bragg.

This is a step in the right direction but does not go nearly far enough. In 1984 a new alliance of terrorists from Belgium, West Germany, France, Portugal and the Netherlands emerged. They shared printing machinery, arms, money and commonly targeted countries and companies that were part of Nato. This was a disturbing development and may mark a turning point – previously co-operation between international terrorists groups has always been very limited.

And, as the terrorists unite, so the allies remain fragmented, unable to agree even upon a common definition of terrorism, let alone upon any coherent policy. Rather than merely having a small unit of Delta based in Europe, Nato members should use that organisation to set up a centre that could co-ordinate the fight against terrorism. With sufficient authority, the centre could act as a clearing house for intelligence and be instrumental in devising a common allied policy, while each individual military response would remain a national one. Without some such common thrust to counter terrorist policy, the bombers and the assassins will continue to hold the initiative in a fight which each year is killing more innocent people.

At the heart of the SOF machine is the equipment used by the special forces. The Soviets have very little that is not standard issue, and they rely on conventional weapons, combined with a higher degree of training than normal, to achieve their aims. In the west, following the United States' lead, there is a greater emphasis on sophisticated equipment. All western special forces retain a research and evaluation unit that specifically tests new ideas. Equally, all of them are able to use special funds to purchase small numbers of specialised equipment outside the normal procurement process.

A complete list of all equipment used by every special force is obviously impossible. Much of it is highly classified and should remain so, but certain items from the SOF capability are unclassified and worth examining in some detail.

SEA

Six nuclear submarines will be dedicated to US SOF by the end of the decade. They include two Ethan Allen class submarines, the *Thomas A. Edison* and the *Thomas Jefferson*, two former Polaris boats, the *Sam Houston* and the *John Marshall*, and two Sturgeon class attack submarines. All will be able to carry a minimum of seventy-five SEALs. A special conversion package attaches a minimum of two pods to the hull of the submarine which house Swimmer Delivery

Vehicles. The SDV was originally conceived as a two-, four-
or six-man underwater chariot that could ferry SOF to a
target area silently and at speed. It can travel at an average
of six knots for six hours.

The US has four types of SDVs currently in service, the
latest of which, the EX-IX, operates on the surface with a
55hp propane fuelled engine and under water with an electric
motor driven by batteries. The two man boat has a computerised Doppler navigation system, and an obstacle avoidance
sonar system provides early warning of hazards ahead.[10]

The new British Type 2400 submarine, which is currently
under construction, will also have a SOF capability. This will
complement the Piranha manufactured by Vickers ship-
building in Barrow, England, specifically for special forces.
The Piranha has a range of 1,500 kilometres submerged and
can carry inflatable craft and frogmen that can be ejected
from the submarine while it remains submerged.

There have been significant developments in underwater
detection systems in recent years (thermal imaging systems
can detect air bubbles, for example) and all underwater
tactics have had to be changed.

All SOF frogmen now use closed circuit breathing apparatus which recycles the air and scrubs it of the carbon
monoxide along the way. The Europeans use a system
developed by the West German Draeger company and the
US uses an Emerson system. Also, instead of men going
directly into a harbour to plant limpet mines or otherwise
destroy shipping, there has been a substantial investment to
improve the ability to attack from long range.

In 1985, the US Navy began a $12.4 million programme
to convert Mark 37 torpedoes for attachment to the EX-IX
two-man SDV. This will give the SEALs the ability to fire at
targets from long distances.

The traditional method of covert sea approach is by Gemini
or Zodiac rubber dinghies with specially silenced outboard
motors. However, there have been new refinements by a
number of companies. For example, the Subskimmer is an

ordinary inflatable with a surface speed of twenty-five knots from a conventional outboard with an operating range of a hundred miles. It can carry two men and a full range of stores including mines and personal weapons. On arriving at the operational area, the engine is stopped, buoyancy tubes are inflated, and the vessel becomes neutrally buoyant. Propelled underwater by electric motors that can be swivelled to control depth and direction, the boat can travel at 2.5 knots for a maximum of five hours.

All underwater SOF are developing remote-controlled vehicles of considerable sophistication. As small as two foot square, these vehicles have a range of around one mile and can remotely attach limpet mines, gather intelligence on the whereabouts and type of enemy underwater defences and even engage in electronic warfare. They are also used to search the bottom of friendly ships in harbour, something that is very unpopular with frogmen. The remote vehicle has powerful disorientating lights and is charged with electricity, so that any attempt to interfere with it results in a stunning shock. This particular weapon is still in its infancy, and major developments will be made over the next few years.

The US Navy have developed the Seafox attack craft specifically for SOF. It is 36 feet long, can carry 10 SEALs at more than 30 knots for 200 nautical miles. The Seafox has a silenced engine and a wide range of electronic countermeasure equipment designed to bypass coastal radars and other defences. Last year, the US Navy also tested the first of eighteen SOF 110 ton hovercraft, although these are unlikely to be used by SEALs as they are too large and too noisy for covert operations.

To communicate with each other or with a host submarine, SOF use a device known as a UTEL that consists of a microphone embedded in the swimmer's face mask and a tiny battery-powered transducer with a range of 10,000 yards that sends a signal through the water. It can also pick up messages or a homing signal from the mother ship to guide the swimmer back to base.

Much of the peacetime work of SOF involves carrying out detailed surveys of likely landing areas in potentially hostile territory. To do this work, the divers carry a small device that samples the sand or rock of the ocean floor and the beach area for later analysis to find out what landing weights can be tolerated. It also records the contours of the bottom so that an accurate map can be produced. A hand-held sonar with both an active and passive mode can chart even shapes that are secure behind impassable defences.

AIR

The most important aircraft in the SOF inventory is the MC-130 Combat Talon which first came into service in the 1960s. The aircraft has a range of 2,800 nautical miles and an average speed of 260 knots. The basic mission of the aircraft is to fly deep behind enemy lines and drop or collect men or equipment. A number of special features have been added to the aircraft.

The Navigation systems include terrain-following radar, precision ground mapping radar, an inertial navigation system, and a retractable forward looking infra-red system. This equipment allows the aircraft to fly in all weathers day or night at heights as low as fifty feet.

The SOF use the Fulton Surface to Air Recovery System. Over sea or land, the aircraft drops a special kit consisting of a helium balloon with a locator beacon, two harnesses and a flexible rope that enables the aircraft to pick up either two men or a 500lb. package without landing. On the first pass, the men on the ground pick up the kit, raise the balloon, and attach the harness. Thirty minutes later the aircraft returns and, guided by the beacon, flies towards the rope supported by the balloon. A yoke on the front of the aircraft engages the rope and lifts the men off the ground. A winch then hauls the men on board via the rear ramp. This is a painful and hazardous method of extraction, since the jerk on the rope when the aircraft connects with it often breaks limbs.

The USAF plans to purchase twenty-one improved MC-

130H Combat Talon IIs which are currently being developed, at a cost of $60 million each. They should have begun entering service five years ago but the USAF has continually delayed the programme. It will have an improved STAR system, currently code-named Project 46, which will be capable of extracting six people at a time.

The 1st Special Operations Wing communications specialists have their own workshops, known as the Skunk Works, for communications and electronic counter measures. All Combat Talons carry an ALQ-8 Electronic Counter-Measures pod under the port wing which can both jam enemy radar and send out a wide range of signals that either convince the enemy that there is a friendly aircraft in the area or that there is no aircraft at all.

In theory the C-130 is the SOF air arm for psychological operations, particularly using the National Guard's Coronet Solo EC-130. However, these craft have a very limited capability. Equipped for television broadcast, they are set for television bands in North America and Canada and do not work at all in Europe, the Middle East or Asia where a different television system is used.[11]

In the AC-130H conversion, the Hercules is a formidable weapons system with an armoury of 20mm, 40mm and 105mm guns to provide fire support. The aircraft can simultaneously track twenty ground targets using on-board computers.

The Defense Advanced Research Projects Agency (DARPA) has commissioned studies into a new SOF aircraft that will be capable of carrying fourteen troops at a cruise speed of 350 knots for 1,200 nautical miles. The aircraft will be required to land on a 1,000 foot runway and be capable of landing on unprepared ground with 18-inch high rocks and plants, ploughed furrows, three feet high grass and snow and ice 18 inches deep. It will have a stall speed of 78 knots compared with 112 knots on the C-130. A 60 per cent scale model began tests in 1986.[12]

The Sikorsky HH-53 Pave Low helicopter is a twin-engined

heavy-lift aircraft designed specifically for night insertion of SOF. Flying at an average speed of 100 knots, the helicopter has a range of 200–300 nautical miles, but with an airborne refuelling capability this can be increased indefinitely, depending only on the endurance of the crew. Nine are currently in service and although they have effective electronics and guidance systems, they are unreliable and very expensive to maintain.

This helicopter uses a special system to extract SOF where landing is impossible. Up to three people can be withdrawn simultaneously with the STABO system, which consists of a rope attached to a harness. For extraction in jungle, a device called the Forest Penetrator, a weighted torpedo-shaped hook with three folding seats, is used.[13]

A new aircraft to replace both the MC-130 and the HH-53 is currently being tested. Originally known as the Joint Service Advanced Vertical Lift Aircraft or JVX, the aircraft has been renamed the V-22 Osprey, and between $25 and $40 billion have been committed to the project. The aircraft uses a revolutionary tilt rotor system: engines on the ends of the wings rotate to convert it into a helicopter with a vertical take off and landing capability. The aircraft should be able to hover like a helicopter and fly like a conventional aircraft.

The aircraft, being developed by Bell Helicopters and Boeing-Vertol, will be supplied to the Marines, the Army, the Navy and the Air Force. The first SOF Osprey is scheduled to be delivered in 1994.

In the short term, the Air Force is funding improvements on the HH-60A Blackhawk, which is already in service, to give the aircraft an improved range and night flying capability, and is purchasing twenty-four HH-60D Nighthawks. The first of the new helicopters will be in service in 1988 and will be used primarily for extraction of SOF. However, although the Nighthawk was originally conceived as an all-weather helicopter with a day and night capability, funding cuts have reduced its capability so that it can now perform only during good weather and preferably in daylight.

Many of the helicopter pilots are trained to use night vision devices such as the Cyclops that give near perfect sight in darkness using thermal imaging techniques. The older type of goggles gave telescopic vision and restricted the view. Newer systems project a holographic image on the front of a visor about two inches from the pilot's eyes. This gives a much wider field of view and better definition. These systems are also used by Army SOF for night fighting.

Although the USAF is committed, like the other services, to a five-year Master Plan to improve SOF capability, the effort remains fragmented and there are serious doubts that the USAF will be able to fulfil their promises. Programmes are split between the Air Force System Command (AFSC), and the Air Force Logistics Command (AFLC), and then are split up again inside those organisations. In July 1985, the Air Force Scientific Advisory Board, in its report entitled 'Enhancement of Special Forces' noted:

'Currently, four aircraft upgrades (Combat Talon 1, Combat Talon II, AC-130, and H-53) are being done *independently* by three different USAF organisations. Unless appropriate, *immediate* action is taken to assure commonality of equipment on these aircraft, any hope of realizing the significant benefits of commonality *will be lost*.' (Original emphasis.)[14]

Since that report was published, there has been no evidence of Air Force action to correct the problems. Instead, historic rivalries continue to waste taxpayers' money and undermine SOF capability.

GROUND
Special forces will very probably take the first step up the nuclear ladder, as many of them are trained to carry and explode portable nuclear bombs. Known as the Special Atomic Demolition Munition (SADM), the bomb is only 35in. wide, 26in. long and 26in. high with a 56lb warhead

with an explosive power of between .01–1 kiloton. Some 300 of these weapons are known to be deployed although the actual numbers are probably far greater.

Training in their use is stressed at Fort Bragg. 'SADM is continuously emphasised. The SADM capability is considered to be an important mission of special forces, and is constantly exercised in quarterly nuclear surety inspections and field exercises. The device can be deployed either by static line, military free fall or by scuba. Scuba mission training is ongoing within each of the special forces groups.'[15] In addition to US special forces, teams from Britain, Belgium, Greece, Italy, the Netherlands, Turkey and West Germany have been trained in the use of SADM.

Army manuals say that the specific targets of 'backpack nukes' are: blocking avenues of approach by cratering defiles and creating rubble; severing routes of communication by destroying tunnels, bridges, canal locks, or cratering roads; creating areas of tree blowdown or forest fires; cratering areas subject to hostile airmobile landings; and creating water barriers by destroying dams and reservoirs.[16]

One of the storage sites for the SADM as well as for nuclear depth charges is a remote RAF base on the Mull of Kintyre in west Scotland. RAF Machrihanish is home to Navy Special Warfare Unit 2, a seventeen-strong team on permanent attachment to the base. At any one time there are an additional twenty SEALs on six-month detachment from the US. The base also houses Mobile Mine Assembly Group 2 and a detachment from the US Naval Aviation weapons facility detachment. Both these units are responsible for maintaining and preparing nuclear depth charges and underwater mines.

In 1981 construction began on an improved runway and additional fuel bunkers, and support facilities were built at a cost of $15m. The airfield now plays a key role as a staging post for reinforcements heading for the European mainland and for special forces planning to deploy on the Soviet mainland.

On a more conventional level, Army SOF tend to use a wide range of weapons that are standard issue to other branches of the forces such as the Uzi sub-machine-gun, the Carl Gustav M-45B sub-machine-gun, the Heckler and Koch MP-5 and the French Mat-49 sub-machine-gun. Snipers use the M-21 weapons system, which is made up of the M-14 National Match Rifle with a variable power telescopic sight.

Both sniper and ordinary weapons are adapted to take the latest thermal imaging sights, which give an effective night/day capability. Some laser sights have been issued which are considered extremely effective. If the user sights the laser dot on the target and squeezes the trigger he is assured of almost 100 per cent success.

If US SOF took all the standard issue equipment with them, each man would be required to carry a pack weighing at least 100lb. But the procurement process has proved unable to cope with the number of items required by SOF. It is also common to find individual soldiers kitted out with a wide range of non-standard equipment purchased from local stores.

In theory, it is the Army that is responsible for psychological operations, via the 4th Psyops Group at Fort Bragg. This should be an essential part of low intensity conflict, particularly in the counter-insurgency role. However, like many other areas of SOF, it has suffered at the expense of more exciting budget demands. The printing presses owned by the 4th are non-portable and produce a very low quality product. The use and specification of the M129EL leaflet bomb that was used extensively in Vietnam is no longer taught to fighter pilots, and the MS-285 audio-visual unit housed in a van is still equipped with 16mm and 35mm slide projectors dating from the Vietnam War.[17]

Communications for ground SOF has also lagged behind the rapid advances that have recently been made elsewhere in micro circuitry. The new AN/PRC-70 radio was issued in the early 1980s as the standard communications equipment for Army SOF. It weighs 45lb and compares unfavourably with the new but not generally available PRC-319, which weighs just 4.8lb and so is truly portable.

In 1978, the Army ordered a new SOF base radio, the AN/TSC-99, which was supposed to have a mean time between failures of 1,200 hours. When it was delivered in 1985, it was found to fail every 5.6 hours and was so bulky that it could only be moved over European roads with special permits. The SOF units refused to take delivery and although some are now in service, the radio remains far too big and still has a failure time double the original requirement.[18]

During the Desert One rescue mission and the Grenada invasion, serious problems were encountered because the different groups involved could not talk to each other. Messages had to be relayed to headquarters and then passed on to the other unit, which was often only a very short distance away. Messages were lost or misinterpreted with alarming frequency. Today, the SEALs and Delta Force units still do not have compatible communications equipment and can only talk to each other via a headquarters unit that has access to both systems. And the SEALs still do not have radios that are compatible with the standard Navy issue.

Delta are actually issued with two radios for each A-Team to communicate with headquarters. However, not only are these radios old-fashioned, unreliable and heavy but no A-Team member is qualified to repair them in the field when they break down, which they do frequently. The batteries that run these radios are required to be kept at temperatures above 40° Fahrenheit, which obviously limits Delta's ability to operate in cold weather.

The reserve SOF are in even worse shape. They are issued with the AN/GRA-71 radio which is so old that production has been stopped and no spare parts at all are available. It is not compatible with current equipment issued to the regular forces or other SOF, so that if the reserves were ever actually deployed the only people they could talk to would be each other.

Of all groups, SOF have the greatest need for a compact

reliable communications system that can operate despite enemy jamming and in burst transmission to prevent early detection. Now, in 1987, Army SOF is at last testing both the British PRC-319 and a similar American system the MRR-50, and a decision on a more modern radio is promised within the next twelve months.

SOF units are supposed to be at a level of readiness both in training and equipment where they can swiftly go to war. The readiness status of a unit is measure in C-ratings and divided into five levels:

C-1 Combat-Ready, no deficiencies
C-2 Combat-Ready, minor deficiencies
C-3 Combat-Ready, major deficiencies
C-4 Not Combat-Ready
C-5 Not Combat-Ready, Training Status

Despite the massive investment that has been made in SOF since the Reagan administration came into office, the majority of SOF units in the Army, Navy and Air Force remain below C-1 and many hover between C-2 and C-3. At C-3 they are really not fit to go to war, particularly for the kind of incisive action required by SOF. The Air Force actually claim that the majority of their SOF personnel are at C-1 but in fact, given the unreliability of the aircraft they fly, this claim is not taken seriously. The Navy say their SEAL teams are not properly qualified because they have been unable to buy the equipment necessary to fill in gaps. Army figures have improved from an almost universal C-3 to include some C-2, but they have moved the goalposts by altering the way they measure readiness.

While readiness is not as good as it should be, the training too remains seriously flawed. There are very few exercises that jointly use conventional and special operations forces. Flintlock is a purely SOF exercise and others such as the annual European Reforger exercise only conventional forces.

When there is a joint exercise, the full range of SOF capability is not tested. For example, during exercise Universal Trek in the Caribbean in 1985, Air Force AC-130 gunships were used to support conventional forces during daylight operations. They are in fact dedicated SOF machines and the pilots are trained to operate mostly at night.

Each theatre command is supposed to produce Target Folders for all its units. Because so few senior officers understand SOF capabilities, the missions are written in the broadest terms, and simply outline general performance (reconnaissance, infiltration, sabotage, etc.). As a result, many Target Folders are so vague as to be useless, while others set out targets that are wholly inappropriate. Moreover, these problems vary between theatres as each CINC interprets the role of SOF differently. The result is confusion, with SOF assets having little idea of what exactly they are supposed to do when the shooting starts.

Until there is some central organisation responsible for the equipment and training of US special forces, these failings will continue. In Grenada they resulted in unnecessary loss of life, and in the future there seems no doubt that the capability of the United States will continue to be undermined.

On past performance, there is little prospect of the military commanders devoting the resources required to bring the training and equipment of special forces up to the required standard. It is hoped that Congress will persevere in its efforts, and will do the job for them.

PART 10: SURROGATE WARFARE

23

A Fist Into Water

During World War II, the actions of anti-Nazi partisans had a critical effect on the course of the conflict. All were supported and supplied with cash and arms by the allies. Immediately after the war, covert support for dissident groups operating in enemy territory continued, with British and American support for rebels operating in the communist bloc. Although these groups had little success, their existence marked the beginning of a post-war campaign of surrogate warfare, whereby the superpowers can sponsor other groups to fight wars on their behalf.

Such warfare allows a country 'plausible deniability' while in fact funding and arming a guerrilla force bent on destabilising another country. This is a useful and increasingly popular foreign policy tool in both west and east, and has brought with it new security needs. So, if Russia seems to be destabilising an area, the United States will generally step in with arms and cash either to prop up the existing government or to support a group that will undermine any Soviet-backed alternative.

This covert warfare takes three forms: the sending of Mobile Training Teams (MTT) of special forces to a country to provide training in counter-insurgency techniques; the sponsorship of other countries or groups to fight on behalf of a major power; or the sponsorship of private individuals to supply training either to the current government or to a group determined on its overthrow.

Guerrilla warfare and terrorism have grown. Although terrorism as a political force has been largely unsuccessful in achieving its stated aims, it has had a profound effect on allied foreign and domestic policy. Every western country in the past twenty years has passed legislation to restrict the activities of terrorists and every one of those Acts has, in some way, infringed on the freedom of the individual. But western societies have accepted that is a small price to pay to control the violence.

Guerrilla warfare, on the other hand, has been politically immensely successful. Since 1945 the Belgian, French and British empires have disintegrated, and indeed the majority of countries that shrugged off the colonial yoke did so by using violence. From Kenya to Angola to Malaya and Zaire, guerrilla movements sprang up to fight the colonialists. In some cases the insurgents were defeated, but even then the colonial power accepted that independence was inevitable and swiftly handed over power. There seems little doubt that the break-up of the colonial empires would not have been so fast without a little help from the guerrilla movements.

Many of these movements were helped by the Soviet Union and her allies. The list of Soviet-aided colonial revolutions is long. In fact, with the possible exception of India, it is difficult to find a single colony that the Soviets did not attempt to influence overtly or covertly with the aim of gaining a new ally. Of course, this was sensible geo-politics and was mirrored by counter-efforts made by the colonial powers and the United States. Throughout, the policy of the Soviet Union was perfectly consistent and demonstrated a determination to win new allies in every possibly part of the world.

During this restless period, United States military policy went through some profound changes. In the immediate aftermath of World War II, the CIA and other intelligence organisations embarked on a campaign of destabilisation that was both inconsistent and often inept. There were some successes (the coup in Iran for example) but generally the arguments seemed to be won by the Soviets.

America was satisfied that nuclear superiority would prevent a world war and until the arrival of John Kennedy in 1961 there had been little thought given to fighting a conventional war with the Soviets. A strategy of flexible response was devised that would allow for a gradual escalation up the nuclear ladder after conventional forces had been exhausted. But at the same time those same conventional forces should be capable of fighting what became known as the 'Two-and-a-Half War' concept. This called for US forces to be ready to deal simultaneously with a war on the Central Front with the Warsaw Pact, a Chinese attack in Asia and another, smaller, conflict elsewhere in the world.

Vietnam provided just that 'Half' war that the planners had considered. But it absorbed far more of America's military capability than had been expected, and – partly in response to military considerations and partly to satisfy political pressure – Richard Nixon devised a new strategy. Known as the Nixon Doctrine, this suggested that in future countries under threat from outside invasion or internal insurgency should be provided with economic and military assistance only. American forces would not be committed as they had been in Vietnam. There was now no need for the 'Two-and-a-Half War' plan, which was therefore reduced to the 'One-and-a-Half War' plan. This allowed for a major communist attack in either Europe or Asia and a lesser conflict elsewhere.

Following the Soviet invasion of Afghanistan in 1979, Jimmy Carter announced that any further aggression in South West Asia 'will be repelled by any means necessary, including military force.' This was a commitment that would have been very difficult for the US to keep, given that any major conflict in the Gulf, for example, must seriously weaken US forces in Europe.

When the Reagan administration took office in 1981, they arrived with the firm conviction that war was unlikely to be the tidy package designed by the strategists; that Soviet ambitions were such that if war broke out in Europe it was unlikely to be confined to that theatre but would immediately spread worldwide. To meet that threat, there would be no 'One-and-a-Half War' or 'Two War' strategy but rather a global concept that required the US to project its power to several different key points in the world simultaneously.

This belief in a limited confrontation between the superpowers in one part of the world automatically leading to global war has severely constrained US and Soviet foreign policy. Both sides will do everything possible to avoid creating an environment where nuclear war is likely.

Throughout these changes in the assessment of the threat to the United States, there was however a continuous common strand to all the policies: containing the expansion of world communism. Instead of United States forces playing a direct role in this work, it has been carried out primarily by the CIA and, more recently, be special operations forces.

When the CIA was first formed immediately after World War II, it was charged with seven objectives including political, psychological, economic and guerrilla warfare, sabotage, escape and evasion and 'other covert operations'. That broad brief enabled the CIA to engage in just about any kind of dirty dealing that took its fancy.

But, as a result of a series of fiascos such as the Bay of Pigs humiliation, Congress introduced restrictive legislation to curb the Agency's paramilitary excesses. At the same time, sophisticated technology emerged that allowed many of the espionage activities normally undertaken by the CIA man on the ground to be taken over by computers and satellites. The CIA purges carried out during the Carter administration cleared the last of the undercover warriors from the Agency's ranks.

In the meantime, the whole nature of covert warfare had changed. Congressional oversight has meant that long-term destabilisation campaigns are very restricted, Castro no longer receives poisoned cigars and, while the CIA still tries to retain its finger in the covert pie, any involvement it has today is more a reflection of historical accident than current ability.

It is, in fact, the military who are the key to today's covert operations. The British were the first to have to deal with the realities of modern warfare. The collapse of the British Empire severely reduced the United Kingdom's influence in world affairs. The ability to change governments through the sending of a single gunboat as an indication of London's displeasure has long gone. Instead a more subtle method of gathering influence has emerged, using the highly-trained special forces of the SAS and SBS.

Soon after the re-emergence of the SAS in the post-war period it was appreciated both by the Ministry of Defence and the Foreign Office that the special forces represented more than a simple force to counter insurgencies by direct action. They could also be used to train special forces in friendly nations to counter their own insurgencies, and to develop units that could guard such nations' leaders against assassination.

Among the emerging nations in the Middle East, Africa and the Far East this was an attractive proposition. The offer was generally subsidised and passed off as foreign aid, and the SAS were discreet and capable. They also were apolitical and trained forces strictly to sustain the existing government.

For the sponsoring government the special forces were a useful force multiplier; there was a considerable effect for a relatively small investment. Countries that had received training from the UK special forces remained allies, unless, of course, the Soviets proved more effective at stirring up revolution. Also, with perhaps the single exception of the South Yemeni government's direct participation in the war in Oman, there was no direct involvement of the sponsoring country's own forces in any conflict.

In the period 1977–80, more than thirty-two different countries had counter-terrorist units set up by the SAS, and other units were set up and trained by the SBS and other British army units. This training is considered a key role for British special forces and is one that continues today.

For the United States, the lessons are obvious. Not only are special forces an obvious tool of foreign policy but it has been asserted repeatedly by senior US officials that spetsnaz units have been sent to countries like Angola, Mozambique, Ethiopia and Nicaragua, either to train guerrilla forces or to support existing left-wing governments. Although British intelligence sources deny that spetsnaz units have been deployed outside of the Warsaw Pact – 'I see absolutely no evidence at all that spetsnaz have been deployed in peacetime. I see them as being a military arm in a much more conventional way,' says one senior source[1] – it would be surprising if the Soviets did not use spetsnaz in an active role overseas.

In fact, however, reports of spetsnaz being used as, for example, a praetorian guard for President Menghistou in Ethiopia remain unconfirmed, and the deployment of Soviet special forces in this way is an article of faith with the US government rather than a judgement supported by evidence.

In part, this article of faith has been used to justify the revitalisation of SOF in the US, and an increase in the presence of US Military Training Teams (MTT) working abroad.

In 1980, the final year of the Carter administration, forty-six MTTs involving 176 men spent 1,161 man weeks in foreign countries; in 1981, the first year of the Reagan administration, eighty-seven teams with 258 men worked 2,550 man weeks abroad; in 1983, a total of 132 MTTs with 562 men spent 5,552 man weeks abroad; and in 1984 that total had risen to 5,787. In the period 1983 to 1984 the numbers of countries visited by MTTs rose from 59 to 65. The vast majority of these teams came from SOF.[2]

In recent years, the US has sent MTTs to Liberia, Colombia, the Lebanon, Somalia, Saudi Arabia, Tunisia, Morocco, the Philippines and Thailand. In mid–1986, there were eighteen MTTs deployed in Chad, Egypt, Sudan, Zimbabwe, Saudi Arabia, the Philippines, Colombia, Costa Rica, El Salvador, Grenada and Honduras.[3]

Each team typically consists of six to eight Green Berets that supply training in five key areas: weapons, demolition, intelligence, communications and medicine. Congress has limited the time each MTT can spend in a country to six months, and notice of the intention to send an MTT abroad must be supplied to the Foreign Affairs Committee of the House and Senate when the budget for the Security Assistance programme is submitted each year. Under the War Powers Resolution, no MTT can be deployed to an area where US personnel are likely to be involved in combat without prior notification to Congress for authority.

The MTTs are the officially authorised training arm of the US government. With less publicity, for the past ten years the United States have been sending teams of counter-terrorist experts, mainly SEALs and Delta Force but including some CIA men, to train friendly governments in measures against hijacks, kidnapping and other terrorist attacks. These teams are sent with the full knowledge of Congress, but extraordinary steps are taken to ensure that news of their deployment is not revealed.

For example, in October 1982 a number of Green Berets were interviewed at the Bordeaux Motor Inn in Fayetteville, near Fort Bragg, for a mission codenamed Operation Quail Shooter. Six men were chosen to go to Honduras to train a forty-man anti-terrorist squad called the Urban Operations Command.[4]

The men were required to shed all identification, including dog tags, grow their hair, and travel to Honduras in civilian clothes using false passports identifying them as civil engineers.

During 1983, two three-man teams rotated through the Honduran army's Special Forces Command at La Venta, north of the country's capital, Tegucigalpa. The Honduran unit was trained in a wide range of counter-terrorist techniques, including house clearing, aircraft assaults and intelligence gathering using sophisticated surveillance devices.

There is considerable sensitivity in the United States over

the role of any US troops in training foreign forces abroad. The US involvement in Vietnam began with the sending of advisers, first to help the French and then to train a new army in South Vietnam. The result of that involvement is well known, and in every commitment that has been openly discussed since then the spectre of Vietnam has been raised. Congressional legislation requires that no US soldier be directly involved in combat without special authority, and all MTT or counter-terrorist training missions are carefully scrutinised to make sure that no American lives are at risk. This caution has been particularly evident in the last few years in Central America.

While guerrilla groups such as UNITA in Angola and the mujahedeen in Afghanistan have benefited from the Reagan administration's determination to fight communism militarily, and to support movements fighting to establish western-style democracy, it has been the conflict in Central America that has provided the main focus of Reagan's interventionist foreign policy.

When Reagan became President in 1981, he inherited a political and military situation in Central America increasingly unsympathetic towards capitalism. The unpopular Nicaraguan dictatorship of President Somoza had been overthrown by a popular revolution in July 1979, the same year that a group of military reformists took power in neighbouring El Salvador.

There is general agreement that Central America is an area of strategic importance to the United States. According to the US State Department, 65 per cent of all ships going through the Panama Canal carry goods to and from the United States; 55 per cent of all crude oil imports to the US pass through the Caribbean between Central America and Cuba; 45 per cent of all US imports and exports transit through the Gulf of Mexico; and 60 per cent of Nato resupplies in time of tension or war will leave from the same place. For American security, Soviet control of Cuba is worrying enough, and a left-wing Central America could place much of America's economic and military power in a communist pincer movement.[5]

Also, the US has always considered itself a country isolated from the pressures that exist in other countries. The mainland US has never been attacked in a world war, and terrorism has left Americans alone. But Central America is Washington's back yard, and communist subversion would only have to spread up through Mexico to reach the porous and vulnerable US southern border. It is a frightening prospect to those who believe that the communists, led by the Soviet Union, are bent on world domination. There are many in the Reagan administration for whom that belief forms the basis of their political philosophy, among them the President himself.

In 1979, while President Carter was in office, perceptions of the Central American situation were in marked contrast to what would follow under Reagan. The new right-wing government in El Salvador was under threat from around 10,000 communist guerrillas who were mostly members of the Farabundo Marti National Liberation Front (FMLN). The guerrillas controlled up to 25 per cent of the country and the government armed forces appeared incapable of combating the insurgency effectively.

The Carter government responded with loans, grants and military aid to the Salvadoran government which totalled a mere $6 million. This had little influence on the guerrilla war, which continued to be characterised by extreme brutality on both sides. The Salvadoran government showed no sign of understanding guerrilla warfare and had no troops properly trained in counter-insurgency tactics. Instead, the government sponsored a number of right-wing death squads that embarked on a campaign of terrorism and assassination against anyone considered to have liberal sympathies. This predictably drove recruits to the FMLN and served to broaden their base of popular support.

Assessments by the CIA and other intelligence agencies suggested that the FMLN were receiving much of their material from the neighbouring new Nicaraguan government.

There has never been any firm evidence setting out the exact level of this support, but there can be no doubt that the Nicaraguan government was supplying a safe haven for the guerrillas, providing some small arms and allowing them the use of territory for training.

None of this was exactly surprising, given that the Nicaraguan revolution had succeeded against a right-wing dictatorship, exactly the kind of government the FMLN now hoped to overthrow.

The US administration originally gave the new Nicaraguan regime a cautious welcome. The overthrow of the Somoza regime had been achieved by a genuinely popular revolution, which had allied businessmen and landowners with youthful revolutionaries. The main military forces had been supplied by the Sandinista National Liberation Front (FSLN), which had about 5,000 men under arms. Leaders of the FSLN had pledged themselves before the Organisation of American States (OAS) to the principles of political pluralism, a mixed economy, and a non-aligned foreign policy. These were laudable aims, with which the United States could hardly take issue. Thus in the first eighteen months of the new government, the US supplied $118 million in economic aid and humanitarian assistance.

But during his last week in office, President Carter suspended a further $14 million in economic aid earmarked for the Nicaraguan government. He had concluded that this was the only way to impress the Sandinistas that the US would not tolerate the export of revolution in Central America. This decision marked a turning point in America's relations with the region. Once economic aid was actually cut off to Nicaragua, the threat of withdrawing that aid, which had always been a useful pressure point, was removed. Only military threats and diplomatic histrionics were left.

The election of Ronald Reagan accelerated an already deteriorating situation. The new administration took office with the firm conviction that communism was on the march, with Cuba acting as point man in the Caribbean and Central

America. Aside from increasing the propaganda offensive against Fidel Castro, there was little the US could do about Cuba. But there were a number of clear measures that could be taken in the hope of countering the guerrilla threat in El Salvador and the influence of the Sandinistas in Nicaragua.

Aid authorised by Congress to El Salvador's dictator rose rapidly from $6 million in 1980 to $35 million in 1981 and $76.7 million the following year. By 1986, the US was giving $484.6 million, including $132.6 million in military aid, and a total of more than $2.5 billion in US aid had poured in to the right-wing government. In addition, the President authorised the deployment of MTTs from the Green Berets to reorganise and train the El Salvador armed forces in fighting a counter-insurgency war. The number of Green Berets was limited to fifty-five by verbal agreement with Congress, but these forces were augmented by up to 150 CIA agents already operating in the country.

In the first stages of their deployment, the MTTs actually attempted to train the 25,000-strong Salvadoran army to fight a conventional war. Using the classic American prescription for all combat, it was decided to meet force with greater force, firepower with massive retaliatory artillery barrages and air bombings. The army was rapidly increased in strength to 43,000, but remained generally unwilling to leave the security of their barracks unless on massive combined arms sweeps. These sweeps through areas thought to be occupied by guerrillas were very similar to many conducted by the US in Vietnam: they used enormous amounts of firepower, involved all the elements of the armed forces, and achieved absolutely nothing except the alienation of the local population whose crops and villages were often destroyed by inaccurate air and ground bombardments. The guerrillas' intelligence was good enough to warn them of these attacks well in advance, and they were invariably clear of the area long before the government troops arrived.

As one Green Beret officer involved in the training in El Salvador puts it: 'We initially adopted a traditional military approach of meeting force with greater force. This was like driving your fist into a bucket of water. You put your fist in, twirl it around and when you'd withdrawn it there was no evidence that you had ever been there. We then changed our policy to develop a more political campaign where influencing the people was seen as the key.'6

This change in tactics in 1984 coincided with presidential elections in El Salvador. The United States had made the establishment of broadly democratic governments in Central America a key part of its policy in the region, and the election of José Napoleon Duarte, in a general election that was remarkably free from electoral malpractice, signified El Salvador's first real attempt at democratic government for forty-five years. Duarte was pledged to introduce economic reforms to reduce the gap between rich and poor, to establish an apolitical military, and to end the guerrilla war. His subsequent failure to achieve the first two of these policy goals has ensured his failure in the third aim.

Under the guidance of the Green Berets, however, the El Salvador armed forces have changed their tactics and training so that they now fight a mobile counter-insurgency war. The new training combines the effective use of helicopters (the government now has sixty US-supplied transport and attack helicopters) to back up commandos launching small-scale raids against known guerrilla forces. The Salvadoran troops are also supplied with timely intelligence by US surveillance aircraft based in Honduras that can intercept and pinpoint guerrilla radio transmissions.

To meet the new threat, the guerrillas too have changed their tactics. Instead of fighting a largely rural war, they have spread their forces over a wider area and taken the battle to the towns and villages.

Both civilian and military officials in the US have repeatedly told this author that the Green Berets 'saved El Salvador for democracy'. This is an over-optimistic assessment and demonstrates a lack of understanding of the nature of guerrilla warfare. It is certainly true that the small contingent of Green

Berets were instrumental in implementing a change in government tactics against the guerrillas. This has resulted in a halving of the number of guerrillas, and has given them some resupply and recruitment problems. This demonstration of military will has also allowed two free elections, for the presidency in 1984 and municipal elections in 1985, both relatively free of intimidation, which confirmed Duarte as President and the Christian Democrats as the party of popular choice. This was a considerable achievement but will be wasted unless more progress is made on the promises Duarte has given to his people.

Ever fearful of a right-wing coup, Duarte has been unable to bring in the economic reforms that are essential if the political support received by the guerrillas is to be undermined. It is a formidable task. Inflation is running at 50 per cent and unemployment at 55 per cent, with the land reforms necessary for even a partial redistribution of the wealth apparently as elusive as ever. Because Duarte has failed to reform, he has been unable to gather the support he needs to set up working militias in the countryside and the small towns to relieve his armed forces of some of their security tasks. As always in any conflict of this type, the ordinary people are sitting on the fence, waiting to see which side is likely to win, and there will be no significant move to the Duarte camp until he backs up his military resolve with a demonstration of political will. It may be a long wait: seemingly the military will never allow the kind of changes that are necessary and neither will the powerful business community, who see their own entrenched and privileged position under threat.

For their part, the guerrillas can afford to wait. They currently have around 5,000 experienced men and women under arms and they can continue the struggle indefinitely. The only development that could significantly change their fortunes would be a new government in Nicaragua. But there too US policy has been poorly executed and the Sandinistas seem as powerful today as they were when elected in 1979, despite six years of economic and military warfare orchestrated by the United States.

After the overthrow of the Somoza regime in 1979, a number of small groups left the country to settle in Costa Rica and Honduras to wage war against the Sandinistas. The groups were composed primarily of former members of Somoza's National Guard, their ranks swelled later by disaffected followers of the Sandinista revolution. Two umbrella organisations, the Democratic National Front (FDN) based in Honduras and the Revolutionary Democratic Alliance (ARDE) in Costa Rica, (known jointly as Contras), controlled most of the rebel activity.

Until 1981, the operations of these groups were more criminal than political. They organised small raiding parties into Nicaragua, burned villages, stole cattle and looted, returning afterwards to their sanctuaries over the border. Without outside support, they would have remained little more than an irritant to the fledgling Sandinista government. But it already had serious problems coping with a failing economy and attempting to deliver the land reforms promised in the first flush of revolutionary enthusiasm, redistribution of wealth, a free press, and elections, and President Reagan appears to have been convinced that an active covert operation against it could force it both to stop the export of revolution to neighbouring El Salvador and to take the steps he thought necessary towards establishing a democratic government.

Officially, the US always insists that it has never been America's intention to overthrow the Nicaraguan government, merely to change its direction and policies. If this intention is taken at face value, the actions of the US government are incomprehensible, since they are clearly aimed at so destabilising the Nicaraguan government that it will be unable to function.

The first turn of the screw came in March 1981, when President Reagan approved a Presidential Finding which made clear that a covert operation was necessary to stop the flow of arms to the guerrillas operating in El Salvador. In November 1981, the CIA came back to the President with a formal plan of action. They proposed a three-tier approach: the formation in Honduras of a 500-man guerrilla force of Cubans and Nicaraguans not associated with the Somoza regime, at a minimum cost of $19.95 million; funding for a fighting group to be formed with the aid of Argentina and Honduras, composed mainly of former Somoza National Guardsmen; and an increase in funding for dissident groups inside Nicaragua. On 23 November the President signed National Security Decision Directive 17 which authorised the CIA to proceed with its plans.

From the few hundred poorly armed and trained guerrilla bands marauding and looting in the border area at the beginning of 1981, the Contras rapidly grew in numbers, from 5,000 in 1983 to around 15,000 in 1986. They were trained by CIA agents, Green Berets, or Cuban exiles who had received paramilitary training in the United States. If the Nicaraguan government had remained passive in the face of this threat, it is possible that the Contras could have formed a credible army that had some chance of military success. But the Nicaraguans embarked on a massive rearmament programme, and it now seems that the Contras have been trained by the Americans to fight the wrong kind of war.

At the time of the revolution, the Nicaraguan government had a 24,000-strong armed force. By 1987, however, they had 72,000 under arms, including active duty reserves, and around 20,500 conscripts on a two year tour. In addition, the Sandinistas can call on another 50,000 men in the militia.[7]

The government has also invested in new arms and equipment, giving them a formidable counter-insurgency capability. Like their neighbours in El Salvador (although in this case with the help of Cuban rather than US advisers) the army has been equipped specifically to fight a guerrilla war. They have formed Irregular Warfare Battalions which use their eighteen Russian Mi-8 transport helicopters backed up by ten Mi-24 Hind helicopter gunships, providing a formidable rapid deployment capability. The Nicaraguans have also requested Mig fighters, but the Soviets have not yet supplied them, perhaps fearing a further escalation in the war.

The Americans have equipped the Contras with Sam-7 missiles to counter the helicopter threat, portable radios, and a wide range of small arms and explosives. Even so, the Contras have never had personnel motivated to fight the kind of war that is required to bring down the Sandinista government.

With the help of their US advisers, the Contras have been trained to fight in a manner reminiscent of the commandos in World War II, rather than been required to live in their area of operations, gaining popular support, and gradually undermining the influence and the will of the existing government. Thus the Contras have learned to fight a war they can never win.

Retired Army General Paul Gorman, the former head of US Southern Command based in Panama, told Congress in January 1987 that the Contras 'are largely a cross-border raiding force, not an unconventional warfare force' and that they are incapable of defeating the Sandinistas. 'You are not going to knock off the Sandinistas with a conventional armed force and that's what the Contras are,' Gorman told the Senate Armed Service Committee. His views are particularly significant because, when head of Southern Command, he was responsible for overseeing US military policy in Central America.[8]

His opinion seems to be supported by the facts. Despite massive funding by the US, the Contras have still not managed to take and hold any significant population centre. There remains little evidence of popular support for them inside the country, no doubt in part because of their consistently alleged looting and brutality. Until the Contras learn to live inside Nicaragua on a permanent basis and the population shows some willingness to support them, they have no chance of making significant gains.

Gorman's views are sharply different from those of civilians in the Reagan administration. In testimony before the Senate Foreign Relations Committee in February 1987, the US Assistant Secretary of State for Inter-American Affairs, Elliott Abrams, said that the Contras could win their guerrilla war in Nicaragua in 'two to four years', provided the United States continues the current levels of military aid. A 'win' in this context was defined not as a 'straight-out military victory, as we won in World War II' but as a 'political victory like the Sandinistas had in 1979'. In other words, the US wishes to see the Sandinista government overthrown.[9]

However victory may be defined, it is difficult to see how the Contras will ever achieve anything significant. From the outset, President Reagan has seen the conflict in Central America as the ultimate surrogate war; an opportunity to take on the twin evils of the Soviet Union and Castro's Cuba and show the world that America is prepared to fight for democracy and the free world. Reagan has described the Contras as 'the moral equivalent of the Founding Fathers', and has subjected the Sandinistas to an unremitting propaganda campaign designed to show them as stooges of the Soviets.

Such starkly drawn arguments have unhelpfully polarised the situation. If Moscow and Havana are named as the main supporters of the Nicaraguan government, then their reputations are laid on the line: they have to support the Sandinistas and be seen to do so if they are to retain credibility in the Third World. It is impossible to disentangle the responsibilities of Moscow and Washington for the military escalation in the region, but there is now no doubt that the war will go on, perhaps indefinitely or, more likely, until the American will to continue disappears.

The war has always been unpopular both with Congress and the American public. Congress has an inherent suspicion of all US commitments overseas, and this consistently undermines the prosecution of a coherent foreign policy. The Tibetans, Laotians, Ukrainians and Montagnards can all

testify to the broken promises made by the US. These promises were always made in good faith, but successive administrations have found themselves unable to sustain the support
of Congress or the people for overseas adventures. This has
been immensely damaging to US credibility and has helped
that of the Soviet Union. The Kremlin does not respond to
an electorate and can therefore afford to take a long view in
seeking influence abroad.

(The US approach to dealing with Cuban involvement in
Central and South America contrasts sharply with that of the
British. In 1983, guerrillas operating in Guatemala were using
the northern part of neighbouring Belize as a safe haven. In
addition, Cubans, using fast motor boats were bringing
supplies – especially RPG–7 grenade launchers, AK–47
assault rifles and ammunition – in to the coast of Belize and
shipping it along a trail hacked through the jungle to the
guerrillas hiding out in the country. They then shipped the
weapons back into Guatemala.

Although officially independent, Belize's security is guaran-
teed by Britain which has troops and Harrier fighter aircraft
stationed there. In addition, it is used as a training ground
for the SAS. They mounted an operation to cut the Cuban
supply line and drive the guerrillas from Belize. Several
Cubans were killed and the route was cut yet the whole
operation was carried out without any publicity and Parliament was certainly not informed.)

It must be said, however, that the execution of the administration's policy in Central America seems almost to have been
designed to cause the maximum alienation of Congress. There
have been periodic attempts at negotiation with the Sandinista government, either directly or using intermediaries in
the OAS and the Contadora Group of Latin American States.
Although these have foundered ostensibly because the
Sandinistas refused to stop their support for the guerrillas in
El Salvador, there has always been the suspicion that the
administration has orchestrated each collapse: the Reagan

policy has clearly been designed to undermine the Sandinista government and compromise has never been on the agenda.

Congress initially supported covert funding of the Contras at fairly modest levels – $21 million in fiscal 1983 and $24 million the next year. However, it cut off funds in June 1984 after revelations that the CIA had been responsible for mining and raids at a number of Nicaragua's ports. This action was condemned as illegal by the International Court of Justice at The Hague – the jurisdiction of which the Reagan administration refused to acknowledge.

In addition, the CIA produced and delivered to the Contras in October 1984 a manual entitled *Psychological Operations in Guerrilla Wars* which was essentially a terrorist handbook, and undermined American claims that it was the Soviets who were behind all terrorism.[10] The eight chapters of the manual cover 'armed propaganda teams', 'massive in-depth support', and 'psychological operations'. The most controversial section actually instructs the reader on how to 'neutralise' selected individuals, with 'neutralise' being a euphemism for assassinate. It was an extraordinary document.

Both the mining and the manual helped to convince an already sceptical Congress that America had lost the moral high ground in Central America. Furthermore, they were fighting a war that was not only unpopular but also showed little prospect of a clear victory. This judgement was reinforced in November 1984, when the Nicaraguan government held the first national elections since the revolution. Although there was some intimidation during the election campaign, the election itself was free of violence. The Sandinistas won 67 per cent of the vote in a 75 per cent turnout and the three opposition parties won only 30 per cent. It was an impressive victory for the Sandinistas and one which clearly demonstrated that the government commanded considerable popular support. Since the election was still dismissed as a sham by the Reagan administration, while similar elections in El Salvador, which had produced a more rightist result, had been welcomed, there was a feeling among commentators and the legislature in Washington that the election result had been dismissed simply because it had not suited the administration line.

In July 1985 Congress grudgingly approved $27 million in non-lethal aid to the Contras and then, after the Soviets had substantially increased the supply of military equipment to Nicaragua and the Sandinista government had suspended civil rights in a new state of emergency, military aid was resumed in November 1986. Even then, Congress only agreed to the President's request for $100 million in military and humanitarian assistance after a lengthy and acrimonious debate.

Although US funding of the Contra campaign is still not at a level appropriate to the war, it is highly unlikely that such funding will remain intact long enough to give the Contras time to develop a proper strategy (even assuming they are capable of fighting a proper unconventional war). Instead, the CIA and the Contras will continue to fight an on-again, off-again war which is therefore doomed to failure.

Not that even the cutting off of funds by Congress in 1984 had reduced the zeal with which the administration attempted to prosecute the war. The propaganda machinery remained in place and the funding and arming of the Contras, no longer carried out officially by the CIA, was continued unofficially by former members of the Agency or the Army's special forces.

There were three key players in this new and possibly illegal covert war: Lt.-Col. Oliver North, Army General John K. Singlaub and Air Force General Richard Secord.

Oliver North was Deputy Director for Political-Military Affairs on the National Security Council, and was responsible for low intensity conflict and counter-terrorism. He had been appointed to the NSC in 1981 aged 38, and swiftly gained himself a reputation as an achiever.

He graduated from the US Naval Academy in 1968 and saw extensive service with the Marine Corps in Vietnam where he was highly decorated. His enthusiasm for and

apparent expertise in unconventional warfare proved useful
to a White House preoccupied with terrorism and communist
subversion. North played key roles in the invasion of Grenada,
where he organised the White House input, and in the
planned Delta Force takeover of the *Achille Lauro* and of the
TWA aircraft hijacked to Beirut by Iranian-sponsored
terrorists.

Among his fellow Marines and within the NSC he had a
reputation for an extraordinary disregard of procedure or
political consequences. His arrogant approach to problem-
solving infuriated many of his colleagues, and upset the Army
hierarchy to the extent that fellow officers believed that, once
out of the White House his career in the Marines was finished.
But Ronald Reagan fondly referred to him as 'My Marine',
and personally recommended him for the Defense Meritorious
Service Medal for his work in the White House.

Jack Singlaub graduated from UCLA in 1942 and was sent
to France just over a year later as a member of a Jedburgh
team in the OSS. After service in Europe he headed for the
Far East and worked behind the lines against the Japanese.
Throughout his service, Singlaub both had a formal military
career and saw extensive action with the CIA. He was
attached to the Agency in China as chief of station in Mukden,
and in Korea as deputy chief of station. He also commanded
the Military Assistance Command, Vietnam – Special Operations Group (MACV-SOG) in Vietnam in 1966–68.[11]

In 1977, Singlaub was relieved of his command as Chief of
Staff for US forces in South Korea after he had criticised
President Carter's plans to withdraw some US troops as 'a
mistake that will lead to war'. Back in the United States he
continued to criticise Carter's defence policy and was asked
to retire from the Army.

For many people with a background in unconventional
warfare or intelligence work, there is really no retirement.
Thus, although formally off the government payroll, Singlaub
continued to see his colleagues, and in 1984 he headed a study
on low intensity conflict for the Pentagon which examined the

situation in Central America. He concluded that low intensity warfare was the most likely form of combat for the future and that the United States should prepare accordingly.

Singlaub had met North in Vietnam and to both of them the encouraging of private enterprise to replace the money cut off from the Contras by Congress seemed a logical solution. North also brought in Richard Secord, whom he had met since his appointment to the White House. (Secord and Singlaub knew each other well from their time in South Asia.)

In the triumvirate, North provided the official backing, Singlaub the network of financiers and Secord the delivery supply network that ensured the arms and cash reached the Contras.

Like Singlaub, Secord was a specialist in covert warfare. His particular expertise was the clandestine movement by air of men and equipment around the world. If you needed an aircraft with dummy log books or no identification, an out-of-the-way airfield and pilots who would keep their mouths shut, then Dick Secord was your man, and the best in the business.

A graduate of West Point, Secord came to the notice of the CIA and covert warfare specialists in 1964 during an operation to evacuate Americans and Belgians from Stanleyville in Zaire. The town was surrounded and the only way in was by air. The evacuation was successful but Secord arrived late after a door on his aircraft blew open in flight and a life raft automatically inflated and wrapped itself around a wing. He successfully landed the plane and received the first of many decorations for a smart piece of flying.

After that initial foray into covert operations, he developed a liking for high-risk, low-profile missions, and United States involvement in Vietnam provided him with just the right opportunity. Although the Vietnam War helped his steady upward progress it also saw one of his less successful missions for the CIA.

The Agency, in their continuing search for an effective way

to block Vietcong supply routes down the Ho Chi Minh trail, had decided to try to make it so slippery that it would become impassable. Secord led a daylight bombing mission on the trail (the CIA insisted on photographs), where a fleet of C–130s deposited hundreds of bags of Calgonate soap flakes, which were supposed to turn to liquid in the rain. This extraordinary plan did not work.

After flying in Laos in the CIA's secret war there, Secord was promoted to colonel and given an office job as the Pentagon's desk officer for Vietnam, Laos and Thailand. In South Asia and in the Pentagon, Secord helped plan operations with the CIA for Southern Air Transport, then a front for the Agency.

In 1975 and still only forty-three, he was sent to Iran as the first head of the Air Force's Military Advisory Group responsible for $60 billion in military equipment sales to the Shah. It was then that he met Edwin Wilson, ex-CIA troubleshooter and now arms supplier at large to everyone, including Colonel Qadaffi. Wilson tried to persuade Secord to sell surveillance systems illegally to the Shah. No deal between the two men resulted, but it was this link that was to destroy Secord's promising Air Force career six years later.

Edwin Wilson was arrested and found guilty of illegal dealing in part on the evidence of a former associate, Douglas Schlachter, who was given a new identity under the Federal Witness Protection programme. Schlachter also alleged that during his time in Iran Secord had helped Wilson sell arms to Iran and had taken some of the profits. Secord, by then the Deputy Assistant Secretary of Defense for the Near East, Africa and South Asia, was suspended while the Justice Department began an investigation. No evidence was found against him and he was reinstated on the personal orders of Frank Carlucci, then number two in the Defense Department. Later, in the fallout from the Iran arms scandal, President Reagan would call on Carlucci to become his new National Security Adviser.

Secord sued Schlachter for libel and won a $1 million

judgement by default. But he was unable to collect, as Schlachter was in hiding under federal protection. Meanwhile the mud that had been thrown at Secord stuck and, realising his rapid climb up the Air Force ladder was over, he resigned and himself joined Stanford Technology.

Shortly before his resignation, Secord was asked to take charge of the planning for Operation Honey Bear, the planned follow up to the Desert One fiasco to rescue the US hostages in Iran. That mission was cancelled after the hostages were released.

In 1983, soon after he retired from the Air Force, Secord fas asked by the Defense Department to join the newly formed Special Operations Advisory Group (SOPAG). This six-strong unit advised senior officials on improving America's covert capability. This was a key position that ensured Secord maintained close links with the intelligence community and with the National Security Council.

His work with SOPAG brought him into regular contact with Ollie North and the two men seemed to have the attraction of opposites. North, ebullient, cigar-smoking and aggressive, was a marked contrast to Secord, who might look like a night club bouncer but was in fact a cautious and thoughtful operator. What united the two men was a fundamental anti-communist philosophy and a 'take that hill' attitude where the ends justified the often dubious means.

In the first year of operation Singlaub raised tens of millions of dollars for the Contras, using a wide array of different organisations to collect the cash. Among them were the US Chapter of the World Anti-Communist League, which Singlaub headed, the Western Goals Foundation, the Council for Inter-American Security, the American Security Council, the Heritage Foundation and the Conservative Caucus. In addition, members of the Saudi royal family and the Sultan of Brunei contributed to the cause.

Secord and his Iranian business partner, Albert Hakim, used their company Stanford Technology, which already had a number of Swiss bank accounts, to organise others through which funds were channelled to the Contras.

Immediately after the Congress cut off the covert funding, Secord bought three STOL (short takeoff and landing) aircraft from an American company, using a part of those Swiss funds. The aircraft were flown to Honduras and handed over to the Contras. The US Customs Service as of June 1987 is investigating to determine if those aircraft can be classified as 'instruments of war' and therefore were illegally exported.

Aircraft were the key to the operations. All supplies had to be flown to the Contras from air bases in Honduras, El Salvador and Costa Rica. Pilots were recruited both on the private mercenary network and through Southern Air Transport, a former CIA proprietary company that had been privatised in 1973 but which still maintained close connections with the Agency. A safe house was set up at 5272 Paseo Escalon in a wealthy suburb of San Salvador. The two-storey building was one of three in which three former CIA agents, led by Felix Ismael Rodriguez (codename Condor), briefed the twenty-four to twenty-six Americans involved in flying in the arms and equipment.

The aircraft were flown from mainly US-built and run airfields, and there is no doubt that gun runners were operating with official knowledge and approval. Singlaub is quoted as saying: 'Now occasionally I make telephone calls to friends (in the administration) and say "Look, old buddy, this is what we're about to do and if you have any objections to this, if you think I am doing the wrong thing, send me a signal. Otherwise this is what I am going to do . . . " and I say, "If at any time you think I'm doing something that's dumb, send me the word." Well until I get some word, I'm going to continue to do what the freedom fighters want me to do.'[12]

Singlaub however, maintains that his involvement in the affair was limited to providing humanitarian assistance to the Contras and to Nicaraguan refugees. He claims that it was mostly Secord who organised the aircraft and the pilots.

News of the private fund-raising and arms supply network began to leak out during 1985 and 1986, causing considerable criticism of the administration in the media and in Congress. What seemed to provoke the most indignation was that business was being done in defiance of Congress but with the authority and backing of the NSC. The affair clearly illustrates how difficult it is for the United States to wage any kind of covert war effectively.

In Europe, should it be politically embarrassing for a national government to be seen to be sending troops to train a foreign army, private companies are cynically encouraged to step in instead. The most reputable of the companies involved in this kind of work is Defence Systems Limited (DSL) which is run by Alastair Morrison, the SAS man who supplied the flash-bang grenades to GSG9 at Mogadishu. In the 1980s the company provided security for the diamond mines in Angola and today it has an extensive operation in Mozambique, as well as supplying guards for US embassies in sensitive areas. DSL uses highly-trained specialists and invariably operates with the full knowledge of the British government. Such companies help provide 'plausible deniability' should the presence of a British training team ever be questioned.

Inevitably, the activities of such companies can become embarrassing – particularly if the sponsoring governments are not kept fully informed of their activities. For example, the Sri Lankan civil war has provided an opportunity for a British company, KMS Ltd., to supply forty people to train a new Sri Lankan police Special Task Force to combat the guerrilla rebels. They have also supplied between ten and twenty pilots for the Sri Lankan Air Force.[13]

Since the British government was anxious not to get directly involved – given that the Indian government allow the Tamils to operate freely in India and has supported their demands for an independent state – KMS did not receive official British permission to go to Sri Lanka. Nothing was done, however, to stop their involvement. But when in 1986, the British High

Commissioner in Colombo complained to the Foreign Office in London about the presence of KMS, one of their directors was told in clear terms that no KMS men should be actually flying missions for the Sri Lankan government. The Foreign Office was assured that only training was being supplied and the company continued its operation.

KMS (the name stands for Keeny Meeny Services, an inside joke that refers to a slang Arabic term for undercover work) was formed in 1977. Since then it has employed ex-SAS, intelligence and regular army men to train foreign armies and provide bodyguards.

KMS has also supplied air crew to Colonel Oliver North for his gun running operation to the Contras in Nicaragua. At least three men were recruited by David Walker, the head of KMS, at their offices in Abingdon Road, west London, and sent to El Salvador. Eyewitnesses at the Ilopongo air base in El Salvador said that at least three mercenaries, two South Africans and one British, were hired. The three arrived in Ilopongo in April 1986 and were assigned to work as crew helping to load and fly transport planes full of military equipment into Nicaragua. American citizens helped direct the loading of the planes but only non-Americans were supposed to fly the planes across the border into Nicaragua. That way, if any crashed or were shot down, the US government could deny any knowledge of the supply operation.[14]

The KMS team was sacked by William Cooper, the man responsible for running the safe house in San Salvador where the mercenaries were based. He said they were incompetent and others claimed they were 'hell raisers' in the bars of the city.

There was no immediate replacement for the sacked crew members. As a result Cooper himself, along with two other Americans, Buzz Sawyer and Eugene Hasenfus, were forced to fly the missions into Nicaragua. On 5 October 1986 a C-123K transport aircraft was shot down by a Sam-7 missile fired by Nicaraguan forces. Cooper and Sawyer were both killed but Hasenfus parachuted to safety and was captured.

Hasenfus and the other crew members had all previously worked for Air America, the CIA front company in South East Asia. That October, Hasenfus had been employed as a 'kicker', the man who loads equipment and then kicks it out of the aircraft over a drop zone. It is a highly skilled task and Hasenfus was being paid $3,000 a month plus a $750 bonus for every flight into Nicaragua.

Hasenfus, plus flight records recovered from the aircraft, gave the Sandinistas a major propaganda coup. Telephone records from the San Salvador safe house showed that the most frequent calls had been to Dick Secord in Virginia and to a number at the White House (202 395–3345). By the time reporters rang this last number, it had been disconnected, but this author and others had used it in the past to contact Ollie North.

The Hasenfus affair exposed for the first time the nature of the secret supply network to the Contras, but by then the job of the underground operation had been done. Soon afterwards Congress finally authorised the money for arms and other assistance demanded by the White House, and business returned to a more legitimate covert footing.

When the Nicaraguan government came to power it showed every sign of being a disorganised but idealistic revolutionary movement. The nation's economy was in chaos and, without substantial injections of cash from groups like the International Monetary Fund, the Sandinistas had no chance of introducing the expensive reforms promised before the revolution. Ironically, the effect of the Contra war has been to unite the population behind the Sandinistas, who have been able to use the war to distract their citizens from the still failing economy. At the same time, the Sandinistas have taken advantage of every pretext to threaten an imminent invasion by US forces (an unlikely prospect), and have used the war as an excuse for suspending a free press and restricting individual liberty. Without the war, there is every chance that the revolution would either have been forced along a more moderate path or would have collapsed in the face of lost support among a disenchanted population.

There now seems little serious prospect of the collapse of the Sandinista government. Even if the population had a dramatic change of heart and began supporting the Contras, who are still identified with the former Somoza regime, the Soviet Union and Cuba would not allow a government into power that was not allied to the eastern bloc. The Reagan administration has made the war in Nicaragua the focus for a surrogate war between the two superpowers. Neither side is likely to emerge with much credit as a victor, but both have invested too much political capital to back down.

As usual, it is the local people who have suffered. In 1980 El Salvador had around 15,000 regular troops, Costa Rica none, Nicaragua 7,100, Guatemala 9,400 and Honduras 4,700.[15] Six years later, El Salvador had 42,640 regular troops, Costa Rica 9,500, Nicaragua 72,500, Guatemala 32,000 and Honduras 19,200.[16] Total troop strengths in the region have gone up from 36,200 to 175,840, a five-fold increase.

This has played havoc with the local economies. According to the International Institute of Strategic Studies' annual survey, El Salvador's Gross Domestic Product, after declining by 25 per cent since 1979, grew by 1.5 per cent in 1984 and perhaps by 2 per cent in 1985, but population growth is 3 per cent and external aid accounts for around 25 per cent of GDP. Nicaragua depends entirely on external assistance for economic survival. Its mounting foreign debt is larger than its declining GDP and debt service payments due in 1985 are equal to over 300 per cent of foreign earnings. Costa Rica's foreign debt is also larger than its GDP and even Honduras grows ever more dependent on US aid.[17]

This destabilising trend will continue for the foreseeable future. Exactly the same mistakes that were made in Vietnam are being made again in Central America. The only difference is that, so far, the commitment of US troops has been kept to a minimum.

There is no doubt that the actions of the Green Berets in

El Salvador, combined with the massive aid programme from the US government, have helped stave off a left-wing takeover of the government. But this is only a temporary success. Unless more is done, and differently, the counter-insurgency war will eat up ever larger portions of the country's already over-stretched budget and the left-wingers' cause will seem increasingly attractive.

To an extent, President Duarte has been made a prisoner of the right wing in his own country, and this has restricted his ability to introduce much needed reforms. However, that is only one part of the story. American military advisers may have improved the capability of the El Salvador armed forces, which now fight a more mobile war, but, just as in Vietnam, they have trained not in counter-insurgency tactics but in search and destroy missions. No real attempt has been made to develop the strategic hamlet concept, or to secure the support of the local people who currently allow the guerrillas to operate among them. Instead, success is counted by the number of people killed. There remains a conviction that there is a quick and easy solution to the war. Unless there is a policy change, this fundamental and tragic error will eventually bring about victory for the communist guerrillas. The United States must introduce new tactics that reflect both the nature of the war that is being fought and the fact that they are involved in a long campaign where there are no easy solutions.

Frustration with the war in El Salvador causes the US government to try and place the blame for the guerrillas' continued presence on Nicaragua. This is exactly what happened in Vietnam, where the Vietcong were seen as being recruited and supplied by the North Vietnamese. Contemporary intelligence estimates did not support that view, and neither do they back today's conviction that without Nicaragua the guerrillas in El Salvador would disappear. That is not the nature of guerrilla warfare. Guerrillas operate with a measure of support from the local people that is obtained either willingly or through terrorism. The support guerrillas receive from outside a country becomes irrelevant if the inside support can be removed.

As the US government has failed to understand this basic fact, it is hardly surprising that they have not proved successful at running their own guerrilla war. In Nicaragua, they are sponsoring a force that does not live among the people but is entirely dependent on outside support. It is therefore reluctant to operate for long periods inside Nicaragua, preferring instead short raids across the border. As a result, there is no chance that the Contras will ever become really effective guerrillas. It is not their fighting abilities that will ultimately decide their fate but the election of a new President in the United States in 1988. In keeping with a long history of United States sponsorship of surrogate wars, the new administration will wish to distance itself from the policies of its predecessor and that will very likely include a reduction in support for the Contras. With a Democrat as President, Reagan's 'Freedom Fighters' who are 'the moral equivalent of our Founding Fathers' will be left to fend for themselves and their war will collapse.

It is right to resist communist subversion around the world. But the method by which that resistance is mounted is critical. The Soviets have one great ally on their side – time. Western democracies have constantly fallen victim to their own democratic systems which every four or five years tend to produce a change of government and policy. Even so, the traffic has not all been in the Soviets' favour. There are countries such as Egypt and Mozambique, supported in their revolutions by the Kremlin, which have moved back or are moving back into the western fold. They turn to the west not because of military action but because the Soviets prove to be mean and oppressive allies.

Military training teams have a vital role to play in winning new friends and gaining influence in developing countries. In the same way the sponsorship of surrogate groups such as UNITA and the Contras may be of questionable morality, but will remain a tool of foreign policy in both west and east.

Given that reality, more must be done to understand the nature of that warfare, to train any surrogate forces suitable, to demonstrate a more consistent political will than has been evident in the past, and to make more use of the economic power available to the western democracies – not to attempt to undermine our enemies (sanctions never work) but to bankroll our friends.

24

Operation Recovery

In February 1986, led by Vice-President George Bush, a task force on combating terrorism published its report. It was the result of months of work and was supposed to provide a definitive statement of US policy on terrorism.

Vice-President Bush spelled out in unequivocal terms current American policy:

'The US government is opposed to domestic and international terrorism and is prepared to act in concert with other nations or unilaterally when necessary to prevent or respond to terrorist acts.

'The US government considers the practice of terrorism by any person or group a potential threat to its national security and will resist the use of terrorism by all legal means available.

'States that practise terrorism or actively support it will not do so without consequence. If there is evidence that a state is mounting or intends to conduct an act of terrorism against this country, the United States will take measures to protect its citizens, property and interests.

'The US government will make no concessions to terrorists. It will not pay ransoms, release prisoners, change its policies or agree to other acts that might encourage additional terrorism. At the same time, the United States will use every available resource to gain the safe return of American citizens who are held hostage by terrorists.

'The United States will act in a strong manner against

terrorists without surrendering basic freedoms or endangering democratic principles, and encourages other governments to take similar stands.

'US policy is based upon the conviction that to give in to terrorists' demands places even more Americans at risk. This no-concessions policy is the best way of ensuring the safety of the greatest number of people.'[1]

Taken at face value, this policy was exemplary. There is ample evidence that countries that fail to stand firm against terrorism simply lead the terrorist to believe that he or she is combating a weak foe. Both Israel and Britain have generally held to an uncompromising counter-terrorist policy while France has regularly capitulated. Both the United Kingdom and Israel continue to experience terrorism, but within their own frontiers it is at least controllable. France, on the other hand, has become a playground for terrorists of all persuasions who wage a freewheeling war against each other and other countries, while the French government constantly seeks accommodations.

But the reality of US counter-terrorist policy has turned out to be rather different. It was Islamic Jihad, an organisation funded and trained by the Iranian government, that was behind the bombing of the Marine barracks in Beirut in 1983 causing the deaths of 241 US servicemen. The terrorists who hijacked the TWA flight in 1985 were also members of Islamic Jihad. Yet when they demanded the release of several hundred Shias imprisoned in Israel as their price for the hostages, the US government secretly applied so much pressure on the Israelis that 735 Shias were in fact released.

This response confusingly went hand-in-hand with an effort to persuade America's allies to adopt a common, tough, policy against terrorists. The Reagan administration applied considerable pressure (without success) on the French government to stop paying money for French hostages held in the Lebanon. The US also led the way in improving the exchange of information between western countries on intelligence matters.

Even so, the western alliance continued to demonstrate a striking lack of united resolve in the fight against terrorism. Rather than co-ordinating policy to meet the threat, it continued to counter terrorism on national lines. Terrorists were fleeing France and finding sanctuary in Belgium, or leaving Ulster to find a home in the United States. Basically, no two countries could even agree on a common definition of the problem, so any concerted policy was regularly hamstrung by political or economic considerations.

Almost 20 per cent of all terrorist attacks in 1985 were aimed at the United States. The attacks killed twenty-seven people and injured hundreds more. Searching for someone to blame for this the US concluded that certain other countries were responsible for funding, arming and training terrorists. In particular, Libya, Iran and Syria were thought to be the most guilty. The question facing the President was: what could be done to deter a state that sponsored terrorism?

One answer was provided at a meeting in December 1985 of terrorist experts at the Defense Intelligence College run by the Defense Intelligence Agency at Bolling Air Force Base, outside Washington DC. The experts from the State Department, the National Security Council and various intelligence agencies were agreed that an armed attack on a state sponsor in retaliation for a terrorist attack was the way forward. Syria and Iran were ruled out because the former was too close to the Soviet Union and the latter because of difficulties in mounting a limited military action. Although the delegates at that December meeting were not there to make policy, all of them were in positions of considerable influence and what was decided there swiftly became official policy.

For the next few months, the US intelligence community placed a high priority on gathering information about Libya and its involvement with terrorism. The National Security Agency, working as always in close harmony with Britain's GCHQ, programmed its computers to eavesdrop upon all matters Libyan. Messages to and from its embassies around the world were tapped. Listening posts in Egypt and on satellites plucked telephone calls out of the air, decoded them and presented the results for human analysis. Some interesting details emerged from this study. Abu Nidal, who is currently the world's most dangerous and successful terrorist, was found to be commuting between Syria and Libya with Qadaffi helping to pay his bills.

But, despite an intensive intelligence gathering effort, hard intelligence on Qadaffi's involvement with terrorism was hard to come by. The CIA submitted one report to the White House that analysed all terrorist attacks in 1985 and was unable to conclude that Libya had been involved in any of them. This did not satisfy the President, who sent the Agency off to look at the matter again. Once more the report came back and this time it was filled with qualifying statements like, 'It is possible that Libya was involved . . .' or 'There is no firm evidence but . . .' Eventually, the White House simply took the report and rewrote it to suit existing prejudices. But then on 4 April 1986, evidence appeared that finally seemed to nail Qadaffi's colours to a terrorist act.

The computers at GCHQ in Britain picked up a message from the Libyan People's Bureau in East Berlin to Tripoli that alerted Colonel Qadaffi to an attack that would be carried out the following morning. A second message then read: 'It will happen soon. The bomb will blow. American soldiers must be hit.' Hours later a bomb planted in La Belle discotheque in West Berlin exploded, killing one American serviceman and wounding 230 others. Immediately after the bombing the People's Bureau reported: 'Action carried out. No trail left.'[2]

This apparently clear evidence was exactly what the United States needed. Since that first interception, however, considerable doubt has been placed on the information and the interpretation put upon it by the United States. The West Germans remain convinced that the Syrians and not the Libyans were behind the attack.

Nevertheless, a plan was devised by the Office for Combating Terrorism in the State Department that would involve using the evidence of Libyan complicity to force the Europeans to unite and to act against the terrorists by imposing economic sanctions and isolating Colonel Qadaffi diplomatically. But the US ambassador to Bonn, Richard Burt, leaked the details of the intercepted messages and the US found itself facing an irate Congress and a frustrated electorate who both demanded more immediate action.

In a series of meetings in the White House over the next four days, a consensus gradually emerged for an armed attack on Libya. The two men who argued most forcefully for an attack was the National Security Adviser, Admiral John Poindexter, and Colonel Oliver North, the member of the National Security Council who had taken on the mantle of counter-terrorist action man in the White House. The only two senior officials who might have opposed armed action were George Bush and Defense Secretary Caspar Weinberger, but both men were out of town when the key decisions were taken.

The result was Operation El Dorado Canyon, an armed attack on Libya by thirteen F-111 fighters and three electronic counter-measures aircraft flown from bases in Great Britain. These were supplemented by an assortment of aircraft from the US Sixth Fleet positioned in the Mediterranean off Libya. Militarily, the attack was a success. The Americans lost one aircraft but caused considerable damage to military installations in Tripoli and Benghazi.

Although several innocent civilians were killed and injured in the attack and the French and Portuguese embassies were hit by bombs, the reaction of the American people to the raid was overwhelmingly supportive. A jubilant White House reported that the switchboard was jammed with calls from people wishing to congratulate the President on his courageous act.

More importantly, the raid had a profoundly adverse effect on American's allies. Even Prime Minister Margaret Thatcher, who had allowed aircraft based in Britain to be used for the raid, was unconvinced that Qadaffi was worth the effort of the raid, and the civilian casualties were a major propaganda coup for the Libyan leader. The other allies were shocked that America would carry out an act of such overt aggression against another nation.

'Although we allowed the raid, there was a general feeling that America had become uncontrollable, that unless we did something Reagan would be even more violent the next time,' said one British intelligence source.[3]

The result was a flurry of diplomatic activity all designed to show the United States that the allies were at long last determined to develop a common counter-terrorist policy. 'For two years prior to the raid we had been trying to get the Europeans to do something about terrorism and they just wanted business as usual,' said one State Department source. 'But the raid acted as a catalyst, which forced them to do something.'[4]

This new resolve was publicly demonstrated at the meeting of seven major democracies in Tokyo at the beginning of May. A statement issued at the end of the summit spelled out for the first time a common policy against terrorism.

'We specify the following as measures open to any government concerned to deny to international terrorists the opportunity and the means to carry out their aims, and to identify and deter those who perpetrate such terrorism. We have decided to apply these measures within the framework of international law and in our own jurisdictions in respect of any state which is clearly involved in sponsoring or supporting international terrorism, and in particular of Libya, until such time as the state concerned abandons its complicity in, or support for, such terrorism. These measures are:

'Refusal to export arms to states which sponsor or support terrorism.

'Strict limits on the size of the diplomatic and consular missions and other official bodies abroad of states which engage in such activities, control of travel of members of such missions and bodies, and, where appropriate, radical reductions in, or even the closure of, such missions and bodies.

'Denial of entry to all persons, including diplomatic

personnel, who have been expelled or excluded from one of our states on suspicion of involvement in international terrorism or who have been convicted of such a terrorist offence.

'Improved extradition procedures within due process of domestic law for bringing to trial those who have perpetrated such acts of terrorism.

'Stricter immigration and visa requirements and procedures in respect of national states which sponsor or support terrorism.

'The closest possible bilateral and multilateral co-operation between police and security organisations and other relevant authorities in the fight against terrorism.'[5]

At a press conference in Tokyo on 6 May, President Reagan made clear that if other countries such as Syria or Iran were found to be involved in state-sponsored terrorism they would be treated in the same way as Libya by those countries which had signed the agreement.

It now emerges, however, that twenty-three days later, a Boeing 707 aircraft left the United States for Israel. On board were Robert McFarlane, the former US National Security Adviser, Oliver North, Howard Teicher, North's immediate superior on the NSC, George Cave, a former CIA station chief in Iran, and a CIA specialist in communications. In Israel, Amiram Nir, an adviser to Prime Minister Peres on terrorism, joined the flight which continued on to Teheran. All the men, including Nir, travelled on false Irish passports.[6]

Also on board the aircraft was a pallet of spare parts for Hawk ground-to-air missiles that the Iranians desperately wanted to help them in their war with Iraq. Adding a personal touch, North took along a cake baked in the shape of a key, to symbolise the opening of a new era in Iranian-American relations, and a pair of Colt pistols.

Their mission was to discuss with Iranian leaders a trade of arms for American hostages then being held by Iranian-sponsored terrorists in the Lebanon. The trip, which was in direct conflict with publicly stated US government policy, was to end in failure. The Americans left Teheran with no agreement but without the cake, pistols or Hawk spare parts.

The origins of that ill-fated flight to Iran began in January 1979 with the overthrow of the Shah and the coming to power of Ayatollah Khomeini. Iran had traditionally been America's key ally in the Middle East. Billions of dollars in arms and aid had been supplied to bolster the Shah's regime which was seen as pro-west and, perhaps more importantly, vehemently anti-Soviet.

Now Iran could no longer be seen as an ally. Indeed, Khomeini and his close followers designated the United States as 'the Great Satan'. But he had also purged the communist Tudeh Party and seemed determined to adopt a strongly isolationist foreign policy.

Instead, paradoxically, the Teheran regime turned its attentions to the moderate Arab countries, such as Kuwait and Saudi Arabia, which it considered to have betrayed the basic tenets of Islam. A string of bombings and assassinations by terrorist groups throughout the Gulf was backed by the Iranian government, and terrorist groups received extensive training and funding from Iran.

A number of terrorist organisations in the Lebanon, variously called Islamic Jihad or Hizbollah, were also known to be directly controlled by Iran. It was those groups that were responsible for the kidnapping of seven Americans between 7 March 1984 and 9 June 1985.

The US intelligence community had no doubt that the hostage-taking was directly linked to Iran. 'We had clear evidence both from Sigint and Humint that Teheran was directing the terrorists. They were behind the bombing of the Marines and many other attacks,' said one US intelligence source.[7]

On 20 January 1984, Secretary of State George Shultz designated Iran a state sponsor of world terrorism. This was more than simple propaganda. Once that designation had been made, the US, which already had a ban on shipping arms to Iran as a result of the embassy takeover, pressured her allies not to ship arms to the country either under a project codenamed Operation Staunch.

Three months later, Iranian-sponsored terrorism in the Lebanon appeared to take a new turn for the worse.

As a result of the bombing of the US embassy in Beirut in 1983 (another attack that was blamed on Iranian-sponsored terrorists) the CIA station at the embassy had been wiped out. The replacement for the station chief was William Buckley, who arrived in the city with the cover of State Department political officer. On 16 March 1984, Buckley came out of his apartment, planning to get into his car and drive to work. A white Renault suddenly stopped in front of him. He was bundled into the car and was never seen again.

The capture alive of the CIA station chief was bad enough but he was also taken with a head full of highly classified material on American contingency plans in the event of terrorist attacks in the area, as well as detailed tactics to be used by special forces in countering hijacks or kidnapping.

The American intelligence community launched one of the most intensive investigations in its history to try to track Buckley down. The CIA, NSA and the DIA pooled their resources and called in all their favours from other friendly intelligence organisations. The investigation failed to discover Buckley's whereabouts or even which organisation was holding him although this was presumed to be Hizbollah.

(Buckley was never found and it is believed he died in June 1985 from injuries he received while being tortured. US intelligence believes that he talked under torture and assumes that all agents and operations in the region have therefore been compromised.)

Two months after Buckley's disappearance, the CIA National Intelligence Officer for the Middle East sent a five-page memo to the NSC and the State Department, suggesting an easing in US relations with Iran, and in particular with moderate members of the government who might be interested in closer ties with the west. It is not clear if the memo was prompted by a need to gain influential contacts in Iran who might help to find Buckley, or if its timing was simply a coincidence. Whatever the reason for its appearance, the memo was the catalyst from which the disasters of the next two years were to flow.

The memorandum was used by the NSC as the basis for a draft National Security Decision Directive (NSDD) that formally proposed improving relations with moderates in Iran, so that the US would have some influence in the country after Khomeini died. The draft paper further suggested that arms could be traded with Iran as a way of gaining influence. National Security Adviser Robert McFarlane sent the draft to Shultz and Weinberger for their comments. Shultz wrote back that he thought the policy proposals 'perverse' while Weinberger wrote in the margin of his copy of the draft: 'This is almost too absurd to comment on.'

Despite this apparently clear dismissal of their ideas, some members of the NSC remained convinced that a new policy on Iran was essential. Then, at the beginning of 1985, the CIA produced a new intelligence assessment on the country that suggested the Soviets might be in a position to exploit faction fighting in Iran that could break out before Khomeini's death or afterwards. It is not clear on what that assessment was based. Most members of the Tudeh party were in jail or had been killed and their influence in any significant area of the country was negligible.

Ollie North was later to tell a friend that the reason the US had tried to talk to moderates in Iran was precisely because of a perceived Soviet threat. The North scenario has it that the Soviets had been deliberately encouraging Iran to launch a 'final offensive' against Iraq. The Soviets had further convinced Iran that it would win such an offensive while, in reality, Moscow expected it to be badly beaten. More than 600 KGB and spetsnaz agents had been infiltrated into the country and were poised to take advantage of the instability that would result from the reversal at the front. In addition, Soviet troops were poised to move over the border once their agents had created a puppet government that would publicly call for their assistance. North claimed that moderate Arab nations-had heard of this plan and asked the United States to intervene. According to North that explained why lines of communication were opened to moderates in Teheran, and why arms were supplied – to give the Iranians a chance of holding their own in their 'final offensive'.[8]

There is not a shred of evidence to support this story. In simple practical terms, it seems extremely unlikely that the Soviets would wish to take over a country in such chaos as Iran while already embroiled in Afghanistan.

The original CIA assessment, however, was used as the basis for a fresh effort by the NSC to get a new policy on Iran adopted. Another NSDD was prepared which argued for closer ties with Iran, and to achieve this the US should 'encourage western allies and friends to help Iran meet its import requirements . . . including provision of selected military equipment.' Once again the proposal foundered on the objections of Shultz and Weinberger.

There the matter might have rested had not the paths of a number of individuals and nations crossed, all of whom were motivated almost entirely by self-interest and were largely unconcerned about the position of the United States or its officials.

First on the scene was Michael Ledeen, a professor at Georgetown University and a part-time NSC consultant known to be extremely close to the Israelis. For many years Ledeen had worked on the periphery of the Washington political scene and he later told the Senate Intelligence Committee that he had proposed to McFarlane in late April that he would ask around in Israel, during a forthcoming trip, to discover if Tel Aviv had any contacts in Teheran.

It was hardly surprising that the answer came back in the affirmative. Since Khomeini came to power the Israelis had for some years been supplying arms to Iran, including tank spares and parts for fighters which had originally been supplied to both countries by the United States. Israel was

anxious that Iran should not be defeated in its war with Iraq
as that would make Iraq a more powerful enemy for Israel.
In any event, the longer the Iran-Iraq war lasted, the less
likely it was that any Arab country would attack Israel.

It was only pressure from the United States in 1984 that
had cut off Israel's arms supplies to Iran. Israel was well
aware of America's wish to free its hostages and of the NSC's
idea of building bridges with the government in Teheran, so
their response was carefully tailored to fit the requirements
of McFarlane and his colleagues on the NSC.

Ledeen told McFarlane that Israel certainly did have lines
open to the Iranian government. This was followed by three
separate contacts by Israeli officials with McFarlane over the
next three months. The Israelis claimed to have opened up
a line to Teheran and that the Iranians were indeed interested
in discussing a new relationship with the United States. The
Israelis also said that the US would have to deal through an
intermediary, Manucher Ghorbanifar, an Iranian
businessman living in France.

The CIA had had dealings with Ghorbanifar since 1980
and had decided that he was too untrustworthy to handle, a
view that was shared by other European intelligence agencies.
When he took a lie detector test in January 1986, the only
question he answered truthfully was his own name. The poly-
graph indicated deception on all other questions – such as
whether he was under the control of the Iranian government,
whether he knew in advance that no American hostages would
be released as a result of any deal with the US, whether he
co-operated with Iranian officials to deceive the United
States, and whether he acted independently to deceive the
US.

Ghorbanifar was an arms dealer who worked closely with
financier Adnan Khashoggi, another arms dealer. Both men
knew that if restrictions on arms sales to Iran were relaxed
there was a fortune to be made. Khashoggi in particular was
in urgent need of additional funds. The collapse in oil prices
had left him short of money and he was in danger of going

bankrupt, so the prospect of an arms deal with Iran that was officially sanctioned by the United States was heaven-sent.

By the beginning of July 1985 the Israelis had stepped up their involvement to include two Israeli arms dealers, Adolph Schwimmer and Yaacov Nimrodi. Schwimmer had been involved in selling arms to Iran before and was anxious to resume the trade, while Nimrodi simply saw an opportunity to make some money.

It is hardly surprising that all the information being fed to McFarlane and his colleagues on the NSC was in favour of a deal with Iran. Every single individual involved had a hidden agenda which either involved making money, advancing Israel's cause, or both. Yet the NSC continued to take at face value the assurances given them that the Iranians truly did want a new relationship.

In July, Ledeen assured McFarlane on behalf of Schwimmer that if a hundred TOW (Tube launched, Optically tracked, Wire guided, anti-tank missiles) were delivered, all seven American hostages being held in Lebanon would be freed.

According to McFarlane, this plan was related to the President in August 1985 and he gave his approval, provided that the amounts were modest and would not influence the outcome of the war with Iraq. He also agreed that the US would replenish Israel's weaponry stocks. In testimony both Shultz and Weinberger say they opposed the deal, while the White House Chief of Staff, Donald Regan, recalls that the President had not approved the sale.

For his part, Reagan first said he had not approved it and then wrote to the Tower Commission: 'In trying to recall events that happened eighteen months ago I'm afraid that I let myself be influenced by others' recollections, not my own. . . . I have no personal notes or records to help my recollection on this matter. The only answer is to state that try as I might, I cannot recall anything whatsoever about whether I approved an Israeli sale in advance or whether I approved replenishment of Israeli stocks around August of 1985. My answer therefore and the simple truth is, "I don't remember – period." '

McFarlane was certainly under the clear impression that he had presidential authorisation for the deal. If asked, it is likely that the President would have agreed, not simply because building bridges to Iran was desirable but because he had become almost obsessed about the fate of the hostages. One of Reagan's great strengths as President is his concern and understanding for the ordinary American and he had been deeply touched by the letters and appeals for help from the hostages' families. In his rather simple view of the world it was almost incomprehensible that a country as powerful as the United States could not rescue a few Americans being held by a terrorist group.

Among those involved in the planning of this first arms deal there is no doubt that the priority was to build a new relationship with Iran. 'We looked at it in pretty hard-nosed geo-strategic terms,' recalled one person involved. 'The first objective was to pump up the moderates and give them some leverage. If some hostages came out, then that would be a bonus.'

But the goal of better relations with Iran was less immediate than the freeing of hostages and it was the latter aim that came to dominate the affair.

On 30 August 1985 Israel delivered a hundred TOW missiles to Iran as a gesture of good faith. This was followed by a further 408 on 14 September. The following day Benjamin Weir was released by his kidnappers in Lebanon. On the face of it, this was a clear demonstration of Iranian goodwill and helped convince the Americans that the deal would work. They had been assured that further hostages would be released very soon after Weir was freed, but this did not happen.

In fact, the release of Weir had not been as straightforward as it had appeared. The Iranian government had indeed told the terrorists to free him but they had ignored the request, and the Iranians had been obliged to send in a unit of Revolutionary Guards to extract him. It now appeared that Iran had far less influence over the terrorists than had originally been believed.

Also, the terrorists in Lebanon had warned the Iranian government that no more hostages would be released until seventeen of their comrades held in jail in Kuwait were freed as well. In particular, the son-in-law of one Lebanese terrorist leader was in a Kuwaiti jail and it was made clear that the three Americans under his control in Baalbeck would not be freed until the Kuwaitis granted his relation a pardon. Over the next year considerable pressure was put on the Kuwaiti government by individuals in the NSC but the Kuwaitis refused to free the men, who had been responsible for a series of bomb explosions and the attempted assassination of the Kuwaiti ruler.

Despite these complications and Iran's failure to release any more hostages, it was decided that Israel would deliver a shipment of eighty Hawk missiles to Iran in exchange for five US hostages. The missiles would be flown in three aircraft to Tabriz in Iran via Portugal to disguise their origin.

Once again, the arrangements went wrong. The lease on the aircraft arranged by the Israeli arms dealer Al Schwimmer ran out and the missiles were stranded in Lisbon. Ollie North arranged for his old friend Richard Secord, who had been in charge of arms shipments to the Contras in Project Democracy, to get an aircraft to fly one load of missiles into Iran. In the event only eighteen were delivered and no hostages came out.

The missiles that did arrive not only had Israeli markings but were not what the Iranians believed they had ordered. The Iranians wanted I-Hawks, an improved variety with longer range and greater accuracy, while the Israelis had supplied the basic version. 'The trouble was that the people acting as intermediaries did not know a Hawk from a sparrow or an elephant,' said one person involved in planning that shipment.[9]

On 30 November McFarlane resigned as National Security Adviser and was replaced by Vice-Admiral John Poindexter. Continuity in dealings with Iran was provided by Ollie North who now took a more aggressive role. On 4 December, the day Poindexter took over, North proposed the transfer of 3,300 Israeli TOWs and fifty Israeli Hawks in exchange for the release of all the hostages. The idea was discussed with the President, Shultz, Weinberger, Regan and John McMahon from the CIA on 7 December, and rejected. It was agreed that McFarlane would travel to London and meet with Ghorbanifar to tell him the deal was off.

At their meeting, Ghorbanifar told McFarlane he would not transmit the message to Teheran as it would almost certainly result in the deaths of the hostages. Of course, it was not in Ghorbanifar's interests to break off the arms-for-hostages arrangement, which looked like making him substantial sums of money.

Although the deal appeared to be dead, Ghorbanifar, Schwimmer, Nir, Ledeen, Secord and North had a number of meetings over the Christmas period to devise a new scheme. On 2 January, Nir proposed to Poindexter that Israel would release twenty Hizbollah prisoners and sell 3,000 TOWs to Iran in exchange for the release of the Americans held in Lebanon.

But there was concern at the role the Israelis had played so far. They had asked for the stocks of missiles already shipped to Iran to be replaced. The Israelis wanted to pay the value of the TOWs they had sent while the US wanted to charge the full price for the current model. Also, it turned out that the Iranians had paid $3 million more than the price charged by the US Department of Defense. A subsequent investigation by the CIA led them to believe that the money had been stolen.

Despite continued opposition from Shultz and Weinberger, on 17 January, the President signed a Covert Action Finding that allowed the operation to officially continue. It read:

'I hereby find that the following operation in a foreign

country (including all support necessary to such operation) is important to the national security of the United States, and due to its extreme sensitivity and security risks, I determine it is essential to limit prior notice, and direct the Director of Central Intelligence to refrain from reporting this Finding to the Congress as provided in Section 501 of the National Security Act of 1947, as amended, until I otherwise direct.

'Scope: Iran

'Description: Assist selected friendly foreign liaison services, third countries, which have established relationships with Iranian elements, groups, and individuals sympathetic to US government interests and which do not conduct or support terrorist actions directed against US persons, property or interests, for the purpose of: 1. establishing a more moderate government in Iran, and 2. obtaining from them significant intelligence not otherwise obtainable, to determine the current Iranian government's intentions with respect to its neighbours and with respect to terrorist acts, and 3. furthering the release of the American hostages held in Beirut and preventing additional terrorist acts by these groups. Provide funds, intelligence, counter-intelligence, training, guidance and communications, and other necessary assistance to these elements, groups, individuals, liaison services and third countries in support of these activities. The USG will act to facilitate efforts by third parties and third countries to establish contact with moderate elements within and outside the government of Iran by providing these elements with arms, equipment and related materiel in order to enhance the credibility of these elements in their effort to achieve a more pro-US government in Iran by demostrating their ability to obtain requisite resources to defend their country against Iraq and intervention by the Soviet Union. This support will be discontinued if the US government learns that these elements have abandoned their goals of moderating their government and appropriated the materiel for purposes other than that provided by this finding.'

President Reagan told the Tower Commission that

although he did not actually read the paper he did have a grasp of its contents. The finding effectively rewrote America's existing policy on Iran and gave the key players in the deal a free hand, which they swiftly exploited.

In February, two loads of 500 TOW missiles were delivered to Iran by Richard Secord, using aircraft supplied by Southern Air Transport, a former CIA proprietary company. In a clear breach of the agreement, no hostages were released. Under the terms of the Presidential Finding the talks should have been broken off immediately, but in fact further arms shipments were arranged.

Following the abortive McFarlane mission to Teheran in May, there was a temporary hiatus in the deals but they received new impetus on 26 July when Father Lawrence Jenco was released. Further Hawk spare parts were delivered the following month but then in September two other Americans, Frank Reed and Joseph Cicippio, were kidnapped in Lebanon. On 12 October, a third American, Edward Tracey, was also taken hostage. After nearly a year of negotiations and arms deliveries, the US now had more hostages in the hands of terrorists than when the discussions began.

Coincidental with this setback, a relation of the Speaker of Iran's parliament, Hojatoleslam Ali Akbar Hashemi Rafsanjani, contacted Richard Secord's business partner, Albert Hakim, via an intermediary. A series of meetings was held to try to exploit this new channel: these basically reiterated the previous demands for arms and intelligence to help Iran's fight with Iraq.

On 5 October, North, Cave and Secord travelled to Frankfurt to meet with an Iranian delegation. North carried with him a Bible that had been inscribed by President Reagan with a handwritten verse from Galatians 3:8 which read, 'And the scripture, foreseeing that God would justify the Gentiles by faith, preached the gospel beforehand to Abraham, saying: "All the nations shall be blessed in you." '

During the meeting North told the following story to the Iranians: 'We inside our government had an enormous debate, a very angry debate inside our government over whether or not my President should authorise me to say, "We accept the Islamic Revolution of Iran as a fact . . . " He (the President) went off one whole weekend and prayed about what the answer should be and he came back almost a year ago with that passage I gave you that he wrote in front of the Bible I gave you. And he said to me, "This is a promise that God gave to Abraham. Who am I to say that we should not do this?" '

This was a complete travesty of what had actually occurred. The President had signed the Bible with the inscription at the request of Poindexter, who told him it was a favourite quotation of the Iranian official North was planning to meet. North compounded the lie by telling the Iranians that the President had told him he wanted the war with Iraq to end on terms 'acceptable to Iran' and that 'Saddam Hussein must go'.

At a second meeting at the end of October, North agreed a plan with the Iranians that included delivery by the US of 500 TOWs, an unspecified number of Hawks, discussion on the seventeen terrorists held in Kuwait, additional arms including 1,000 more TOWs and the provision of military intelligence – in exchange for which Iran promised to release one or two hostages and use its best efforts to free the rest.

On 29 October, the 500 TOWs were delivered and on 2 November hostage David Jacobson was released. The following day a pro-Syrian magazine in Beirut published details of the negotiations, and on 4 November Rafsanjani publicly announced details of the McFarlane mission to Teheran, which effectively ended any further talk of an arms-for-hostages deal.

From the outset there had been serious doubts that the deal could ever work. There was no clear evidence of a 'moderate' faction inside Iran that could deliver any kind of new relationship with the United States. Suggestions that the Iranian government could actually influence the terrorists holding the US hostages in the Lebanon seem to have originated with

Ghorbanifar and the Israelis, both of whom had their own reasons for advancing that argument: Ghorbanifar wanted to make money and the Israelis wanted to keep Iran fighting Iraq for as long as possible, and to do that the US had to be persuaded to lift its arms embargo. In fact, analysis conducted by both the CIA and the DIA independent of the negotiations suggested that as the terrorists gained power and influence in Lebanon so they were becoming daily more independent of their original sponsors in Teheran. But these analyses were never asked for. Indeed, the need for secrecy was such that none of the normal checks and balances that go into making US foreign policy came into play.

As one Arabist in the State Department, with extensive experience in counter-terrorism, puts it: 'We tried to say "Goddammit, look at the implications", but as we weren't supposed to know what was happening it was impossible to influence things.'[10]

In fact, the policy vacuum was filled largely by Ollie North. With no experience of formulating US foreign policy, he nonetheless attempted to forge a new relationship with Iran which would have had profound implications for US policy in the Middle East and for its counter-terrorist policy worldwide.

North, too, had a hidden agenda in the shape of his commitment to the Contras. In connection with his Project Democracy, North, with the help of like-minded people such as Richard Secord and General John Singlaub, was raising funds for the Contras that were then channelled through Switzerland to Honduras and Costa Rica.

The cash paid by Iran for the arms was around $23 million in excess of the value of the weapons delivered. $20 million of that had been directly controlled by the United States and was put into Swiss bank accounts controlled by Richard Secord's company, Lake Resources. The cash went into the same accounts that were used to send money to the Contras.

In February 1987 Secord was telling friends that no money had been transferred to the Contras, but by April he was saying that it was possible some money had reached them.

In June, Secord's business partner Albert Hakim, told a Congressional committee that Secord had used some of the money to buy himself a Porsche car. Certainly, there remains a substantial discrepancy in the accounts. Part of this may be accounted for by the dealings of middlemen. Documents which include copies of bank statements and cancelled cheques held by this author show that in August and September 1985 Ghorbanifar paid $4 million to Adnan Khashoggi and then from February to April 1986 a further $12 million passed through Khashoggi's accounts. Given that the Israelis would have taken a substantial commission on the deal, it is possible that the missing money simply ended up lining the pockets of those who were involved in brokering the sales.

Although a transfer of funds to the Contras would very probably have been illegal, the Iran affair was more important than simple financial duplicity.

There is no doubt that the United States government was the victim of a substantial confidence trick by a wide range of people, including Israelis, arms dealers and members of the Iranian government. For different reasons, all were interested in getting the US to relax its arms embargo with Iran and succeeded in doing so. In direct contradiction of its stated position as an independent broker of US government policy, the NSC and in particular the National Security Adviser and his immediate aides, formulated government policy without any reference either to Congress or to those experts in the State Department and the intelligence community who were available to offer informed advice.

The result was an amateurish shambles that undermined the position of the United States in the Middle East and called into question its whole counter-terrorist policy.

Responsibility for the affair must ultimately lie with the President. His grasp of day-to-day events was fragmentary at best and he showed no clear understanding of the implications of what he was authorising. As President, his style had been in marked contrast to that of his predecessor, President

Carter, who had an obsession with detail. Reagan preferred to deal in generalities and leave his staff to get on with the nuts and bolts of policy execution. This was an effective leadership style but it proved fatally flawed on this occasion.

Clearly the President allowed himself to be overly influenced by the fate of the hostages. Opening up new channels to the Iranian government was sensible foreign policy, but the President's concern for the fate of the hostages was well known to all his staff and came to be the primary motive for talking with the Iranians. The President made a distinction between dealing with terrorists and dealing with those who had influence with terrorists. But this subtle distinction had previously eluded the State Department, the CIA, the DIA and the White House itself, all of whom had repeatedly stated that Iran was a sponsor of terrorism.

It is too early to judge the extent of the damage to the United States resulting from the Iran affair. Fears of a collapse of America's Middle East policy appear to be ill-founded. Although its lost neutrality in the Iran-Iraq war and its involvement with Israel, a country that is hated and feared by all America's allies in the Gulf, must have raised problems, the Arabs appear to have taken a pragmatic view of the whole matter. Apart from some mild protests from Jordan and Saudi Arabia there have been no serious diplomatic difficulties. Possibly the Arab nations recognise that what went on was an aberration and not official US policy.

For Iran and their terrorist allies matters are less clear. If there ever were any moderates in the Iranian government they will now be forced to wait until Khomeini's death before any overt lines are opened to Washington. In theory, this unlocks the door for the Soviets, but in practice it is highly unlikely that Moscow will find it any easier to deal with a new government in Teheran than will Washington.

The terrorists in the Lebanon were quite specifically told by the Archbishop of Canterbury's representative, Terry Waite, acting on behalf of North, that their Kuwaiti comrades would be released from jail. This has not happened and it is probable that Waite's kidnapping in Lebanon in January 1987 was a direct result of his independence being compromised by his dealings with North.

Any possibility of influencing Hizbollah has vanished. Indeed, after an unprecendented effort throughout 1986 and 1987, the US intelligence community still knows very little about the organisation. They have no idea of their numbers, bases or structure and no indication who is holding any of the terrorists or where.

There was hard intelligence in February 1987 that some of the American hostages were going to be executed by their captors. Only a clear warning that if just one hostage died American aircraft would bomb specific targets in Lebanon in a re-run of Operation El Dorado Canyon in Libya the previous year prevented this. But the hostages represent power to the terrorists, and to remain credible they will have to demonstrate their willingness to kill. Because the Iran negotiations were so badly handled more American lives will surely be lost and the United States will have only one option: to retaliate with ever larger measures of destabilising military force.

25

Conclusion

Low intensity conflict, whether guerrilla warfare, counter-insurgency or terrorism, is here to stay. Of the forty-three wars taking place around the world today only that between Iran and Iraq could be described as conventional. The balance, while in some cases as costly in cash and human suffering, are less easy to define and present a new challenge to the political and military leaders of the world.

Since World War II, the prospect of a major conventional confrontation between the superpowers has steadily diminished as the possibility of a nuclear holocaust has ensured that both sides have kept their distance in case a small war between them should rapidly become a conflict that both recognise would mean the end of the world as we know it today.

Although a conventional war may be the least likely eventuality, it is essential that both west and east maintain their substantial regular forces. Without them there would be no steps to climb up the escalatory ladder to nuclear war. Any reduction in the conventional force levels, unless matched by both sides, would upset the delicate balance between west and east and make war not less but more likely. The fact that deterrence has worked is sufficient reason to keep those forces in place.

But if the conventional status quo has remained largely unchanged, almost every other level of combat has altered dramatically over the past thirty years.

Since the defeat of Hitler's Germany, both west and east have battled for control and influence of countries around the world. This battle for territory has been spurred on by the rapid disintegration of the old colonial empires of Britain, France, Holland and Belgium which has given dozens of countries independence. That freedom was often won through revolution or a protracted guerrilla war. In Algeria, Malaya, and Aden for example, the colonial country engaged in protracted and rarely successful defence of the existing order before handing over the reins of power. Clear lessons were learned from those early campaigns:

Guerrilla warfare has as its aim the overthrow of an existing order and this is achieved by creating a military and political environment where it becomes impossible for the government to function effectively. In the early stages of an unconventional war, the guerrillas will operate in small units, living off the land and depending on the local people both for support and intelligence. The co-operation of the local people is gained in the first instance either through propaganda or intimidation.

If the government under attack can be provoked into responding with conventional means, the guerrillas are assured of victory. The massive use of ordinary firepower, mass bombings by aircraft, search and destroy missions or the widespread use of denial munitions such as napalm and defoliants, simply support the guerrillas' case that the government is oppressive. Recruits rush to join the guerrilla forces which begin to take on the shape and numbers of a more conventional force. However, while the government continues to seek a conventional solution to the conflict, the guerrilla will dictate the time and place of any confrontation and will retain the initiative.

Eventually, after a process that may take many years, the guerrillas will emerge into the open and pose a direct threat to the government. The people, who over the years have seen the guerrillas make steady gains against the government forces, are now more likely to support the revolutionaries, who have always won victories, rather than the government, which has been steadily defeated.

The course of such wars has been seen time and again in the past thirty years and lessons can be drawn from the occasions where the guerrillas have been defeated and where they have triumphed. Malaya is often seen as the classic counter-insurgency campaign. The communist guerrillas, who wished to overthrow the existing government, had built up a comprehensive network of villages and provinces where they could rely on receiving food, medical supplies and, where necessary, sanctuary.

At that time, Malaya was a British colony and the government committed troops to the country to fight the guerrillas. The war that was fought was largely dictated by the SAS and not by the conventional forces, who were there in a supporting role. Developing what became known as the Oil Spot theory, the SAS operated in small units deep in the jungle to encourage the local people to look after their own community. These local people were armed and trained by the British and, once one area was secured, so the message was spread in ever widening circles to the next village and the next.

The communist guerrillas were rapidly denied their traditional sanctuaries and sources of supply. With the local people well-armed and prepared to defend their territory, the movements of the guerrillas became increasingly difficult, and eventually they were driven to operate in ever smaller areas where killing or capturing them was a relatively simple job.

From this campaign, a number of points can be made that hold good for any counter-insurgency war.

The guerrilla can afford to fight a long war. He is invariably highly committed and is fighting for a cause. The defending forces, on the other hand, rarely feel similar enthusiasm. This commitment ensures that the guerrilla takes a long time to defeat (the Malaya campaign lasted ten years and the war in Oman six). That means there are no easy victories and no quick answers.

Although the guerrilla invariably receives some support

from outside the country where he operates, his survival depends on the local people. If they can be convinced that the guerrilla is fighting a lost cause, then support for him will swiftly dry up. But that conviction can only come from the government demonstrating a clear and consistent political will to defeat him and by giving responsibility to the local people to defend themselves.

The guerrilla's strength is his mobility and flexibility, while the potential weakness of the government is its over-dependence on conventional weapons. It is always the case that the government forces possess more modern and powerful weapons than the guerrillas. But to be effective, they must be properly used, and many of the weapons in a nation's armoury are anyway totally unsuited to a counter-guerrilla war.

The guerrilla will portray the government as the enemy of the people and as an aggressive and oppressive power. If the government responds to the guerrilla threat by using the massive conventional power at its disposal, the guerrilla's propaganda will appear to be confirmed. If deployed conventionally, government forces invariably overreact to the threat and innocent civilian lives are lost, crops destroyed and villages levelled. This pushes the local people to join the growing guerrilla army.

Both east and west have had to deal with guerrilla warfare on two levels: as sponsors and as defenders of existing governments. In the struggle for influence and power, both the United States and the Soviet Union have practised widespread destabilisation of foreign countries. Guerrilla warfare is cheap and effective and has the added advantage of avoiding any direct involvement. But both countries still have lessons to learn in the conduct of such warfare.

The Soviets have trained and supported a large number of guerrilla armies, from South Yemen to Zimbabwe, Mozambique and Nicaragua. The training they supply seems to be effective and they are liberal with both cash and arms. A number of successful coups, revolutions and guerrilla campaigns would not have been as successful without Soviet support.

The United States, on the other hand, has been less successful. The Ukraine, Albania, Tibet and Laos (among others) are testimony to a failed strategy. The reasons for that failure are twofold. There has been a consistent lack of understanding of the nature of unconventional warfare and, because political support has always been uncertain, there has been a lack of a coherent policy. This in turn has led to a search for quick answers in campaigns that require long term commitment.

Curiously, both superpowers seem to have made exactly the same mistakes when defending their allies from a guerrilla threat. Whether it is the Soviets in Angola backing the government in its fight against the CIA-backed UNITA guerrillas, or the Americans backing the El Salvador government against communist guerrillas, the response has been identical. Both have supplied huge quantities of bigger and better arms in the apparent belief that weapons alone will solve the problem.

But again it is the Soviets who are learning more quickly. The commitment of their forces in Afghanistan to fighting a classic guerrilla war has given them the practical experience they had previously been lacking. Immediately after their invasion, they introduced troops designed to fight a conventional war. Their tanks and armoured personnel carriers moved around the country in large convoys that were easy targets for the guerrillas. The opportunity to meet the mujahedeen in battle was rare as the approach of the Soviet forces was so slow that the guerrillas were long gone before they arrived at the planned battleground. The introduction of Soviet special forces or spetsnaz has dramatically changed the course of the Afghani war. Combined unconventional tactics, including the extensive use of helicopters for rapid deployment, have proved very successful. Western intelligence believes that those tactics are already being adapted for their forces in Europe. It also seems likely that the Soviets will pass on the benefit of their experience to the governments they support in the Third World.

Unfortunately, the United States has failed to learn from the conflicts where US forces have been directly involved. In Korea and in Vietnam special forces were either not used or used incorrectly. In Vietnam, which was essentially an unconventional war, the military insisted on fighting a conventional war, which inevitably led to victory for the Vietcong.

From the evidence of recent years, the same mistakes will be repeated for the foreseeable future. In the attempted hostage rescue mission in Iran, the invasion of Grenada and the current conflict in Central America, the US military still demonstrates a lack of understanding of the nature of modern warfare. In Iran, special forces were used for a plan that grew in complexity as ever greater numbers of individual services became involved, not for sound military reasons but to give each part of the bureaucracy a slice of the pie. A reluctance to train and equip special forces also ensured that the right men and machinery were not available on the day. In Grenada and Central America the confrontations have been characterised by the overwhelming application of force in an environment that required subtlety and a far greater understanding of the type of war being fought.

Terrorism is at the lowest end of the conflict spectrum and there too the west has been found wanting. Each country has responded to the terrorist threat with new laws and a more powerful police force. The common factor uniting the west has been the establishment of special forces designed specifically to combat the terrorist threat. On occasion these have worked spectacularly well; Mogadishu and the Iranian embassy seige, for example. But at other times, in Karachi or the Malta hijack, there has been heavy loss of life among hostages.

Special forces are an essential part of the counter-terrorist effort, but they are only as good as the intelligence and training they receive. There has been a lamentable lack of intelligence-sharing in the past. However, as terrorism has affected more countries, so the situation has improved. Today, relations between the Europeans and the United States are generally very good and co-operation is at a consistently high level. Israel has been less forthcoming, both because of a reduced capability and in response to a growing feeling among western intelligence officers that she cannot be trusted. Much work still needs to be done, and as long as each nation follows its own path in countering terrorism, so the initiative will remain with the terrorist. New policies need to be designed that take the fight to the terrorist, that make counter-terrorism pro-active instead of reactive as it is today.

It is special forces that provide the essential reactive element in countering terrorism. Their role is certain to grow over the next few years as terrorism continues to expand. All the more important, then, that government confidence in the need for special forces grows and that they continue to receive the political support they need.

In Europe, there has been no shortage of political support, and groups like the SAS, GSG9 and the GIGN are well trained and armed. In the United States, the special forces have not been so fortunate. During the Kennedy years there was a resurgence of interest in special forces in order to meet what the President saw as the threat of Soviet subversion around the world. After his assassination, the special forces fell out of favour.

President Reagan, however, has authorised the biggest expansion of special operations forces in America's history and has increased spending from $400 million a year to $1.5 billion. Even so, money alone has not proved enough. While the service chiefs continue to pay lip service to low intensity conflict by establishing numerous study centres and new commands, they continue to resist any attempt to give the SOF the resources they need.

US special operations forces still lack a clear doctrine, they have glaring gaps in their equipment, and their training is inadequate for the roles they are supposed to play. Congress has tried to improve matters by ordering comprehensive changes but these too the military have resisted.

This continued obsessive commitment to a conventional war on the Central Front will, in the long term, do immense damage to the interests of the United States and her allies. There is clear evidence that the Soviets are showing a greater understanding of unconventional war. The United States, as the leader of the free world, has the task of opposing communist expansion and trying to sustain democracies where they exist, but if the US response to the unconventional threat continues to be one that was designed for a conventional war in Europe, the Soviets will be able to build on the successes they have already achieved.

Greater and more consistent political leadership is needed from the United States government to force change upon the military. Plans to bring the SOF under one command and under the political control of a new Assistant Secretary for Special Operations and Low Intensity Conflict must be right. It must also be sensible to take the budget for SOF away from each individual service and place it in a central fund. But, until the military structure is reformed, the US commanders will, like the guerrillas, play a waiting game. They know that administrations change and with them the priority given to SOF. So a programme of positive discrimination should be introduced without delay to bring officers with SOF experience into the highest levels of command, including the Joint Chiefs of Staff. Only then will the bias in favour of conventional warfare be corrected.

The Soviets recognised long ago that low intensity conflict is just the opening move in a potentially much bigger game. If World War III should ever occur, the role of special forces will be critical. The Soviets have always invested in special forces and currently have around 25,000 available. In time of tension or at the outbreak of war, these forces would be sent to the United States and Europe to wage a campaign of sabotage, assassination and psychological warfare. Western intelligence believes that campaign will play a key part in undermining the will of the west to prosecute the war, and may even cripple our nuclear capability before war has officially begun. It is an alarming prospect but one that is made serious by the view widely held in the US military that unconventional warfare is an irrelevance to the bigger conflict.

As has been seen in Vietnam, Laos and countless other conflicts of recent times, the ability to fight and win a low intensity conflict can decide the fate of millions. In the endless struggle between communism and democracy, it is unconventional warfare that is the key. Who fights best will win. Today the west, led by the United States, is on the defensive.

Notes

CHAPTER 1

1. *Ann Arbor News*, 27.10.86 and 'The World at War – 1987', *The Defense Monitor*, the Center for Defense Information, Washington DC, 1983. The Center does an annual survey of small wars around the world which is considered definitive on the subject.
2. Maurice Tugwell and David Charters, 'Special Operations and the Threats to United States Interests in the 1980s', in Frank R. Barnett, (ed.) *Special Operations in US Strategy*, National Defense University Press, Washington, 1984, p.37.
3. Steven E. Daskal, 'The Insurgency Threat and Ways to Defeat It', *Military Review*, January 1986, pp. 28–41. Similar points are made in a particularly prescient article by Donald B. Vought entitled 'Preparing for the Wrong War' in *Military Review*, May 1977.
4. No single definition of a terrorist has been agreed between western nations so all such figures are open to different interpretations. Others will suggest that terrorism is actually increasing at around 15% per annum rather than the 5% I suggest. All are agreed that the numbers are increasing and the acts are getting more violent.
5. Information supplied to the author April 1987.
6. *US Army operational concept for low intensity conflict*, TRADOC pamphlet No. 525–44, Department of the Army, Fort Monroe, VA 23651–5000, 10 February 1986, p.2.
7. Keynote address by John O. Marsh in *Special Operations in US Strategy*, op. cit., p.24.
8. George Shultz, 'Low Intensity Warfare: The Challenge of Ambiguity' in *Proceedings of the Low Intensity Warfare Conference*, 14–15 January 1986, Department of Defense, Washington DC, pp. 9–12.

CHAPTER 2

1. Quoted by Slavko N. Bjelajac, 'Soviet Unconventional Warfare Capabilities', *Military Review*, November 1959, pp.30–37.
2. Richard Simpkin, *Deep Battle*, Brasseys Defence Publishers, London, 1987.
3. John J. Dziak, 'The Soviety Approach to Special Operations' in

Special Operations in US Strategy, edited by Frank Barnett, National Defense University Press, Washington DC, 1984, p.101.
4. Pospolev et.al. *The Great Patriotic War of the Soviet Union, 1941–45*, Progress Publishers, Moscow, 1974, p.459. Quoted in John Dziak op. cit., p.103.

CHAPTER 3

1. Unless otherwise stated, information on special forces activity in World War II comes from: John Strawson, *The SAS Regiment*, Secker and Warburg, London, 1984; William Seymour, *British Special Forces*, Sidgwick and Jackson, London, 1985; Philip Warner, *The Secret Forces of World War II*, Granada, London, 1985; Aaron Bank, *From OSS to Green Berets*, Presidio Press, Novato, 1986; Alfred Paddock, *US Army Special Warfare*, National Defense University, Washington DC, 1982; Barrie Pitt, *The Special Boat Squadron*, Century, London, 1983. The best account of the SAS remains Tony Geraghty's *Who Dares Wins*, Arms and Armour Press, London, 1980.
2. Quoted in Strawson, *A History of the SAS Regiment*, op.cit., pp.247–248.
3. Bradley F. Smith, *The Shadow Warriors*, Andrew Deutsch, London, 1983, pp.86–87.

CHAPTER 4

1. John Ranelagh, *The Agency, The Rise and Decline of the CIA*, Simon and Schuster, New York, 1986, pp.45–46.
2. Aaron Bank, *From OSS to Green Berets*, Presidio, Novato, 1986, p.15.

CHAPTER 5

1. Quoted in John Prados, *The President's Secret Wars*, op.cit., p.22.
2. John Ranelagh, *The Agency*, op.cit., p.130.
3. Alfred Paddock, *US Army Special Warfare*, op.cit., p.73.

CHAPTER 6

1. Aaron Bank, *From OSS to Green Berets*, op.cit., p.151.
2. ibid., p.163.
3. Roger Hilsman, 'Two American Counterstrategies to Guerrilla Warfare: The case of Vietnam' in Tsang Tsou (ed.) *China in Crisis*, Vol.2, University of Chicago Press, Chicago, 1965, pp.289–309. Charles M. Simpson III, *Inside the Green Berets*, Berkley Books, New York, 1984.

CHAPTER 7

1. Harry Summers, *On Strategy*, Dell Publishing, New York, 1984, p.21.
2. Aside from works cited in the bibliography, a number of particularly thoughtful articles have addressed the way the war was fought in

Vietnam, among them: Guenther Lewy, 'Some Political-Military Lessons of the Vietnam War', *Parameters*, Spring 1984, pp.2–14; George C. Herring, 'American Strategy in Vietnam: The Postwar Debate', *Military Affairs*, April 1982, pp.57–63; George K. Tanham and Dennis J. Duncanson, 'Some Dilemmas of Counterinsurgency', *Foreign Affairs*, October 1969, pp.113–122; Peter Dunn, 'The American Army: The Vietnam War, 1965–1973', in *Armed Forces and Modern Counter-Insurgency*, Ian Beckett, John Pimlott (eds.) Croom Helm, London; 1985, pp.77–111.

3. Andrew F. Krepinevich, Jr., *The Army and Vietnam*, Johns Hopkins University Press, Boston, 1986. This book is particularly critical of the failure of the US military in Vietnam.

4. *Special Forces Handbook*, Headquarters, Department of the Army, January, 1965, p.II–1.

5. Simpson, *Inside the Green Berets*, op.cit., p.173.

6. Krepinevich, op.cit., p.84.

7. Roger Hilsman, 'Two American Counterstrategies to Guerrilla Warfare', op.cit., p.299.

8. Guenther Lewy, *America in Vietnam*, Oxford University Press, New York, 1978, p.38.

9. Patrick McGarvey, *Visions of Victory: Selected Vietnamese Military Writings, 1964–1968*, Hoover Institutuion Press, Stanford, 1969, p.43.

10. Sir Robert Thompson, 'Squaring the Error', *Foreign Affairs*, April 1968, pp.442–453.

11. An excellent account of the Son Tay raid appears in Benjamin Schemmer, *The Raid*, Harper and Row, New York, 1976. Other accounts are in Richard Gabriel, *Military Incompetence*, Hill and Wang, New York, 1985; Peter Kelly, 'Raid and National Command: Mutually Exclusive', *Military Review*, April 1980, pp.20–26; John Prados, *The President's Secret Wars*, op.cit., pp.304–305.

CHAPTER 8

1. Quoted in Harriet Scott and William Scott, *The Armed Forces of the USSR*, Westview Press, Boulder, Colorado, 1979, p.57.

2. Details of this period come from Frantisek August and David Rees, *Red Star Over Prague*, The Sherwood Press, London, 1984; Aleksei Myagkov, 'Soviet Sabotage Training for World War III', *Soviet Analyst*, 20 December 1979, pp. 2–6; John Dziak, *The Soviet Approach to Special Operations*, op.cit.; Jiri Valenta, 'From Prague to Kabul', *International Security*, Fall 1980, pp.114–141; Zdenek Mlynar, *Nightfrost in Prague*, Karz Publishers, New York, 1980; and interviews with intelligence sources in London and Washington, 1986.

CHAPTER 9

1. A great deal of confusion surrounds terrorist statistics. The ones I have cited come from the US State Department and a statistical database prepared by Clandestine Tactics and Technology, a US company specialising in terrorism. There is no common definition of terrorism and therefore no agreed way of preparing the statistics. However, what is agreed is that terrorism is increasing at between 5 and 15 per cent per annum and that acts are getting much more violent.

CHAPTER 10

1. The best account of the Munich massacre as well as of GSG9 is by Rolf Tophoven in *GSG9, German Response to Terrorism*, Bernard and Graefe Verlag, Bonn, 1984. Also, George Rosie has produced an excellent source work in his *Dictionary of International Terrorism*, Mainstream Publishing, Edinburgh, 1986.
2. Details of the Egyptair hijacking come from the following sources: unpublished files written by *Sunday Times* journalists working on the story at the time; numerous press accounts; *Time*, 9 December 1985, pp. 42–45; *Newsweek*, 9 December 1985, pp.36–39; *Counter-Terrorism and Security*, Fall 1986, pp.16–26; intelligence sources.
3. Information supplied to the author March 1987.

CHAPTER 11

1. Beckwith has written (with Donald Knox) a detailed account of his time in special forces in a book entitled *Delta Force* (Harcourt Brace Jovanovich, New York, 1983). This is the most comprehensive account currently available on the formation of Delta Force. However, all those special forces personnel spoken to by the author question, in broad terms, many of the facts and conclusions drawn by Beckwith. Specific criticisms, however, are hard to come by and it may be that Beckwith is simply the victim of the petty feuds and jealousies that seem to afflict the armed services.
2. Beckwith, *Delta Force*, op.cit., p.20.
3. ibid., pp.36–37.
4. ibid., p.123.
5. ibid., p.143.
6. *Defence Systems Review*, undated, pp.31–37. Other details on parachutes come from *Special Forces Journal*, undated, pp.26–28 and special forces sources.

CHAPTER 12

1. Information for this chapter comes from the following sources: Beckwith, *Delta Force*, op.cit.; Brzezinski, Zbigniew, *Power and Principle: Memoirs of the National Security Adviser, 1977–1981*, Farrar, Straus and

Giroux, New York, 1983; Carter, Jimmy, *Keeping Faith*, Bantam Books, New York, 1982; Hadley, Arthur T., *The Straw Giant*, Random House, New York, 1986; Gabriel, *Military Incompetence*, op.cit.; Logan Fitch, 'Death at Desert One', *Penthouse*, undated, pp.67–69, 166–173; numerous press accounts of the time; *Rescue Mission Report* by Admiral James L. Holloway III, August, 1980; and interviews with special forces personnel.

2. Beckwith, *Delta Force*, p.8.
3. Interview, April 1987.
4. *Penthouse*, op.cit., p.170.
5. Beckwith, *Delta Force*, op.cit., p.290.
6. ibid., p.295.
7. The Holloway Report, op.cit., pp.61–62.

CHAPTER 13

1. Details of the invasion come from *Time* Magazine, 22 November 1982, pp.25–26; Jiri Valenta, 'From Prague to Kabul', *International Security*, Fall, 1980, pp.114–141; Major Joseph J. Collins, *The Soviet-Afghan War*, unpublished manuscript of United States Military Academy, undated; John Dziak, *The Soviet Approach to Special Operations*, op.cit.; and intelligence sources in the US and Britain.
2. This was reported in the *Newsweek* article which was allegedly written by a Soviet defector, Vladimir Kuzichkin, a former KGB major. Much of what he says is confirmed by other, more independent, intelligence sources but other information seems likely to have been deliberately inserted into the article by western intelligence. For example, the idea that the Soviet soldiers, particularly spetsnaz, would shoot their own commanding officer seems unlikely. Instead of going outside to verbally summon reinforcement he would call them up on his radio. Also, the article tends to support the idea that Afghanistan will be the Soviet Union's Vietnam, a popular propaganda line but one that is not generally supported by serious analysts.
3. Thomas T. Hammond, *Red Flag Over Afghanistan*, Westview Press, Boulder Colorado, 1984, p.100.
4. Collins, *The Soviet-Afghan War*, op.cit., p.4; Hammond, *Red Flag over Afghanistan*, op.cit., p.74.
5. Jay Peterzell, *Reagan's Secret Wars*, Center for National Security Studies, Washington DC, 1984, pp.11–12.
6. Conversations with intelligence sources in the US and Britain suggest this very high figure which sources in Pakistan tend to confirm.

CHAPTER 14

1. This story has been repeated to the author by both US and Pakistani officials but it has been impossible to verify independently. Certainly,

the Soviets were active in Baluchistan prior to the invasion. (The Soviets published a photograph of soldiers being taught languages, and that language was Baluch.) But, the Pakistanis have always been anxious to play up Soviet involvement with the Baluch to persuade the US to give them more aid.

2. *Afghanistan: Six Years of Occupation*, The US State Department, Washington DC, 1985, p.14.

3. Told to the author by a member of the group concerned, April 1986.

4. *Soldier of Fortune*, June 1985, pp.59–86.

5. *Jane's Defence Weekly*, 31 March 1984, p.483.

6. *International Herald Tribune*, 6 April 1987, p.4.

7. Claude Malhuret, 'Report from Afghanistan', *Foreign Affairs*, undated, pp.426–435.

8. *Air Force Magazine*, March 1982, pp.38–42; Collins, *The Soviet-Afghan War*, op.cit., p.19; State Department sources.

9. Unless otherwise specified, details on spetsnaz in Afghanistan comes primarily from intelligence sources in Europe and the United States in briefings given in 1986.

10. As told to the late Italian journalist Almerigo Grilz during a three month stay in Afghanistan which ended in December 1986.

11. *Los Angeles Times*, 24 May 1986.

12. The *Washington Post*, 5 October 1985; *New York Times*, 11 October 1985; *Free Afghanistan Report*, Number 9, December 1985; *Washington Times*, 2 December 1985; intelligence sources.

13. Information supplied to the author by a US doctor who spent two years in the area, returning to America in late 1986.

14. The *Sunday Times*, 3 November 1985; intelligence sources.

15. This comes from a translation of an article entitled 'A Creative Approach to Tactics' by Army General Mikhail Zaitsev, 6 March 1982.

16. This appeared in an intelligence paper on Zaitsev given to the author in 1985. The quote comes from the writings of army general I. M. Tretyak who used to command Zaitsev. The reference is not dated.

17. Conversation with the author, April 1986.

18. Translation of an article entitled 'Once and Always' by Captain S. Dyshev in *SV*, November 1985, p.7.

CHAPTER 15

1. Quoted in William R Bode, 'The Reagan Doctrine', *Strategic Review*, Winter 1986, pp.21–29.

2. John Strawson, *The SAS Regiment*, op.cit., p.221. An excellent account of this affair comes in a book by the *Sunday Times* Insight team, *Seige!*, Hamlyn Paperbacks, London, 1980. Additional material comes from Tony Geraghty, *Who Dares Wins*, op.cit., pp.177–181 and SAS sources.

3. To the author March 1987.

CHAPTER 16

1. Reports on the attempted coup come from contemporary press reports of the time. The SAS involvement has been described to the author by individuals familiar with the operation.

CHAPTER 17

1. Max Hastings and Simon Jenkins, *The Battle for the Falklands*, Michael Joseph, London, 1983, p.85.
2. Nick Vaux, *March to the South Atlantic*, Buchan and Enright, London, 1986.
3. Quoted in Strawson, *The SAS Regiment*, op.cit., p.230.
4. Supplement to the *London Gazette*, 8 October 1982, p.12847.
5. The mission on the mainland was first reported by John Witherow in *The Times*, 3 July 1982; further details come from Rodney A. Burden et.al. *Falklands: The Air War*, Arms and Armour Press, London, 1986; and from those involved with the mission.
6. Hastings and Jenkins, *The Battle for the Falklands*, op.cit., p.265.
7. Quoted in Strawson, *The SAS Regiment*, op.cit., p.234.
8. In an interview February 1987.

CHAPTER 18

1. Colonel A. Tsvetkov, *Zarubezhnoye Voyennoye Obozreniye*, Moscow, 8 June 1982, pp.9–14.
2. An excellent exposition of the tactical problems generated by the OMG and Airland Battle can be found in Richard Simpkin, *Race to the Swift*, Brassey's Defence Publishers, London, 1985.
3. Fred C. Ikle, a speech to the Inland Empire of Southern California, World Affairs Council, 30 January 1986.
4. Robert Kupperman Associates Inc., *Low Intensity Conflict*, Volume 1, prepared for the US Army Training and Doctrine Command, 30 July 1983, p.2.
5. The *Guardian*, 10 June 1982; *New York Times* 21 August 1982; Department of Defense Appropriations, hearings before a subcommittee on Appropriations of the House of Representatives, US government Printing Office, Washington DC, 1987, No. 60–489 0, p.562. The hearings include a detailed look at the recent history of US special forces.
6. Information supplied under the FOIA by the Department of the Air Force, 12 October 1983.
7. Ashley Brown (ed.) *The Green Berets, US Special Forces*, Orbis Publishing, London, 1986, p.91.
8. The JSOC mission statement was released under the Freedom of Information Act in May 1983.
9. Joint Chiefs of Staff, *Military Posture for FY 1983*, US Government Printing Office, Washington DC, 1982, p.99.

10. *Washington Post*, 23 August 1983; information supplied to the author November 1986.

11. *Los Angeles Times*, 15 May 1983; *New York Times*, 11 May 1983; other information on ISA comes from conversations the author had with intelligence, Pentagon and special forces personnel in July, September, October and November 1986.

12. Department of Defense Appropriations 1987 hearings, op cit., p.633–634.

13. The best account of Gritz's mission comes from the *Boston Globe*, 7 July 1981.

14. Related to the author on 31 October 1986.

15. Reports on the investigations appeared in *Washington Post*, 20 November 1985, 21 November 1985, 26 November 1985, 29 November 1985, 30 November 1985, 26 January 1986, 18 November 1986; *Detroit News*, 30 November 1985; *Newsweek*, 16 November 1985, p.28; *Washington Post*, 20 November 1984; *Los Angeles Times*, 19 October 1984. Other information from interviews conducted by the author with Pentagon, DIA and State Department officials in 1985 and 1986.

16. Interview on 28 July 1986.

17. ibid.

18. Information comes from interviews conducted with participants in November 1986, February and March 1987.

CHAPTER 19

1. Department of Defense Appropriations 1987, hearings before the committee of appropriations of the House of Representatives, US Government Printing Office, 1986, No. 59–248 0, pp.161–163.

2. Department of State, *The Soviet-Cuban Connection in Central America and the Caribbean*, published by the Department of State and the Department of Defense in March 1985, Washington DC, pp.11–17.

3. *International Herald Tribune*, 1 March 1983.

4. Text of the Full Committee Hearing of the House of Representatives Armed Services Committee on the *Lessons Learned as a Result of the US Military Operations in Grenada*, US Government Printing Office, Washington DC, 1984, pp.10–11.

5. ibid.

6. Much of the information in this chapter comes from interviews with those who took part in Operation Urgent Fury or with those who were privy to the after-action reports. Understandably, none of those interviewed wishes to be mentioned by name and, indeed, none of the people mentioned in the text should be seen as sources for this chapter.

7. In conversation with the author, November 1986.

8. *Lessons Learned as a Result of the US Military Operations in Grenada*, op.cit., p.12.

9. Interview March 1987.

10. These and other details of the operation come from interviews conducted by the author with personnel who took part in Urgent Fury. The interviews were conducted in 1985 and 1986 in Washington and London.

11. Testimony to the House of Representatives, 25 February 1986.

12. The most detailed account so far on special forces operations on Grenada can be found in Richard Gabriel's *Military Incompetence*, Hill and Wang, New York, 1985, pp.149–186.

13. Major Scott R. McMichael, 'Urgent Fury: Looking Back and Looking Forward', *Field Artillery Journal*, March-April, pp.8–13.

14. *Washington Post*, 20 February 1986.

15. Michael Duffy, 'Grenada: Rampant Confusion', *Military Logistics Forum*, July/August 1985, pp.20–28.

16. *Gung Ho*, October 84, pp.74–79.

17. Michael Duffy, 'Grenada', op.cit., p.23.

18. Marine Corps documents quoted in the Providence *Sunday Journal*, 26 October 1986.

19. A comment made to the author in November 1986.

20. Interview April 1987

CHAPTER 20

1. *Adequacy of US Marine Corps Security in Beirut*, Report of the Investigations Subcommittee, Committee on Armed Services, House of Representatives, No. 28–647 0, US Government Printing Office, Washington DC, 19 December 1983, p.11.

2. Michael Petit, *Peacekeepers at War*, Faber and Faber, London, 1986, pp.3–6.

3. Report of the Department of Defense Commission on Beirut International Airport Terrorist Act, 23 October 1983, released in typescript on 23 December 1983.

4. ibid., p.60.

5. *National Journal*, 25 October 1986, p.2567.

6. The Long Commission, op.cit. p.68.

7. *Washington Post*, 5 December 1986.

8. Interview in July 1986.

9. Statement by Major-General Wesley Rice, before the Subcommittee of the Committee on Appropriations, 10 April 1984, US Government Printing Office, Washington DC, 1984, No.35–272 0, p.799

10. Department of Defense Appropriations for 1987, Hearings before the Defense Subcommittee on the Committee of Appropriations, House of Representatives, US Government Printing Office, Washington DC, No.60–489 0, March 12, 1986, pp.623–624.

11. *Defense Week*, 2 April 1984, p.12.

12. Statement by Noel Koch, Principal Deputy Assistant Secretary of Defense (International Security Affairs) before the Subcommittee on Defense, Committee of Appropriations, House of Representatives, 10 April 1984.

13. Interview with House official July 1986. He was quoting the original remark made by a critic of Initiative 17 in the *Armed Forces Journal*.

14. In an interview in July 1986.

15. *Military Logistics Forum*, April 1986, p.41.

16. Interview in January 1987.

17. *Defense Week*, 10 February 1986, pp.1,20.

18. *New York Times*, 23 December 1984; *New York News*, 1 August 1984.

19. Quoted in *Military Logistics Forum*, April 1986, p.41.

20. Statement to the Special Operations Panel, Subcommittee on Readiness, House of Representatives, 6 September 1984.

21. Information on the hijacking comes from numerous press accounts at the time and counter-terrorist sources involved in planning the rescue of the hostages.

22. Details on the hijack comes from the *Observer* and the *Sunday Times*, 13 October 1985; the *Washington Post*, 12 October 1985; *Newsweek*, 21 October 1985; CBS evening news broadcast 10 October 1985; and intelligence sources.

23. *Newsweek* of 21 October 1985, pp.14–18 gives an account of this conversation.

24. *Armed Forces Journal*, August 1985, pp.71–74.

25. Statement by Admiral William J. Crowe, chairman of the JCS before the Subcommittee on Sea Power and Force Projection of the Senate Committee on Armed Services, 5 August 1986.

26. Statement by Richard Armitage before the Subcommmittee on Seapower and Force Projection, Committee on the Armed Services, US Senate, 5 August 1986.

27. Stilwell's letter is in the author's possession.

28. A copy of the memo is in the author's possession.

29. Hearings before a Subcommittee of the Committee of Appropriations, House of Representatives, on the Department of Defense Appropriations for 1986, US Government Printing Office, 1985, No.47–926 0, p.606.

CHAPTER 21

1. Information supplied from intelligence sources, March 1987.

2. Information on spetsnaz comes from the following sources: three undated and unsigned assessments of Soviet special forces carried out by the British entitled *Operations in the Enemy Rear: Soviet Doctrine and Tactics, The Soviet Threat to Europe in the 1980s, Unconventional Warfare*

Operations: a draft copy of the latest British Army Field Manual prepared in 1985; and Nato intelligence sources.

3. Quoted in USAF Joint Special Operations Planning Workshop, Special Operations School, February 1986, p.8–1.

4. *New York Times*, 4 November 1986.

5. *Jane's Defence Weekly*, 25 January 1986, p.83.

6. In an interview 7 August 1986.

7. In an interview in September 1986.

8. 'Parachute Drop Reconnaissance Deep Behind Enemy Lines' by Evgeny Mesyatser, special correspondent of *Smena*, translated in 1973.

9. 'Soviet Sabotage Training for World War III', by Aleksei Myagkov in *Soviet Analyst*, 20 December 1979, pp.2–6.

10. The most detailed account of spetsnaz operations in the Baltic comes in a study prepared for the US Department of Defense entitled *Soviet Navy Spetsnaz Operations on the Northern Flank: Implications for the Defense of Western Europe*, by Lynn M Hansen, The Center for Strategic Technology, Texas A & M University, April 1984, no. SS84–2.

11. ibid., pp.20–21

12. *Jane's Defence Weekly*, 15 September 1984, p.435, and intelligence sources.

13. An interesting analysis of Soviet midget submarine capability appears in Captain J. E. Moore and Commander R. Compton-Hall, *Submarine Warfare Today and Tomorrow*, Michael Joseph, London, 1986, pp.222–229.

14. *Military Technology*, June 1986, p.69; *Defense Week*, March 25, 1985, p.13; undated *Jane's Defence Weekly*.

15. L. G. Gref, A. L. Latter, E. A. Martinelli and H. P. Smith, *A Soviet Paramilitary Attack on US Nuclear Forces – A Concept*, DARPA project No. 048–4S–13665, November 1974, pp.2–1, 2–2.

16. Statement to the Senate Armed Services Committee, Washington DC, 1 March 1985.

17. ibid.

CHAPTER 22

1. Frank Barnett (ed). *Special Operations in US Strategy*, op.cit., pp.32–33; *US Army Operational Concept for Low Intensity Conflict*, Department of the Army Training and Doctrine Command, pamphlet No. 525–44, 10 February 1986.

2. A detailed account of Green Beret training appears in *Gung Ho*, December 1983.

3. The *Washington Post*, 18 May 1980.

4. John Strawson, *The SAS Regiment*, op.cit., p.170.

5. Defense Department Authorization and Oversight hearings before

the House Armed Services Committee, US Government Printing Office, Washington DC 1983, p.654.

6. John Wiseman, *The SAS Survival Handbook*, Collins Harvill, London, 1986.

7. Interview with the author in November 1986.

8. Briefing distributed to participants in Flintlock 83 by Headquarters Special Operations Task Force, Europe, 10 January 1983.

9. In an interview in Washington, November 1986.

10. *US Navy SEAL Combat Manual*, Lancer Militaria, Sims, Arkansas, January 1974.

11. *Defense and Foreign Affairs*, November 1984.

12. *Aviation Week*, 13 October 1986, p.28; briefing by Lockheed staff November 1986.

13. *Special Forces Air Operations*, FM 31-24, July 1982.

14. Hearings before a Subcommittee on Appropriations of the House of Representatives, March 12 1986, US Government Printing Office, 1986, No. 60-489 0, p.608.

15. Transcript of a command briefing at the John F. Kennedy Centre for military assistance at Fort Bragg.

16. *Bulletin of the Atomic Scientists*, April 1985, pp.4-5.

17. *Defense and Foreign Affairs*, November 1984.

18. Hearings before the Subcommittee on Appropriations of the House of Representatives, March 12 1986, US Government Printing Office, 1986, No. 60-489 0, p.19.

CHAPTER 23

1. In an interview, September 1986.

2. *The Defense Monitor*, Vol XIV, Number 2, 1985, p.12; hearings before the Subcommittee on the Department of Defense, House of Representatives, US Government Printing Office, Washington DC, 1986, p.573.

3. Information supplied by the Department of Defense.

4. *Washington Post*, 24 March 1985.

5. *The Challenge to Democracy in Central America*, Department of Defense/Department of State, US Government Printing Office, Washington DC, June 1986, p.5.

6. In an interview with the author, November 1986.

7. *The Military Balance, 1986-1987*, The International Institute for Strategic Studies, London, p.191.

8. *Washington Post*, 29 January 1987.

9. *Los Angeles Times*, 6 February 1987.

10. Tayacan, *Operaciones Sicologicas en Guerra de Guerrillas*, neither publisher nor date of publication is listed.

11. The *Guardian*, 7 October 1986; *The New Republic*, 30 September 1985, pp.11-13; *Soldier of Fortune*, February 1987, pp.68-71; *Financial*

Times, 10 November 1986; John Prados, *The President's Secret Wars*, op.cit., p.399.

12. *Common Cause Magazine*, September/October 1985, p.28.

13. *Soldier of Fortune*, February 1987, p.45.

14. KMS is mentioned in the report of the Tower Commission on the Iran affair published in March 1987. Other information comes from sources in Washington and El Salvador interviewed in February 1987.

15. Colonel T. N. Dupuy, Colonel John C. Andrews and Grace P. Hayes, *The Almanac of World Military Power*, Presidio Press, San Rafael, California, 1980.

16. *The Military Balance 1986–87*, The International Institute of Strategic Studies, London.

17. *Strategic Survey 1985–1986*, The International Institute for Strategic Studies, London, p.206.

CHAPTER 24

1. *Public Report of the Vice-President's Task Force on Combating Terrorism*, US Government Printing Office, Washington DC 20402, February 1986, p.7.

2. The author attended the unclassified part of the conference at Bolling Air Force Base in December 1985. He also conducted interviews in Washington on state terrorism in April 1986. Details of American and British surveillance come from interviews in London and Washington, April 1986 and March 1987.

3. To the author, November 1986.

4. Interview, April 1987.

5. Taken from the official text following the Tokyo summit.

6. Information on the Iran affair is drawn principally from four sources: the Report of the President's Special Review Board (otherwise known as the Tower Commission), published on 26 February 1987; the report of the Select Committee on Secret Military Assistance to Iran and the Nicaraguan Opposition of the United States Senate (otherwise known as the Senate Intelligence Committee report), published on 29 January 1987; interviews with Pentagon and State Department officials who took part in the planning and execution of the operation; numerous press accounts that appeared between November 1986 and May 1987.

7. Interview in Washington, November 1986.

8. North told this story to author Neil Livingstone on 14 November 1986 who repeated it to this author that same month. He also wrote about it in the *National Review*, 30 January 1987, pp.37–38, 67–68.

9. Interview in Washington, December 1986.

10. Interview in Washington, November 1986.

Definitions

Guerrilla Warfare is military and paramilitary combat operations conducted in enemy-held or hostile territory by irregular, predominantly indigenous forces.

Insurgency is a form of revolutionary warfare involving a resistance movement by a disaffected portion of the population against the incumbent government. An insurgency usually consists of a methodically conducted, protracted struggle which seeks the support of the population and eventual overthrow of the incumbent government. The conflict usually involves insurgent initiated guerrilla warfare which may be supported by an external power.

Low Intensity Conflict is a limited political-military struggle to achieve political, social, economic, or psychological objectives. It is often protracted and ranges from diplomatic, economic, and psycho-social pressures through terrorism and insurgency. Low intensity conflict is generally confined to a geographic area and is often characterised by constraints on the weaponry, tactics and level of violence.

Paramilitary Forces are forces or groups which are distinct from the regular armed forces of any country, but resembling them in organisation, equipment, training, or mission.

Propaganda is any form of communication in support of national objectives designed to influence the opinions, emotions, attitudes or behaviour of any gorup in order to benefit the sponsor, either directly or indirectly.

Psychological Operations are political/military activities planned and conducted to influence the attitudes and behaviour of a specific population.

Psychological Warfare is the planned use of propaganda and other psychological actions having the primary purpose of influencing the opinions, emotions, attitudes, and behaviour of hostile foreign groups in such a way as to support the achievement of national objectives.

Sabotage is an act with an intent to injure, interfere with, or obstruct the national defence of a country by wilfully injuring or destroying, or attempting to injure or destroy, any national defence or war material, premises or utilities to include human or natural resources.

Special Operations as defined by the US military are those military operations conducted by specially trained, equipped and organised forces against strategic or tactical targets in pursuit of national military, political, economic, or psychological objectives. These operations may be conducted during periods of peace or hostilities. They may be conducted in conjunction with conventional operations, or they may be prosecuted independently when use of conventional forces is either inappropriate or unfeasible.

Another version describes Special Operations as 'small scale, clandestine, covert or overt operations of an unorthodox and frequently high risk nature, undertaken to achieve significant political or military objectives in support of foreign policy. Special operations are characterized by either simplicity or complexity, by subtlety and imagination, by the discriminate use of violence, and by oversight at the highest level. Military and non-military resources, including intelligence assets, may be used in concert.'

Special Activities are defined in the US as intelligence activities conducted in support of national foreign policy objectives abroad which are planned and executed so that the role of the United States government is not apparent or acknowledged publicly, and actions in support of such activities, but which are not intended to influence United States political processes, public opinion, policies, or media and do not include diplomatic activities or the collection and production of intelligence or related support functions.

Terrorist is an individual or member of a group that wishes to achieve political ends using violent means, often at the cost of casualties to innocent civilians and with the support of only a minority of the people he or she claims to represent.

Unconventional Warfare is a broad spectrum of military and paramilitary operations conducted in enemy, enemy-held, enemy-controlled, or politically sensitive territory. It includes, but is not limited to, the interrelated fields of guerrilla warfare, evasion and escape, subversion, sabotage and other operations of a low visibility, cover, or clandestine nature. These interrelated aspects of unconventional warfare may be prosecuted singly or collectively by predominantly indigenous personnel, usually supported and directed in various degrees by external sources during all conditions or war and peace.

The definitions in this section come from a number of sources:

1. *The Joint Special Operations Planning Workshop* of the USAF Special Operations School, Hulbert Field, Florida, February 1986.
2. Frank Barnett (ed.), *Special Operations in U.S. Strategy*, National Defense University Press, Washington D.C., 1984.
3. James Adams, *The Financing of Terror*, Simon and Schuster, New York, 1986.

Glossary

CIA	Central Intelligence Agency
CIDG	Civil Irregular Defense Group
CINC	Commander-in-Chief
CINCLANT	Comander-in-Chief Atlantic
COMSUBIN	Commando Raggruppamento Subacqueri ed Incursori
CRW	Counter Revolutionary Warfare
DARPA	Defense Advanced Research Projects Agency
DIA	Defense Intelligence Agency
DOD	Department of Defense
ECM	Electronic Counter Measures
ELINT	Electronic Intelligence
ETA	Euskadi Ta Askatasuna (Basque)
EW	Electronic Warfare
FDR	Frente Democratico Revolucionario (El Salvador)
FID	Foreign Internal Defence
FLIR	Forward-Looking Infra-Red
FMLN	Frente Farabundo Marti para la Liberacion Nacional (El Salvador)
FNLA	Frente National da Libertacao de Angola
FOIA	Freedom of Information Act
FSLN	Frente Sandinista de Liberacion Nacional (Nicaragua)
GIG	Gruppi Interventi Speciali
GIGN	Groupe D'Intervention de la Gendarmerie Nationale
GSG9	Grenzschutzgruppe 9
HAHO	High Altitude High Opening
HALO	High Altitude Low Opening
HUMINT	Human Intelligence
INSCOM	Intelligence and Security Command
ISA	Intelligence Support Activity
JCS	Joint Chiefs of Staff
JSOA	Joint Special Operations Agency
JSOC	Joint Special Operations Command
JSOSE	Joint Special Operations Support Element

LIC	Low Intesity Conflict
MAC	Military Airlift Command
MAU	Marine Amphibious Unit
MIA	Missing in Action
MOD	Ministry of Defence
MPLA	Movimento Popular para a Libertacao de Angola
NATO	North Atlantic Treaty Organisation
NAVSOECWAR	Naval Special Warfare Unit (NSWU)
NSWU	Naval Special Warfare Unit
OMG	Operational Manoeuvre Group
OPC	Office of Policy Co-ordination
OPSEC	Operations Security
OSS	Office of Strategic Services
PFLP	Popular Front for the Liberation of Palestine
PINS	Palletised Inertial Navigation System
PLO	Palestine Liberation Organisation
PSYOP	Psychological Operation
RPG	Rocket Propelled Grenade
RUC	Royal Ulster Constabulary
SADM	Special Atomic Demolition Munition
SAS	Special Air Service
SBS	Special Boat Squadron
SBU	Special Boat Unit
SCUBA	Self-Contained Underwater Breathing Appartus
SDV	Swimmer Delivery Vehicle
SDVT	Swimmer Delivery Vehicle Team
SEAL	Sea Air Land Team
SECDEF	Secretary of Defense
SERE	Survival, Evasion, Resistance and Escape
SIGINT	Signals Intelligence
SOCOM	Special Operations Command
SOE	Special Operations Executive
SOF	Special Operations Forces
SOPAG	Special Operations Advisory Group
STABO	Stabilised Tactical Airborne Body Operations
STAR	Surface To Air Recovery
STOL	Short Take Off and Landing
TOW	Tube-launched Optically-tracked Wire command-linked guided anti-tank missile
TRADOC	Training and Doctrine Command
UNITA	Uniao Nacional para a Independencia Total de Angola
USAF	United States Air Force

Bibliography

ADAMS, James, *The Financing of Terror*, Simon and Schuster, New York, 1986.

ADAN, Avraham, *On The Banks of the Suez*, Arms and Armour Press, London, 1980.

AUGUST, Frantisec and David Rees, *Red Star Over Prague*, Sherwood Press, London, 1984.

BAMFORD, James, *The Puzzle Palace*, Sidgwick and Jackson, London, 1982.

BANK, Aaron, *From OSS to Green Berets*, Presidio, Novato, California, 1986.

BARNETT, Frank R., B. Hugh Tovar and Richard H. Schultz, *Special Operations in US Strategy*, National Defense University Press, Washington DC, 1984.

BARRON, John, *KGB Today, The Hidden Hand*, Readers Digest Press, New York, 1983.

BECKWITH, Col. Charlie L. and Donald Knox, *Delta Force*, Harcourt Brace Jovanovich, New York, 1983.

BISHOP, Patrick and John Witherow, *The Winter War*, Quartet, London, 1982.

BLOCH, Jonathan and Patrick Fitzgerald, *British Intelligence and Covert Action*, Brandon Junction, London, 1983.

BROWN, Ashley, *Elite Forces, Israeli Paras*, Orbis, London, 1986.

BURDEN, Rodney A., Michael I. Draper, Douglas A. Rough, Colin R. Smith, David L. Wilton, and *Falklands, The Air War*, Arms and Armour Press, London, 1986.

COWLES, Virginia, *The Phantom Major*, Collins, London, 1958.

COCHRAN, Thomas B., William N. Arkin and Milton N. Hoenig, *US Nuclear Forces and Capabilities, Volume I*, Ballinger, Cambridge Mass., 1984.

DALY, Lt.-Col. Ron Reid, *Selous Scouts, Top Secret War*, Galligo Publishing, Alberton, South Africa, 1982.

DEWAR, Lt.-Col. Michael, *The British Army in Northern Ireland*, Arms and Armour Press, London, 1985.

DEPARTMENT of the Army, *US Army Special Forces 1961–1971*, Department of the Army, Washington DC, 1973.

DICKENS, Peter, *SAS The Jungle Frontier*, Arms and Armour Press, London, 1983.

DICKIE, Christopher, *With the Contras*, Faber and Faber, London, 1985.

EARLE, Edward Mead, *Makers of Modern Strategy*, Princeton University Press, Princeton N.J., 1971.

ESHEL, David, *Elite Fighting Units*, Arms and Armour Press, London, 1984.

FARRINGDON, Hugh, *Confrontation*, Routledge, Kegan and Paul, London, 1986.

FIENNES, Ranulph, *Where Soldiers Fear to Tread*, Hodder and Stoughton, London, 1975.

FULLERTON, Alexander, *Special Deliverance*, Macmillan, London, 1986.

GABRIEL, Richard A., *Military Incompetence*, Hill and Wang, New York, 1985. *Operation Peace for Galilee*, Hill and Wang, New York, 1984.

GERAGHTY, Tony, *March or Die*, Grafton Books, London, 1986. *Who Dares Wins*, Arms and Armour Press, London, 1980.

GODSON, Roy, *Intelligence Requirements for the 1980s: Covert Action*, National Strategy Information Center, Washington DC, 1981.

GOULDEN, Joseph C., *The Death Merchant*, Simon and Schuster, New York, 1984.

HADLEY, Arthur T., *The Straw Giant*, Random House, New York, 1986.

HAMMOND, Thomas T., *Red Flag Over Afghanistan*, Westview Press, Boulder, Col., 1984.

HARCLERODE, Peter, (ed.), *The Elite and Their Support*, Strategic Publishing, Basingstoke, England, 1986.

HARRISON, Selig S., *In Afghanistan's Shadow: Baluch Nationalism and Soviet Temptation*, Carnegie Endowment, New York, 1981.

HASTINGS, Max and Simon Jenkins, *The Battle for the Falklands*, Michael Joseph, London, 1983.

HERMAN, Edward S., *The Real Terror Network*, South End Press, Boston, 1982.

INTERNATIONAL Institute for Strategic Studies, *Military Balance, 1985–1986, 1986–1987*, IISS, London, 1985, 1986.

——*Strategic Survey, 1983–1984, 1984–1985, 1985–86*, IISS, London.

JACKSON, Robert, *Strike Force*, Robson Books, London, 1986.

JANKE, Peter, *Guerrilla and Terrorist Organisations: A World Directory and Bibliography*, Macmillan, London, 1983.

KITSON, Frank, *Gangs and Counter-gangs*, Barrie and Rockliff, London, 1960. *Warfare as a Whole*, Faber and Faber, London, 1987.

KREPINEVICH, Andrew F. Jr., *The Army and Vietnam*, The Johns Hopkins University Press, Boston, 1986.

LEVY, 'Yank' Bert, *Guerrilla Warfare*, Paladin Press, Boulder, Col., 1964.

LEWY, Guenther, *America in Vietnam*, Oxford University Press, New York, 1978.

LINDSAY, Kennedy, *The British Intelligence Services in Action*, Dunrod, Irish Republic, 1981.

MAAS, Peter, *Manhunt*, Harrap, London, 1986.

MACDONALD, Callum A., *Korea: The War Before Vietnam*, Macmillan Press, London, 1986.

MACKSEY, Kenneth, *First Clash*, Arms and Armour Press, London, 1985.

MARCHETTI, Victor and John D. Marks, *The CIA and The Cult of Intelligence*, Laurel, New York, 1974.

BIBLIOGRAPHY

419

MOORE, Capt. J. E. and Commander R. Compton-Hall, *Submarine Warfare*, Michael Joseph, London, 1986.

MOYER, SGM Frank A., *Special Forces Foreign Weapons Handbook*, Paladin Press, Boulder, Col., 1983.

O'BALLANCE, Edgar, *No Victor, No Vanquished*, Barrie and Jenkins, London, 1979.

PADDOCK, Alfred H. Jr., *US Army Special Warfare*, National Defense University Press, Washington DC, 1982.

PETERZELL, Jay, *Reagan's Secret Wars*, Center for National Security Studies, Washington DC, 1984.

PETIT, Michael, *Peacekeepers at War*, Faber and Faber, London, 1986.

PITT, Barrie, *Special Boat Squadron*, Century, London, 1983.

PRADOS, John, *The President's Secret Wars*, William Morrow and Co., New York, 1986.

RANELAGH, John, *The Agency*, Simon and Schuster, New York, 1986.

RECORD, Jeffrey, *Revising US Military Strategy*, Pergamon Brassey's, Washington, 1984.

RICHELSON, Jeffrey T., *Sword and the Shield*, Ballinger, Cambridge, Mass., 1986. *The US Intelligence Community*, Ballinger, Cambridge, Mass., 1985.

RICHEY, George, *Britain's Strategic Role in NATO*, Macmillan, London, 1986.

ROSIE, George, *The Directory of International Terrorism*, Mainstream Publishing, Edinburgh, 1986.

RYAN, Paul B., *The Iranian Rescue Mission, Why it Failed*, The Naval Institute Press, Annapolis, Maryland, 1985.

SCHEMMER, Benjamin, *The Raid*, Harper and Row, New York, 1976.

SCHIFF, Ze'ev and Ehud Ya'ari, *Israel's Lebanon War*, Simon and Schuster, New York, 1984.

SCOTT, Harriet Fast and William F. Scott, *The Armed Forces of the USSR*, Westview Press, Boulder, Col., 1984.

SEATON, Albert and Joan Seaton, *The Soviet Army*, Bodley Head, London, 1986.

SEYMOUR, William, *British Special Forces*, Grafton, London, 1985.

SHEEHAN, Michael and James Wyllie, *The Economist Pocket Guide to Defence*, Basil Blackwell, Oxford, 1986.

SIMPSON, Charles M. III, *Inside the Green Berets*, Berkley Books, New York, 1984.

SIMPKIN, Richard, *Race to the Swift*, Brassey Defence Publishers, London, 1985. *Deep Battle*, Brassey Defence Publishers, London, 1986.

SIPRI, *World Armaments and Disarmament*, Oxford University Press, Oxford, 1986.

SMITH, Bradley F. *The Shadow Warriors*, Andre Deutsch, London, 1983.

STOHL, Michael and George A. Lopez, *The State as Terrorist*, Greenwood Press, Westport, Conn., 1984.

STRAWSON, John, *A History of the SAS Regiment*, Secker and Warburg, London, 1984.

SUMMERS, Colonel Harry, *On Strategy, A Critical Analysis of the Vietnam War*, Presidio Press, Novato, California, 1982.

SUN TZU, *The Art of War*, Delacorte Press, New York, 1983.

SUVOROV, Viktor, *Soviet Military Intelligence*, Hamish Hamilton, London, 1984.

TOPHOVEN, Rolf, and Bernard and Graefe Verlag, *GSG9, German Responses to Terrorism*, Bernard and Graefe Verlag, West Germany, 1984.

VAUX, Nick, *March to the South Atlantic*, Buchan and Enright, London, 1986.

WARNER, Philip, *The Secret Forces of World War II*, Grenada, London, 1985.

WISEMAN, John, *The SAS Survival Handbook*, Collins Harvill, London, 1986.

YOUNG, John Robert, *The French Foreign Legion*, Thames and Hudson, London, 1984.

Field Manuals

FM 31–24 *Special Forces Air Operations*, Department of the Army, Washington DC, July 1982.

FM 31–25 *Special Forces Waterborne Operations*, Department of the Army, Washington DC, September 1982.

FM 31–19 *Special Forces Military Free-Fall Parachuting*, Department of the Army, Washington DC, August 1977.

Documents

HOUSE COMMITTEE ON APPROPRIATIONS, Hearings before the subcommittee on the Department of Defense, Part 6, US Government Printing Office, Washington DC, 1985.

——Hearings before the subcommittee on the Department of Defense, Part 1 and Part 6, US Government Printing Office, Washington DC, 1986.

SENATE COMMITTEE ON THE ARMED SERVICES, Omnibus Defense Authorization Act, 1984, US Government Printing Office, Washington DC, 1983.

Defense Organisation: The need for Change, US Government Printing Office, Washington DC, 1985.

Soviet Military Power, September 1981, March 1983, April 1984, April 1985, March 1986, US Government Printing Office, Washington DC.

Appendix

This is not intended as a comprehensive list of special operations forces (a book in itself) but it does set out some information for easy reference. I have been detailed with the names and locations of different United States units as they will be more in the news in the future. I have included a command structure for Spetsnaz which, as far as I know, has not been published before and a structure for the SAS which is also new.

Australia

The Australian *Special Air Service Regiment (SASR)* is modelled on Britain's SAS and, like them, has both a wartime and a counter-terrorist role. Unlike many other such units, the *SASR* has seen a significant amount of combat since it was formed in 1957 and has fought in Vietnam, Thailand, Papua New Guinea and Borneo. Currently the Regiment is organized into three sabre squadrons and a base squadron with one unit at permanent readiness to deal with a terrorist threat.

Belgium

The *Escadron Special D'Intervention (ESI)* is the country's principal counter-terrorist unit. Although it comes under the Ministry of Defence, the unit carries out protection duties of senior government officials and has an advisory role in suggesting methods of improving security for embassies abroad. The *ESI* has played a major part in breaking up the Cellules Communistes Combattantes (CCC), the Belgian terrorist group that first emerged in 1984. Until the arrival of the CCC Belgium had paid lip-service to the need for a counter-terrorist unit and the *ESI* was poorly funded and suffered from recruiting difficulties. Training and morale are now much improved.

The country's main special forces unit is the airborne *Paracommando Regiment* which is made up of three battalions with supporting artillery, light armoured reconnaissance, anti-tank and administrative units. Their role, similar to that of the US Ranger, requires them to operate in battalion-size units behind enemy lines to seize key points.

Denmark

Funding for the Danish armed forces has been a serious problem in recent years and its small special forces units have suffered by being given an enormous range of tasks with insufficient cash for training or personnel. However, within those constraints both the Navy's *Fromandskorpset* and the Army's *Jaegerkorps* are considered highly professional.

Both units are around 50 strong, although the Navy have been given the main counter-terrorist role which is similar to that given to the British Royal Marines *Comachio Company*. In addition both units are expected to be expert in sabotage and reconnaissance both on land and underwater. The duplication in the roles of the two units means that there is a great deal of shared training.

Federal Republic of Germany

West Germany's principal counter-terrorist weapon is the *Grenzschutzgruppe 9 (GSG-9)*, which was formed after the disaster at the 1972 Munich Olympics when 11 Israeli athletes were massacred. *GSG-9* is currently based in Hangelar, 30 minutes north of the West German capital, Bonn. The 210-strong unit has 120 combat troops. They have their own separate compound inside the one-mile square Federal Border Guard base. Behind wire fences and a battery of surveillance cameras, the men live in a five-storey light-brown building and train in a number of low modern buildings that form a square, in the centre of which is a grass-covered parade and exercise ground.

Their headquarters is a mixture of high technology equipment where money is clearly no object and living conditions that are less lavish. The mess is spartan with cheap pine furniture and the food served to the men is of exceptionally poor quality. In an ironic piece of disinformation the main painting on the mess wall is of the Mogadishu mission. However, it is highly inaccurate, no doubt so that any visitor will not gain a useful insight into *GSG-9*'s operational techniques.

The men wear the green uniforms of the Border Guard with only the narrow white badge of the German eagle flanked by oak leaves to distinguish them. As their operations are strictly limited to counter-terrorism, their structure and training are different from other special operations forces which often have a wartime role.

Their structure is based on the five-man combat team. However, although all these men are trained in hostage rescue and detailed expertise in explosives, communications and documentation are kept in different units and are drawn on as and when necessary. In the event of an incident, the commander of *GSG-9* (currently

GRENZSCHUTZGRUPPE 9 (GSG9)

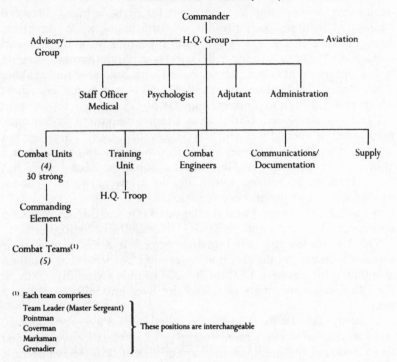

(1) Each team comprises:
Team Leader (Master Sergeant)
Pointman
Coverman
Marksman
Grenadier
} These positions are interchangeable

Colonel Uwe Dee) forms a special advisory group drawn from civilian, military and border guard experts to handle the crisis. At the same time, the combat unit is alerted and a lieutenant from the command element is put in charge. A civilian psychologist is permanently attached to the unit both to screen applicants and to advise on tactics in kidnappings.

Each applicant is psychologically examined, and is put through a series of endurance and reaction tests as well as an obstacle course designed to test mental and physical agility. Senior officers in *GSG-9* claim it takes between two and three years before a recruit is fully trained. There is no rotation of members into other Border Guard units and as long as an individual remains fit he is allowed to stay. However, the average age of *GSG-9* members is 29 and very few stay in the unit once they have reached 40.

GSG-9 recruits are paid an extra 200 Deutschmarks a month which, after tax, just about pays for the additional insurance premium each member takes out.

Each member of a combat team is issued two sets of identical equipment, one for day and tte other for night fighting. Personal equipment includes body armour, a 9 mm pistol, a .357 magnum pistol, a Heckler and Koch MP5 sub-machinegun, a Heckler and Koch G3 7.62 mm sniping rifle with laser and thermal imaging sights and pump action shotguns loaded with solid shot for breaking down doors. They also have available 40 mm grenade launchers which can fire high explosives, tear gas or CS gas.

For road transport, *GSG-9* uses either anonymous volkswagen mini-buses or specially tuned Mercedes 280SE cars. These are not armoured as the men prefer speed to protection and the cars are able to reach 145 mph on Germany's autobahns. Each vehicle has three different scrambled telephones to allow car-to-car, car-to-headquarters and general conversations.

A special air transport unit is integrated into the *GSG-9* command structure. They use Puma, Bell UH1D or Bell 212 helicopters.

The budget for the unit remains secret but a measure of their support is shown by the fact that an average border guard batallion of 600 men fire between 120 and 200,000 rounds a year. By contrast, the 120 combat members of *GSG-9* fire over one million rounds a year.

Until the late 1970s *GSG-9* were called out on average about 20 times a year. However, more recently the terrorists have changed their tactics as the methods and capabilities of *GSG-9* have become known. As one senior *GSG-9* officer put it in May 1987: 'The reconnaisance that the terrorists carry out before each act has improved and so has their use of escape routes. They kill and bomb and have left the scene before we even hear about it. All we can do is sit here.'

Some members of *GSG-9* have been arguing to be allowed to take the fight to the terrorists by infiltrating their gangs and having a more reactive policy. To date, this sensitive course of action has been vetoed by the governments.

Like the SAS, with whom they co-operate closely, the *GSG-9* are trained to carry out assaults on embassies and aircraft, provide protection for VIPs and carry out long-term undercover work against terrorist groups.

Unlike other Nato countries, West Germany has developed a unit specifically for long-range reconnaissance. A long-range reconnaissance company, the *Fernspahkompanie*, is attached to each German Army Corps. The company is expected to work independently of air or ground support deep behind enemy lines. The *Fernspahkompanie* are each 150 strong, divided into a headquarters, two reconnaissance platoons, a communications detachment and a logistics unit. Each platoon is divided into a three-man headquarters and ten four-man patrols.

France

Plans for reorganization of the French army were announced in June 1983 and by 1985 the 47,000-strong *Force D'Action Rapide (FAR)* had been established. The *FAR* is made up of five divisions: one marine infantry, one parachute, one Alpine, one light-armoured and one air-mobile.

There are four key areas of operation for the *FAR*: overseas in districts or territories or at the request of nations bound to France by defence agreements; to reinforce existing defences inside France; to reinforce elsewhere in Europe in time of crisis.

France formed its own counter-terrorist unit, the *Groupe d'Intervention de la Gendarmerie Nationale (GIGN)*, in 1973 after it was realized the police were incapable of handling effectively a major terrorist attack. The *GIGN* gets its authority from the Ministry of Defence but has powers of arrest and carries out attacks on pure criminals as well as terrorists.

The organization has 54 members, divided into four twelve-man teams and a headquarters. Each team is sub-divided into two teams of five and a dog handler and, like comparable units elsewhere, they are trained parachutists, scuba divers, climbers and experts in shooting and hand to hand combat. *GIGN* is based at a barracks near Paris where all the team members and their families live.

Israel

The intelligence services, the police and the armed forces all contain units which carry out active measures. However, the *Parachute Corps* is the principal source of special operations forces. They have a long and distinguished record in battle and a special counter-terrorist force drawn from the Corps, *Unit 269*, was responsible for the raid on Entebbe. There are currently five parachute brigades in the Israeli Defence Forces with two kept at full strength and the others manned by reservists.

Italy

Perhaps more than any other European nation, Italy has suffered most from terrorism. As a result, a number of different units have sprung up to deal with the problem. The three most important are the *Comando Raggruppamento Subacqueri ed Incursori* known as *COMSUBIN*, the *Gruppi Interventi Speciali* and the *Nucleo Operativo Centrale do Sicurezza (NOCS)*.

COMSUBIN are the equivalent of the US *SEALS* or the British SBS and have a similar role. They are trained in reconnaissance, sabotage and small unit raiding as well as hand to hand combat, parachuting and the use of explosives.

The *GIS* comes under the paramilitary police and Italy's Ministry of Defense. The *NOCS* were formed after the kidnapping of Italian Premier Aldo Moro in 1978 and are part of the regular police. Around 50 strong, both groups are known as 'Leatherheads' after their habit of wearing tight leather masks to cover their face and neck when in action. The masks serve as a disguise and provide some protection.

In addition to their counter-terrorist units, the Italians have formed the *9th Airborne Assault (Saboteur)* Battalion of the *Folgore Airborne Brigade* which has a similar wartime role to the US Rangers, including behind the lines raiding and reconnaissance.

Netherlands

The Netherlands have a vital role in protecting Britain's Northern Flank in the event of a Soviet invasion. They have also placed considerable emphasis on protecting their oil rigs in the North Sea from terrorist attack. It is hardly surprising, therefore, that their special forces are similar to Britain's Royal Marines and their counter-terrorist forces train with and have similar roles to the Royal Navy's Special Boat Squadron.

The *Royal Netherlands Marine Corps* is mainly organized into the *1st Amphibious Combat Group (ACG)*, which in war would combine with the British Marines to form the *United Kingdom/Netherlands Landing Force*.

A special unit of the Netherlands Marine Corps, *The Special Assistance Unit – Marines (BBE)*, is responsible for combatting terrorism and for some reconnaissance and sabotage in war. The *BBE* has three operational 30 man platoons organized into five man teams. The most spectacular operation carried out by the *BBE* occurred in May 1977 when South Moluccan terrorists simultaneously seized a school and a train. Both groups of terrorists were attacked by units of the *BBE* and the hostages released.

Norway

Norway, like Britain, is concerned about the possible sabotage of her oil fields in the North Sea and has formed a joint counter terrorism force with units drawn from the Army, Navy and police. The Norwegian National Police have a 48 strong *Readiness Troop* divided into four 12-man squads broken down into five two-man units with a small headquarters. These are supported by men from the 30 strong Marine *Jaeger* and the 100 strong Parachute *Jaeger*. Both groups are required to have a wartime special operations role as well as a peacetime counter-terrorist mission.

Soviet Union

The Spetsnaz command structure is set out below.

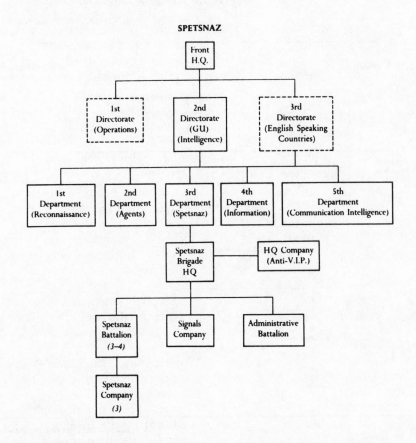

Spain

Counter-terrorism is carried out by the *Grupo Especiale Para Los Operaciones (GEO)*. They are recruited from and run by the civilian police and undergo training similar to the *SAS*. Both countries have a similar terrorist problem from groups that use the same tactics. *GEO* has had some considerable successes against ETA and against right-wing groups.

United Kingdom

The *SAS* command structure is set out below.

Each of the squadrons have a particular area of responsibility (Northern Flank, counter terrorism) but those responsibilities are rotated between squadrons to ensure an overall competence.

SPECIAL AIR SERVICE

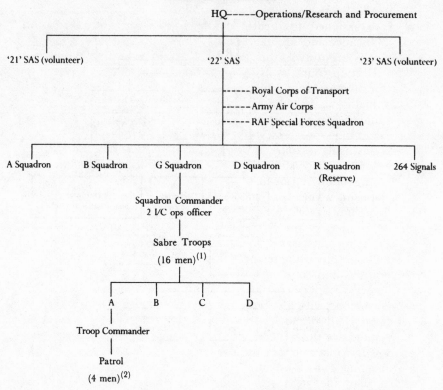

HQ-----Operations/Research and Procurement

'21' SAS (volunteer)   '22' SAS   '23' SAS (volunteer)

------ Royal Corps of Transport
------ Army Air Corps
------ RAF Special Forces Squadron

A Squadron   B Squadron   G Squadron   D Squadron   R Squadron   264 Signals
                                                                (Reserve)

Squadron Commander
2 I/C ops officer

Sabre Troops
(16 men)[1]

A   B   C   D

Troop Commander

Patrol
(4 men)[2]

	current location
HQ Command	Duke of York's Barracks, Knightsbridge
Sabre Squadrons	Stirling Barracks, Hereford
RAF Special Forces Squadron	Lyneham, Wiltshire

[1] Each troop has a speciality —
either mountain warfare, high altitude/low opening parachuting,
motor vehicles or boats.
[2] Each member has a speciality —
either signals, medicine, languages or demolition.

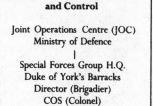

**UK Special Forces Command
and Control**

Joint Operations Centre (JOC)
Ministry of Defence

Special Forces Group H.Q.
Duke of York's Barracks
Director (Brigadier)
COS (Colonel)
18 staff

SBS   SAS

The *Special Boat Squadron (SBS)* is about the size of an infantry rifle company but its numbers are supplemented by specialist communications and logistics support. In war, the Squadron breaks down into Section groups, each with their own communications, and are assigned to theatre commanders for deep penetration reconnaissance and sabotage.

Recruits are drawn from the Royal Marines and an initial two week selection course tests physical stamina, intelligence and aptitude for diving. Around fifty per cent fail at this stage.

To qualify as a swimmer/canoeist, *SBS* recruits are expected to learn underwater navigation and the use of oxygen rebreather sets. As the course progresses, they develop skills as canoeists and coxswains using a canoe, the German Klepper Aerius Mark XIII. They have to successfully negotiate a surf zone and navigate a 30 mile course along an open coast. They also practice infiltrating to a target using a variety of 'mother' ships including aircraft, helicopters, merchant vessels, naval ships and, more regularly, submarines.

The trainee swimmer/canoeist must understand the detailed aspects of reconnaissance, basic land and underwater demolitions, still photography using telephoto lenses, the principles of equipment recognitions and communications.

The *SBS* armoury contains a selection of 9 mm and 5.56 calibre weapons along with a variety of support weapons and sniper rifles. The Colt CAR16 and AR16 with M203 40 mm grenade launcher underslung are the weapons used in the Nato theatre and for their counter-terrorist role they use the Beckler and Koch range of 9 mm sub-machine guns. The emphasis in training is on instinctive firing rather than the measured shot as they train to operate without detection so must respond quickly to a surprise attack.

On completion of the basic course, a swimmer/canoeist joins an operational section which vary in size but are generally 16 strong. Within the section each operating team is led by a swimmer/canoeist first class. He graduates to first class status via a series of upgrading courses the final of which places a heavy emphasis on operational planning and training supervision. Before going on that course, the candidate has to pass the Royal Marines Senior Command Course at the Commando Training Centre.

Most ordinary ranks, aside from an occasional return to more normal duties will spend the rest of his career in the Royal Marines with the *SBS*. Officers do a four year tour of duty.

There are two additional special units within the Royal Marines. *Comacchio Group* was formed in May 1980 to provide special forces to guard Britain's offshore oil installations in the North Sea. As an additional task, detachments are rotated through the Clyde

Submarine base at Faslane to guard Britain's nuclear deterrent from sabotage by Spetsnaz or other foreign agents. Their role has recently been expanded to include ship assaults to counter terrorist attacks. All ships under British flag has been reconnoitered by men from Comacchio. The Group is based in Abroath and currently numbers 400 officers and men under the command of the Major General Royal Marines Training, Reserve and Special Forces Royal Marines who has his headquarters in Royal Marines, Eastney, Hampshire.

Operational control in the event of an attack on an oil rig rests with the local chief of police. *Comacchio* would assist the Civil Power only at the formal written request of the police and with the approval of ministers.

The third group within the Royal Marines is the *Mountain and Arctic Warfare Cadre* (M&AW) which is responsible for cold weather training for the Marines. The Cadre also acts as the Marines Reconnaissance Troop to provide both strategic and tactical intelligence.

USA
The three command structures are set out below.

Source: US and Soviet Special Operations, Draft Committee
Print for the Special Operations Panel of House Armed Services Committee, proposed by John M. Collins, Congressional Research Service, Library of Congress, December 23, 1986.

Sources
I am particularly grateful to Ross Kelly for sharing with me his knowledge of special forces worldwide. His series on special forces written for the magazine *Defence and Foreign Affairs* was very informative. In addition I have drawn from material published in *The Elite and Their Support*, Strategic Publishing, Hartley Wintney, England, 1986. Finally, various special forces were kind enough to help with information.

U.S. NAVY SOF
(Special Operations Forces)

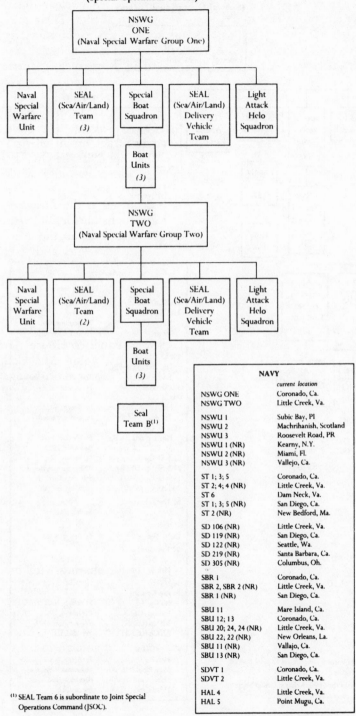

```
                    NSWG
                    ONE
         (Naval Special Warfare Group One)
```

| Naval Special Warfare Unit | SEAL (Sea/Air/Land) Team (3) | Special Boat Squadron | SEAL (Sea/Air/Land) Delivery Vehicle Team | Light Attack Helo Squadron |

```
                    Boat
                    Units
                    (3)
```

```
                    NSWG
                    TWO
         (Naval Special Warfare Group Two)
```

| Naval Special Warfare Unit | SEAL (Sea/Air/Land) Team (2) | Special Boat Squadron | SEAL (Sea/Air/Land) Delivery Vehicle Team | Light Attack Helo Squadron |

```
                    Boat
                    Units
                    (3)
```

```
                    Seal
                    Team B⁽¹⁾
```

(1) SEAL Team 6 is subordinate to Joint Special Operations Command (JSOC).

NAVY	current location
NSWG ONE	Coronado, Ca.
NSWG TWO	Little Creek, Va.
NSWU 1	Subic Bay, PI
NSWU 2	Machrihanish, Scotland
NSWU 3	Roosevelt Road, PR
NSWU 1 (NR)	Kearny, N.Y.
NSWU 2 (NR)	Miami, Fl.
NSWU 3 (NR)	Vallejo, Ca.
ST 1; 3; 5	Coronado, Ca.
ST 2; 4; 4 (NR)	Little Creek, Va.
ST 6	Dam Neck, Va.
ST 1; 3; 5 (NR)	San Diego, Ca.
ST 2 (NR)	New Bedford, Ma.
SD 106 (NR)	Little Creek, Va.
SD 119 (NR)	San Diego, Ca.
SD 122 (NR)	Seattle, Wa.
SD 219 (NR)	Santa Barbara, Ca.
SD 305 (NR)	Columbus, Oh.
SBR 1	Coronado, Ca.
SBR 2, SBR 2 (NR)	Little Creek, Va.
SBR 1 (NR)	San Diego, Ca.
SBU 11	Mare Island, Ca.
SBU 12; 13	Coronado, Ca.
SBU 20; 24, 24 (NR)	Little Creek, Va.
SBU 22; 22 (NR)	New Orleans, La.
SBU 11 (NR)	Vallajo, Ca.
SBU 13 (NR)	San Diego, Ca.
SDVT 1	Coronado, Ca.
SDVT 2	Little Creek, Va.
HAL 4	Little Creek, Va.
HAL 5	Point Mugu, Ca.

U.S. ARMY SOF
(Special Operational Forces)

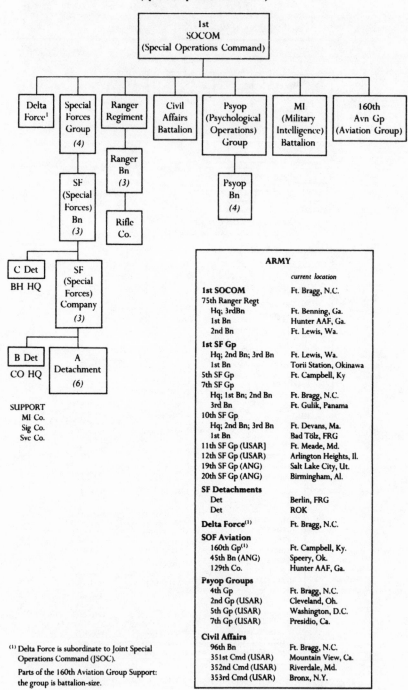

ARMY	
	current location
1st SOCOM	Ft. Bragg, N.C.
75th Ranger Regt	
Hq; 3rdBn	Ft. Benning, Ga.
1st Bn	Hunter AAF, Ga.
2nd Bn	Ft. Lewis, Wa.
1st SF Gp	
Hq; 2nd Bn; 3rd Bn	Ft. Lewis, Wa.
1st Bn	Torii Station, Okinawa
5th SF Gp	Ft. Campbell, Ky
7th SF Gp	
Hq; 1st Bn; 2nd Bn	Ft. Bragg, N.C.
3rd Bn	Ft. Gulik, Panama
10th SF Gp	
Hq; 2nd Bn; 3rd Bn	Ft. Devans, Ma.
1st Bn	Bad Tölz, FRG
11th SF Gp (USAR]	Ft. Meade, Md.
12th SF Gp (USAR)	Arlington Heights, Il.
19th SF Gp (ANG)	Salt Lake City, Ut.
20th SF Gp (ANG)	Birmingham, Al.
SF Detachments	
Det	Berlin, FRG
Det	ROK
Delta Force[1]	Ft. Bragg, N.C.
SOF Aviation	
160th Gp[1]	Ft. Campbell, Ky.
45th Bn (ANG)	Speery, Ok.
129th Co.	Hunter AAF, Ga.
Psyop Groups	
4th Gp	Ft. Bragg, N.C.
2nd Gp (USAR)	Cleveland, Oh.
5th Gp (USAR)	Washington, D.C.
7th Gp (USAR)	Presidio, Ca.
Civil Affairs	
96th Bn	Ft. Bragg, N.C.
351st Cmd (USAR)	Mountain View, Ca.
352nd Cmd (USAR)	Riverdale, Md.
353rd Cmd (USAR)	Bronx, N.Y.

[1] Delta Force is subordinate to Joint Special Operations Command (JSOC).

Parts of the 160th Aviation Group Support: the group is battalion-size.

U.S. AIR FORCE SOF
(Special Operations Forces)

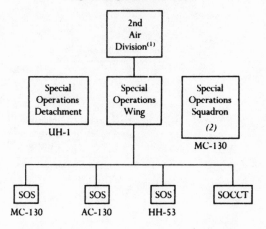

	NUMBER OF AIRCRAFT[2]			
	Active	AFR	ANG	Total
Core SOP				
MC-130 Combat Talon	14			14
AC-130 Spectre	10	10		20
EC-130 Volant Solo			4	4
HH-53 Pave Low	8			8
UH-1 Huey	4			4
CH-3		6		6
Augmentation				
C-141 (SOLL II)[3]	9			9
C-130 (SOLL II)[3]	9			9
HC-130	8			8
HH-53	8			8
HH-60	8			8

AIRFORCE	
authorized aircraft	*current location*
	Hurlburt Fld, Fl
	Hurlburt Fld, Fl
6 MC-103E	
10 AC-100H	
8 HH-53H	
4 HC-130E	Clark AB, Pl
4 MC-103E	Rhein-Main AB, FRG
6 CH-3	Luke AFB, Ar.
8 EG-130E	Harrisburg, Pa.
10 AC-130A	Duke Fld, Fl
4 UH-1N	Howard AFB, Panama
	Hurlburt Fld, Fl.
9 C-130E Crews	Pope AFB, NC
9 C-141B Crews	Charleston, SC
4 HC-130; 8 H-60	Eglin AFB, Fl
4 HC-130; 8 HH-53	McClelland AFB, Ca.

[1] Elements of 2d Air Division respond to Joint Special Operations Command (JSOC).
[2] Search and rescue (SAR) units worldwide are not shown. EC-130E Volant Solos are psyop.

Index